Chinese for Living in China 2

真实生活汉语 2

吴德安 （De-an Wu Swihart）
刘宪民 （Xianmin Liu）
魏久安 （Julian K. Wheatley） 编著
梁新欣 （Hsin-hsin Liang）
李金玉 （Jinyu Li）
胡龙华 （Lung-hua Hu）

配有录音光盘

北京大学出版社
PEKING UNIVERSITY PRESS

图书在版编目(CIP)数据

真实生活汉语. 2/吴德安等编著. —北京：北京大学出版社，2016.7
ISBN 978-7-301-27127-8

Ⅰ.①真… Ⅱ.①吴… Ⅲ.①汉语—对外汉语教学—教材 Ⅳ.①H195.4

中国版本图书馆CIP数据核字 (2016) 第 100146 号

封面图片由 http://www.123rf.com 提供
Copyright: <a href='http://www.123rf.com/profile_boggy22'>boggy22 / 123RF Stock Photo</a> = 25155450 TIFF
书中照片由吴德安（De-an Wu Swihart）拍摄

书　　名	真实生活汉语 2 ZHENSHI SHENGHUO HANYU 2
著作责任者	吴德安（De-an Wu Swihart）　刘宪民（Xianmin Liu）　魏久安（Julian K. Wheatley） 梁新欣（Hsin-hsin Liang）　李金玉（Jinyu Li）　胡龙华（Lung-hua Hu）　编著
责任编辑	周　鹂　邓晓霞
标准书号	ISBN 978-7-301-27127-8
出版发行	北京大学出版社
地　　址	北京市海淀区成府路205号　100871
网　　址	http://www.pup.cn　新浪微博：@北京大学出版社
电子信箱	zpup@pup.cn
电　　话	邮购部 62752015　发行部 62750672　编辑部 62767349
印 刷 者	北京大学印刷厂
经 销 者	新华书店
	889毫米×1194毫米　16开本　20.25印张　465千字
	2016年7月第1版　2016年7月第1次印刷
定　　价	115.00元（配有录音光盘）

未经许可，不得以任何方式复制或抄袭本书之部分或全部内容。
版权所有，侵权必究
举报电话：010-62752024　电子信箱：fd@pup.pku.edu.cn
图书如有印装质量问题，请与出版部联系，电话：010-62756370

Contents 目录

Preface
前言
Qiányán i

Abbreviations
缩略语
Suōlüèyǔ viii

Lesson Eleven   In a Chinese School
第十一课   在中国学校 1
Dì-shíyī Kè   Zài Zhōngguó Xuéxiào

In this lesson you will learn how to do the following
- Introduce yourself
- Talk about your schedule of classes
- Ask about adding and dropping classes
- Talk about classroom facilities

Grammar
- Complements of manner: V + "得 de" + Adjective Phrase
- Potential compounds: "看得懂 kàn de dǒng" "看不懂 kàn bu dǒng"
- Cause: "因为 yīnwèi……所以 suǒyǐ……" (because… [so…])
- The auxiliary verb "会 huì" (ability, likelihood)
- "除了 chúle……以外 yǐwài, 还 hái/也 yě/都 dōu……" (in addition to, besides)
- The "把 bǎ" construction
- Verbs with resultative complements
- Destination expressed with "到 dào"

Culture Notes
- Schools and other educational institutions
- School administration
- The school year
- A sample school calendar

Lesson Twelve   At the Supermarket
第十二课   在超市 30
Dì-shí'èr Kè   Zài Chāoshì

In this lesson you will learn how to do the following
- Invite friends or colleagues to dinner
- Ask where you can shop for items
- Locate items in a supermarket

Grammar
- Duration phrases and objects
- Pivotal constructions
- Alternative questions with "还是 háishi" (or); alternatives with "或者 huòzhě" (or)
- "又 yòu……又 yòu……" ([both]… and…)
- Resolution with "就 jiù……了 le"
- Movement to a location: V + "在 zài"/"到 dào"

Culture Notes
- Traditional Chinese weight and liquid measures
- Discounts
- Morning markets and street markets
- Bargaining

Lesson Thirteen   Taking the Bus
第十三课   坐车 55
Dì-shísān Kè   Zuò Chē

In this lesson you will learn how to do the following
- Talk about where you work or study
- Ask how to get places by bus
- Talk about changing buses
- Buy bus tickets

Grammar
- Adverbs "又 yòu" versus "再 zài"
- The suffix "极了 jí le" (extremely)
- "多 duō" and "几 jǐ" in questions and statements
- More on conditional sentences: "如果 rúguǒ……就 jiù……" (if… [then]…
- Expressing direction with "从 cóng" (from), "到 dào" (to) and "往 wǎng" (to, towards)
- Adverbs expressing degree of intensity
- "让 ràng" (to let, to allow) as a pre-pivotal verb

Culture Notes
- Public buses in China
- Taxis

Lesson Fourteen   Getting a Haircut
第十四课   理发 80
Dì-shísì Kè   Lǐ Fà

In this lesson you will learn how to do the following
- Request services at a barbershop or hairdresser
- Describe the sort of shampoo and cut that you want
- Discuss getting a shave
- Consider issues about hair coloring

Grammar
- The verb suffix "过 guo" (usually with neutral tone)
- "的 de" used as a nominalizer
- The verb suffix "着 zhe"
- The verbs "掉 diào" and "成 chéng" used as resultative complements
- Omitted subjects and objects
- Same or different: "A 跟 gēn B (不 bù) 一样 yíyàng"

Culture Notes
- Shampooing
- Massage

i

真实生活汉语
Chinese for Living in China 2

Lesson Fifteen Shopping for Clothes
第十五课 买衣服 107
Dì-shíwǔ Kè Mǎi Yīfu

In this lesson you will learn how to do the following
- Find out what sort of clothes are appropriate for particular occasions
- Find out where to buy clothes
- Talk about size and color
- Compare items
- Request slightly different sizes or colors
- Bargain

Grammar
- The position of question words
- More examples of the adverb "就 jiù"
- Coordinate verb phrases
- Questions with "多 duō"
- Comparison: "比 bǐ" and "没有 méiyǒu" patterns
- "还可以 hái kěyǐ" as an expression of acceptance

Culture Notes
- Weights and measures: Length and distance
- Height
- Converting metric to non-metric
- International shoe sizes
- Receipts: "小票 xiǎopiào"

Lesson Sixteen At the Hospital
第十六课 在医院 131
Dì-shíliù Kè Zài Yīyuàn

In this lesson you will learn how to do the following
- Explain your symptoms to a doctor
- Explain how you hurt yourself or got injured
- List any medicines you are taking
- Get instructions for your prescription

Grammar
- Resultative complements
- Events in succession: "先 xiān……然后 ránhòu……" (first... then...)
- Expressing uncertainty with "不知道 bù zhīdào" ([I] don't know if/whether)
- Directional complements ("下来 xiàlai", down here; "上去 shàngqu", up there, etc.)
- Ongoing action: the adverbs "正 zhèng", "在 zài" and "正在 zhèngzài"
- The intensifying suffix "得很 de hěn"

Culture Notes
- Registering at the hospital
- The medical examination room
- Payments
- The pharmacy

Lesson Seventeen Mary's Apartment
第十七课 玛丽的公寓 158
Dì-shíqī Kè Mǎlì de Gōngyù

In this lesson you will learn how to do the following
- Talk about your co-worker(s) or classmates
- Describe your place of work
- Describe where you live in terms of rooms, furniture, utility bills, etc.
- Talk about preparing a meal and the kitchen implements you use

Grammar
- The preposition "被 bèi" (by)
- The three "de's": "的", "地", and "得"
- Purpose with "为了 wèile" (in order to)
- Concession, with "虽然 suīrán……但是 dànshì……" (although... [but]...)
- Coordination, with "不但 búdàn……而且 érqiě……" (not only... but also...)
- Simultaneous actions, with "一边 yìbiān……一边 yìbiān……" (while..., as well as...)

Culture Notes
- How to address people
- Visitors who come by unannounced
- What to bring as a gift
- Work units and the provision of daily-use items

Lesson Eighteen Traveling over Chinese New Year
第十八课 春运 185
Dì-shíbā Kè Chūnyùn

In this lesson you will learn how to do the following
- Talk about vacation plans
- Talk about the problems of traveling over the "Spring Rush" period
- Discuss train and other forms of transportation in China
- Buy train tickets, and choose types of seat or berth, etc.

Grammar
- The adverb "才 cái" (only then, not until)
- The paired adverbs "一 yī……就 jiù……" (once, as soon as, whenever)
- Complete action with "了 le" and "没(有) méi (yǒu)"
- Double negatives, expressing insistence: "不能不 bù néng bù", etc.
- "只要 zhǐyào……就 jiù……" (so long as... [then]...)
- "为什么不 wèi shénme bù……" (why don't..., how come [you] don't...)

Culture Notes
- How to buy a train or airplane ticket
- Types of trains in China
- Types of ticket
- Round-trip and one-way tickets
- Things to take when you travel by train
- Meals or snacks on the train

目录 Contents

Lesson Nineteen — How's the Weather?
第十九课　天气怎么样？　　215
Dì-shíjiǔ Kè　Tiānqì Zěnmeyàng?

In this lesson you will learn how to do the following
- Talk about the weather and the seasons
- Become familiar with the language of weather reports
- Compare the weather in different areas

Grammar
- The scope of negation (e.g. "不都 bù dōu" versus "都不 dōu bù")
- Ambient sentences: describing the weather
- Vivid reduplication
- Comparison with "有 yǒu" and "没有 méiyǒu"
- The construction "以 yǐ……为 wéi……" (take…as…)
- Four-syllable expressions: a favorite type

Culture Notes
- "The 24 Solar Terms" of the traditional Chinese seasonal calendar
- Centigrade to Fahrenheit conversion table

Lesson Twenty — Celebrating the New Year
第二十课　过　年　　240
Dì-èrshí Kè　Guò Nián

In this lesson you will learn how to do the following
- Talk about family
- Talk about preparations for the Chinese New Year
- Describe the various activities associated with the New Year
- Talk about the significance of the various foods eaten at the New Year

Grammar
- Topic-comment
- Providing reassurance with "没什么(不) méi shénme (bù)"
- Comparison with "不如 bùrú" (not as [good as], be inferior to)
- Elliptical "的 de" phrases
- Rhetorical questions, with "不是 bú shì……吗 ma?"
- Coordinate clauses

Culture Notes
- "春节 Chūn Jié": The Spring Festival
- "压岁钱 yāsuìqián" (New Year's money)
- "拜年 bài nián" (Paying New Year's calls)

Vocabulary
词汇表　　265
Cíhuì Biǎo

Listening Scripts
录音文本　　290
Lùyīn Wénběn

前 言 Qiányán

《真实生活汉语》全套共4册，每册10课，是适合欧美外国学生使用的初级到中级的汉语教材。本套教材也适用于准备去中国学习、工作、旅行，希望尽快掌握一些在中国生活所需中文的外国人，或已经生活在中国且需要开始或继续学习生活所需中文的外国人。

一、本书缘起

这套《真实生活汉语》系列教材是在《外国人实用生活汉语》（上、下）（北京大学出版社，2004年）的基础上重新编写的。《外国人实用生活汉语》是为参加CTLC（组织英语国家大学毕业生去中国教英语的美国教育组织）与北京大学外国语学院合作的暑期外教强化培训（1997年开始）的外教编写的。这些外教在培训后去深圳的公立中小学担任英语老师，在中国至少住一年。他们是英语为母语的外国人，有的学过中文，有的没有学过，有不同的学习需求。《外国人实用生活汉语》的编写反映了他们的需要，是一套直接与他们在中国的日常生活紧密相关的汉语课本，所以很受他们的欢迎。至今为止，已有1000多名学生使用过那套教材。另外，《外国人实用生活汉语》也适合在中国留学或在中国工作居住一年以上的外国人。

经过10年的积累，这套全新的《真实生活汉语》把原教材扩充至4册，课文内容根据当前的生活用语重新编写，增加一倍，足够使用两年。一般的汉语教材在第二年时会从对话课文过渡到阅读课文，更强调汉字读写，本书则继续以对话交流为主。这套新教材已经在北京大学暑期强化中文课和深圳大学对外汉语课上试用了3年，反映良好。

基于上千学生的使用经验，我们希望《真实生活汉语》系列教材将为在中国生活的外国人继续提供有益的帮助。

二、编写理念

1. 口语交流 —— 培养学生听和说的能力

外国人在中国生活的关键是能与中国人进行口头交流，本书在设计上首先注重的是外国人在中国生活的会话需要，也就是注重培养学生听和说的实践能力。要培养这一能力，就需要精选生活在中国的外国人会遇到的典型情景会话。在中国的外国人都希望在课堂学到的汉语可以马上用到现实生活中去，这套书可以说满足了他们的需要。书中每课都与他们的现实生活有直接关系：换钱、买东西、理发、上饭馆、打的、看病、住宾馆、在学校上课或教书、在公司上班、租房、坐火车、飞机、地铁，安排在中国的旅游、文化参观，等等。本书作者根据多年对外国人在中国生活的调查，按照来华外国人的需要进行了精心选择，把他们最迫切需要的话题及用语都收入此书。因此《真实生活汉语》不但对话内容具有很强的真实性和实用性，而且对话语言简洁、生动、自然，非常适合学习者到中国后的生活需求。这些特点能极大地提高学生学习汉语的兴趣，增强他们的学习动力，使他们学得更快更好。教学实践表明，本教材受到了已经在华或准备来华学习汉语的外国人的喜爱。

2. 汉字学习——培养学生读和写的能力

怎样解决英语为母语的外国人学习汉字困难的问题？本书采取了一些教学策略。

首先，为了不让汉语学习变成"老牛拉着汽车走"，要想办法不让缓慢的汉字读写速度拖住他们快速学会汉语会话的步伐。《真实生活汉语》是为英语为母语，而且没有汉语学习经验的人设计的。所以最开始是拼音会话，比如第一册中每课的语音中大量运用拼音练习词汇发音和对话；再逐渐进入到汉字加拼音，让他们先学会说话；最后逐渐进入汉字学习。对于母语为拼音文字的人来说，有这样一个从拼音到汉字的渐进过程会比较容易接受，而且可以帮助他们准确发音。本系列4册课本都是拼音与汉字同时出现，就是为了减轻英语为母语的学生在学汉语时读写汉字的负担。学生需要较长时间才能把汉字的形状和声音联系起来并记住；按他们母语的习惯，记住了每个汉字的声音才能帮

真实生活汉语
Chinese for Living in China 2

助他们阅读中文。我们认为这个过程大约需要两年的时间。

其次，汉字的读写不是要学生们死记硬背，而是强调让他们学会如何在生活实践中使用这些学过的汉字。本书所有汉字下面都附有拼音，学生可以把拼音用作拐杖。比如学习对话时，老师可以让学生盖住课文的拼音部分，利用已经熟悉了的对话内容，只看汉字来试着复述课文内容。当然，老师应该为学生分析每个汉字的结构和细节，这样可以帮助他们认出和记住一些字的相同偏旁部首，也可以要求学生们手写汉字帮助记忆。老师还应尽量将已经学过的汉字搭配成新词组，以帮助学生加深对汉字的理解并扩大词汇量。

本书采用的是标准简体字，但是在每课的词汇表中，如果出现的简体汉字同时有繁体字写法，就把繁体字并列在旁边。学生应该了解哪些汉字是有繁简两种字形的，并能辨认两种字形，因为在中国香港、中国台湾和海外的中国城都还使用繁体字。每课词汇表以外的其他部分则仅使用简体字。本书没有全书采用繁简字体对照是因为：其一是两种字形并用占用的空间太大，影响可读性；其二，也是最主要的原因，本书的主要目的是训练学生适应在中国大陆的生活，而中国大陆很少看到繁体字。由于本书强调培养学生的阅读能力，如果是已经学过繁体字的学生，应该能迅速适应用简体字阅读，并逐渐学会用简体字写作。

三、教材结构形式

1. 课文：本书每课的课文几乎都是对话。比如：在饭馆里顾客和服务员之间的交谈，中国学校里外教和中国老师之间的交谈，外国人在超市向服务员询问并付款，外国病人在中国医院和大夫谈病情，外国旅行者在机场寻找丢失的行李或购买火车票、飞机票，等等。

2. 生词：每课的新词在词汇表中列出，包括汉字、拼音、词性及英文翻译，并提供繁体字以便对照。

3. 用译文复述课文：每课的课文后面有英文译文，但那不是单纯地给课文提供翻译，而是希望学生借助英文提示的会话情景，用中文复述本课的对话内容。

4. 语法点：每课都详细讲解本课对话中出现的重要语法点，以便学生充分理解中文的句子结构。同时为学生设计句型练习，帮助他们利用句型自己生成新句子。

5. 练习：每课设计了丰富的练习和课堂活动帮助学生进一步掌握本课所学内容。练习包括：句式操练、发音训练、听力训练、交际活动、角色扮演，以及各种复习等。

6. 中国日常生活文化：每课介绍三四个与课文内容相关的，在中国生活必须了解的中国文化常识，比如：怎样在医院挂号，如何寻找丢失的行李，如何存取款等。

7. 拼音卡片（只在第一册有）：第1册书后附有拼音卡片，由石安妮（Anne Swihart）设计。每张卡片正面是拼音字母，背面讲如何发音——用英文的近似发音进行说明，并带有插图提示。比如解释"b"的发音用"similar to boh in boy"，插图提示是一个男孩（boy），这样就更容易被学生接受。学生可以把所有卡片剪切下来使用。

对老师来说，把每课的内容材料转化为课堂活动的过程是一个挑战。课堂活动的重点应放在与口语交流相关的练习活动上，以提高学生在实际生活中与中国人交流的能力，满足学生的需要。

四、作者简介

吴德安（De-an Wu Swihart）博士：毕业于北京大学中文系，在普林斯顿大学获得博士学位。在美国和加拿大教授汉语、中国文学和文化20多年，任教学校包括明德大学和麦基尔大学暑期学校、罗德大学、孟菲斯大学等。曾经任CTLC与北京大学外语学院合作的暑期外教强化培训项目主任15年。现为美国大学中国教学中心主任。出版过意大利文版和德文版两本中文教材，还是其他两套汉语系列课本的主要作者，也出版过3本中英文诗歌小说。主要负责《真实生活汉语》系列教材的总体设计及初稿编写。

刘宪民（Xianmin Liu）博士：美国明尼苏达大学汉语语言学博士。在美执教20余年。目前任教于美国范德堡大学，是该校汉语语言教学项目主任及范德堡大学在中国的暑期项目主任。在此之前，曾任教于明尼苏达大学、俄勒冈大学、俄亥俄大学及哈佛大学。曾多次担任美国CET留华暑期项目教学主任。主要研究方向为汉语句法、语义、语用学及汉语教学语法。曾合著其他对外汉语教材。是《真实生活汉语》第1册第三作者和第2册第二作者。

魏久安 (Julian K. Wheatley) 博士：曾在康奈尔大学任教11年，在麻省理工大学任教9年，还曾在美国杜兰大学、新加坡南洋理工大学国立教育学院和香港教育学院任教。目前是美国大学中国教学中心的负责人之一。专门研究东南亚大陆及中国的语言和语言学（特别是缅甸语和汉语）。是《真实生活汉语》1–4册的作者之一。

　　梁新欣 (Hsin-hsin Liang) 博士：美国密执安大学语言学博士。曾任教于美国威斯康辛大学、密执安大学、康奈尔大学、明德大学中文暑校，以及美国各大学联合汉语中心（ACC）。现为美国弗吉尼亚大学东亚语言文学及文化系副教授、现代中国语言项目主任，同时也是"弗大在上海"暑期中文项目主任。是《真实生活汉语》系列教材第3、4册的第二作者，以及第1、2册作者之一。

　　李金玉 (Jinyu Li)：毕业于南京大学和澳大利亚国立大学，在美国莱斯大学获得硕士学位。在美国从事大学汉语教学20多年，在任教于哈佛大学的十几年间曾任多门中文课主任教师。现为塔芙茨大学中文部高级讲师。主要研究方向为中英文句法特点的比较、文化与语言、词汇教学。是《真实生活汉语》第2、3、4册作者之一。

　　胡龙华 (Lung-Hua Hu)：美国哥伦比亚大学英语教学硕士，曾任教于美国国务院外交学院台北华语学校、明德暑校、普林斯顿大学、普林斯顿北京培训班、哥伦比亚大学北京暑期培训班、杜克大学北京暑期培训班，现任布朗大学高级讲师及中文部主任、新英格兰中文教师协会副会长及执行长。在美国从事汉语教学二十余年，其"中级汉语课程"曾遴选为美国大学理事会美国十大最佳汉语课程之一。主要研究方向为汉语语音、语法、词汇教学。是《真实生活汉语》第2册作者之一。

五、鸣谢

　　衷心感谢帮助《真实生活汉语》成功出版的同事及朋友们，他们是：北京大学英语系的马乃强博士、于莹教授、陈冰老师，中国人民大学的陆姚老师，重庆大学的范红娟老师，深圳大学的朱庆红教授、贾陆依教授。他们曾为此书的编写提供过建议和修改意见，并且协助收集学生对此书的意见。此外，石安妮 (Anne Swihart) 女士设计了第1册的插图。我们在此向他们表示诚挚的感谢。

　　同时也要衷心感谢北京大学出版社，多位编辑对此书提供了很多宝贵建议，为本系列教材的出版作出了很大贡献，在此一并表示感谢。

主笔：吴德安(De-an Wu Swihart)
参编作者：刘宪民 (Xianmin Liu)
　　　　　魏久安 (Julian K. Wheatley)
　　　　　梁新欣 (Hsin-hsin Liang)
　　　　　李金玉 (Jinyu Li)
　　　　　胡龙华 (Lung-hua Hu)

Preface

Chinese for Living in China is a textbook series in four volumes, each with ten lessons, which serves as a foundation for beginning and intermediate levels of language instruction and learning. It is designed for people studying Chinese with the intention of going to China to work or to continue their studies; and for people already in China, starting or continuing to learn the language there.

Conversational skills

Chinese for Living in China is designed for speakers of English who have no prior knowledge of Chinese. Since the key ingredient for living successfully in China is being able to talk to people – to communicate orally, *Chinese for Living in China* is organized first by conversational needs (listening and speaking). Initial conversational instruction proceeds incrementally, with *Pinyin* transcription providing access to language material and to correct pronunciation.

Lessons cover topics that are typically encountered by foreigners living in China: buying things, eating out, taking or teaching classes, mobile phones, banks, changing money, transportation, hotels and airports, doctor's visits, finding a place to stay, working in an office, making travel arrangements, finding employment, and so on. Many of these topics have immediate application in the daily lives of foreigners living in China and, as such, provide a powerful learning incentive which speeds up the process of mastery. The topics have been selected on the basis of the authors' own experiences, living, traveling, and working in China and observing the needs of their students.

Reading skills

The ability to communicate in Chinese can, with proper practice, proceed quite quickly. This provides learners with a sense of accomplishment. Learning the literary skills of reading and writing in characters, on the other hand, is much more challenging. It simply takes a long time to learn to reliably associate characters with sound. (Learners are doubly handicapped by not being able to utilize the sound hints found in the phonetic components of many characters which prove so useful to native speakers.)

Chinese for Living in China deals with the character problem in this way: In the first place, it does not let character recognition dictate the pace of spoken language learning. The dialogues that begin each lesson are natural, cover the topic sufficiently, and introduce new material at a rate that can be absorbed and utilized in conversation. In the second place, *Chinese for Living in China* emphasizes recognition of characters in context. Almost all Chinese material in the series is introduced in both characters and *Pinyin*. In the case of the narratives and dialogues, *Pinyin* is written below the character lines as continuous script. As learners become more familiar with the language through speaking practice in and out of class, they can cover the *Pinyin* lines and try to read the characters, using their familiarity with the text as a crutch, and checking the *Pinyin* as much as necessary. Naturally, a lot of attention will still need to be paid to hand-writing and character analysis to ensure proper attention to character detail. But as much as possible, characters will be learned by reading familiar material, where the focus can be on finding ways to associate characters with known words.

For character reading, *Chinese for Living in China* uses the simplified set of characters that is standard on the Mainland (as well as in Singapore). In vocabulary lists, whenever two forms exist, traditional characters are given alongside simplified ones. But elsewhere, only the simplified set is used. There are several reasons for the limited use of the traditional set. One is space and readability; having two versions of character material takes up excessive space and can be confusing. The main reason, however, is that the series is specifically geared to life on the Mainland where the traditional characters are rarely seen. In any case, given the emphasis on reading over writing in *Chinese for Living in China*, even those students who have started their study with traditional characters should be able to quickly adapt to reading the simplified, even if they cannot write them.

Organization

1. The dialogues: Lessons begin with a dialogue that illustrates the lesson's subject matter: a conversation between a customer ordering a meal and a waiter, for example; or one between two teachers (one foreign, one Chinese) and a supermarket worker about finding items and about check-out procedures; or a conversation between a foreign patient and a Chinese doctor in China; or a foreigner looking for lost luggage at an airport or buying train tickets; and so on.

2. Vocabulary: Individual words for each lesson are listed with characters, *Pinyin*, part-of-speech and English equivalents. For those cases in which the traditional form of the character differs from the simplified, the two are placed together in the vocabulary lists.

3. Re-enacting the dialogue: Along with the Chinese version of the texts, a fluid English translation is provided so that learners can cue the Chinese and, as a first step, practice producing Chinese, not just reading it.

4. Grammatical points: Important grammatical topics introduced in the course of the dialogues are discussed and further illustrated individually to help learners understand Chinese sentence structure and start to produce novel sentences themselves.

5. Exercises: Each lesson provides exercises and activities designed to help learners internalize new material. These include practice with sentence patterns, pronunciation drills, listening practice, and a host of communicative activities involving role play and group work.

6. Chinese everyday culture: Each lesson ends with three or four cultural notes relevant to the dialogues. These provide information crucial to everyday life in China: how to check in at a hospital, for example, how to find lost luggage, or how to deposit and withdraw money, etc.

7. *Pinyin* cards (Only Book I): At the back of the book there are ten pages of *Pinyin* cards, designed by Anne Swihart. On one side of each card is a letter – given in upper and lower case. On the other side is a picture of an object whose name in English begins with that letter. "Ff" is matched to the number "four" (Ff=f); "Qq", is matched to a wedge of "cheese" (Qq=ch). Along with the illustration is a hint (with color coding) that explains in terms of English spelling how the letter (on the front) is pronounced in *Pinyin*. So for "Qq", along with the picture of "cheese" is the hint "similar to chee in cheese"; with "Ff" and the picture of "4" is the hint "similar to foeh in four". The cards can be cut out and joined together to make *Pinyin* syllables (words) for self-testing.

For teachers, the process of transforming textbook material into classroom activities that serve the learner's needs is facilitated by the focus on the spoken language and the provision of communicatively relevant activities in each lesson.

Origins

Chinese for Living in China is based on an earlier two-volume series that was also published by the Peking University Press. It was called *Practical Chinese for English Speakers*, written by De-an Wu Swihart and Cong Meng, and edited by William H. O'Donnell. That series was written for overseas teachers participating in the Center for Teaching and Learning in China (CTLC). Since 1997, CTLC has been recruiting English teachers from English speaking countries to teach for at least a year in the Shenzhen school system. In collaboration with the Peking University School of Foreign Languages, CTLC has provided these teachers with an initial period of intensive training in the teaching of English in China, as well as intensive instruction in Mandarin. Practical Chinese for English Speakers was written to respond to the need for a textbook that would allow these teachers to make use of Chinese in their everyday lives.

The new *Chinese for Living in China* series has been completely revamped, with all content – including dialogues – rewritten to reflect changes in language usage and in society since the earlier volumes were written. The new series, with four volumes rather than the earlier two, doubles the amount of material and allows teachers and learners to use one series over the equivalent of two years of non-intensive language study. One of the unique features of the new series is that, while many texts shift from a conversational approach to a focus on reading and character recognition at the intermediate level, *Chinese for Living in China* retains the conversational format through all four volumes. Initial drafts of the new series have been tried and tested to good effect by over 1000 students over the last three years in CLTC's intensive language course at Peking University, and in the regular Chinese courses for foreigners at Shenzhen University. It is our hope that the series will continue to serve the many new learners who have plans to study, travel or work in China.

真实生活汉语
Chinese for Living in China 2

The authors

Dr. De-an Wu Swihart graduated from the Chinese Department at Peking University and received her Ph.D. from Princeton University. She has taught courses in Chinese language, literature and culture for over 20 years at a variety of institutions in the United States and Canada, including the University of Memphis, Rhodes College, Middlebury College Summer School, and McGill University Summer School. She has been director of the Summer Intensive Foreign Teachers' Training Program at Peking University, School of Foreign Languages for 15 years. She has been co-director of the Center for Teaching & Learning in China since 1997. She has published two Chinese textbooks in Italian and German and has been the main author of two other Chinese textbook series. She is also the author of three books on English and Chinese poetry and fiction. Dr. Swihart designed the *Chinese for Living in China* series and was responsible for initial drafts of all four volumes.

Dr. Xianmin Liu received her Ph.D. in Chinese linguistics from the University of Minnesota. She has taught for over twenty years in the U.S. She is currently teaching at Vanderbilt University, where she is the coordinator of the Chinese language program and director of the Vanderbilt Summer-in-China Program. Before joining the Vanderbilt faculty, she also taught at Minnesota, Oregon, Ohio and Harvard Universities. She has also served a number of times as the academic director for CET summer immersion programs in China. Her research interests include Chinese grammar, semantics and pragmatics, as well as Chinese language pedagogy. She has co-authored several Chinese textbooks for English speakers. She is third author for volume 1 of *Chinese for Living in China*, and second author for volume 2.

Dr. Julian K. Wheatley taught for eleven years at Cornell University and for nine years at MIT. More recently, he has been a guest teacher at the Singapore National Institute of Education, at the Hong Kong Institute of Education and at Tulane University. He is currently one of the directors of the CTLC program. His research and publications involve the languages and linguistics of mainland Southeast Asia and China (particularly Burmese and Chinese). He is co-author of all four volumes of *Chinese for Living in China*.

Dr. Hsin-hsin Liang received her doctorate in linguistics from the University of Michigan. She has taught at a number of institutions, including the University of Wisconsin, the University of Michigan, Cornell University, Middlebury Summer Program, and the Language Center of the Associated Colleges in China (ACC). She is currently associate professor of Chinese in the Department of East Asian Languages, Literatures and Cultures at the University of Virginia, where she is director of the modern Chinese language program and field director of the UVA-in-Shanghai Chinese language program. She is second author of volumes 3 and 4 of *Chinese for Living in China*, as well as one of the co-authors of volumes 1 and 2.

Jinyu Li received B.A. degrees from Nanjing University and from Australian National University, and an M.A. from Rice University. She has been involved with Chinese language teaching in the U.S. for almost 30 years. Before taking up her current position as senior lecturer at Tufts University, she was a preceptor at Harvard University, where she taught a variety of courses in the Chinese program. Her main areas of interest are Chinese-English comparative grammar, culture and language, and the teaching of vocabulary. She is one of the authors of volumes 2, 3 and 4 of *Chinese for Living in China*.

Lung-Hua Hu received her Master's degree in TESOL (Teaching English to Speakers of Other Languages) at Teachers College, Columbia University in New York City. She taught at CLASS (the Chinese Language and Area Studies School under FSI) before moving to the United States in 1994. She is senior lecturer and coordinator of the Chinese Language Program at Brown University, and had taught at Princeton University and its intensive summer program PiB (Princeton in Beijing), Middlebury College Summer Chinese School, Columbia University's summer program in Beijing, and Duke University's Beijing summer program. She currently serves as Vice President and Executive Director of NECLTA (New England Chinese Language Teachers Association), and will begin to serve as its President in October 2016. Her "Intermediate Chinese" course was identified as one of the ten Best Practices in Teaching Chinese in the US by the College Board in 2006. Her research focuses on Chinese phonetics and phonology, syntax, and lexicon. She is a co-author of *Chinese for Living in China*, Volume 2.

Acknowledgments

The authors wish to express sincere thanks to colleagues and friends who have made the publication of *Chinese for Living in China* possible, and who provided valuable advice and suggestions for improvement, as well as helping to collect student feedback on draft versions of this book. They are: Dr. Ma Naiqiang, Professor Yu Ying and Senior Lecturer Chen Bin all from the English Department at Peking University; Lu Yao from Renmin University of China and Fan Hongjuan from Chongqing University; Professors Zhu Qinghong and Jia Luyi from Shenzhen University. In addition, artist Anne Swihart

designed the illustrations for the first volume of the series. We are deeply grateful for the help and support these people have provided towards making *Chinese for Living in China* a success.

The authors would also like to thank the people at Peking University Press, several edieors provided useful suggestions for the series and we deeply appreciate their help and support.

Editor in chief: De-an Wu Swihart
Participating authors: Xianmin Liu
Julian K. Wheatley
Hsin-hsin Liang
Jinyu Li
Lung-hua Hu

Abbreviations 缩略语 Suōlüèyǔ

Abbreviation	English	*Pinyin*	Chinese
Adj	Adjective	xíngróngcí	形容词
Adv	Adverb	fùcí	副词
Attr	Attributive	dìngyǔ	定语*
Aux	Auxiliary	zhùdòngcí	助动词
BF	Bound Form	zǔhé xíngshì	组合形式
Conj	Conjunction	liáncí	连词
Det	Determiner	xiàndìngcí	限定词
DirC	Directional Complement	qūxiàng bǔyǔ	趋向补语
Exp	Expression	xíguàn yòngyǔ	习惯用语
Intj	Interjection	tàncí	叹词
IntPron	Interrogative Pronoun	yíwèn dàicí	疑问代词
Meas	Measure Word	liàngcí	量词
N	Noun	míngcí	名词
Num	Numeral	shùcí	数词
Part	Particle	zhùcí	助词
Pot	Potential Form	kěnéng bǔyǔ	可能补语
Pref	Prefix	qiánzhuì	前缀
Prep	Preposition	jiècí	介词
Pron	Pronoun	dàicí	代词
PropN	Proper Noun	zhuānyǒu míngcí	专有名词
PW	Position Word	fāngwèicí	方位词
RC	Resultative Complement	jiéguǒ bǔyǔ	结果补语
Q	Quantifier	shùliàngcí	数量词
Suf	Suffix	hòuzhuì	后缀
V	Verb	dòngcí	动词
VO	Verb-object	dòngbīn jiégòu	动宾结构

*本书的"定语"就是一般所说的"非谓形容词"。
The "Attributive" in this book means what is generally called "non-predicative adjective".

Lesson Eleven   In a Chinese School

第十一课   在中国学校
Dì-shíyī Kè   Zài Zhōngguó Xuéxiào

In this lesson you will learn how to do the following
- Introduce yourself
- Talk about your schedule of classes
- Ask about adding and dropping classes
- Talk about classroom facilities

Grammar
- Complements of manner: V + "得 de" + Adjective Phrase
- Potential compounds: "看得懂 kàn de dǒng" "看不懂 kàn bu dǒng"
- Cause: "因为 yīnwèi……所以 suǒyǐ……" (because… [so…])
- The auxiliary verb "会 huì" (ability, likelihood)
- "除了 chúle……以外 yǐwài, 还 hái/也 yě/都 dōu……" (in addition to, besides)
- The "把 bǎ" construction
- Verbs with resultative complements
- Destination expressed with "到 dào"

Culture Notes
- Schools and other educational institutions
- School administration
- The school year
- A sample school calendar

真实生活汉语 2
Chinese for Living in China

Dialogue

A：习文，日本留学生 B：白老师，英语老师 C：技术人员
Xí Wén, Rìběn liúxuéshēng Bái lǎoshī, Yīngyǔ lǎoshī jìshù rényuán

习文是日本留学生。他在中国读本科学位。这个学期他选了四门课：中级汉语、世界历史、中国文学和英语口语。他的英语老师是美国人，姓白。今天他去找白老师问英语课的问题。

Xí Wén shì Rìběn liúxuéshēng. Tā zài Zhōngguó dú běnkē xuéwèi. Zhège xuéqī tā xuǎnle sì mén kè: zhōngjí Hànyǔ、shìjiè lìshǐ、Zhōngguó wénxué hé Yīngyǔ kǒuyǔ. Tā de Yīngyǔ lǎoshī shì Měiguórén, xìng Bái. Jīntiān tā qù zhǎo Bái lǎoshī wèn Yīngyǔkè de wèntí.

A：白老师，您好！我是日本留学生，可以问您几个问题吗？
Bái lǎoshī, nín hǎo! Wǒ shì Rìběn liúxuéshēng, kěyǐ wèn nín jǐ ge wèntí ma?

B：可以。请进。你叫什么？
Kěyǐ. Qǐng jìn. Nǐ jiào shénme?

A：我姓习，叫习文。我注册了您的英语口语课。我汉字认得不太多[G1]，看不懂[G2]这个课表。我们什么时候上课？
Wǒ xìng Xí, jiào Xí Wén. Wǒ zhùcèle nín de Yīngyǔ kǒuyǔkè. Wǒ Hànzì rèn de bú tài duō[G1], kàn bu dǒng[G2] zhège kèbiǎo. Wǒmen shénme shíhou shàng kè?

B：英语口语班一周有三节课：星期一、三、五上午的第[1]三节上课。今天第三节就有课。
Yīngyǔ kǒuyǔbān yì zhōu yǒu sān jié kè: xīngqīyī、sān、wǔ shàngwǔ de dì[1]-sān jié shàng kè. Jīntiān dì-sān jié jiù yǒu kè.

A：我们的教室在哪儿？
Wǒmen de jiàoshì zài nǎr?

B：教学楼二楼207室，在汉语教室对面。
Jiàoxuélóu èr lóu èrlíngqī shì, zài Hànyǔ jiàoshì duìmiàn.

A：我们用什么教材呢？
Wǒmen yòng shénme jiàocái ne?

Notes

1. Ordinal numbers (1st, 2nd, 3rd…) are formed by the addition of prefix "第 dì" to the cardinal number: "第一课 dì-yī kè" (the first lesson); "第三节 dì-sān jié" (the third period). Notice that in *Pinyin*, ordinal numbers are written with hyphens: dì-yī, dì-èr. (In its ordinal form "yī" is always first tone.)

第十一课　在中国学校
Lesson Eleven　In a Chinese School

B：因为是口语课，所以我们没有教材[G3]。我每次[2]上课会[G4]发材料给你们。
Yīnwèi shì kǒuyǔkè, suǒyǐ wǒmen méiyǒu jiàocái[G3]. Wǒ měi cì[2] shàng kè huì[G4] fā cáiliào gěi nǐmen.

A：这门课有考试吗？
Zhè mén kè yǒu kǎoshì ma?

B：有。每星期有一次小考，期末有大考。平时的课堂表现和出勤率也算分。
Yǒu. Měi xīngqī yǒu yí cì xiǎokǎo, qīmò yǒu dàkǎo. Píngshí de kètáng biǎoxiàn hé chūqínlǜ yě suàn fēn.

A：我的室友也想上您的口语课，还可以加课吗？
Wǒ de shìyǒu yě xiǎng shàng nín de kǒuyǔkè, hái kěyǐ jiā kè ma?

B：我不太清楚加课和退课的日期，你们可以去查一下儿[3]校历，或者问一下儿教务处。
Wǒ bú tài qīngchu jiā kè hé tuì kè de rìqī, nǐmen kěyǐ qù chá yíxiàr[3] xiàolì, huòzhě wèn yíxiàr jiàowùchù.

A：您有没有办公室时间？
Nín yǒu méiyǒu bàngōngshì shíjiān?

B：在中国，教师没有固定的办公室时间。除了上课，我都在办公室[G5]。你随时可以来。
Zài Zhōngguó, jiàoshī méiyǒu gùdìng de bàngōngshì shíjiān. Chúle shàng kè, wǒ dōu zài bàngōngshì[G5]. Nǐ suíshí kěyǐ lái.

A：好。谢谢您。
Hǎo. Xièxie nín.

（在教室 Zài jiàoshì）

B：师傅，我一会儿就要上课了，这间教室太热了，是不是空调坏了？
Shīfu, wǒ yíhuìr jiù yào shàng kè le, zhè jiān jiàoshì tài rè le, shì bu shì kōngtiáo huài le?

C：我来看看。空调没有坏。我把[G6]空调的温度调低[G7]，关上门和窗户，等一会儿就不热了。
Wǒ lái kànkan. Kōngtiáo méiyǒu huài. Wǒ bǎ[G6] kōngtiáo de wēndù tiáodī[G7], guānshang mén hé chuānghu, děng yíhuìr jiù bú rè le.

---

2. "次 cì" is a verbal measure, meaning "times, occurrences": "去过一次 qùguo yí cì" (have gone there once). "每 měi" combines with nominal or verbal measure words to mean "every, each": "每天 měi tiān" (every day); "每本书 měi běn shū" (every book); "每次 měi cì" (every time).

B：谢谢。我上课时要用PPT，还要上网，这间教室有没有投影仪和能上网的电脑？

Xièxie. Wǒ shàng kè shí yào yòng PPT, hái yào shàng wǎng, zhè jiān jiàoshì yǒu méiyǒu tóuyǐngyí hé néng shàng wǎng de diànnǎo?

C：有，在这儿。我们学校的教室都是多媒体的⁴。

Yǒu, zài zhèr. Wǒmen xuéxiào de jiàoshì dōu shì duōméitǐ de⁴.

B：这支水笔干了，在白板上写不出字。我应该到^G8哪儿去要水笔？

Zhè zhī shuǐbǐ gān le, zài báibǎn shang xiě bu chū zì. Wǒ yīnggāi dào^G8 nǎr qù yào shuǐbǐ?

C：系办公室有水笔和板擦儿，可以跟秘书要⁵。

Xì bàngōngshì yǒu shuǐbǐ hé bǎncār, kěyǐ gēn mìshū yào⁵.

B：教室里的桌子、椅子都可以移动吗？我上口语课时学生们需要面对面坐。

Jiàoshì li de zhuōzi、yǐzi dōu kěyǐ yídòng ma? Wǒ shàng kǒuyǔkè shí xuéshēngmen xūyào miàn duì miàn zuò.

C：这个教室的桌椅都是可以移动的。我现在就帮您摆好吧。

Zhège jiàoshì de zhuōyǐ dōu shì kěyǐ yídòng de. Wǒ xiànzài jiù bāng nín bǎihǎo ba.

B：谢谢。

Xièxie.

C：不客气。

Bú kèqi.

New Words

1	日本	Rìběn	PropN	Japan
2	英语/英語	Yīngyǔ	PropN	English, the English language (esp. spoken)
3	技术/技術	jìshù	N	technique, skill, technology
4	人员/人員	rényuán	N	personnel, staff

3. "一下儿 yíxiàr" (the r-suffix indicates northern pronunciation) is a measure phrase that frequently appears after verbs to indicate brevity or casualness: "查一下儿 chá yíxiàr" (to look it up); "看一下儿 kàn yíxiàr" (to take a look).

4. "多媒体" (multimedia) is a noun that frequently acts as an attributive, that is, it modifies a following noun: "多媒体的教室 duōméitǐ de jiàoshì" (multimedia classroom); "多媒体的卡 duōméitǐ de kǎ" (multimedia card). When the head noun is understood, the noun behind "的 de" can be omitted. Cf. "我们的 [ ] wǒmen de [ ]" (ours [=books]); "平时的 [ ] píngshí de [ ]" (ordinary ones [ones = classrooms]).

5. "跟秘书要 gēn mìshū yào" (to get it from the secretary): The verb "要 yào" (here, meaning "ask for") takes "跟 gēn" (with) to indicate the person to which the request is directed: "跟她要钱 gēn tā yào qián" (to ask her for money).

第十一课　在中国学校
Lesson Eleven　In a Chinese School

5	读 / 讀	dú	V	to read aloud, to read, to study (a subject in school)
6	本科	běnkē	N	undergraduate, undergraduate course
	科	kē	N	branch of learning, administrative section
7	学位/學位	xuéwèi	N	academic degree
8	学期/學期	xuéqī	N	academic semester, school term
9	选/選	xuǎn	V	to choose, to select
10	门/門	mén	Meas/N	*for courses in school, skills*; door
11	中级/中級	zhōngjí	Attr	intermediate level, middle rank, secondary
12	世界	shìjiè	N	world
13	历史/歷史	lìshǐ	N	history
14	文学/文學	wénxué	N	literature
15	口语/口語	kǒuyǔ	N	spoken language
16	问题/問題	wèntí	N	question, issue, problem
17	注册/註冊	zhùcè	V	to register
18	汉字/漢字	Hànzì	PropN	Chinese character
	字	zì	N	character, word, letter
19	认/認	rèn	V	to recognize, to know
20	懂	dǒng	V	to understand, to comprehend ("不懂 bù dǒng", not to understand)
21	课表/課表	kèbiǎo	N	schedule of classes, school timetable
22	班	bān	N	class
23	第	dì	Pref	*attached to cardinal numbers to form ordinals*, e.g.: "第三 dì-sān" (3rd)
24	教室	jiàoshì	N	classroom
	室	shì	N	room, chamber
25	教材	jiàocái	N	teaching material
26	因为/因為	yīnwèi	Conj	because, for, on account of
27	所以	suǒyǐ	Conj	so, therefore, as a result
28	次	cì	Meas	occasion, time
29	发/發	fā	V	to send out, to issue, to launch, to produce

30	材料	cáiliào	N	material, data, ingredients
31	考试/考試	kǎoshì	V/N	to take an exam or test; test, examination
32	小考	xiǎokǎo	N	quiz
33	期末	qīmò	N	end of the school term
34	大考	dàkǎo	N	final examination
35	平时/平時	píngshí	N	(in) ordinary times
36	课堂/課堂	kètáng	N	classroom
37	表现/表現	biǎoxiàn	V/N	to show, to display, to do; performance, expression
38	出勤率	chūqínlǜ	N	rate of attendance, amount of participation
39	算	suàn	V	to count, to include, to consider as, to calculate
40	室友	shìyǒu	N	roommate
41	加课/加課	jiā kè	Phrase	to add a class
42	清楚	qīngchu	Adj	clear, distinct
43	退课/退課	tuì kè	Phrase	to drop a class
	退	tuì	V	to withdraw, to quit, to return (goods, money, etc.)
44	日期	rìqī	N	date
45	查	chá	V	to check, to examine, to inspect
46	一下儿/一下兒	yíxiàr	Q	a bit, for a while (minimizing)
47	校历/校曆	xiàolì	N	school calendar
48	或者	huòzhě	Conj	or, either
49	教务处/教務處	jiàowùchù	N	the dean's office, the administration office
50	办公室/辦公室	bàngōngshì	N	office
51	教师/教師	jiàoshī	N	teacher
52	固定	gùdìng	Adj	fixed, regular, scheduled
53	除了	chúle	Prep	except for, besides
54	随时/隨時	suíshí	Adv	from time to time, as necessary, at all times
55	师傅/師傅	shīfu	N	master (worker)
56	把	bǎ	Prep	*spotlights objects*

第十一课　在中国学校

Lesson Eleven　In a Chinese School

57	温度	wēndù	N	temperature
58	调/調	tiáo	V	to adjust, to mix, to blend
59	低	dī	Adj/V	low; to lower (e.g. one's head)
60	关上/關上	guānshang	V-RC	to close, to lock (a door, window, etc.)
	关/關	guān	V	to close
61	窗户	chuānghu	N	window
62	投影仪/投影儀	tóuyǐngyí	N	projector
63	上网/上網	shàng wǎng	VO	to go online, to get on the Internet
	网/網	wǎng	N	net, network
64	电脑/電腦	diànnǎo	N	computer
65	多媒体/多媒體	duōméitǐ	N	multimedia
66	支	zhī	Meas	*for long, thin, inflexible objects*
67	水笔/水筆	shuǐbǐ	N	marker, water-color brush, fountain pen
68	干/乾	gān	Adj	dry, dried up, dried out
69	白板	báibǎn	N	whiteboard, white bulletin board
70	写/寫	xiě	V	to write, to compose, to draw
71	到	dào	V/Prep	to arrive, to succeed in; to, until
72	板擦儿/板擦兒	bǎncār	N	(chalkboard or whiteboard) eraser
73	秘书/秘書	mìshū	N	secretary
74	桌子	zhuōzi	N	table, desk
75	椅子	yǐzi	N	chair
76	移动/移動	yídòng	V	to move, to shift
77	面对面/面對面	miàn duì miàn	Phrase	face-to-face
78	帮/幫	bāng	V	to help, to lend a hand
79	摆/擺	bǎi	V	to arrange, to lay out

Re-enacting the Dialogue*

A: Xi Wen, a Japanese overseas student
B: Prof. White, an English teacher
C: A technician

Xi Wen is a Japanese student. He's in China, studying for an undergraduate degree. He's taking four courses this semester: Intermediate Chinese, World History, Chinese Literature and Conversational English. His English teacher is an American, (sur)named White. Today, he's gone to find his English teacher to ask him some questions about the English class.

A: Prof. White, how do you do? I'm a Japanese overseas student. May I ask you some questions?

B: Sure. Come on in. What's your name, please?

A: My surname's Xi, my full name's Xi Wen. I've registered for your English conversational course. I don't know that many Chinese characters, so I haven't been able to read the schedule. What time is the class?

B: The conversational English classes meet three times a week. We meet Monday, Wednesday and Friday morning, third period. We have class third period today.

A: Where's the classroom?

B: It's on the second floor of the Classroom Building, Room 207, opposite the Chinese classroom.

A: What textbook do we use?

B: Because it's a conversational class, we don't have a textbook. Every class, I'll hand out materials for you.

A: Does this course have any examinations?

B: Yes, it does. Every week, there's a quiz and there's an examination at the end of the term. Regular class performance and effort also count.

A: My roommate also wants to take your conversational class, can he add it?

B: I'm not certain about the add and drop dates, you can go and check the catalogue, or ask at the dean's office.

A: Do you have office hours?

B: In China, teachers don't have regular office hours. When I'm not in class, I'm always in my office. You can come by any time.

A: Fine, thank you.

---

* As in Volume I, a translation of the main text is provided to help you retell or re-enact the conversation. As noted in Volume I: "The dialogues are not reading exercises; they provide conversational material. For this reason, they are designed for you to be able to access them easily, with *Pinyin* provided along with vocabulary and grammatical explanations. A first step in trying to internalize the conversational material is to practice re-enacting the dialogues. To help you do this, a translation is provided. You can glance at the English to remind yourself of what you want to say, then try to say it, and finally, check yourself against the Chinese. The first time you do this, you will find it quite difficult; but by the third time, you should find yourself close to fluency. Once you reach that point, you will be much more successful in trying out variations on the basic themes in and out of class."

Lesson Eleven In a Chinese School

(In the classroom)

B: Sir, I'm having class here in a little while. The classroom's too hot – is the air-conditioning broken?

C: Let me take a look. The air-conditioning's fine. I've turned the temperature down and closed the doors and windows. It'll get cooler shortly.

B: Thanks. I need to use PowerPoint and go online. Does this classroom have overhead facilities and a computer that I can use to go online?

C: Yes, it's here. Our classrooms are all multimedia.

B: This white board marker's dry, it won't write on the whiteboard. Where should I go for white board markers?

C: The departmental office has white board markers and erasers, you can get them from the secretary.

B: Can desks and chairs in the classroom be moved around? The students in my conversational class need to sit facing each other.

C: Desks and chairs in this classroom can all be moved around. Let me help you set them up now.

B: Thanks.

C: You're welcome.

Grammar

▶ G1. Complements of manner or result: V + "得 de" + Adjectival Phrase

The following example, taken from the main dialogue in this lesson, illustrates a particular kind of verb complementation in which the verb is linked to an adjectival phrase with the particle "de", written with character "得" (the same character used to write the auxiliary verb "děi" — must, have to). Generally speaking, the complement expresses manner ("how", "to what degree") or result.

① 我汉字认得不多。 I don't know many characters.
　 Wǒ Hànzì rèn de bù duō.

("认 rèn" in this case is short for the verb "认识 rènshi" — know in the sense of "recognize".)
Here is another example — one you will probably hear a lot in China:

② 你汉语说得很好！ You speak Chinese very well!
　 Nǐ Hànyǔ shuō de hěn hǎo!

Notice that the adjectival phrase in Chinese (hěn hǎo) often corresponds to an adverbial phrase in English (very well). Complements of manner form questions or negatives as follows:

③ A: 她们说得好不好？ How well do they speak?
　　 Tāmen shuō de hǎo bu hǎo?

　 B: 她们说得不太清楚。 They don't speak very clearly.
　　 Tāmen shuō de bú tài qīngchu.

For the negative, note that in English, it is the first verb that is negated: "don't speak clearly"; while in Chinese, it is the complement "speak not very clearly".

Notice also that, in this construction, objects never appear directly after "得 de", which is always followed by an adjectival phrase. In the first example, above, the object appears before the verb (and after the subject): "我汉字认得不多 Wǒ Hànzì rèn de bù duō". The same is true of the second example: "你汉语说得很好 Nǐ Hànyǔ shuō de hěn hǎo". However, with objects that are tightly bound to verbs, like the "觉 jiào" of "睡觉 shuìjiào" or the "饭 fàn" of "吃饭 chī fàn", the verb is often expressed twice, first with the object, then with "得 de":

④ 我睡觉睡得很好。 I sleep quite well.
　 Wǒ shuì jiào shuì de hěn hǎo.

So to sum up, here are the various options, illustrated by means of a sentence praising someone's Chinese. The components are: "他 tā", "说 shuō", "汉语 Hànyǔ", and "很好 hěn hǎo":

⑤ 他说得很好。 "Hànyǔ" is unexpressed – it is understood from context.

　 他汉语说得很好。 "Hànyǔ" is mentioned before the verb.

　 他说汉语说得很好。 "Hànyǔ" appears after its verb, which is then repeated with "得 de".

G2. Potential compounds: "看得懂 kàn de dǒng" "看不懂 kàn bu dǒng"

Potential compounds can be illustrated by the following short interchange, which could be initiated by your teacher:

A: 听得懂吗？　Could you understand?
　　Tīng de dǒng ma?

B: 我听不懂，她说得太快！　No, I couldn't. She was speaking too fast.
　　Wǒ tīng bu dǒng, tā shuō de tài kuài!

The final phrase, "说得太快 shuō de tài kuài", is another illustration of the complement of result, just introduced in G1 above. But the first phrase, even though it also involves the particle "得 de", is different. In "听得懂 tīng de dǒng", "得 de" is followed not by an adjective, but by another verb (懂 dǒng), expressing result. In the response, the negative replaces "得 de": "听不懂 tīng bu dǒng".

In both cases – "听得懂 tīng de dǒng" and "听不懂 tīng bu dǒng" – the construction indicates possibility rather than actuality. Not "did you understand" but "could you understand" or "can you understand", which is why compounds of this type are called potential compounds. Another example with "懂 dǒng" is "看得懂 kàn de dǒng" (can or could read and understand), with the negative "看不懂 kàn bu dǒng" (can't or couldn't read and understand).

Potential compounds can be contrasted with actual (or plain) versions, which are discussed more fully in section G7 below. These involve the same combination of verbs without the infixed "得 de" or "不 bù". The options can be summarized as follows:

Actual		Potential	
他们听懂了。	understood or understand	他们听得懂。	can or could understand
他们没听懂。	didn't or don't understand	他们听不懂。	can't or couldn't understand

The number of possible second verbs in actual or potential compounds of this type is quite large, but many are restricted in their ability to combine with particular first verbs. "懂 dǒng", for example, is limited to the combinations already illustrated (with "听" and "看"), plus a few more that are rarer. "完 wán" (finish), on the other hand, combines with almost any action verb, e.g.: "工作做不完 gōngzuò zuò bu wán" (cannot finish the work); "我怎么喝得完呢？Wǒ zěnme hē de wán ne?" (How can I finish drinking all of it?)

G3. Cause: "因为 yīnwèi……所以 suǒyǐ……" (because ... [so…])

The conjunctions "因为 yīnwèi" (because, since) and "所以 suǒyǐ" (so, therefore) can appear singly, or they can appear together, linking two clauses in a causal relationship.

① 因为是口语课，所以我们没有教材。
　　Yīnwèi shì kǒuyǔkè, suǒyǐ wǒmen méiyǒu jiàocái.
　　Because it's a conversational class, we don't have a textbook.

② 我的汉语不太好，所以看不懂课表。
　　Wǒ de Hànyǔ bú tài hǎo, suǒyǐ kàn bu dǒng kèbiǎo.
　　My Chinese isn't very good, so I haven't been able to read the schedule.

③ 因为我们的教室都是多媒体的，所以能在教室上网。
　　Yīnwèi wǒmen de jiàoshì dōu shì duōméitǐ de, suǒyǐ néng zài jiàoshì shàng wǎng.
　　Because our classroom is multimedia, we can get online in the classroom.

"因为 yīnwèi" can occur before or after the subject of the first clause ("因为我 yīnwèi wǒ……" or 我因为 wǒ yīnwèi……"), but "所以 suǒyǐ" always appears at the head of the second ("所以我们 suǒyǐ wǒmen……"). One of the conjunctions can be omitted in Chinese, and if so, it is almost always "因为 yīnwèi", the first of the two, not "所以 suǒyǐ", as in the second example above. In English, either the causal clause may be marked ("Because it's a…") or the result ("It's a conversational class, so…"), but not usually both.

▶ **G4.** The auxiliary verb "会 huì" (ability, likelihood)

"会 huì" was introduced in Lesson 9 (G2) in Volume I, along with other auxiliary verbs such as "要 yào" (want, need, will) and "想 xiǎng" (be thinking of, intend to, want to). In fact, "会 huì" can function as a full verb (followed by an object) meaning "to know" or "to understand": "我会日文，不会英文 Wǒ huì Rìwén, bú huì Yīngwén" (I know Japanese, but not English). But more commonly, it functions as a modal auxiliary (i.e. followed by another verb or verb phrase). As an auxiliary, it indicates:

(1) Ability: "know how to, have the ability to, be able to, can":

① 他很会用电脑！　He really knows how to use computers!
　　Tā hěn huì yòng diànnǎo!

(2) Likelihood, possibility, intention: "will, would, be probable or likely":

② 他会不会已经走了？　Could it be he's already left?
　　Tā huì bu huì yǐjīng zǒu le?

③ 我每次上课会发材料给你们。　Every class, I'll hand out materials for you all.
　　Wǒ měi cì shàng kè huì fā cáiliào gěi nǐmen.

④ 课堂表现和出勤率也会算分。　Regular class performance and effort will also count.
　　Kètáng biǎoxiàn hé chūqínlǜ yě huì suàn fēn.

Questions with "会 huì" are formed in the regular patterns, either with final "吗 ma", or as below, with "会不会 huì bu huì":

⑤ 你会去中国学校学习吗？　Will you be attending a Chinese school?
　　Nǐ huì qù Zhōngguó xuéxiào xuéxí ma?

⑥ 今天会不会很热？　Is it going to be hot today?
　　Jīntiān huì bu huì hěn rè?

"会 huì" should be contrasted with "能 néng", which can also be translated as "can". But while "会 huì" expresses learned ability or likelihood, "能 néng" generally indicates external circumstances or permission: "不能这样做 bù néng zhèyàng zuò" (you can't do that); "不能去上课 bù néng qù shàng kè" (unable to make it to class due to some circumstances).

第十一课　在中国学校
Lesson Eleven　In a Chinese School

▶ **G5.** 除了 chúle……以外 yǐwài……, S 都 dōu (except for…)

The construction "除了 chúle……以外 yǐwài" (whose literal meaning is "removed… out") serves as a complex preposition that corresponds to English "apart from, in addition to, except for, besides":

① 除了上课以外，我都在办公室。　Except for when I'm teaching, I'm always in my office.
　　Chúle shàng kè yǐwài, wǒ dōu zài bàngōngshì.

② 除了他以外，我们都去银行换钱了。
　　Chúle tā yǐwài, wǒmen dōu qù yínháng huàn qián le.
　　Except for him, we all went to the bank to exchange money.

除了 chúle……以外 yǐwài……, S 还/也/hái/yě (in addition to; besides…)

③ 除了电脑外，我还要买手机。
　　Chúle diànnǎo yǐwài, wǒ hái yào mǎi shǒujī.
　　Besides a computer, I also need to buy a cell phone.

④ 除了英文以外，他也看得懂法文。　He reads French in addition to English.
　　Chúle Yīngwén yǐwài, tā yě kàn de dǒng Fǎwén.

▶ **G6.** The "把 bǎ" construction

Giving orders (about where to put furniture, for example) or instructions (say, a recipe) often involves picking out a series of items and then putting, moving, measuring or otherwise manipulating them. In Chinese, the things "picked out" are typically marked by the preposition "把 bǎ":

① A: 请把电脑放在桌子上。Please put the computer on the table.
　　　Qǐng bǎ diànnǎo fàng zài zhuōzi shang.

　　B: 我已经把它放在桌子上了。I've already put it on the table.
　　　Wǒ yǐjīng bǎ tā fàng zài zhuōzi shang le.

② 请把椅子摆在那边。Please put the chair over there.
　　Qǐng bǎ yǐzi bǎi zài nàbian.

③ 他把电脑卖掉了。He sold his computer.
　　Tā bǎ diànnǎo màidiàole.

④ 请不要把电视关上。Please don't switch off your television.
　　Qǐng bú yào bǎ diànshì guānshang.

Historically, "把 bǎ" derives from a verb meaning "to grasp, to hold"; and in some cases, translating "把 bǎ" as "to take" can give you a feel for its function in picking out or spotlighting a noun phrase prior to doing something to it – manipulating it. Thus, the first example above might be translated as: "Please take the computer and put it on the table".

⑤ 她没把房间钥匙给我。She didn't give me the room key.
　　Tā méi bǎ fángjiān yàoshi gěi wǒ.

Notice that the negative appears before "把 bǎ" rather than before the main verb, as shown in example 5.

The function of "把 bǎ" in spotlighting the object of interest has certain consequences. First of all, such objects will be definite: "the key" not "a key". Contrast examples with the following, in which the "key" is not highlighted with "把 bǎ" and is best translated as "a" key.

⑥ 她给了我房间钥匙。 She gave me a room key.
  Tā gěile wǒ fángjiān yàoshi.

Another feature of sentences with "把 bǎ" is that since they express some sort of manipulation or transformation, such sentences cannot contain simple, unadorned verbs: not just "卖 mài" (to sell), but at least "卖了 màile" (sold) or "卖掉 màidiào" (sell-fall); not just "关 guān" (to close), but "关上 guānshang" (close-up); not just "放 fàng" (to put), but "放在桌子上 fàng zài zhuōzi shang" (to put on the table).

A final note: verbs that do not perform any manipulation on their objects – no movement, transformation, or change – do not take "把 bǎ". Verbs of emotion, for example, like "喜欢 xǐhuan" (to be fond of), verbs of cognition such as "懂 dǒng" (to understand) and potential resultative-verb compounds, such as "喝不完 hē bu wán" (can/could not finish drinking), do not normally appear with "把 bǎ".

▶ G7. Verbs with resultative complements

In G2 above, combinations of action and resultative verbs were illustrated in both their potential form (听得懂 tīng de dǒng) and their plain, or actual, form (听懂 tīngdǒng). Several other resultative verbs occur in this lesson: "低 dī" (low) in "调低 tiáodī" – to turn down (adjust-lower); "上 shàng" (on; to go up) in "关上 guānshang" – close (close-up); and "好 hǎo" (good) in "摆好 bǎihǎo" – to arrange (set out-satisfactorily). Recall that "好 hǎo" in this same resultative complement function was introduced in Lesson 7 (G5):

① 这是押金收据，请收好。 This is your deposit receipt; please keep it safe.
  Zhè shì yājīn shōujù, qǐng shōuhǎo.

The examples from this lesson's dialogue are reproduced below. Since resultative complements typically encode movement or manipulation, they often appear with "把 bǎ".

② 我把空调的温度调低了。 I've lowered the air-conditioning.
  Wǒ bǎ kōngtiáo de wēndù tiáodī le.

③ 你把门和窗户都关上了吗？ Did you close the doors and windows?
  Nǐ bǎ mén hé chuānghu dōu guānshang le ma?

④ 教室里的桌子和椅子都摆好了。
  Jiàoshì li de zhuōzi hé yǐzi dōu bǎihǎo le.
  The classroom tables and chairs have all been arranged properly.

The familiar word "到 dào" (to arrive; to) is a particularly productive resultative complement. After action verbs, it indicates the achievement of the verbal action: "manage to, succeed in". The following examples illustrate both the potential and the actual usage:

⑤ 没买到火车票，怎么办？ We didn't get the train tickets, what will we do?
  Méi mǎi dào huǒchēpiào, zěnme bàn?

Lesson Eleven In a Chinese School

⑥ 我已经买到了。 I've already bought them.
　Wǒ yǐjīng mǎidào le.

⑦ 今天学到第十二课。 We can get to Lesson 12 today.
　Jīntiān xué dào dì-shí'èr kè.

⑧ 她还没找到工作呢。 She hasn't managed to find a job yet.
　Tā hái méi zhǎodào gōngzuò ne.

Verbs with resultative complements, like those illustrated in this section, are comparable to English "phrasal verbs", that consist of a verb and one of the little words that are categorized as adverbs or prepositions: "hand in", "hand out", "clam up", "wind down", etc. Like the second verb in the Chinese compounds, the adverbs and prepositions in the English are drawn from a limited set, and many of the combinations are idiosyncratic and have to be learned (thus "goof off" not "goof up", "mess up" not "mess off"). Given the range and unpredictability of verb plus complement compounds in Chinese, you will need to build up your repertoire slowly as examples appear in each lesson.

▶ **G8.** Destination expressed with "到 dào"

In Lesson 8 (G3) of Volume I, the verbs "来 lái" and "去 qù" were introduced with the destination following immediately: "去北京 qù Běijīng" (go to Beijing); "来中国 lái Zhōngguó" (come to China). There is another option, however, that is probably more common among northern speakers: that is, to introduce the destination with "到 dào" (to reach, to arrive), functioning as a preposition corresponding to English "to". Like other prepositions in Chinese, "到 dào" is placed before the verb:

① 去银行 = 到银行去   go to the bank
　qù yínháng = dào yínháng qù

In both cases, the direct pattern (去银行 qù yínháng) and the prepositional pattern (到银行去 dào yínháng qù), the purpose follows:

② 去超市买水果　　　　→ 到超市去买水果
　qù chāoshì mǎi shuǐguǒ　　dào chāoshì qù mǎi shuǐguǒ
　go to the market to buy fruit

③ 来中国教英文　　　　→ 到中国来教英文
　lái Zhōngguó jiāo Yīngwén　　dào Zhōngguó lái jiāo Yīngwén
　come to China to teach English

④ 去系办公室要水笔和板擦儿　→ 到系办公室去要水笔和板擦儿
　qù xì bàngōngshì yào shuǐbǐ hé bǎncār　　dào xì bàngōngshì qù yào shuǐbǐ hé bǎncār
　go to the departmental office to get felt pens and erasers

The choice of the direct pattern (去银行 qù yínháng) over the prepositional pattern (到银行去 dào yínháng qù) can be a matter of style and balance; "去 qù" provides a nice pivot between the destination and the purpose in examples like the last one. However, in most cases, the choice is free. Historically, the prepositional pattern is northern; the direct pattern seems to have been introduced into Mandarin by way of southern dialects such as Cantonese, where the direct pattern is the norm.

Consolidation & Practice

1. Practice with "V + 得 de + Adjective Phrase"

    (1) Incorporate the phrases provided using the above construction

    Example: 她说得很好。
    Tā shuō de hěn hǎo.

    她汉语说得很好。
    Tā Hànyǔ shuō de hěn hǎo.

    她说汉语说得很好。
    Tā shuō Hànyǔ shuō de hěn hǎo.

    } She speaks (Chinese) very well.

选课 xuǎn kè	很多 hěn duō
写汉字 xiě Hànzì	不多 bù duō
发材料 fā cáiliào	很多 hěn duō
摆桌子和椅子 bǎi zhuōzi hé yǐzi	不整齐 bù zhěngqí

说汉语 shuō hànyǔ	不错 búcuò
上课 shàng kè	很早 hěn zǎo
调温度 tiáo wēndù	太低 tài dī

    (2) Comment on how your family members or friends play sports, drive, sing or read

    Example: 我妈妈做饭做得很好吃。
    Wǒ māma zuò fàn zuò de hěn hǎochī.

    ① 我爸爸 _____。
    Wǒ bàba

    ② 我弟弟 _____。
    Wǒ dìdi

    ③ 我朋友 _____。
    Wǒ péngyou

    ④ 我的中国朋友 _____。
    Wǒ de Zhōngguó péngyou

2. Practice with potential compounds

    Example: 你要的菜太多，我们吃不完。
    Nǐ yào de cài tài duō, wǒmen chī bu wán.

Lesson Eleven In a Chinese School

(1) Make suitable potential compounds by selecting from the list of complements; then translate the phrases into idiomatic English

进去 jìnqu   好 hǎo   出来 chūlai   到 dào   完 wán   清楚 qīngchu

① 看得 _____   _____
   kàn de

② 吃得 _____   _____
   chī de

③ 听不 _____   _____
   tīng bu

④ 找不 _____   _____
   zhǎo bu

⑤ 做得 _____   _____
   zuò de

⑥ 写得 _____   _____
   xiě de

⑦ 放不 _____   _____
   fàng bu

⑧ 修得 _____   _____
   xiū de

⑨ 买得 _____   _____
   mǎi de

⑩ 看不 _____   _____
   kàn bu

⑪ 睡得 _____   _____
   shuì de

(2) Following the English cues, fill in the blanks with appropriate potential complements

V_1 得/不 V_2

① A: 你可以用这支水笔吗?
      Nǐ kěyǐ yòng zhè zhī shuǐbǐ ma?

   B: 这支水笔干了,写不出字了。
      Zhè zhī shuǐbǐ gān le, xiě bu chū zì le.

   A: 那试一下儿这支,写得出字吗?
      Nà shì yíxiàr zhè zhī, xiě de chū zì ma?

B: 这支可以，_____。 (Yes, this one's OK, it writes.)
　　Zhè zhī kěyǐ, _____.

② A: 老师，你的PPT上面的字太小了，我看不清楚。
　　Lǎoshī, nǐ de PPT shàngmiàn de zì tài xiǎo le, wǒ kàn bu qīngchu.

B: 你可以坐在前边。现在看得清楚吗？
　　Nǐ kěyǐ zuò zài qiánbian. Xiànzài kàn de qīngchu ma?

A: _____。 (Yes, I can.)

③ A: 我们的课表都是中文的，有的学生看得懂，可是有的学生看不懂。
　　Wǒmen de kèbiǎo dōu shì Zhōngwén de, yǒude xuésheng kàn de dǒng, kěshì yǒude xuésheng kàn bu dǒng.

B: 要是学生 _____ 怎么办呢？ (can't read [and understand] it)
　　Yàoshi xuésheng _____ zěnme bàn ne?

B: 那我们就给他们英文课表。
　　Nà wǒmen jiù gěi tāmen Yīngwén kèbiǎo.

④ A: 在哪儿能换美元？
　　Zài nǎr néng huàn měiyuán?

B: 在大宾馆都 _____ 美元。 (can exchange)
　　Zài dà bīnguǎn dōu _____ měiyuán.

⑤ A: 我写在白板上的字，你们看得清楚吗？
　　Wǒ xiě zài báibǎn shang de zì, nǐmen kàn de qīngchu ma?

B: 字很大，我们都 _____。 (can read them clearly)
　　Zì hěn dà, wǒmen dōu _____.

⑥ A: 你去办公室找两支水笔，好吗？
　　Nǐ qù bàngōngshì zhǎo liǎng zhī shuǐbǐ, hǎo ma?

B: 秘书不在，我可能 _____ 水笔。 (won't be able to find any)
　　Mìshū bú zài, wǒ kěnéng _____ shuǐbǐ.

⑦ A: 你怎么没有英语口语的教科书？
　　Nǐ zěnme méiyǒu Yīngyǔ kǒuyǔ de jiàokēshū?

B: 我忘了把书放在哪儿了，我常常 _____ 我的东西。 (can't find)
　　Wǒ wàngle bǎ shū fàng zài nǎr le, wǒ chángcháng _____ wǒ de dōngxi.

第十一课　在中国学校
Lesson Eleven　In a Chinese School

3. Use the "因为 yīnwèi……所以 suǒyǐ……" construction to respond to the following questions.

   (1) A: 我们怎么没有教科书？
   　　 Wǒmen zěnme méiyǒu jiàokēshū?

   　　 B: _____
   　　 (Because it is a conversational class, we don't use a textbook.)

   (2) A: 你怎么不知道哪天退课？
   　　 Nǐ zěnme bù zhīdào nǎ tiān tuì kè?

   　　 B: _____
   　　 (Because I can't read the school calendar, I don't know the last day for dropping classes.)

   (3) A: 你为什么每天都起得那么早？
   　　 Nǐ wèi shénme měi tiān dōu qǐ de nàme zǎo?

   　　 B: _____
   　　 (I get up so early every day because I have class at 8:00 a.m.)

   (4) A: 老师为什么不用PPT？
   　　 Lǎoshī wèi shénme bú yòng PPT?

   　　 B: _____
   　　 (It's not a multimedia classroom, so the teacher can't use PPT.)

   (5) A: 你为什么要当翻译？
   　　 Nǐ wèi shénme yào dāng fānyì?

   　　 B: _____
   　　 (I have to work as a translator because I need money.)

4. Fill in the blanks, using the auxiliary verb "会 huì"

   (1) A: 你明年想要做什么？
   　　 Nǐ míngnián xiǎng yào zuò shénme?

   　　 B: _____
   　　 (I'm probably going to China.)

   (2) A: 我们怎么还没有课表？
   　　 Wǒmen zěnme hái méiyǒu kèbiǎo?

   　　 B: _____
   　　 (The instructor will be handing it out in the first class.)

   (3) A: 明天你有事儿吗？我们一起去买东西好吗？
   　　 Míngtiān nǐ yǒu shìr ma? Wǒmen yìqǐ qù mǎi dōngxi hǎo ma?

   　　 B: _____
   　　 (I can't go. A friend of mine is coming over tomorrow.)

(4) A: 北京八月的天气怎么样？
　　　Běijīng bāyuè de tiānqì zěnmeyàng?

　　B: _____
　　　(It's likely to be very warm.)

(5) A: 中级汉语课会不会很难？你上过这门课吗？
　　　Zhōngjí Hànyǔkè huì bu huì hěn nán? Nǐ shàngguo zhè mén kè ma?

　　B: _____
　　　(As long as you practice a lot, it won't be very difficult.)

5. **Except or besides. Following the English cues, fill in the blanks, incorporating the "除了 chúle……以外 yǐwài" construction**

(1) A: 你星期三只上中文课吗？
　　　Nǐ xīngqīsān zhǐ shàng Zhōngwénkè ma?

　　B: _____
　　　(Besides going to the Chinese class, I also have tutoring.)

(2) A: 这个周末你忙不忙？
　　　Zhège zhōumò nǐ máng bu máng?

　　B: 我这个周末很忙。_____
　　　Wǒ zhège zhōumò hěn máng. (Besides doing laundry, I also have to clean up my (dorm) room.)

(3) A: 昨天你和男朋友约会吃饭，吃了什么？
　　　Zuótiān nǐ hé nánpéngyou yuēhuì chī fàn, chīle shénme?

　　B: _____
　　　(We ordered four dishes, and on top of that, we also ordered two glasses of beer.)

(4) A: 你为什么要退文学课？
　　　Nǐ wèi shénme yào tuì wénxuékè?

　　B: _____
　　　(Because I am taking too many classes (courses); in addition to Chinese conversational class and Chinese History, I'm also taking American History.)

(5) A: 你怎么一到中国就花了几千块钱？
　　　Nǐ zěnme yí dào Zhōngguó jiù huāle jǐqiān kuài qián?

　　B: _____
　　　(Since my laptop was broken, I had to buy a new one as well as a new cellphone.)

(6) A: 中级汉语课难吗？
　　　Zhōngjí Hànyǔkè nán ma?

　　B: _____
　　　(I find it difficult. Besides homework and tests, the professor also looks at classroom performance.)

第十一课　在中国学校
Lesson Eleven　In a Chinese School

Listening Comprehension

1. Listen to the dialogue and then answer the questions

    (1) Did David take any Chinese before he came to China?
    (2) What Chinese class is David taking now?
    (3) How does David feel about his class?
    (4) What is David's first question?
    (5) What does Ms. Zhang recommend?
    (6) When are they going to meet again?
    (7) What is David's second question?
    (8) What does Ms. Zhang suggest that he do?

2. As you listen to the passage, fill in the missing parts of Lucy's schedule and answer the questions

    (1) Fill out Lucy's schedule, based on what you hear.

Lucy's daily schedule	Activities
8:00–9:00 a.m.	
9:00–10:00 a.m.	
10:00–11:00 a.m.	
11:00–12:00 noon	
12:00–1:00 p.m.	
1:00–2:00 p.m.	
Afternoon	
11:00 p.m.	

New Words

休息 xiūxi V to rest
发现 fāxiàn V to discover, to find, to notice

    (2) What does Lucy do in China?
    (3) What does Lucy think of Chinese students?
    (4) What does Lucy do after dinner?

3. Fill out the chart below based on information provided in the dialogue

    (1) Why are classrooms usually so large in China?
    (2) In the table below, check off items found in Chinese or US classrooms by placing a Y (for "yes") and N (for "no") in the appropriate boxes.
    (3) What are the main differences between classrooms in China and the US?

New Words

下边 xiàbian PW below
有用 yǒuyòng Adj useful
电扇 diànshàn N electric fan

Countries	Whiteboard	Markers	Whiteboard Eraser	PPT	A/C	Internet
China						
U.S.A.						

21

真实生活汉语 2
Chinese for Living in China

Communication Activities

Pair Work

Scenario I: Using questions such as those listed below, get to know your partner and find out about his or her classes – schedules, classrooms, teachers, etc.

姓什么？／贵姓？
Xìng shénme? / Guìxìng?

哪国人？
Nǎ guó rén?

知道不知道退课／加课的时间？
Zhīdào bù zhīdào tuì kè / jiā kè de shíjiān?

教室在哪儿？／是不是多媒体的？／有空调吗？
Jiàoshì zài nǎr? / Shì bu shì duōméitǐ de? /
Yǒu kōngtiáo ma?

老师说话说得快不快？
Lǎoshī shuō huà shuō de kuài bu kuài?

老师的办公室时间是什么时候？
Lǎoshī de bàngōngshì shíjiān shì shénme shíhou?

叫什么？
Jiào shénme?

注册了几门课？
Zhùcèle jǐ mén kè?

一周有几节课？
Yì zhōu yǒu jǐ jié kè?

用什么教科书？
Yòng shénme jiàokēshū?

看得懂吗？／听得懂吗？
Kàn de dǒng ma? / Tīng de dǒng ma?

Scenario II: a. You've met a Chinese student – male or female – who knows some English. Start by praising the student's English then, following the English cues given below, find out all you can about him or her.

- Where he or she is from.
- Where the student learned English.
- How many classes he or she has every day.
- How many students there are in the class.
- How many classes he or she is taking this semester.
- If he or she is taking any Chinese classes in addition to the English one.
- If his or her teacher is American.
- If the teacher speaks too fast.

b. Then ask the student if he or she can tutor you in Chinese in exchange for English conversation a couple of times a week. Exchange phone numbers and say it's fine to phone anytime. Make use of the following:

| 帮 | 清楚 | 快 | 每星期 | 次 |
| bāng | qīngchu | kuài | měi xīngqī | cì |

把你的电话号码给我　　　　　　　　　　随时
bǎ nǐ de diànhuà hàomǎ gěi wǒ　　　　　suíshí

第十一课　在中国学校
Lesson Eleven　In a Chinese School

Scenario III: Working in pairs, comment on people or actions using the construction:

$$\text{Subject} + (V + \text{Object}) + V \text{ 得} + \text{Adj.}$$

Example: 这个餐厅 / 做饭 / 很好
zhège cāntīng / zuò fàn / hěn hǎo

→ 这个餐厅做饭做得很好。
zhège cāntīng zuò fàn zuò de hěn hǎo.

(1) 美国人 / 喝咖啡 / 多 → _____
    Měiguórén / hē kāfēi / duō

(2) 那个学生 / 问问题 / 很好 → _____
    nàge xuésheng / wèn wèntí / hěn hǎo

(3) 马丽莎 / 教英文 / 不错 → _____
    Mǎ Lìshā / jiāo Yīngwén / búcuò

(4) 汉语班的学生 / 学中文 / 快 → _____
    Hànyǔbān de xuésheng / xué Zhōngwén / kuài

(5) 很多学生 / 上网玩儿 / 多 → _____
    hěn duō xuésheng / shàng wǎng wánr / duō

(6) 中国老师 / 考试 / 太难 → _____
    Zhōngguó lǎoshī / kǎoshì / tài nán

(7) 我 / 认汉字 / 不多 → _____
    wǒ / rèn Hànzì / bù duō

(8) 宾馆里边的餐厅 / 卖冷饮 / 太贵 → _____
    bīnguǎn lǐbian de cāntīng / mài lěngyǐn / tài guì

(9) 留学生 / 休息 / 太晚了 → _____
    liúxuéshēng / xiūxi / tài wǎn le

Role-Play

Scenario I: Work in pairs, with each one of you taking the role of foreign English teachers (one from the US, one from Canada) working at Shenzhen University. Introduce yourselves, then talk about your classroom facilities and students. Try to incorporate the following expressions:

姓	叫	哪个班	教室	在几楼
xìng	jiào	nǎge bān	jiàoshì	zài jǐ lóu
空调	投影仪	黑板/白板	问问题	看得清楚
kōngtiáo	tóuyǐngyí	hēibǎn/báibǎn	wèn wèntí	kàn de qīngchu
听得懂	看不清楚	听不懂		
tīng de dǒng	kàn bu qīngchu	tīng bu dǒng		

真实生活汉语
Chinese for Living in China 2

Scenario II: Study the chart below and report on the different teaching styles and activities of Teacher Wang, a senior teacher, and Teacher Li, a new teacher. Critique the various activities from the point of view of learners like yourselves.

王老师, 60岁　Wáng lǎoshī, liùshí suì	李老师, 29岁　Lǐ lǎoshī, èrshíjiǔ suì
中级汉语 zhōngjí Hànyǔ	口语课 kǒuyǔkè
黑板 hēibǎn	白板 báibǎn
发很多材料 fā hěn duō cáiliào	不经常发材料（学生上网找材料） bù jīngcháng fā cáiliào (xuésheng shàng wǎng zhǎo cáiliào)
不喜欢学生问问题 bù xǐhuan xuésheng wèn wèntí	喜欢学生问问题，常请学生到前边讲 xǐhuan xuésheng wèn wèntí, cháng qǐng xuésheng dào qiánbian jiǎng
有时候放幻灯片 yǒu shíhou fàng huàndēngpiàn	每节课都上网看一个小电影，然后学生讨论 měi jié kè dōu shàng wǎng kàn yí ge xiǎo diànyǐng, ránhòu xuésheng tǎolùn
很多翻译练习 hěn duō fānyì liànxí	没有翻译练习，学生自己写对话 méiyǒu fānyì liànxí, xuésheng zìjǐ xiě duìhuà
教室不开空调 jiàoshì bù kāi kōngtiáo	空调开得很冷 kōngtiáo kāi de hěn lěng
很多学生退课（有12个人） hěn duō xuésheng tuì kè (yǒu shí'èr ge rén)	很多学生加课（有35个人） hěn duō xuésheng jiā kè (yǒu sānshíwǔ ge rén)

Group Activities

One student takes the part of (A), a language coordinator in charge of teaching and room assignments for a group of language teachers (B, C, D) from overseas teaching in China. They want to find out what to expect. Use the expressions listed.

The Language Coordinator A: Gives the teachers their schedules and explains which classes they will each be teaching, when they meet, how many students they'll have, where they'll meet, and what sort of equipment they will have access to.

课表 kèbiǎo	每天 měi tiān	教 jiāo	第 dì	节 jié
教室 jiàoshì	上班 shàngbān	办公室 bàngōngshì	幻灯片 huàndēngpiàn	板擦儿 bǎncār
粉笔 fěnbǐ	空调 kōngtiáo	投影仪 tóuyǐngyí	黑板 hēibǎn	

第十一课 在中国学校
Lesson Eleven   In a Chinese School

Teacher B: Wants to know where the English department is, and where the classrooms are exactly; also how many students are in the class and how good their English is.

系	教	第	节	几点
xì	jiāo	dì	jié	jǐ diǎn
班	听得懂	每个	一共	
bān	tīng de dǒng	měi ge	yígòng	

Teacher C: This teacher is also studying Chinese. He or she is concerned about how little time there is between classes – English class and Chinese – and wants to find out if the classrooms are across from each other and if not, how many minutes it will take to walk from one to the other.

对面	教学楼	办公室	附近	可以
duìmiàn	jiàoxuélóu	bàngōngshì	fùjìn	kěyǐ
换	走	分钟	走不到	远
huàn	zǒu	fēnzhōng	zǒu bu dào	yuǎn

Teacher D: She or he has seen the room already, is a little unhappy about the room facilities, and tries to get the coordinator to change the room.

空调	投影仪	黑板	电扇	桌子	椅子
kōngtiáo	tóuyǐngyí	hēibǎn	diànshàn	zhuōzi	yǐzi
窗户	板擦儿	粉笔	电脑	灯	坏了
chuānghu	bǎncār	fěnbǐ	diànnǎo	dēng	huài le

Review Exercises

1. You and your classmates are volunteering for a conference. Using the "把 bǎ" construction wherever you can, make a list of things you need to do

    (Subject +) 把 bǎ + Object + V + Complement.

    Example: 我们把白板擦干净吧。 Let's wipe the whiteboard clean.
              Wǒmen bǎ báibǎn cā gānjing ba.

空调	桌子	椅子	白板	水笔	板擦儿	投影仪
kōngtiáo	zhuōzi	yǐzi	báibǎn	shuǐbǐ	bǎncār	tóuyǐngyí
窗户	材料	饮料	电脑	调好	放整齐	摆好
chuānghu	cáiliào	yǐnliào	diànnǎo	tiáohǎo	fàng zhěngqí	bǎihǎo
摆整齐	关上	打开	买好	放在桌子上边		
bǎi zhěngqí	guānshang	dǎkāi	mǎihǎo	fàng zài zhuōzi shàngbian		

真实生活汉语
Chinese for Living in China 2

2. List 10 people you know. Comment on their strong points. Then think of 5 things that Chinese tend to do differently from Americans. The list below provides some guidance

   Example: ① 奥巴马讲话讲得很好。
   Àobāmǎ jiǎng huà jiǎng de hěn hǎo.

   ② 中国人起床起得很早。
   Zhōngguórén qǐchuáng qǐ de hěn zǎo.

   | 做饭……好 | 开车……慢 |
   | zuò fàn……hǎo | kāi chē……màn |

   | 旅游……多 | 教英文……好 |
   | lǚyóu……duō | jiāo Yīngwén……hǎo |

   | 说中文……好 | 吃饭……不多 |
   | shuō Zhōngwén……hǎo | chī fàn……bù duō |

3. What would you say in each of the following situations?

   (1) Meeting a new instructor for the first time.
   (2) You want to find out from a Chinese student where the classroom building is.
   (3) You want to find out the date of the final exam from your instructor.
   (4) You wish to ask your instructor for her office hours.
   (5) You want to ask your instructor if he could speak more slowly – you're having trouble understanding.
   (6) It's hot in the classroom so you request that the air-conditioner be turned down a bit.

4. Create a weekly schedule based on the following classes

课程表 kèchéngbiǎo
中级汉语精读 Zhōngjí Hànyǔ Jīngdú
汉语作文 Hànyǔ Zuòwén
中国历史 Zhōngguó Lìshǐ
电脑 Diànnǎo
汉语口语 Hànyǔ Kǒuyǔ
汉语语法 Hànyǔ Yǔfǎ

第十一课　在中国学校
Lesson Eleven　In a Chinese School

Culture Notes

1. Schools and other educational institutions

Schools		China	U.S.A.	Age
Elementary schools (小学 xiǎoxué)		Grades 1–6	Grades 1–6	6–11 year-olds
Secondary schools (中学 zhōngxué)	Middle Schools (初中 chūzhōng)	Junior 1–3	Grades 7–9	12–14 year-olds
	High Schools (高中 gāozhōng)	Senior 1–3	Grades 10–12	15–17 year-olds
Two-year professional training schools – an alternative to high school (中专 zhōngzhuān)				
Three-year professional training colleges (大专 dàzhuān)				
Four-year colleges and universities (大学 dàxué), some of which are specialized professional colleges, e.g.: Beijing Foreign Language University (for training foreign-language experts) and Beijing Normal University (for training teachers)				

2. School administration

The secretary of the general party branch is the official head of the school; in most schools the principal also holds this post. The principal (校长 xiàozhǎng) makes all final decisions at the school. The vice-principal (副校长 fùxiàozhǎng) is in charge of the day-to-day administration. Department chairs (系主任 xìzhǔrèn) are in charge of particular subject areas, such as English, Mathematics, or Chinese.

The Office of Educational Administration (教务处 Jiàowùchù) is in charge of faculty, curricula, teaching materials, examinations, student records, and the school library.

The Office of Student Affairs (学生处 Xuéshēngchù) is in charge of student affairs and counseling.

3. The school year

September 1	Fall (Autumn) semester begins
September 10	Teacher's Day
Late September	The Mid-Autumn Festival (a one-day holiday)
October 1	National Day (a three-day holiday)
January or February	Chinese New Year or Spring Festival (a three-day holiday, but usually coincides with school winter vacation, which is about a month)
March 1	Spring semester begins
March 8	Women's Day (female employees have a half-day vacation)
April	Qingming Festival (a one-day holiday)
Early May	The Dragon Boat Festival (a one-day holiday)
May 1	Labor Day (a one-day holiday)

| June 1 | Children's Day (a one-day holiday for children) |
| July 10 – August 31 (approximately) | Summer vacation |

4. A sample school calendar

深圳市2014—2015学年义务教育阶段学校校历

深圳市教育局　2014年5月印发

第一学期				第二学期				说明
日　期	学年周次	学期周次	内　容	日　期	学年周次	学期周次	内　容	
7月20日—26日	1		暑假，学年开始，2014年暑假起始时间为7月13日	1月18日—24日	27	21	上课	1．全学年52周。其中教学时间（周一至周五）为39周，含机动时间2周，由各区教育行政部门或学校视具体情况自行安排（可用于安排学校传统文化科技艺术节、运动会、社会实践等）。
7月27日—8月2日	2		暑假	1月25日—31日	28	22	上课，学期复习考试	
8月3日—9日	3		暑假	2月1日—7日	29		寒假	
8月10日—16日	4		暑假	2月8日—14日	30		寒假	
8月17日—23日	5		暑假	2月15日—21日	31		寒假，2月19日春节	
8月24日—30日	6		暑假	2月22日—28日	32		寒假	
8月31日—9月6日	7	1	上课，9月1日开学	3月1日—7日	33	1	上课，3月2日开学	
9月7日—13日	8	2	上课，中秋节放假1天	3月8日—14日	34	2	上课，妇女节妇女放假半天	
9月14日—20日	9	3	上课	3月15日—21日	35	3	上课	
9月21日—27日	10	4	上课	3月22日—28日	36	4	上课	
9月28日—10月4日	11	5	上课，国庆节放假3天	3月29日—4月4日	37	5	上课	
10月5日—11日	12	6	上课	4月5日—11日	38	6	上课，清明节放假1天	
10月12日—18日	13	7	上课	4月12日—18日	39	7	上课	
10月19日—25日	14	8	上课	4月19日—25日	40	8	上课	

第十一课　在中国学校
Lesson Eleven　In a Chinese School

续表 Continued

第一学期				第二学期				说　明
日　期	学年周次	学期周次	内　容	日　期	学年周次	学期周次	内　容	
10月26日—11月1日	15	9	上课	4月26日—5月2日	41	9	上课，劳动节放假1天	2．寒暑假、国家法定节假日共13周,法定节假日按国务院和省政府安排的时间执行。寒假起始时间为2015年2月1日；暑假起始时间为2015年7月12日。
11月2日—8日	16	10	上课	5月3日—9日	42	10	上课	
11月9日—15日	17	11	上课	5月10日—16日	43	11	上课	
11月16日—22日	18	12	上课	5月17日—23日	44	12	上课	
11月23日—29日	19	13	上课	5月24日—30日	45	13	上课	
11月30日—12月6日	20	14	上课	5月31日—6月6日	46	14	上课，儿童节小学放假1天	
12月7日—13日	21	15	上课	6月7日—13日	47	15	上课	
12月14日—20日	22	16	上课	6月14日—20日	48	16	上课，端午节放假1天	
12月21日—27日	23	17	上课	6月21日—27日	49	17	上课	
12月28日—2015年1月3日	24	18	上课，元旦放假1天	6月28日—7月4日	50	18	上课	
1月4日—10日	25	19	上课	7月5日—11日	51	19	上课，学年复习考试	

Lesson Twelve   At the Supermarket

第十二课   在超市
Dì-shí'èr Kè   Zài Chāoshì

In this lesson you will learn how to do the following
- Invite friends or colleagues to dinner
- Ask where you can shop for items
- Locate items in a supermarket

Grammar
- Duration phrases and objects
- Pivotal constructions
- Alternative questions with "还是 háishi" (or); alternatives with "或者 huòzhě" (or)
- "又 yòu……又 yòu……" ([both]... and…)
- Resolution with "就 jiù……了 le"
- Movement to a location: V + "在 zài"/"到 dào"

Culture Notes
- Traditional Chinese weight and liquid measures
- Discounts
- Morning markets and street markets
- Bargaining

第十二课　在超市
Lesson Twelve　At the Supermarket

Dialogue

A：大伟，英语老师 Dàwěi, Yīngyǔ lǎoshī　　　B：毛老师 Máo lǎoshī

C、D：服务员 fúwùyuán

今年大伟到深圳的一所中学教英语。他要在学校的教师公寓住一年^{G1}。他想他应该¹交一些²中国朋友，所以³这个周末他想请英文教研组的同事和邻居一起吃饭^{G2}。他去找同事毛老师。

Jīnnián Dàwěi dào Shēnzhèn de yì suǒ zhōngxué jiāo Yīngyǔ. Tā yào zài xuéxiào de jiàoshī gōngyù zhù yì nián^{G1}. Tā xiǎng tā yīnggāi¹ jiāo yìxiē Zhōngguó péngyou, suǒyǐ³ zhège zhōumò tā xiǎng qǐng Yīngwén jiàoyánzǔ de tóngshì hé línjū yìqǐ chī fàn^{G2}. Tā qù zhǎo tóngshì Máo lǎoshī.

A：毛老师，这个周末我想请您和其他几⁴位同事一起去我那儿吃个饭。您能来吗？
Máo lǎoshī, zhège zhōumò wǒ xiǎng qǐng nín hé qítā jǐ⁴ wèi tóngshì yìqǐ qù wǒ nàr chī ge fàn⁵. Nín néng lái ma?

B：您太客气了。是星期六还是^{G3}星期日？
Nín tài kèqi le. Shì xīngqīliù háishi^{G3} xīngqīrì?

A：星期六晚上，好吗？
Xīngqīliù wǎnshang, hǎo ma?

B：好，我一定去。
Hǎo, wǒ yídìng qù.

A：请问，我应该到哪儿去买菜？
Qǐngwèn, wǒ yīnggāi dào nǎr qù mǎi cài?

B：附近有个早市，蔬菜又新鲜又便宜^{G4}，还可以砍价。我常常去那儿买菜。
Fùjìn yǒu ge zǎoshì, shūcài yòu xīnxian yòu piányi^{G4}, hái kěyǐ kǎn jià. Wǒ chángcháng qù nàr mǎi cài.

Notes

1. "应该 yīnggāi" is an auxiliary verb that expresses obligation (should, ought, must), e.g.: "不应该 bù yīnggāi" (one shouldn't). It is sometimes reduced to "该" in speech: "该走了 gāi zǒu le" (time to get going).
2. "一些 yìxiē" (some, a few, a little), sometimes shortened to "些 xiē", substitutes for a measure phrase when multiplicity is meant: "交（一）些朋友 jiāo (yì) xiē péngyou" (make some friends).
3. "所以 suǒyǐ" appeared in Lesson 11 in conjunction with "因为 yīnwèi" (because). However, it can also be used independently as a conjunction introducing a consequence, often translated as English "so".
4. "几 jǐ" has several functions in addition to its role in questions. Here, it indicates "a small number of, several (fewer than ten)".

A：早市几点开门？
Zǎoshì jǐ diǎn kāi mén?

B：早上六点开门，九点关门。
Zǎoshang liù diǎn kāi mén, jiǔ diǎn guān mén.

A：现在太晚了。早市已经关门了。
Xiànzài tài wǎn le. Zǎoshì yǐjīng guān mén le.

B：现在你可以去超市，或者[G3]去对面小区的菜市场买。
Xiànzài nǐ kěyǐ qù chāoshì, huòzhě[G3] qù duìmiàn xiǎoqū de càishìchǎng mǎi.

A：哪个比较近？
Nǎge bǐjiào jìn?

B：超市最近。你出了校门往右走，过三个路口就到了[G5]。
Chāoshì zuì jìn. Nǐ chūle xiàomén wǎng yòu zǒu, guò sān ge lùkǒu jiù dào le[G5].

A：那我就去超市。除了买菜，我还要买日用品。
Nà wǒ jiù qù chāoshì. Chúle mǎi cài, wǒ hái yào mǎi rìyòngpǐn.

（在超市 Zài chāoshì）

A：请问，卫生纸和洗衣粉在哪儿？
Qǐngwèn, wèishēngzhǐ hé xǐyīfěn zài nǎr?

C：在日用品那行。
Zài rìyòngpǐn nà háng.

A：蔬菜和调料呢？
Shūcài hé tiáoliào ne?

C：调料在中间那行，蔬菜在那边，往右走到[G6]头。
Tiáoliào zài zhōngjiān nà háng, shūcài zài nàbian, wǎng yòu zǒudào[G6] tóu.

A：肉和海鲜也在那边吗？
Ròu hé hǎixiān yě zài nàbian ma?

C：肉在左边那行，海鲜在蔬菜前边。
Ròu zài zuǒbian nà háng, hǎixiān zài shūcài qiánbian.

A：请问，青椒多少钱一斤？
Qǐngwèn, qīngjiāo duōshao qián yì jīn?

---

5. "最 zuì" appears before adjectives (as well as verbs such as "喜欢 xǐhuan"— to like) to indicate extreme or superlative degree, e.g.: "最好 zuì hǎo" (best); "最高 zuì gāo" (tallest); "最便宜的 zuì piányi de" (the cheapest one, the most inexpensive one).

第十二课　在超市
Lesson Twelve　At the Supermarket

D：蔬菜上面都有价格标签。您挑了菜，放在塑料袋里，拿给我称。
Shūcài shàngmiàn dōu yǒu jiàgé biāoqiān. Nín tiāole cài, fàng zài sùliàodài li, ná gěi wǒ chēng.

A：这是我要的菜。
Zhè shì wǒ yào de cài.

D：黄瓜10元，番茄5元，生菜5元，青椒8元，西蓝花12元，洋葱3元。
Huángguā shí yuán, fānqié wǔ yuán, shēngcài wǔ yuán, qīngjiāo bā yuán, xīlánhuā shí'èr yuán, yángcōng sān yuán.

A：一共多少钱？
Yígòng duōshao qián?

D：我们这里不收钱。请你到前面收银台一起算账、付款。
Wǒmen zhèli bù shōu qián. Qǐng nǐ dào qiánmiàn shōuyíntái yìqǐ suàn zhàng、fù kuǎn.

A：请问，牛奶和鸡蛋在哪行？我还要去拿面包，然后再一起付款。
Qǐngwèn, niúnǎi hé jīdàn zài nǎ háng? Wǒ hái yào qù ná miànbāo, ránhòu zài yìqǐ fù kuǎn.

D：牛奶、鸡蛋在第一行，面包在旁边。
Niúnǎi、jīdàn zài dì-yī háng, miànbāo zài pángbiān.

A：谢谢。
Xièxie.

New Words

1	深圳	Shēnzhèn	PropN	Shenzhen (a city in Guangdong Province)
2	所	suǒ	Meas	*for houses, schools, hospitals*
3	中学/中學	zhōngxué	N	middle school, high school, secondary education
4	公寓	gōngyù	N	apartment house, boarding house, rooming house ("教师公寓 jiàoshī gōngyù", teacher's dorm)
5	一些	yìxiē	Q	some, a few, several, a number of, a little
	些	xiē	Meas	some, a few, several
6	教研组/教研組	jiàoyánzǔ	N	teaching and research department or group
7	同事	tóngshì	N	colleague, fellow worker ("同事们 tóngshì men", colleagues, fellow workers)
8	邻居/鄰居	línjū	N	neighbor

真实生活汉语
Chinese for Living in China 2

9	其他	qítā	Pron	others, the rest, other
10	位	wèi	Meas	*for people* ("几位 jǐ wèi", several people)
11	客气/客氣	kèqi	Adj	polite, courteous
12	买菜/買菜	mǎi cài	Phrase	to buy vegetables, to buy groceries
	菜	cài	N	vegetables, dish; (in a meal)
13	早市	zǎoshì	N	morning market
14	蔬菜	shūcài	N	vegetables, greens
15	又……又……	yòu……yòu……	Construction	(both) … and…
	又	yòu	Adv	again, moreover, and
16	新鲜/新鮮	xīnxian	Adj	fresh (of food, air, etc.), new
17	砍价/砍價	kǎn jià	VO	to bargain
18	开门/開門	kāi mén	VO	to open the door (literal or figurative)
	开/開	kāi	V	to open, to start
19	关门/關門	guān mén	VO	to close the door (literal or figurative)
20	小区/小區	xiǎoqū	N	area, a residential neighbourhood
21	菜市场/菜市場	càishìchǎng	N	food market, grocery store
22	哪个/哪個	nǎge	IntPron	which (of them), which one
23	比较/比較	bǐjiào	Adv/V	comparatively, relatively; to compare, to contrast
24	最近	zuì jìn	Phrase	nearest
25	校门/校門	xiàomén	N	school gate
26	路口	lùkǒu	N	street intersection
27	日用品	rìyòngpǐn	N	items of daily use, daily necessities
28	卫生纸/衛生紙	wèishēngzhǐ	N	toilet paper, sanitary paper
29	洗衣粉	xǐyīfěn	N	washing powder, laundry powder
30	行	háng	Meas	line, row
31	调料/調料	tiáoliào	N	seasoning, flavoring
32	头/頭	tóu	N	head, top, end of something
33	肉	ròu	N	meat (default is "pork")
34	海鲜/海鮮	hǎixiān	N	seafood

第十二课 在超市
Lesson Twelve   At the Supermarket

35	前边/前邊	qiánbian	PW	in front, ahead, preceding
36	青椒	qīngjiāo	N	green peppers
37	上面	shàngmiàn	PW	above, on top of, on
38	价格/價格	jiàgé	N	price, cost
39	标签/標簽	biāoqiān	N	label, tag (with the price, proof of inspection, etc.)
40	挑	tiāo	V	to select, to choose
41	放	fàng	V	to put down, to place ("放在 fàng zài", to put or place into or onto)
42	塑料袋	sùliàodài	N	plastic bag
	塑料	sùliào	N	plastic
43	拿	ná	V	to hold, to grasp, to take
44	称/稱	chēng	V	to weigh
45	黄瓜	huángguā	N	cucumber
46	番茄	fānqié	N	tomato ("番茄 fānqié" in Guangdong and Hong Kong, "西红柿 xīhóngshì" in North China)
47	生菜	shēngcài	N	lettuce, romaine lettuce
48	西蓝花/西藍花	xīlánhuā	N	broccoli
49	洋葱/洋蔥	yángcōng	N	onion
50	这里/這裡	zhèli	PW	here, this place
51	收钱/收錢	shōu qián	Phrase	to receive money, to collect debts
52	前面	qiánmiàn	PW	in front, ahead
53	收银台/收銀臺	shōuyíntái	N	cashier
54	算账/算賬	suàn zhàng	VO	to square or settle accounts (with sb.), to get even
	账/賬	zhàng	N	accounts, bill
55	付款	fù kuǎn	Phrase	to pay a sum of money
	付	fù	V	to pay
56	牛奶	niúnǎi	N	milk
57	面包/麵包	miànbāo	N	bread

Re-enacting the Dialogue

A: David, an English teacher   B: Mao laoshi   C、D: supermarket attendants

This year, David's gone to a middle school in Shenzhen to teach English. He'll be staying at the teachers' dorm for a year. He feels he should make some Chinese friends. So this weekend, he's planning to invite some colleagues from the English Language Teaching and Research Department and some neighbors over for a meal. He goes to look for his colleague, Mao laoshi.

A: Mao laoshi, I'd like to invite you and some other teachers from our office to come for a meal at my place this weekend. Can you make it?

B: You're too kind. Is it on Saturday, or Sunday?

A: How about Saturday evening?

B: Fine, I'll be there.

A: May I ask where I should go to buy vegetables?

B: There's a morning market nearby where vegetables are fresh and inexpensive, you can also bargain there. I often go there to buy vegetables.

A: What time does the morning market open?

B: It opens at 6:00 a.m. and closes at 9:00 a.m.

A: It's too late now; the morning market's already closed.

B: Now, you can go to the supermarket or to the neighborhood vegetable market across the street.

A: Which is closer?

B: The supermarket is closest. You go out the gate, turn to the right, go three blocks and you're there.

A: OK, then I'll go to the supermarket. Besides buying vegetables, I also need to get some everyday items.

(At the supermarket)

A: Excuse me, where are the toilet paper and the laundry powder, please?

C: They're in the everyday items aisle.

A: And vegetables and seasonings?

C: Seasonings are in that middle aisle; vegetables are over there, to the right – walk to the end.

A: Are meats and seafood also in that area?

C: Meat is the aisle to the left; seafood is in front of vegetables.

A: Excuse me, how much for a catty of green peppers?

D: The vegetables all have a price tag; after you choose your vegetables, put them in a plastic bag and bring them to me to weigh.

A: These are the vegetables I want.

D: Cucumber, 10 *yuan*; tomatoes, 5 *yuan*; lettuce, 5 *yuan*; green peppers, 8 *yuan*; broccoli, 12 *yuan*; onions, 3 *yuan*.

A: How much altogether?

D: We don't accept payment here; please go to the cashier in front to check out and pay.

A: Where are milk and eggs? I still have to get milk, eggs and bread, then I'll pay for them all together.

D: Milk and eggs are in aisle one; bread is on the side.

A: Thanks.

Lesson Twelve At the Supermarket
第十二课 在超市

Grammar

▶ **G1.** Duration phrases and objects

In Lesson 7 (G5), you encountered duration phrases such as "三天 sān tiān" (three days), "五年 wǔ nián" (five years), "一会儿 yíhuìr" (a while) and "很久 hěn jiǔ" (a long time) and it was noted that they appeared directly after the verb. The question of how a verb with its object ("教英语 jiāo Yīngyǔ", for example or "看电视 kàn diànshì") would accommodate a duration phrase was postponed – until now.

If an object is present, there are two options, with slightly different nuances of meaning. You can place the duration phrase between the verb and object:

① 教了一年英语　taught a year's English
　　jiāole yì nián Yīngyǔ

The modifying relationship between the duration phrase (一年 yì nián) and the object (英语 Yīngyǔ) in this construction can be made explicit by the addition of "的 de", which makes the expression parallel to English "taught a year's English", with "的 de" corresponding to the apostrophe "s":

② 教了一年的英语　taught a year's English
　　jiāole yì nián de Yīngyǔ

The other option is to state the verb with its object first (but without "了 le" or any other verbal suffix), then repeat the verb with the duration phrase – but without the object.

③ 教英语，教了一年　taught English for a year
　　jiāo Yīngyǔ, jiāole yì nián

See if you can apply the pattern to "看电视 kàn diànshì" (watch television) for an hour everyday ("hour" is "一个小时 yí ge xiǎoshí" or colloquially, "yì xiǎoshí"). There are two possibilities:

④ 她每天看一个小时（的）电视。　She watches an hour's TV everyday.
　　Tā měi tiān kàn yí ge xiǎoshí (de) diànshì.

⑤ 她每天看电视看一个小时。　She watches TV for an hour everyday.
　　Tā měi tiān kàn diànshì kàn yí ge xiǎoshí.

Here, for reference, are some of the units of duration (cf. Lesson 10, G1): "天 tiān" (三天); "年 nián" (五年); "月 yuè" (三个月); "星期 xīngqī"(两个星期); "小时 xiǎoshí" (三 [个] 小时). Notice that "天 tiān" and "年 nián" are themselves measures, while "月 yuè" and "星期 xīngqī" require the measure "个 gè"; and "小时 xiǎoshí" can appear with "个 gè" or without (一小时).

▶ **G2.** Pivotal constructions

Sentences containing pivotal constructions were introduced in Lesson 7 (G8). They involve a series of verbs, but unlike "verbs in series" (Lesson 4, G2), verbs in a pivotal construction share a noun phrase that is the object of the first verb and the subject of the second:

① 他叫我去打球。 He asked me to play bau game..
　Tā jiào wǒ qù dǎ qiú.

② 她请我帮忙。 She asked me for help.
　Tā qǐng wǒ bāng máng.

③ 技术人员教我们用投影仪。 The technician is teaching us to use the projector.
　Jìshù rényuán jiāo wǒmen yòng tóuyǐngyí.

In these examples, the pivots are, respectively: "我 wǒ", and "我们 wǒmen". Each is the object of the previous verb – the pre-pivotal verb – and the subject of the following verb. English does not allow you to have it both ways. In English, the equivalent of the pivot is clearly an object and the second verb is explicitly subordinated to the first ("to play", "to help"). Chinese forgoes grammatical complexity, simply juxtaposes the verbs, and lets the shared noun phrase pivot!

▶ **G3.** Alternative questions with "还是 háishi"(or); alternatives with "或者 huòzhě" (or)

Alternate question in Chinese – "or" questions – are formed with "还是 háishi". See the following examples:

① 是星期六好，还是星期日好？ Is Saturday best (,) or Sunday?
　Shì xīngqīliù hǎo, háishi xīngqīrì hǎo?

② 你喝茶，还是喝咖啡？ Would you like tea (,) or coffee?
　Nǐ hē chá, háishi hē kāfēi?

However, "或者 huòzhě" is used to give options in a declarative sentence. "或者 huòzhě", sometimes reduced to "或"; "或是 huòshi" is also an alternative. The following is the sort of question you often get asked at breakfast, where "tea or coffee" is considered a single option, as opposed to nothing, or to fruit juice. Notice that in English "tea or coffee" has high, questioning intonation.

③ 我喝茶或者咖啡。 I'd like to have tea or coffee.
　Wǒ hē chá huòzhě kāfēi.

④ 今天或者明天都行。 Today or tomorrow (either one) will be fine.
　Jīntiān huòzhě míngtiān dōu xíng.

⑤ 他想到广州或者深圳去工作。 He's thinking of going to Guangzhou or Shenzhen to work.
　Tā xiǎng dào Guǎngzhōu huòzhě Shēnzhèn qù gōngzuò.

⑥ 你现在可以去超市，或者去对面小区的菜市场买。
　Nǐ xiànzài kěyǐ qù chāoshì, huòzhě qù duìmiàn xiǎoqū de càishìchǎng mǎi.
　At this time, you can go to the supermarket or to the neighborhood vegetable market across the way.

"或者 huòzhě" may also be doubled or multiplied, meaning "or …or … or …":

⑦ 或者你爸爸去，或者你妈妈去，或者你的老师去，没关系。
　Huòzhě nǐ bàba qù, huòzhě nǐ māma qù, huòzhě nǐ de lǎoshī qù, méi guānxi.
　Whether your dad goes, or your mom, or your teacher – it doesn't matter.

G4. "又 yòu……又 yòu……" ([both] ... and...)

"又 yòu" as an adverb means "once again" or "go on to (do something else)" – for events that have already taken place:

① 你看，他又来了。 Look, here he is again.
　　Nǐ kàn, tā yòu lái le.

② 她从银行出来，又进了超市。 She came out of the bank, then went into the supermarket.
　　Tā cóng yínháng chūlai, yòu jìnle chāoshì.

"又 yòu" may also be paired with consecutive adjectives or verbs to indicate that both states or events are so:

③ 那个早市的蔬菜又便宜又新鲜。
　　Nàge zǎoshì de shūcài yòu piányi yòu xīnxian.
　　The vegetables at that morning market are cheap and fresh.

④ 我周末又要买菜，又要洗衣服。
　　Wǒ zhōumò yòu yào mǎi cài, yòu yào xǐ yīfu.
　　This weekend, I have to shop for groceries and wash the clothes.

⑤ 上课的时候学生们又说又写。 In class, the students do reading and writing.
　　Shàng kè de shíhou xuéshengmen yòu shuō yòu xiě.

G5. Resolution with "就 jiù……了 le"

"就 jiù" was first introduced in Lesson 8 (G5), where it appeared in conjunction with "如果 rúguǒ" (if):

① 如果您用电话卡就很便宜。 It's quite cheap – if you use a phone card.
　　Rúguǒ nín yòng diànhuàkǎ jiù hěn piányi.

"就 jiù" is associated with something that follows naturally from the condition – which in the example is "making use of a phone card". In a similar example, also from Lesson 8, the speaker has been listening to all the advantages of a particular phone card, and says in the end:

② 好。我就要这个卡。 OK. Then [it follows that] I'll have this one.
　　Hǎo. Wǒ jiù yào zhège kǎ.

"就 jiù" appears again in the grammar notes of Lesson 9 (G4). The example there is much the same: conditions are stated (after class gets out), from which it follows that there are certain consequences (the speaker feels tired) that involve a change of state (了 le):

③ 下班以后我就累了。 I get quite tired after work.
　　Xià bān yǐhòu wǒ jiù lèi le.

Other examples in which the resolution involves a change of state:

④ 过三个路口就到了。 Go three blocks and you're there.
　　Guò sān ge lùkǒu jiù dào le.

⑤ 开了空调就不热了。 Once you put the aircon on, you won't be hot.
　　Kāile kōngtiáo jiù bú rè le.

⑥ 九点早市就关门了。 The morning market will be closed by 9:00 a.m.
Jiǔ diǎn zǎoshì jiù guānmén le.

▶ **G6.** Movement to a location: V + "在 zài" / "到 dào"

Location in the sense of where something takes place – the site of an event – is placed *before* the associated verb in Chinese, as the following examples from this lesson show:

① 他要在学校的教师公寓住一年。 He'll be staying at the teacher's dorm for a year.
Tā yào zài xuéxiào de jiàoshī gōngyù zhù yì nián.

② 我想请您在我那儿吃个便饭。 I'd like to invite you to come for a meal at my place.
Wǒ xiǎng qǐng nín zài wǒ nàr chī ge biànfàn.

However, with verbs that involve movement, the location where the person or thing ends up – the goal or destination – is marked by "在 zài" or "到 dào" (often in the neutral tone) placed directly after the verb:, e.g.: "放在 fàng zài", "走到 zǒudào". "在 zài" is usual with verbs that involve momentary movements, such as "放 fàng" (to put), "坐 zuò" (to sit), "停 tíng" (to stop, to park), and "掉 diào" (to drop):

③ 放在桌子上   to put on the table
fàng zài zhuōzi shang

④ 坐在椅子上   to sit on the chair
zuò zài yǐzi shang

⑤ 停在学校前边   to park in front of school
tíng zài xuéxiào qiánbian

⑥ 掉在地上   to drop on the floor
diào zài dì shang

⑦ 您挑了菜，放在塑料袋里，拿给我称。
Nín tiāole cài, fàng zài sùliàodài li, ná gěi wǒ chēng.
After you choose your vegetables, put them in a plastic bag and bring them to me to weigh.

"到 dào" follows verbs of locomotion, such as "走 zǒu" (to walk) or "开 kāi" (in its meaning of "to drive"), or "坐 zuò" (in its meaning of "to take [a bus or train]"), or verbs of movement that involve a long trajectory, like "拿 ná" (to take, to bring) or "搬 bān" (to move [house], to remove, to take away).

⑧ 往右走到头   go to the right, all the way to the end
wǎng yòu zǒudào tóu

⑨ 走到二楼   go to the second floor
zǒudào èr lóu

⑩ 坐到南京路   take it to Nanjing Road
zuòdào Nánjīng Lù

⑪ 拿到外头   take it outside
nádào wàitou

第十二课　在超市
Lesson Twelve　At the Supermarket

Time can also be treated as an end point, following "到 dào":

⑫ 走到中午　walk until noon
　 zǒudào zhōngwǔ

But notice that people are not locations unless they are buttressed with "这儿 zhèr/这里 zhèli" or "那儿 nàr/那里 nàli":

⑬ 放在她那儿　put it over by her
　 fàng zài tā nàr

⑭ 走到我这儿　come over by me
　 zǒudào wǒ zhèr

Consolidation & Practice

1. Observe the sample sentences and then answer the questions based on your own situation

    Example: ① 他在中国学习了一年。　　　③ 他上星期病了两天。
    　　　　　Tā zài Zhōngguó xuéxíle yì nián.　　Tā shàng xīngqī bìngle liǎng tiān.

    　　　　　② 请在外边等一会儿。　　　　④ 我们来中国一个月了。
    　　　　　Qǐng zài wàibian děng yíhuìr.　　Wǒmen lái Zhōngguó yí ge yuè le.

    (1) A: 超市每天开门开几个小时？　　　B: 超市每天开门开_____。
    　　　Chāoshì měi tiān kāi mén kāi jǐ ge xiǎoshí?　　Chāoshì měi tiān kāi mén kāi____.

    (2) A: 早市每天开门开几个小时？　　　B: 早市每天开门开_____。
    　　　Zǎoshì měi tiān kāi mén kāi jǐ ge xiǎoshí?　　Zǎoshì měitiān kāi mén kāi____.

    (3) A: 你每天上课上几个小时？　　　　B: _____。
    　　　Nǐ měi tiān shàng kè shàng jǐ ge xiǎoshí?

    (4) A: 你每天上网上几个小时？　　　　B: _____。
    　　　Nǐ měi tiān shàng wǎng shàng jǐ ge xiǎoshí?

    (5) A: How long do you sleep every day?　　B: _____。

    (6) A: How long have you studied Chinese?　　B: _____。

2. Following the English cues, make sentences that incorporate the phrases listed in a pivotal construction; you may have to reorder the phrases

    Subject + V + Pivot / noun + V + Object.

    Example: 他 / 英文教研组的同事和邻居 / 饭 / 请 / 吃
    　　　　　tā / Yīngwén jiàoyánzǔ de tóngshì hé línjū / fàn / qǐng / chī

    　　　　　→ 他请英文教研组的同事和邻居吃饭。
    　　　　　Tā qǐng Yīngwén jiàoyánzǔ de tóngshì hé línjū chī fàn.

    (1) 大卫 / 朋友 / 菜 / 请 / 点 → _____
    　　Dàwèi / péngyou / cài / qǐng / diǎn
    　　(David asked his friend to order some food.)

    (2) 你 / 服务员 / 空调 / 叫 / 修 → _____
    　　nǐ / fúwùyuán / kōngtiáo / jiào / xiū
    　　(Call the service clerk to fix the AC.)

    (3) 老师 / 学生 / 作业 / 告诉 / 交 → _____
    　　lǎoshī / xuésheng / zuòyè / gàosu / jiāo
    　　(The teacher told her students to hand in their work.)

第十二课　在超市
Lesson Twelve　At the Supermarket

(4) 我 / 美国朋友 / 英文信 / 请 / 翻译 → _____
wǒ / Měiguó péngyou / Yīngwén xìn / qǐng / fānyì
(I asked my American friend to translate the English letter.)

(5) 客人 / 服务员 / 床单 / 叫 / 换 → _____
kèren / fúwùyuán / chuángdān / jiào / huàn
(The guest asked the maid to change the sheets.)

(6) 美国朋友 / 我 / 家教 / 请 / 做 → _____
Měiguó péngyou / wǒ / jiājiào / qǐng / zuò
(My American friend invited me to be his/her tutor.)

(7) 张老师 / 我 / 给外教 / 房间 / 让 / 预订 → _____
Zhāng lǎoshī / wǒ / gěi wàijiào / fángjiān / ràng / yùdìng
(Teacher Zhang told me to make a reservation for the foreign expert.)

(8) 妈妈 / 我 / 日用品和调料 / 让 / 去超市 / 买 → _____
māma / wǒ / rìyòngpǐn hé tiáoliào / ràng / qù chāoshì / mǎi
(Mom told me to go to the supermarket to get some daily necessities and seasoning.)

3. Observe the different functions of "还是 háishi" and "或者 huòzhě" (both translatable as "or") in the following mini dialogues and then fill in the blanks with the correct word

Example:　① A: 超市近还是菜场近？　　　B: 菜场近。
　　　　　　　Chāoshì jìn háishi càichǎng jìn?　　Càichǎng jìn.

② A: 我想下个星期五或者星期六请你来我这儿吃晚饭，你有时间吗？
Wǒ xiǎng xià ge xīngqīwǔ huòzhě xīngqīliù qǐng nǐ lái wǒ zhèr chī wǎnfàn, nǐ yǒu shíjiān ma?

B: 你太客气了！有时间，没问题。
Nǐ tài kèqi le! Yǒu shíjiān, méi wèntí.

(1) A: 你买日用品 _____ 食品？　　　B: 日用品。
　　　Nǐ mǎi rìyòngpǐn _____ shípǐn?　　　Rìyòngpǐn.

(2) A: 早市六点 _____ 七点开门？　　B: 七点开门。
　　　Zǎoshì liù diǎn _____ qī diǎn kāi mén?　　Qī diǎn kāi mén.

(3) A: 超市八点 _____ 九点关门？　　B: 九点关门。
　　　Chāoshì bā diǎn _____ jiǔ diǎn guān mén?　　Jiǔ diǎn guān mén.

(4) A: 你常常在早市 _____ 在超市买菜？
　　　Nǐ chángcháng zài zǎoshì _____ zài chāoshì mǎi cài?

B: 在早市买菜，那儿的菜便宜一点儿。
Zài zǎoshì mǎi cài, nàr de cài piányi yìdiǎnr.

(5) A: 你喜欢吃什么菜？
Nǐ xǐhuan chī shénme cài?

B: 素菜我都喜欢，生菜 _____ 西蓝花都可以。
Sùcài wǒ dōu xǐhuan, shēngcài _____ xīlánhuā dōu kěyǐ.

(6) A: 你今年夏天打算做什么？   B: 我想去北京 _____ 上海。
Nǐ jīnnián xiàtiān dǎsuàn zuò shénme?   Wǒ xiǎng qù Běijīng _____ Shànghǎi.

(7) A: 你下学期想修什么课？
Nǐ xià xuéqī xiǎng xiū shénme kè?

B: 还没想好。除了汉语课，还想修一门历史课 _____ 文学课。
Hái méi xiǎnghǎo. Chúle Hànyǔkè, hái xiǎng xiū yì mén lìshǐkè _____ wénxuékè.

(8) A: 你知道退课的日期吗？
Nǐ zhīdào tuì kè de rìqī ma?

B: 不太清楚，这个星期五 _____ 下个星期一。
Bú tài qīngchu, zhège xīngqīwǔ _____ xià ge xīngqīyī.

4. Fill in the blanks making use of "又 yòu……又 yòu……" and incorporating the verbs given in parentheses

(1) A: 你怎么又去早市买菜？
Nǐ zěnme yòu qù zǎoshì mǎi cài?

B: 那儿的菜_____。(好/便宜)
Nàr de cài _____ . (hǎo/piányi)

(2) A: 学校对面的饭馆怎么样？
Xuéxiào duìmiàn de fànguǎn zěnmeyàng?

B: 我不太喜欢，那儿的菜_____。(不好吃/贵)
Wǒ bú tài xǐhuan, nàr de cài _____ . (bù hǎochī/guì)

(3) 超市刚来的鱼真好，_____。(新鲜/便宜)
Chāoshì gāng lái de yú zhēn hǎo, _____ . (xīnxian/piányi)

(4) 我们班今天新来的女同学_____。(高/漂亮)
Wǒmen bān jīntiān xīn lái de nǚ tóngxué _____ . (gāo/piàoliang)

(5) 八月的北京_____。(干/热)
Bāyuè de Běijīng _____ . (gān/rè)

(6) 这个周末我会很忙，_____。(要买菜/要做饭)
Zhège zhōumò wǒ huì hěn máng, _____ . (yào mǎi cài/yào zuò fàn)

(7) 他现在很忙，_____。(上课/做家教)
Tā xiànzài hěn máng, _____ . (shàng kè/zuò jiājiào)

第十二课　在超市
Lesson Twelve At the Supermarket

(8) 昨天她十九岁，我们都来给她过生日，她高兴得_____。(唱/跳)
　　Zuótiān tā shíjiǔ suì, wǒmen dōu lái gěi tā guò shēngri, tā gāoxìng de _____ .
　　(chàng/tiào)

(9) 我的宿舍又_____又_____。(describe your dorm)
　　Wǒ de sùshè yòu _____ yòu _____ .

(10) 我的同学又_____又_____。(describe your classmate(s))
　　Wǒ de tóngxué yòu _____ yòu _____ .

5. Examine the examples in which a changed state (with "了 le") is introduced by "就 jiù" (and then). Then, taking your cue from the English and incorporating the items given in parentheses, fill in the blanks

   Example: ① 你开了空调就不热了。 You'll cool off once you turn on the air-conditioner.
   　　　　　　Nǐ kāile kōngtiáo jiù bú rè le.

   　　　　　② 你多放一点儿调料就好吃了。 It'll taste fine if you add more seasoning.
   　　　　　　Nǐ duō fàng yìdiǎnr tiáoliào jiù hǎochī le.

(1) 我们俩_____。(要三个菜/够)
　　Wǒmen liǎ _____ . (yào sān ge cài/gòu)

(2) A: 你知道退课的日期吗？
　　　Nǐ zhīdào tuì kè de rìqī ma?

　　B:_____。(看看校历/知道)
　　　_____ . (kànkan xiàolì/zhīdào)

(3) A: 我需要卫生纸和日用品，还想买点儿水果。
　　　Wǒ xūyào wèishēngzhǐ hé rìyòngpǐn, hái xiǎng mǎi diǎnr shuǐguǒ.

　　B: 明天我们 _____。(去超市/都买)
　　　Míngtiān wǒmen _____ . (qù chāoshì/dōu mǎi)

(4) A: 水笔在哪儿？
　　　Shuǐbǐ zài nǎr?

　　B: 你去 _____。(问一下儿秘书/知道)
　　　Nǐ qù _____ . (wèn yíxiàr mìshū/zhīdào)

(5) A: 在哪儿付款？
　　　Zài nǎr fù kuǎn?

　　B:_____。(往前一走/看到)
　　　_____ . (wǎng qián yì zǒu/kàndào)

6. Examine the examples, then following the English cues, fill in the blanks with final locations

Example: ① 坐在椅子上　sit on the chair
　　　　　　 zuò zài yǐzi shang

④ 停在学校前边　park in front of the school
　 tíng zài xuéxiào qiánbian

② 放在桌子上　put on the table
　 fàng zài zhuōzi shang

⑤ 掉在地上　drop on the floor
　 diào zài dì shang

③ 交到前台　hand over to the front desk
　 jiāodào qiántái

(1) 把车停_____。(Park the car on the other side of the road.)
　　Bǎ chē tíng_____.

(2) 把水果放_____。(Put the fruit in the refrigerator.)
　　Bǎ shuǐguǒ fàng_____.

(3) 把电脑放_____。(Put your laptop in your backpack.)
　　Bǎ diànnǎo fàng_____.

(4) 把这个坏空调搬_____。(Take the broken AC outside.)
　　Bǎ zhège huài kōngtiáo bān_____.

(5) 把书交_____。(Deliver the book to the instructor's office.)
　　Bǎ shū jiāo_____.

(6) 别把鱼_____。(Don't drop the fish onto the floor.)
　　Bié bǎ yú_____.

(7) 别把你的鞋放_____。(Don't put your shoes in the room.)
　　Bié bǎ nǐ de xié fàng_____.

(8) 你把钥匙交_____。(Take the key to the front desk.)
　　Nǐ bǎ yàoshi jiāo_____.

(9) 别坐_____。(Don't sit on my roommate's bed.)
　　Bié zuò_____.

(10) 你可以坐_____。(You can sit on that small desk.)
　　 Nǐ kěyǐ zuò_____.

(11) 把海鲜放_____。(Put the seafood into the plastic bag.)
　　 Bǎ hǎixiān fàng_____.

(12) 你可以把洗衣粉放_____。(You can leave your laundry powder here.)
　　 Nǐ kěyǐ bǎ xǐyīfěn fàng_____.

(13) How would you tell someone: "Take your groceries to the cashier"?

_____

第十二课 在超市
Lesson Twelve At the Supermarket

Listening Comprehension

1. Listen to the narrative and then answer the questions

   (1) What did Ma Lisha do differently today?

   (2) Where did Ma Lisha go this morning?

   (3) Mention three items that she bought.

   (4) What did she eat for lunch today?

   (5) What kinds of fruit did she get this afternoon? (Mention three kinds.)

   (6) What did she buy at the supermarket? (Mention two things.)

   (7) What will Ma Lisha do tonight?

New Words

食堂　shítáng　N　canteen
扁豆　biǎndòu　N　lentil
肉菜　ròucài　N　meat diet
样　yàng　Meas　kind, type

2. Listen to the dialogue and then answer the questions

   (1) Where did they go shopping?

   (2) What was Qian Ming hoping to buy?

   (3) Mention three daily necessities that Tom wanted to buy.

   (4) What food did Tom buy?

   (5) What did Qian Ming buy?

   (6) Did they buy any clothing? Why or why not?

New Words

卷　juǎn　Meas　roll
包　bāo　Meas　bag
肥皂　féizào　N　soap
罐头　guàntou　N　tin, can

Communication Activities

Pair Work

Scenario I: Explain the following to a friend or partner, using the constructions indicated

A. Use "或者 huòzhě" or "还是 háishi" and "又 yòu……又 yòu……"

(1) Your literature instructor speaks too fast and isn't clear – you're either going to drop the course, or switch to another section.

....

....

(2) You just bought some tomatoes at the morning market. They're cheap, and fresh. They're so good, you're going to go and get some more either this afternoon, or this evening.

....

....

B. Use a pivotal sentence and "就好了 jiù hǎo le"

You would like to invite your friend over for dinner this Friday; explain that there's no need to bring anything, but if he/she wants, he/she could bring some fruit.

....

....

C. Use a pivotal construction, "什么都不 shénme dōu bù + V", and "就好了 jiù hǎo le"

Tomorrow is your birthday. The only present you want from your friend is a Chinese textbook – nothing else. That would be terrific.

....

....

Lesson Twelve   At the Supermarket

第十二课　在超市

Scenario II: Compare and contrast the sort of things that can be bought in a supermarket in the US, and China; and the sort of things that can be bought in a farmer's market in the US, and China. Use the following expressions:

什么地方	又……又……	什么都……	或者
shénme dìfang	yòu……yòu……	shénme dōu……	huòzhě
还是	砍价	开门	关门
háishi	kǎn jià	kāi mén	guān mén
水果	蔬菜	饮料	
shuǐguǒ	shūcài	yǐnliào	

Scenario III: Checking your receipt. Work in pairs: After you do your shopping, you and your friend get together to double-check your receipt. First time: one of you reads the items, the other, the price. Second time: one of you reads the item and price, the other, repeats both and checks off the item.

(1)	5	oranges	￥3.49
(2)	2.5 *jin*	tomatoes	￥4.50
(3)	2	fish	￥11.47
(4)	3 *jin*	broccoli	￥8.00
(5)	1 *jin*	egg	￥5.06
(6)	3	bread	￥10.50
(7)	4	toilet paper	￥12.00
(8)	5	daily necessities	￥16.75 altogether
(9)	2	laundry powder	￥8.60 each
(10)	2 bottles	milk	￥20.12

Scenario IV: Shopping lists: Work in pairs: One of you has been shopping at a supermarket and now needs to know what else to buy. Your partner – your Chinese roommate – is at home. Phone your roommate and explain what you've already bought; then your roommate will explain what is still needed. Use the lists below.

Already bought	Still needed
(1) canned green beans	(1) canned meat
(2) fresh vegetables	(2) orange candy
(3) banana bread	(3) fruit salad
(4) green apples	(4) vegetable soup
(5) green peppers	(5) apple vinegar

Role-Play

Scenario I: In a supermarket. One person takes the part of a salesperson; the other plays the customer. The customer is shopping for various things: fruit, vegetables, drinks, canned food, etc. Try to use the following expressions in your conversation.

食品	水果	蔬菜	饮料	怎么卖
shípǐn	shuǐguǒ	shūcài	yǐnliào	zěnme mài
找钱	哪行	走到头儿	把……放在……里	
zhǎo qián	nǎ háng	zǒudào tóur	bǎ……fàng zài……li	

Scenario II: Shopping. One of you does your shopping at the morning market, the other, prefers shopping at supermarkets. Give reasons for your preferences and make use of the following expressions.

到……去	什么地方	砍价	可以
dào……qù	shénme dìfang	kǎn jià	kěyǐ
等	又……又……	最	新鲜
děng	yòu……yòu……	zuì	xīnxian
贵得多	便宜一点儿	开门	关门
guì de duō	piányi yìdiǎnr	kāi mén	guān mén

Scenario III: Buying fruit. One of you, takes the part of a customer, the other, a fruit seller at the morning market. Make use of the following expressions:

(1) Bargain over the price of apples: 太贵了，便宜一点儿，就行了
  tài guì le, piányi yìdiǎnr, jiù xíng le

(2) Ask for better bananas – fresher ones: 新鲜，换，最
  xīnxian, huàn, zuì

(3) Ask for the correct change: 找钱，不对，少找了……
  zhǎo qián, bú duì, shǎo zhǎo le……

Group Activities

Your group is having a potluck dinner today.

a. Each comes up with a shopping list for your particular dish. Make sure your selection includes vegetables, fruit, meat, beverages and seasonings. Also ask someone to buy household items for cleaning up afterward. Use the following:

第十二课　在超市
Lesson Twelve　At the Supermarket

食品	日用品	水果	饮料
shípǐn	rìyòngpǐn	shuǐguǒ	yǐnliào
怎么样	就……了	Pivotal verb	
zěnmeyàng	jiù……le		

b. Choose where you want to shop and give reasons for your decision. Use the following:

附近	又……又……	新鲜	很贵
fùjìn	yòu……yòu……	xīnxian	hěn guì
砍价	便宜一点儿	可以	开门
kǎn jià	piányi yìdiǎnr	kěyǐ	kāi mén
关门	最		
guān mén	zuì		

Review Exercises

1. Following the English cues, complete the sentences with "又 yòu……又 yòu……"

   Example: 菜市场的青椒又好又新鲜，买三个。
   Càishìchǎng de qīngjiāo yòu hǎo yòu xīnxian, mǎi sān ge.

   (1) 早市的扁豆 ＿＿＿＿＿＿＿＿，来五块钱的。(cheap and fresh)
   　　Zǎoshì de biǎndòu ＿＿＿＿＿＿＿＿, lái wǔ kuài qián de.

   (2) 房间的毛巾 ＿＿＿＿＿＿＿＿，我们找服务员换两条。(old and not clean)
   　　Fángjiān de máojīn ＿＿＿＿＿＿＿＿, wǒmen zhǎo fúwùyuán huàn liǎng tiáo.

   (3) 超市的日用品 ＿＿＿＿＿＿＿＿，我不在这儿买。(expensive and cannot be bargained for)
   　　Chāoshì de rìyòngpǐn ＿＿＿＿＿＿＿＿, wǒ bú zài zhèr mǎi.

   (4) 对面的超市 ＿＿＿＿＿＿＿＿，我们到那儿去。(large and inexpensive)
   　　Duìmiàn de chāoshì ＿＿＿＿＿＿＿＿, wǒmen dào nàr qù.

   (5) 新餐厅的饭 ＿＿＿＿＿＿＿＿，我们今天可以到那儿去吃。(delicious and cheap)
   　　Xīn cāntīng de fàn ＿＿＿＿＿＿＿＿, wǒmen jīntiān kěyǐ dào nàr qù chī.

   (6) 这个学生 ＿＿＿＿＿＿＿＿，学得真好。(intelligent and hardworking)
   　　Zhège xuésheng ＿＿＿＿＿＿＿＿, xué de zhēn hǎo.

2. Complete the following dialogue following the English cues

   A: ＿＿＿＿＿＿＿＿ 怎么卖？(green peppers)
   　　＿＿＿＿＿＿＿＿ zěnme mài?

51

真实生活汉语
Chinese for Living in China 2

B: 十块钱三斤。_____? (How many *jin* do you want?)
Shí kuài qián sān jìn. _____?

A: 来两斤。
Lái liǎng jīn.

B: 好。两斤。_____? (Anything else?)
Hǎo. Liǎng jīn. _____?

A: 苹果、橘子_____? (How much are they per *jin*?)
Píngguǒ、júzi _____?

B: 苹果_____, (3.50 per *jin*) 橘子_____。 (3.00 per *jin*)
Píngguǒ _____, júzi _____.

A: _____。 (3 *jins* of each.)

B: 好。_____。 (That's 19.50 *yuan* altogether.)
Hǎo. _____.

3. Use "最 zuì" (most) to describe each of the situations by using the words provided

   Example: 苹果五元一斤, 香蕉四块五一斤, 橘子三块三一斤。
   Píngguǒ wǔ yuán yì jīn, xiāngjiāo sì kuài wǔ yì jīn, júzi sān kuài sān yì jīn.

   → 苹果最贵, 橘子最便宜。
   Píngguǒ zuì guì, júzi zuì piányi.

(1) 菜市场八点开门, 超市九点开门, 早市六点开门。
   Càishìchǎng bā diǎn kāi mén, chāoshì jiǔ diǎn kāi mén, zǎoshì liù diǎn kāi mén.

   → 早市开门_____, 超市开门_____ (早 zǎo/晚 wǎn)
   Zǎoshì kāi mén _____, chāoshì kāi mén _____.

(2) 水果罐头是八月买的, 蔬菜罐头是十月买的, 面包是昨天买的。
   Shuǐguǒ guàntou shì bāyuè mǎi de, shūcài guàntou shì shíyuè mǎi de, miànbāo shì zuótiān mǎi de.

   → 面包_____, 水果罐头_____。(早 zǎo/新鲜 xīnxian)
   Miànbāo _____, shuǐguǒ guàntou _____.

(3) 去银行用十分钟, 去邮局用十五分钟, 去商店用五分钟。
   Qù yínháng yòng shí fēnzhōng, qù yóujú yòng shíwǔ fēnzhōng, qù shāngdiàn yòng wǔ fēnzhōng.

   → 邮局_____, 商店_____。(远 yuǎn/近 jìn)
   Yóujú _____, shāngdiàn _____.

(4) Tell your Chinese friend that Chinese Conversation is your favorite class. (喜欢 xǐhuan)

_____

52

第十二课 在超市
Lesson Twelve   At the Supermarket

(5) Tell your teacher that you feel that Lesson 12 was the most useful. (有用 yǒuyòng)

_____

(6) Ask your roommate what the most interesting place in Beijing is. (有意思 yǒu yìsi)

_____

4. **You've just arrived in Beijing and don't know your way around yet. Incorporating the expressions in parentheses in your questions, find out or do the following**

   (1) Where the nearest bank is. (最近 zuì jìn, 在 zài)

   ....

   (2) If there's a supermarket next to the university. (旁边 pángbiān)

   ....

   (3) If there's a morning market around, and if so, when it opens. (有 yǒu, 开门 kāimén)

   ....

   (4) How much apples, oranges, and bananas are, per *jin*. (多少钱 duōshao qián, 一斤 yì jīn)

   ....

   (5) Where you can find canned food and milk. (买到 mǎidào)

   ....

   (6) Which is the cheaper place to get fresh groceries, the morning market or the supermarket. (还是 háishi)

   ....

   (7) Tell your friend that you are excited (兴奋 xīngfèn) and nervous (紧张 jǐnzhāng). (又 yòu……又 yòu……)

   ....

   (8) Invite your friend to eat out with you (and mention that you'll pick up the bill). (请 qǐng)

   ....

Culture Notes

1. Traditional Chinese weight and liquid measures

Although China officially uses the metric system, informally, the traditional system of weights and measures is also used. It is called "the market system" (市制 shìzhì). The chart below shows conversion values for weight and liquid volume in three systems: the traditional "market system", the Metric System, and the American System:

Weight	1 jīn (斤)	0.5 kilogram, 1.1 pounds
	1 liǎng (两)	0.05 kilogram/50 grams, 1.8 ounces
Liquid/Volume	1 shēng (升)	1 liter, 1.12 quarts

2. Discounts

When stores offer a discount, they indicate not the reduction, but the remaining price, using the character "折 zhé" (cut). "八折 bā zhé", literally an "8 cut" (that is, 8 of 10 or 80%) means 20% off. A 10% discount would be "九折 jiǔ zhé". 15% off would be "八五折 bā-wǔ zhé".

3. Morning markets and street markets

Farmers often sell their vegetables and other homegrown produce at morning markets, which can be found in cities, towns and villages all over China. They usually open for business at sunrise and close at mid-morning, between 6:00 a.m. and 9:00 a.m. Street markets are also very common. They usually specialize in one type of product, such as clothes, antiques or arts and crafts.

4. Bargaining

At morning markets and street markets, bargaining is the norm. Sellers will start with relatively higher prices so as to leave room for customers to haggle. A rule of thumb is to offer half the starting price, but in markets that cater to tourists, the asking price may be much higher than even double. Most government-owned department stores have fixed prices, with no possibility of bargaining. (But one can always try.)

Lesson Thirteen   Taking the Bus

第十三课   坐 车
Dì-shísān Kè   Zuò Chē

In this lesson you will learn how to do the following
- Talk about where you work or study
- Ask how to get places by bus
- Talk about changing buses
- Buy bus tickets

Grammar
- Adverbs "又 yòu" versus "再 zài"
- The suffix "极了 jí le" (extremely)
- "多 duō" and "几 jǐ" in questions and statements
- More on conditional sentences: "如果 rúguǒ……就 jiù……" (if... [then]...)
- Expressing direction with "从 cóng" (from), "到 dào" (to) and "往 wǎng" (to, towards)
- Adverbs expressing degree of intensity
- "让 ràng" (to let, to allow) as a pre-pivotal verb

Culture Notes
- Public buses in China
- Taxis

真实生活汉语 2
Chinese for Living in China

Dialogue

A：丽莎，美国留学生 　　B：小王，系秘书 　　C：售票员
　Lìshā, Měiguó liúxuéshēng　 Xiǎo Wáng, xì mìshū　　shòupiàoyuán

丽莎在师范大学留学。她是美国人，又^{G1}是师范大学的学生，所以请她教英语的人多极了^{G2}。因为她只学汉语，上课时间不多，所以她每星期可以抽出几^{G3}个小时去教英语。又学习又教书，她还可以更多地了解中国。最近有个外语学校请她每星期去上三次课，工资很高，她接受了。今天下课后她就要去外语学校教英语了。怎么去呢？她去问系办公室的秘书小王。

Lìshā zài Shīfàn Dàxué liúxué. Tā shì Měiguórén, yòu^{G1} shì Shīfàn Dàxué de xuésheng, suǒyǐ qǐng tā jiāo Yīngyǔ de rén duōjí le^{G2}. Yīnwèi tā zhǐ xué Hànyǔ, shàng kè shíjiān bù duō, suǒyǐ měi xīngqī kěyǐ chōuchū jǐ^{G3} ge xiǎoshí qù jiāo Yīngyǔ. Yòu xuéxí yòu jiāo shū, tā hái kěyǐ gèng duō de liǎojiě Zhōngguó. Zuìjìn yǒu ge wàiyǔ xuéxiào qǐng tā měi xīngqī qù shàng sān cì kè, gōngzī hěn gāo, tā jiēshòu le. Jīntiān xiàkè hòu tā jiù yào qù Wàiyǔ Xuéxiào jiāo Yīngyǔ le. Zěnme qù ne? Tā qù wèn xì bàngōngshì de mìshū Xiǎo Wáng.

A：小王，外语学校怎么去？
　Xiǎo Wáng, Wàiyǔ Xuéxiào zěnme qù?

B：你可以坐公共汽车去，或者打车去。不过[1]，坐公共汽车便宜得多。
　Nǐ kěyǐ zuò gōnggòng qìchē qù, huòzhě dǎ chē qù. Búguò[1], zuò gōnggòng qìchē piányi de duō.

A：坐公共汽车到那儿要多长时间？
　Zuò gōnggòng qìchē dào nàr yào duō cháng shíjiān?

B：如果不堵车，二十分钟就到了^{G4}。
　Rúguǒ bù dǔ chē, èrshí fēnzhōng jiù dào le^{G4}.

A：我还有一个多^{G3}小时才上课，还来得及[2]。从^{G5}这儿到外语学校坐几路车？
　Wǒ hái yǒu yí ge duō^{G3} xiǎoshí cái shàng kè, hái láidejí[2]. Cóng^{G5} zhèr dào Wàiyǔ Xuéxiào zuò jǐ lù chē?

Notes

1. "不过 búguò", literally "not-pass", is a conjunction that indicates a degree of reservation, hence translations like "but, however, only". It overlaps with two other common conjunctions, "可是 kěshì" and "但是 dànshì", also often translated "but".
2. "来得及 láidejí" (able to get there, be in time for) and its negative, "来不及 láibují" (not able to get there, not be in time for) derive from potential compounds (cf. Lesson 11, G2) formed from the verbs "来 lái" (to come) and "及 jí" (to reach) – the latter used as a resultative complement. They have become idiomatized and are now listed in dictionaries as words.

第十三课 坐车

Lesson Thirteen Taking the Bus

B：你坐2路，是空调大巴，很舒服。校门外边就有一个2路站牌，坐到南京路换车。
　　Nǐ zuò èr lù, shì kōngtiáo dàbā, hěn shūfu. Xiàomén wàibian jiù yǒu yí ge èr lù zhànpái, zuòdào Nánjīng Lù huàn chē.

A：今天真热，我一定要坐有空调的大巴。到了南京路再换几路？
　　Jīntiān zhēn rè, wǒ yídìng yào zuò yǒu kōngtiáo de dàbā. Dàole Nánjīng Lù zài huàn jǐ lù?

B：到南京路后换6路，坐到人民公园下车。
　　Dào Nánjīng Lù hòu huàn liù lù, zuòdào Rénmín Gōngyuán xià chē.

A：要坐几站？
　　Yào zuò jǐ zhàn?

B：坐两站。
　　Zuò liǎng zhàn.

A：公共汽车多长时间来一班？
　　Gōnggòng qìchē duō cháng shíjiān lái yì bān?

B：车非常[G6]多，每五分钟就来一班。
　　Chē fēicháng[G6] duō, měi wǔ fēnzhōng jiù lái yì bān.

A：谢谢！
　　Xièxie!

B：不谢。
　　Bú xiè.

（在车上 Zài chē shang）

A：师傅，我去南京路，车票多少钱？
　　Shīfu, wǒ qù Nánjīng Lù, chēpiào duōshao qián?

C：两块五。
　　Liǎng kuài wǔ.

A：我到南京路后要换6路，请问在哪儿换？
　　Wǒ dào Nánjīng Lù hòu yào huàn liù lù, qǐngwèn zài nǎr huàn?

C：您往[G5]哪个方向坐？
　　Nín wǎng[G5] nǎge fāngxiàng zuò?

A：去人民公园的方向。
　　Qù Rénmín Gōngyuán de fāngxiàng.

C：您下车后过马路，往左边走一点儿就是6路站牌。
　　Nín xià chē hòu guò mǎlù, wǎng zuǒbian zǒu yìdiǎnr jiù shì liù lù zhànpái.

真实生活汉语
Chinese for Living in China 2

A：谢谢您。到南京路那站时，请告诉我，可以吗？
　　Xièxie nín. Dào Nánjīng Lù nà zhàn shí, qǐng gàosu wǒ, kěyǐ ma?

C：没问题。请您往后走走，让[G7]要下车的人到门口来。
　　Méi wèntí. Qǐng nín wǎng hòu zǒuzou, ràng[G7] yào xià chē de rén dào ménkǒu lái.

A：好。劳驾[3]，让我过一下儿。
　　Hǎo. Láojià[3], ràng wǒ guò yíxiàr.

New Words

1	车/車	chē	N	bus, car, vehicle ("坐车 zuò chē", by bus, car, etc.)
2	小	xiǎo	Adj/Pref	little, small; prefixed to a "姓 xìng", or when added to a last name, it indicates familiarity or endearment
3	售票员/售票員	shòupiàoyuán	N	ticket seller, bus conductor (female or male)
4	师范/師範	shīfàn	Attr	a "normal" or teacher's (college)
5	大学/大學	dàxué	N	university, college
6	极了/極了	jí le	Phrase	extremely, very (after adjectives)
	极/極	jí	Adv	extremely
7	抽出	chōuchū	V-DirC	to draw out, to extract, to find (time)
	抽	chōu	V	to take out, to draw forth, to obtain
8	学习/學習	xuéxí	V	to study, to learn, to learn from
9	教书/教書	jiāo shū	VO	to teach
10	了解	liǎojiě	V	to understand, to find out about, to look into, to learn about
11	最近	zuìjìn	Adv	recently, of late, lately, in the near future
12	外语/外語	wàiyǔ	N	foreign language
13	工资/工資	gōngzī	N	salary, wages, pay
14	接受	jiēshòu	V	to accept, to receive (honors), to get ("接受采访 jiēshòu cǎifǎng", to be interviewed)

3. "劳驾 láojià", is a polite and rather courtly phrase, more common in northern China, that is often translated as "excuse me" but has the tone of English "would you mind if …".

第十三课 坐车
Lesson Thirteen Taking the Bus

15	公共汽车/公共汽車	gōnggòng qìchē	Phrase	public bus
	公共	gōnggòng	Attr	public, common, communal
	汽车/汽車	qìchē	N	motor vehicle, car, bus
16	打车/打車	dǎ chē	VO	to go by taxi, to take a taxi
17	不过/不過	búguò	Conj	but, however, nevertheless
18	多长时间/多長時間	duō cháng shíjiān	Phrase	how long
	多长/多長	duō cháng	Phrase	how long (with "多 duō" here meaning "to what degree")
19	堵车/堵車	dǔ chē	VO	for there to be traffic jams, for traffic to be bad
20	才	cái	Adv	only then, just now, only (in reference to age or duration)
21	来得及/來得及	láidejí	Pot	can make it (in time) (the negative is "来不及 láibují")
22	几路/幾路	jǐ lù	Phrase	bus number what, which bus
	路	lù	N	road, path, (bus) route, line
23	大巴	dàbā	N	large bus, big bus ("空调大巴 kōngtiáo dàbā", *air-conditioned bus*)
24	舒服	shūfu	Adj	comfortable, feel well
25	外边/外邊	wàibian	PW	the outside, away from home, outside
26	站牌	zhànpái	N	sign identifying a bus stop (or train station, subway station, etc.)
27	南京	Nánjīng	PropN	Nanjing (a city in "江苏 Jiāngsū") ("南京路 Nánjīng Lù", *Nanjing Road*)
28	换车/換車	huàn chē	Phrase	to change vehicles (bus, train, etc.), to transfer, to switch
29	人民	rénmín	N	the people (of a country)
30	公园/公園	gōngyuán	N	public park, town green
31	下车/下車	xià chē	Phrase	to get off of a vehicle (bus, train, etc.) (cf. "上车 shàng chē", *to get on a vehicle*)
32	站	zhàn	V/N	to stand, to stop; station
33	班	bān	Meas	*for scheduled buses, trains, airplanes*
34	非常	fēicháng	Adv	very, extremely
35	车票/車票	chēpiào	N	ticket (for bus, train)

36	方向	fāngxiàng	N	direction, orientation, bearing
37	就是	jiù shì	Phrase	to be right at, then it's, and that is
38	时/時	shí	N	time, when, at (a certain time)
39	让/讓	ràng	V/Prep	to let, to allow, to have or make (sb. do sth.); by
40	门口/門口	ménkǒu	N	doorway, entrance
41	劳驾/勞駕	láojià	Intj	excuse me (when asking sb. to move out of the way, etc.), would you mind…

Re-enacting the Dialogue

A: Lisa, an American woman studying in China
B: Young Wang, departmental secretary
C: A bus conductor

Lisa is studying abroad at Normal University. Because she's American and a student at Normal, there are lots and lots of people asking her to teach English. Since she's only taking Chinese and doesn't spend a lot of time in class, she can find a few hours each week to go and teach English. By teaching as well as studying, she'll be even more knowledgeable about China. Recently, a foreign language school has asked her to teach three classes a week; it pays quite well, so she's accepted. Today, after she gets out of class, she's going to the School of Foreign Languages to teach English. How is she going to get there? She asks the secretary in the department office – young Wang – how to get to the School of Foreign Languages.

A: Xiao Wang, how do I get to the School of Foreign Languages?
B: You can take a bus, or you can go by taxi; but taking the bus is a lot cheaper.
A: How long will it take on the bus?
B: If there's no traffic, it'll take 20 minutes to get there.
A: I still have more than an hour before teaching – there is still time. Which bus do I take from here to the School of Foreign Languages?
B: Take the #2, it's a comfortable air-conditioned bus. There's a #2 bus-stop right outside the university gate; change at Nanjing Road.
A: It's really hot today, for sure I'm going to take an air-conditioned bus. Which bus do I change to at Nanjing Road?
B: When you get to Nanjing Road, change to the #6 and get off at People's Park.
A: How many stops is that?
B: Two.
A: How often do the buses come?
B: There are lots of buses; one comes every five minutes.

第十三课 坐 车
Lesson Thirteen　Taking the Bus

A: Thanks.

B: You're welcome.

(on the bus)

A: Sir, I'm going to Nanjing Road; how much is the ticket?

C: ¥2.50.

A: When I get to Nanjing Road, I need to change to the #6 bus; where do I change, please?

C: Which direction are you going in?

A: I'm going towards People's Park.

C: After you get off the bus, cross the road and the #6 stop is a short walk to the left.

A: Thank you. Would you mind telling me when we get to Nanjing Road?

C: No problem. Please move to the back and let people who want to get off get to the door.

A: Fine. Excuse me, let me through please.

Grammar

▶ G1. Adverbs "又 yòu" versus "再 zài"

A rough translation of these adverbs as "again" distorts their differences. "又 yòu" may indicate repetition, sometimes with a slight tone of irritation:

① 他又病了，又不能来上课了。 He's ill again, and once again, can't come to class.
Tā yòu bìng le, yòu bù néng lái shàng kè le.

② 她怎么又来了？ How come she's back again?
Tā zěnme yòu lái le?

"又 yòu" may also indicate an addition:

③ 她学中国历史，又学世界历史。
Tā xué Zhōngguó lìshǐ, yòu xué shìjiè lìshǐ.
She's studying world history, as well as Chinese history.

④ 她是美国人，又是师范大学的学生。
Tā shì Měiguórén, yòu shì Shīfàn Dàxué de xuésheng.
She's an American, and a Normal university student too.

"又 yòu" is used with actual events that have happened. "再 zài", on the other hand, anticipates an event, either as a repeat or as postponement.

⑤ 有空请再来玩儿。 Please come again, if you have the time.
Yǒu kòng qǐng zài lái wánr.

⑥ 你先在人民路换车，到了南京路再换一次车。
Nǐ xiān zài Rémnín Lù huàn chē, dàole Nánjīng Lù zài huàn yí cì chē.
You change buses at Renmin Road and change again at Nanjing Road.

⑦ 我去过一次，可是后来没有再去。 I went once, but haven't been again.
Wǒ qùguo yí cì, kěshì hòulái méiyǒu zài qù.

⑧ 明天再来，好不好？ Come back tomorrow, OK?
Míngtiān zài lái, hǎo bu hǎo?

▶ G2. The suffix "极了 jí le" (extremely)

With adjectives, there are various ways of indicating degree or intensity. Adding "很 hěn" is the least intense. Adding "非常 fēicháng" (see G6 below) is more intense. Adding the suffix "极了 jí le" after the adjective also indicates a high degree of intensity: "好极了！Hǎojí le!" (Great!) "极 jí" originally meant the "ridgepole" of a house (hence the "wood" radical in the character). It was also applied to the poles of the earth, the "北极 Běijí" (North Pole) and "南极 Nánjí" (South Pole). By extension, it came to mean "extreme". The final "了 le" probably derives from the sense of crossing a boundary into a "new state" (cf. "太好了 tài hǎo le", That's great). The combination can now be treated as a single unit, a suffix. Here are some additional examples:

Lesson Thirteen　Taking the Bus

① 今天热极了！　It's extremely hot today!
Jīntiān rèjí le!

② 请她教英语的人多极了！　So many people are asking her to teach English!
Qǐng tā jiāo Yīngyǔ de rén duōjí le!

③ 那工作容易极了！　That work's so easy!
Nà gōngzuò róngyì jí le!

④ 她汉语说得好极了！　She speaks Chinese really well!
Tā Hànyǔ shuō de hǎojí le!

▶ **G3.** "多 duō" and "几 jǐ" in questions and statements

"多 duō" occurs in the question word "多少 duōshao" (how much) and in the interrogative phrase "多长时间 duō cháng shíjiān" (how much time, how long). It may also occur alone before an adjective to question the degree or amount:

① A: 他多高？　How tall is he?
　　Tā duō gāo?

B: 他高极了！　He's really tall!
　　Tā gāojí le!

"几 jǐ" is also a question word (or interrogative pronoun), but unlike "多少 duōshao", it implies an answer with a relatively low number, usually less than ten:

② A: 有几个老师？　How many teachers are there?
　　Yǒu jǐ ge lǎoshī?

B: 有两个。　There are two.
　　Yǒu liǎng ge.

③ A: 有多少学生？　How many students are there?
　　Yǒu duōshao xuésheng?

B: 有三十个。　There are thirty.
　　Yǒu sānshí ge.

④ A: 几块钱？　How much is it?
　　Jǐ kuài qián?

B: 三块八。　3.80 *yuan*.
　　Sān kuài bā.

"多 duō" and "几 jǐ" also appear in statements. "多 duō" may appear after measure words, or after multiples of ten ("十 shí", "百 bǎi", "千 qiān", etc.) to mean "over, more than": "一个多 yí ge duō" (slightly more than one); "十多个 shí duō ge" (a few more than 10); "三百多个 sānbǎi duō ge" (over 300); "三斤多 sān jīn duō" (a little over 3 *jin*). Here is an example from the main dialogue:

⑤ 我还有一个多小时才上课，来得及。
　　Wǒ hái yǒu yí ge duō xiǎoshí cái shàngkè, láidejí.
　　I still have more than an hour before teaching – there is still time.

Notice that "多 duō" only follows measure words or multiples of ten (which can be considered a type of measure word). The amount over is indeterminate, but with measures, it will be a fraction of a whole: "两个多星期 liǎng ge duō xīngqī" (a bit over two weeks); with multiples of ten, it will be a fraction of the next unit: "两千多块钱 liǎngqiān duō kuài qián" (over 2000 *yuan* [by perhaps one or two hundreds]).

"几 jǐ" in statements can mean "several":

⑥ 几个月前　several months ago
　　jǐ ge yuè qián

⑦ 几个咖啡杯　several coffee cups
　　jǐ ge kāfēibēi

In a similar usage, "几 jǐ" also occurs before or after numbers to indicate "and several more": "十几个 shíjǐ ge" (several more than ten); "几十个 jǐshí ge" (several tens of) ; "几千块钱 jǐqiān kuài qián" (several thousand dollars). Here are some examples using lesson material:

⑧ 教室里有十几个人。　There are more than ten people in the classroom.
　　Jiàoshì li yǒu shíjǐ ge rén.

⑨ 她每星期可以抽出几个小时去教英语。
　　Tā měi xīngqī kěyǐ chōuchū jǐ ge xiǎoshí qù jiāo Yīngyǔ.
　　She can take off several hours each week to teach English.

▶ **G4.** More on conditional sentences: "如果 rúguǒ……就 jiù……" (if... [then]…)

Conditional sentences, with the condition introduced by "如果 rúguǒ" and the conclusion (or resolution) marked by "就 jiù", were first introduced in Lesson 8 (G4) of Volume I in this series. They are revisited in this lesson.

"如果 rúguǒ" can be placed before or after the subject. "就 jiù" does not always appear in the following clause, but if it does, since it is a regular adverb, it goes before the verb. So the only options for sentences such as the following one involve the relative positions of "如果 rúguǒ" and "时间 shíjiān":

① 如果时间来不及，我就打的去。/ 时间如果来不及，我就打的去。
　　Rúguǒ shíjiān láibují, wǒ jiù dǎdī qù. / Shíjiān rúguǒ láibují, wǒ jiù dǎdī qù.
　　If time's too short, I'll take a taxi.

Two other examples:

② 如果不堵车，二十分钟就到了。　If there's no traffic, we'll be there in 20 minutes.
　　Rúguǒ bù dǔchē, èrshí fēnzhōng jiù dào le.

③ 你如果有问题，就来问老师。　If you have any questions, come and ask your teacher.
　　Nǐ rúguǒ yǒu wèntí, jiù lái wèn lǎoshī.

Notice that there is generally no English word corresponding to Chinese "就 jiù" in the translations. In Chinese, by contrast, "如果 rúguǒ" is often omitted so that "就 jiù" carries the weight of the conditional.

    ④ 用电话卡就很便宜。 If you use a phone card, it's cheap.
       Yòng diànhuàkǎ jiù hěn piányi.

▶ G5. Expressing direction with "从 cóng" (from), "到 dào" (to) and "往 wǎng" (to, towards)

The expression of direction involves the prepositions "从 cóng" (from), "到 dào" (to) and "往 wǎng" (to, towards). All three have been introduced in earlier lessons (cf. Lesson 6, G7 and G8; Lesson 11, G8). "从 cóng" introduces a starting point, which may be a location or a time:

    ① 你能从北京大学来找我吗？ Can you come from Peking University to see me?
       Nǐ néng cóng Běijīng Dàxué lái zhǎo wǒ ma?

    ② 他从小就喜欢吃辣的。 He's liked spicy food from an early age.
       Tā cóng xiǎo jiù xǐhuan chī là de.

"到 dào" indicates the destination or end point. It is frequently paired with "从 cóng".

    ③ 他们从北京坐火车到上海去。 They're taking the train from Beijing to Shanghai.
       Tāmen cóng Běijīng zuò huǒchē dào Shànghǎi qù.

    ④ 我从八点半到十一点都有课。 I have class from 8:30 to 11:00.
       Wǒ cóng bā diǎn bàn dào shí'yī diǎn dōu yǒu kè.

    ⑤ 从这儿到外语学校坐几路车？
       Cóng zhèr dào Wàiyǔ Xuéxiào zuò jǐ lù chē?
       Which bus do I take from here to the School of Foreign Languages?

    ⑥ 从这儿到车站怎么走？ How do I get from here to the bus station?
       Cóng zhèr dào chēzhàn zěnme zǒu?

"往 wǎng" indicates general direction and can be followed by left or right ("左 zuǒ" or "右 yòu"), by directions such as front and back ("前 qián" and "后 hòu"), and by the cardinal directions, "东 dōng", "南 nán", "西 xī" and "北 běi" (east, south, west, north).

    ⑦ A: 往哪个方向走？ Which direction do I walk in?
       Wǎng nǎge fāngxiàng zǒu?

      B: 往前走。 Walk straight ahead.
       Wǎng qián zǒu.

▶ G6. Adverbs expressing degree of intensity

This is a good time to take stock of some adverbs of degree. Some have appeared in previous lessons, others are new: "更 gèng" (even more, still more), "很 hěn" (quite, very), "真 zhēn" (really, truly), "非常 fēicháng" (unusually, exceptionally). Examples:

① 更多地了解中国　to understand China better
　gèng duō de liǎojiě Zhōngguó

② 工资很高。　The salary's quite good.
　Gōngzī hěn gāo.

③ 今天真热。　It's really hot today.
　Jīntiān zhēn rè.

④ 车非常多。　There are an unusually large number of cars.
　Chē fēicháng duō.

The suffixial intensifier, "极了 jí le", described in G2 of this lesson, has a similar effect to adverbial intensifiers such as "非常 fēicháng".

▶ **G7.** "让 ràng" (to let, to allow) as a pre-pivotal verb

This lesson introduces an important pre-pivotal verb (cf. Lesson 12, G2), "让 ràng" (to let, to allow). Recall that pre-pivotal verbs introduce noun phrases (the pivots) that serve two verbs, the first as object, the second as subject. Earlier examples included "请 qǐng" (to invite) and "告诉 gàosu" (to tell).

① 大家让要下车的人到门口来。　Let people who want to get off get to the door.
　Dàjiā ràng yào xià chē de rén dào ménkǒu lái.

② 劳驾，让我过一下儿。　Excuse me, let me through please.
　Láojià, ràng wǒ guò yíxiàr.

③ 我朋友让我在宿舍等她。　My friend asked me to wait for her in my dorm.
　Wǒ péngyou ràng wǒ zài sùshè děng tā.

第十三课　坐　车
Lesson Thirteen　Taking the Bus

Consolidation & Practice

1. **Fill in the blanks with "又 yòu" or "再 zài"**

   (1) 你先坐6路车, 到了人民公园（　　　）换2路车。
   　　Nǐ xiān zuò liù lù chē, dàole Rénmín Gōngyuán (　　　) huàn èr lù chē.

   (2) 昨天我去超市买了一条鱼, 真新鲜！今天上午我（　　　）去买了两条。
   　　Zuótiān wǒ qù chāoshì mǎile yì tiáo yú, zhēn xīnxian! Jīntiān shàngwǔ wǒ (　　　) qù mǎile liǎng tiáo.

   (3) 上个星期二空调刚修好, 今天（　　　）坏了。
   　　Shàng ge xīngqī'èr kōngtiáo gāng xiūhǎo, jīntiān (　　　) huài le.

   (4) 丽莎在中国留学三个月, 今天就要回美国了, 她说明年还会（　　　）来。
   　　Lìshā zài Zhōngguó liúxué sān ge yuè, jīntiān jiù yào huí Měiguó le, tā shuō míngnián hái huì (　　　) lái.

   (5) 昨天我去外语学校坐错车了, 今天我要打的去, 不会（　　　）坐错了。
   　　Zuótiān wǒ qù Wàiyǔ Xuéxiào zuòcuò chē le, jīntiān wǒ yào dǎdī qù, bú huì (　　　) zuòcuò le.

   (6) A: 你想去对面的饭馆吃饭吗？
   　　　Nǐ xiǎng qù duìmiàn de fànguǎn chī fàn ma?

   　　B: 我昨天刚去过, 周末（　　　）去吧。
   　　　Wǒ zuótiān gāng qùguo, zhōumò (　　　) qù ba.

2. **Complete the following sentences, incorporating the suffix "极了 jí le"**

   Example: 今天热极了。　It is extremely hot today.
   　　　　 Jīntiān rèjí le.

   (1) 北京的公共汽车＿＿＿＿＿＿。(方便 fāngbiàn)
   　　Běijīng de gōnggòng qìchē ＿＿＿＿＿＿.

   (2) 早市的青菜＿＿＿＿＿＿。(新鲜 xīnxian)
   　　Zǎoshì de qīngcài ＿＿＿＿＿＿.

   (3) 我的邻居做饭做得＿＿＿＿＿＿。(好吃 hǎochī, delicious)
   　　Wǒ de línjū zuò fàn zuò de ＿＿＿＿＿＿.

   (4) 在中国学英文的人＿＿＿＿＿＿。(多 duō)
   　　Zài Zhōngguó xué Yīngwén de rén ＿＿＿＿＿＿.

真实生活汉语 2
Chinese for Living in China

(5) 我的同学告诉我，中国历史课＿＿＿＿＿＿。（难 nán）
　　Wǒ de tóngxué gàosu wǒ, Zhōngguó lìshǐ kè ＿＿＿＿＿.

(6) 我听说英文家教的工资＿＿＿＿＿＿。（高 gāo）
　　Wǒ tīngshuō Yīngwén jiājiào de gōngzī ＿＿＿＿＿.

(7) Using "极了 jí le", comment (in Chinese) that "Shanghai is a really interesting city!"
　　＿＿＿＿＿＿＿＿＿＿＿＿＿＿＿＿＿＿＿＿＿＿＿＿＿＿＿

(8) Tell your partner that the movie you watched was extremely impressive.
　　＿＿＿＿＿＿＿＿＿＿＿＿＿＿＿＿＿＿＿＿＿＿＿＿＿＿＿

(9) Tell your partner that the food in the restaurant across the street is really good.
　　＿＿＿＿＿＿＿＿＿＿＿＿＿＿＿＿＿＿＿＿＿＿＿＿＿＿＿

3. Fill in the blanks with either "几 jǐ" or "多 duō"

   Example: ① 教室里有十几个人。　There are a few more than ten people in the classroom.
   　　　　　　Jiàoshì li yǒu shíjǐ ge rén.

   　　　　　② 我还有一个多小时才上课，还来得及。
   　　　　　　Wǒ hái yǒu yí ge duō xiǎoshí cái shàngkè, hái láidejí.
   　　　　　　I still have more than an hour before teaching – there is still time.

(1) 今天我去早市买了很多蔬菜和水果，现在只有两块＿＿＿＿钱了。
　　Jīntiān wǒ qù zǎoshì mǎile hěn duō shūcài hé shuǐguǒ, xiànzài zhǐ yǒu liǎng kuài ＿＿＿ qián le.

(2) 选汉语口语课的学生很多，所以我们有＿＿＿＿个班。
　　Xuǎn Hànyǔ kǒuyǔkè de xuésheng hěn duō, suǒyǐ wǒmen yǒu ＿＿＿ ge bān.

(3) 从师范大学到外语学校，如果堵车要一个＿＿＿＿小时才能到。
　　Cóng Shīfàn Dàxué dào Wàiyǔ Xuéxiào, rúguǒ dǔchē yào yí ge ＿＿＿＿ xiǎoshí cái néng dào.

(4) 今天菜市场的青椒真新鲜，我想下午再去买＿＿＿＿个。
　　Jīntiān càishìchǎng de qīngjiāo zhēn xīnxian, wǒ xiǎng xiàwǔ zài qù mǎi ＿＿＿ ge.

(5) 他学了三个＿＿＿＿月的中文了，还看不懂课表。
　　Tā xuéle sān ge ＿＿＿ yuè de Zhōngwén le, hái kàn bu dǒng kèbiǎo.

(6) 听说英语家教的工资很高，一个小时＿＿＿＿百块人民币。
　　Tīngshuō Yīngyǔ jiājiào de gōngzī hěn gāo, yí ge xiǎoshí ＿＿＿ bǎi kuài rénmínbì.

第十三课 坐 车
Lesson Thirteen   Taking the Bus

4. Connect the phrases with the conditional (if) pattern (如果 rúguǒ……就 jiù……)

Example: 没有苹果 / 买橘子 → 如果没有苹果，我们就买橘子吧。
méiyǒu píngguǒ/mǎi júzi　Rúguǒ méiyǒu píngguǒ, wǒmen jiù mǎi júzi ba.
　　　　　　　　　　　　If they don't have any apples, we'll buy oranges, OK?

(1) 超市的水果太贵 / 去早市买水果
chāoshì de shuǐguǒ tài guì / qù zǎoshì mǎi shuǐguǒ

→ _____

(2) 没有新鲜的鱼 / 买鸡
méiyǒu xīnxian de yú / mǎi jī

→ _____

(3) 没有菠菜 / 买大白菜
méiyǒu bōcài / mǎi dàbáicài

→ _____

(4) 没有西红柿 / 买胡萝卜
méiyǒu xīhóngshì / mǎi húluóbo

→ _____

(5) 坐汽车堵车/我们坐地铁
zuò qìchē dǔchē / wǒmen zuò dìtiě

→ _____

(6) 学习太忙/别做家教
xuéxí tài máng / bié zuò jiājiào

→ _____

5. Following the cues given, create short two-way exchanges that involve asking and giving directions, expressing direction with "从 cóng", "到 dào" and "往 wǎng"

Example: ① A: 从这儿到医院应该往哪个方向坐车？
Cóng zhèr dào yīyuàn yīnggāi wǎng nǎge fāngxiàng zuò chē?
Which direction should I go to get to the hospital from here?

B: 往东坐。 Go east.
Wǎng dōng zuò.

② A: 从师范大学到银行怎么走？ How do I get from Normal University to the bank?
Cóng Shīfàn Dàxué dào yínháng zěnme zǒu?

真实生活汉语 2
Chinese for Living in China

B: 过了马路往前走一点儿就到了。
Guòle mǎlù wǎng qián zǒu yìdiǎnr jiù dào le.
Cross the road, go straight for a while, and you'll be there.

A	B
(1) 宿舍 → 超市，走 sùshè → chāoshì, zǒu	南，走 nán, zǒu
(2) 师范大学 → 外语学院，坐车 Shīfàn Dàxué → Wàiyǔ Xuéyuàn, zuò chē	西，坐，4 站 xī, zuò, sì zhàn
(3) 这儿 → 人民公园，走 zhèr → Rénmín Gōngyuán, zǒu	前，走一会儿，就到了 qián, zǒu yíhuìr, jiù dào le
(4) 这儿 → 332 车站，走 zhèr → sān-sān-èr chēzhàn, zǒu	前，走五分钟，就到了 qián, zǒu wǔ fēnzhōng, jiù dào le
(5) 这儿 → 超市，走 zhèr → chāoshì, zǒu	南，走一点儿，就看见超市了 nán, zǒu yìdiǎnr, jiù kànjiàn chāoshì le

6. Choose "更 gèng", "真 zhēn" or "非常 fēicháng" to fill in the blanks in the following exchanges

(1) A: 我听说早市的水果_____新鲜，明天你能不能跟我去早市看看？
　　Wǒ tīngshuō zǎoshì de shuǐguǒ _____ xīnxian, míngtiān nǐ néng bu néng gēn wǒ qù zǎoshì kànkan?

B: 对，早市的水果_____新鲜，明天我们一起去早市吧！
　　Duì, zǎoshì de shuǐguǒ _____ xīnxian, míngtiān wǒmen yìqǐ qù zǎoshì ba!

A: 你想几点去？
　　Nǐ xiǎng jǐ diǎn qù?

B: 六点半，怎么样？
　　Liù diǎn bàn, zěnmeyàng?

A: _____早！
　　_____ zǎo!

B: 六点半不早。如果我自己去，去得_____早。
　　Liù diǎn bàn bù zǎo. Rúguǒ wǒ zìjǐ qù, qù de _____ zǎo.

(2) A: 昨天小王请我和几个同学去她家吃饭。她做饭做得_____好吃！
　　Zuótiān Xiǎo Wáng qǐng wǒ hé jǐ ge tóngxué qù tā jiā chī fàn. Tā zuò fàn zuò de _____ hǎochī!

B: 听说她先生做饭做得_____好吃。
　　Tīngshuō tā xiānsheng zuò fàn zuò de _____ hǎochī.

A: 我发现很多中国人都_____会做饭。我这次一定得学学做中国饭。
　　Wǒ fāxiàn hěn duō Zhōngguórén dōu _____ huì zuò fàn. Wǒ zhè cì yídìng děi xuéxue zuò zhōngguófàn.

第十三课 坐 车
Lesson Thirteen   Taking the Bus

(3) A: 今天我在地铁里听两个上海人说话，_____ 难懂！
  Jīntiān wǒ zài dìtiě li tīng liǎng ge Shànghǎirén shuō huà, _____ nán dǒng!

  B: 当然了，上海话 _____ 难懂。
  Dāngrán le, Shànghǎihuà _____ nán dǒng.

  A: 可是别人告诉我广东话 _____ 难懂！你知道中国什么地方的话最难懂吗？我的中国同学告诉我是温州话。以后我希望能学温州话。
  Kěshì biéren gàosu wǒ Guǎngdōnghuà _____ nán dǒng! Nǐ zhīdào Zhōngguó shénme dìfang de huà zuì nán dǒng ma? Wǒ de Zhōngguó tóngxué gàosu wǒ shì Wēnzhōuhuà. Yǐhòu wǒ xīwàng néng xué Wēnzhōuhuà.

  B: 我 _____ 希望说好北京话。
  Wǒ _____ xīwàng shuōhǎo Běijīnghuà.

7. Make sentences incorporating the pivotal verb "让 ràng", then translate your sentences into English

  Examples: ① 门口的人让下车的人过一下儿。
      Ménkǒu de rén ràng xià chē de rén guò yíxiàr.

    ② 每次丽莎去外语学校教英文，回家都很晚。她男朋友让她以后打的回家。
      Měi cì Lìshā qù Wàiyǔ Xuéxiào jiāo Yīngwén, huí jiā dōu hěn wǎn. Tā nánpéngyou ràng tā yǐhòu dǎdī huí jiā.

  (1) 司机 / 前边的人 / 往后 / 让 / 走 → _____
    sījī / qiánbian de rén / wǎng hòu / ràng / zǒu

  (2) 秘书 / 丽莎 / 英文信 / 让 / 翻译 → _____
    mìshū / Lìshā / Yīngwén xìn / ràng / fānyì

  (3) 丽莎 / 男朋友 / 药 / 给她 / 让 / 买 → _____
    Lìshā / nánpéngyou / yào / gěi tā / ràng / mǎi

  (4) 我 / 我的中国朋友 / 我家 / 让 / 来 / 吃饭 → _____
    wǒ / wǒ de Zhōngguó péngyou / wǒ jiā / ràng / lái / chī fàn

  (5) 客人 / 清洁工 / 房间 / 让 / 打扫 → _____
    kèren / qīngjiégōng / fángjiān / ràng / dǎsǎo

  (6) 老师 / 我们 / 教科书 / 让 / 看 → _____
    lǎoshī / wǒmen / jiàokēshū / ràng / kàn

  (7) 我 / 我朋友 / 给我 / 不让 / 晚上 / 打电话 → _____
    wǒ / wǒ péngyou / gěi wǒ / bú ràng / wǎnshang / dǎ diànhuà

  (8) 医生 / 我 / 海鲜 / 不让 / 吃 → _____
    yīshēng / wǒ / hǎixiān / bú ràng / chī

Listening Comprehension

1. Listen to the dialogue and then answer the questions

   (1) How many buses go to Peking University? Which ones?

   (2) Which is the cheapest bus?

   (3) Which bus doesn't have air-conditioning?

   (4) Do you need to change buses to get to Peking University?

   (5) If the man takes the 802, how many stops before he gets off?

   (6) In which direction should the man go after he gets off the bus?

2. Listen to the narrative and then answer the questions

   (1) Which is the best form of transportation for getting around at rush hour?

   (2) What's the best thing to do to avoid getting stuck in traffic in a taxi?

   (3) What is the most economic and efficient way to travel if you have an emergency and need to travel across the city?

   (4) How frequently does the subway run?

   (5) In which directions does the subway run?

   (6) Where are subway stations usually located?

New Words

停 tíng V to stop
路口 lùkǒu N intersection
出租车 chūzū chē N taxi
打表 dǎ biǎo VO to use the meter

第十三课　坐　车
Lesson Thirteen　Taking the Bus

Communication Activities

Pair Work

Scenario I: Tell a newcomer about your experiences taking buses in Beijing. Incorporate as many of the following items as you can:

汽车站	等	先……再……	换车
qìchēzhàn	děng	xiān……zài……	huàn chē
如果……就……	堵车	来不及	一直坐到……
rúguǒ……jiù……	dǔ chē	láibují	yìzhí zuòdào……

Scenario II: Tell your friend about your first experience taking a taxi in China. Use the following items:

出租汽车站	打的	司机	打表
chūzū qìchēzhàn	dǎdī	sījī	dǎ biǎo
如果……就……	开快一点儿	堵车	在路口停下
rúguǒ……jiù……	kāi kuài yìdiǎnr	dǔ chē	zài lùkǒu tíngxià

Scenario III: Explain to a new student how to use the Beijing subway. Make use of the following items:

路口	地铁站	坐几站	上车
lùkǒu	dìtiězhàn	zuò jǐ zhàn	shàng chē
下车	换车	到站	堵车
xià chē	huàn chē	dào zhàn	dǔ chē

Role-Play

Scenario I: A is an American. B is a Beijing taxi driver. A is in a hurry to get to the Bank of China but unfortunately, the traffic is very slow. A and B start chatting with each other. Try to use the following items:

多长时间	堵车	打表	开快点儿	好像
duō cháng shíjiān	dǔ chē	dǎ biǎo	kāi kuài diǎnr	hǎoxiàng
街	路口	走路	最快	
jiē	lùkǒu	zǒu lù	zuì kuài	

Scenario II: One of you is a Canadian tourist, the other is a local Chinese waiting for a bus. The tourist has a map and wants to go to the Mud Market (also known as "潘家园 Pānjiāyuán" Antique Market, in the south-eastern part of Beijing). The tourist and the local talk about how to get there.

真实生活汉语 2
Chinese for Living in China

地图	指	地方	知道	看不懂
dìtú	zhǐ	dìfang	zhīdào	kàn bu dǒng
等	公共汽车	还有……路	几站	下车
děng	gōnggòng qìchē	hái yǒu……lù	jǐ zhàn	xià chē
往东	方向			
wǎng dōng	fāngxiàng			

Group Activities

Scenario I: You are writing a report on Beijing's public transit system. Interview a group of Beijing residents to find out how they get around everyday, then fill out the following form.

	Transportation means	Waiting time	Number of changes	With air-conditioning	Cost of transportation
Person A					
Person B					
Person C					
Person D					
Person E					
Person F					
Person G					

Scenario II: A and B are from New York and Chicago, C and D are from small towns in the United States. Compare and contrast how people get around in these places. Use the following items:

地图	堵车	如果……就……	急事	来不及
dìtú	dǔ chē	rúguǒ……jiù……	jíshì	láibují
走路	上车	下车	换车	停车
zǒu lù	shàng chē	xià chē	huàn chē	tíngchē
街	路口	到站	开车	
jiē	lùkǒu	dào zhàn	kāi chē	

Lesson Thirteen Taking the Bus

Review Exercises

1. Write the following in Chinese in the spaces provided

(1) north of your dorm _____

(2) south of your dorm _____

(3) east of your dorm _____

(4) west of your dorm _____

(5) northwest of your dorm _____

(6) northeast of your dorm _____

(7) southwest of your dorm _____

(8) southeast of your dorm _____

(9) opposite of your dorm _____

(10) next to your dorm _____

2. Make sentences following the English cues, incorporating the conditional pattern with "如果 rúguǒ……就 jiù……" and the given phrases

(1) 有急事 / 打的 → _____
yǒu jíshì / dǎdī
(If you're in a rush, then get a taxi.)

(2) 不堵车 / 一会儿就到了 → _____
bù dǔ chē / yíhuìr jiù dào le
(If there isn't a traffic jam, it won't take long.)

(3) 堵车 / 在路口下车，走回家 → _____
dǔ chē / zài lùkǒu xià chē, zǒuhuí jiā
(If there's a traffic jam, we'll get off at the intersection and walk home.)

(4) 鱼不新鲜 / 买鸡 → _____
yú bù xīnxian / mǎi jī
(If the fish isn't fresh, we'll get chicken.)

(5) 扁豆太老 / 青椒 → _____
biǎndòu tài lǎo / qīngjiāo
(If the green beans are too old, we'll buy some green peppers.)

(6) 有地图 / 知道怎么走 → _____
yǒu dìtú / zhīdào zěnme zǒu
(If we have a map, we'll figure out how to get there.)

真实生活汉语
Chinese for Living in China 2

(7) 到站 / 告诉我 → _____
dào zhàn / gàosu wǒ
(Let me know when we get there.)

(8) How do you say in Chinese, "If you can't find the subway station, ask someone"?
(找不到 zhǎo bu dào, 别人 biéren)
_____

(9) How do you say in Chinese, "If my salary were a little higher, I would be happy to tutor your child in English"? (高一点儿 gāo yìdiǎnr, 做英文家教 zuò Yīngwén jiājiào)
_____

3. **Following the English cues, use "来不及了 láibují le" to finish the sentences**

   Example: 现在十点了，去超市来不及了。
   Xiànzài shí diǎn le, qù chāoshì láibují le.

   (1) 我今天起床起晚了，_____。 (didn't have time for breakfast)
   Wǒ jīntiān qǐ chuáng qǐwǎn le, _____.

   (2) 银行五点就关门了，_____。 (I didn't have time to exchange money)
   Yínháng wǔ diǎn jiù guān mén le, _____.

   (3) 我一直工作到十点钟，_____。 (I didn't have time to call you)
   Wǒ yìzhí gōngzuò dào shí diǎnzhōng, _____.

   (4) 超市太远了，_____。 (we don't have enough time to go there today)
   Chāoshì tài yuǎn le, _____.

   (5) 走到外事处要花十五分钟，_____。 (we can't make it before lunch)
   Zǒu dào Wàishìchù yào huā shíwǔ fēnzhōng, _____.

   (6) 如果等网吧开门，_____。 (we won't make it to our Chinese literature class in time)
   Rúguǒ děng wǎngbā kāi mén, _____.

   (7) 今天下课晚了，_____。 (we don't have enough time to make it to the post office)
   Jīntiān xià kè wǎn le, _____.

4. **Fill in the blanks using the cues provided in parentheses**

   (1) A: 我要去食品超市，_____? (which bus to take)
   Wǒ yào qù shípǐn chāoshì _____?

   B: 113 路和 800 路 _____。 (both go to the food market)
   Yāo-yāo-sān lù hé bā-líng-líng lù _____.

   A: _____? (Which of the two buses has Aircon?)

76

第十三课 坐车
Lesson Thirteen Taking the Bus

B: 800 路又快又有空调。
　　Bā-líng-líng lù yòu kuài yòu yǒu kōngtiáo,_____.
　　　　　　　　　　　　　　　　　　　　　(you get off the bus at Nanjing Rd.)

(2) A: 我去邮局，_____? (which direction should I take?)
　　　Wǒ qù yóujú,_____?

　　B: 先往东走，_____。 (then turn south at the intersection.)
　　　Xiān wǎng dōng zǒu,_____.

　　A: _____? (How long do I have to walk?)

　　B: _____。
　　(Not far. If you don't want to walk, you can take bus No.2 for one stop.)

(3) A: 师傅，我要去南京北路。_____? (How much is the bus fare?)
　　　Shīfu, wǒ yào qù Nánjīng Běi Lù._____?

　　B: 一块一张。
　　　Yí kuài yì zhāng.

　　A: _____，好吗? (Please tell me when we get to the stop.)
　　　_____, hǎo ma?

　　B: 没问题。
　　　Méi wèntí.

(4) A: 师傅，_____。 (I'd like to go to the vegetable market.)
　　　Shīfu,_____.

　　B: _____? (Which one? The eastern one or the southern?)

　　A: 马路南边的那个。
　　　Mǎlù nánbian de nàge.

　　B: 好，_____。(get in) 真糟糕_____! (another traffic jam.)
　　　Hǎo,_____. Zhēn zāogāo,_____!

　　A: _____。 (How much will it be?)

　　B: _____. (I use the meter.)

　　A: 到了！_____。谢谢，多少钱? (Please stop in front of this building.)
　　　Dào le!_____. Xièxie, duōshao qián?

　　B: 十四块。
　　　Shísì kuài.

　　A: _____. (Here's 15, keep the change.) (不用 búyòng, need not)

5. What would you say in the following situations?

(1) It's your first time in Beijing. You are a bit nervous, but proud to find that you are managing to use your newly acquired language skills to get around.

① You are waiting at a bus stop. Ask someone which bus goes to Peking University, how frequently the bus runs, and if you need to change buses.

(多长时间 duō cháng shíjiān, 班 bān, 换 huàn)

....

② You're taking a bus to the Bank of China. Ask the bus attendant how much the fare is, and politely request that he/she let you know when it is time for you to get off.

(多少 duōshao, 到站 dào zhàn, 告诉 gàosu)

....

③ You're in a taxi; explain that you're in a hurry – and ask the driver to go faster. When you run into a traffic jam, ask the driver to turn right at the next intersection.

(有急事 yǒu jíshì, 快一点儿 kuài yìdiǎnr, 好像 hǎoxiàng, 堵车 dǔ chē, 往右转 wǎng yòu zhuǎn)

....

(2) You've met a student who's just come from France to study Chinese. He/she has lots of questions for you, and you do your best to help:

① He/she'd like to go to Peking University to visit her friend. Tell him/her to go out the West Gate, then take the 808 air-conditioned big bus, and get off at the front gate of Peking University.

(出西门 chū xīmén, 有空调 yǒu kōngtiáo, 到了 dào le, 下车 xià chē)

....

② He/she wants to go to a supermarket somewhere in the vicinity. Explain that he/she should cross the road first, then walk straight ahead, and turn left at the intersection; the supermarket will be right there.

(过马路 guò mǎlù, 一直 yìzhí, 往前 wǎng qián, 到了路口 dàole lùkǒu, 往 wǎng……拐 guǎi, 在 zài)

....

③ He/she also has to go to the Bank of China. Advise him/her to take a taxi, otherwise he/she won't make it before the bank closes at five.

(打的 dǎdī, 关门 guān mén, 如果 rúguǒ, 来不及 láibují)

....

Lesson Thirteen Taking the Bus

第十三课 坐车

Culture Notes

1. Public buses in China

There are several types of public buses in China.

a. Regular buses: Their fares are much lower than those in the U.S. In Beijing, for example, less that $0.50 will take you from one end of a bus line to the other.

b. Trolley buses: Their fares are similar to those on regular buses, but they run more slowly.

c. Mini-buses: They usually run on routes parallel to those of regular buses. Fares range from one *yuan* to six (less than a dollar), which is more than regular buses; but mini-buses are faster than public buses and no one stands.

d. Air-conditioned buses: Their fares are higher than regular buses, ranging from two to twelve *yuan*, depending on distance.

e. Tour buses: These are special buses serving tourist attractions. Tickets are sold at hotels or travel agencies.

2. Taxis

In China, taxis are usually distinctively painted and have a sign on the roof. Taxis charges/costs per kilometer differ according to type of car. They are written on the side window, e.g. 1.60, or 2.00, i.e., 1.20 *yuan* or 1.60 *yuan* – per kilometer (0.6 mile).

Lesson Fourteen   Getting a Haircut

第十四课   理发
Dì-shísì Kè   Lǐ Fà

In this lesson you will learn how to do the following
- Request services at a barbershop or hairdresser
- Describe the sort of shampoo and cut that you want
- Discuss getting a shave
- Consider issues about hair coloring

Grammar
- The verb suffix "过 guo" (usually with neutral tone)
- "的 de" used as a nominalizer
- The verb suffix "着 zhe"
- The verbs "掉 diào" and "成 chéng" used as resultative complements
- Omitted subjects and objects
- Same or different: "A 跟 gēn B (不 bù) 一样 yíyàng"

Culture Notes
- Shampooing
- Massage

第十四课　理发
Lesson Fourteen　Getting a Haircut

Dialogue

A：乔治　　　　B：一号理发师　　　C：三号理发师　　　D：琳达
　　Qiáozhì　　　　yī hào lǐfàshī　　　 sān hào lǐfàshī　　　　Líndá

琳达和乔治在广州一家瑞士公司工作。他们在广州住了一个多月了，还没有去过[G1]理发店。现在他们的头发已经长得太长了，琳达也需要染发了。他们就在附近找了一家理发店，看看人不多就进去了。

Líndá hé Qiáozhì zài Guǎngzhōu yì jiā Ruìshì gōngsī gōngzuò. Tāmen zài Guǎngzhōu zhùle yí ge duō yuè le, hái méiyǒu qùguo[G1] lǐfàdiàn. Xiànzài tāmen de tóufa yǐjīng zhǎng de tài cháng le, Líndá yě xūyào rǎn fà le. Tāmen jiù zài fùjìn zhǎole yì jiā lǐfàdiàn, kànkan rén bù duō jiù jìnqu le.

A：师傅，我们要理发，需要等很久吗？
　　Shīfu, wǒmen yào lǐ fà, xūyào děng hěn jiǔ ma?

B：不用。我们这里美发师很多。我是一号美发师，为[1]您服务。您两位都理发吗？
　　Búyòng. Wǒmen zhèli měifàshī hěn duō. Wǒ shì yī hào měifàshī, wèi[1] nín fúwù. Nín liǎng wèi dōu lǐfà ma?

A：我要理发、修面，她要染发。
　　Wǒ yào lǐ fà、xiū miàn, tā yào rǎn fà.

B：我可以先给您理发、修面，等一会儿专业染发的师傅来了，再给您太太染发，好吗？
　　Wǒ kěyǐ xiān gěi nín lǐ fà、xiū miàn, děng yíhuìr zhuānyè rǎn fà de shīfu lái le, zài gěi nín tàitai rǎn fà, hǎo ma?

A：好。琳达，今天不能"女士优先"了。
　　Hǎo. Líndá, jīntiān bù néng "nǚshì yōuxiān" le.

D：没关系。我等一会儿。
　　Méi guānxi. Wǒ děng yíhuìr.

Notes

1. "为 wèi" is a preposition with the meaning of "for (the sake of), on (behalf of)". Cf. "为什么 wèi shénme", literally "for the sake of what", and the common phrase "为人民服务 wèi rénmín fúwù" (serve the people). The character "为" also represents a rising toned "wéi" that appears in certain compounds and in formal language with the meaning of "be" or "do", e.g "以为 yǐwéi" (consider [sth.] to be).

真实生活汉语
Chinese for Living in China 2

B： 请您到这边坐。您是洗剪吹都要吗?
Qǐng nín dào zhèbian zuò. Nín shì xǐ-jiǎn-chuī dōu yào ma?

A： 请您说慢一点儿². 什么是"洗剪吹"?
Qǐng nín shuōmàn yìdiǎnr². Shénme shì "xǐ-jiǎn-chuī"?

B： "洗剪吹"就是洗头、剪发和吹风。您都要吗?
"Xǐ-jiǎn-chuī" jiù shì xǐ tóu, jiǎn fà hé chuī fēng. Nín dōu yào ma?

A： 对。我能不能看看你们用什么洗发剂?
Duì. Wǒ néng bu néng kànkan nǐmen yòng shénme xǐfàjì?

B： 可以。我们有国产的[G2]，也有韩国和德国进口的。
Kěyǐ. Wǒmen yǒu guóchǎn de[G2], yě yǒu Hánguó hé Déguó jìnkǒu de.

A： 德国进口的是不是很贵?
Déguó jìnkǒu de shì bu shì hěn guì?

B： 洗发剂不收费。水洗都是二十元。如果干洗才按³洗发剂价格收费。
Xǐfàjì bù shōu fèi. Shuǐxǐ dōu shì èrshí yuán. Rúguǒ gānxǐ cái àn³ xǐfàjì jiàgé shōu fèi.

A： 我要水洗，请您用德国进口的洗发剂。
Wǒ yào shuǐxǐ, qǐng nín yòng Déguó jìnkǒu de xǐfàjì.

B： 您洗头时要不要按摩? 是免费的。
Nín xǐ tóu shí yào bu yào ànmó? Shì miǎnfèi de.

A： 免费的? 当然要。
Miǎnfèi de? Dāngrán yào.

B： 您只按³头部，还是后背、肩膀都按?
Nín zhǐ àn³ tóubù, háishi hòubèi, jiānbǎng dōu àn?

A： 都按。
Dōu àn.

……

---

2. "说慢一点儿 shuōmàn yìdiǎnr" (to speak a bit more slowly): While the expression "有一点儿慢 yǒu yìdiǎnr màn" would mean "be rather slow", "慢一点儿 màn yìdiǎnr", with "一点儿" after the adjective, implies a comparison: "more slowly". Placing the whole adjective phrase (慢一点儿 màn yìdiǎnr) after the verb makes it a result: "speak so it is slower". Cf. "走慢一点儿 zǒu màn yìdiǎnr" (walk slower), "走快一点儿 zǒukuài yìdiǎnr" (walk faster). The same construction, with "一些 yìxiē" (a few) substituting for "一点儿 yìdiǎnr" appears in the sentence, "两鬓剪短一些 liǎngbìn jiǎnduǎn yìxiē" (cut the two sides a bit shorter).

3. "按 àn" is a preposition with the meaning "according to, based on". It appears before its associated verb, followed by an object, as the example from the dialogue illustrates: "如果干洗才按洗发剂价格收费 Rúguǒ gānxǐ cái àn xǐfàjì jiàgé shōufèi" (If you want a dry wash, then it's priced according to the shampoo). "洗发剂价格 xǐfàjì jiàgé" (the cost of the shampoo) is the object of "按 àn". Note that "按 àn" also appears in the dialogue as a full verb, meaning "to press, to push down" – or in the context, "to massage": "后背、肩膀都按 hòubèi、jiānbǎng dōu àn" (massage the back and shoulders as well).

第十四课　理发
Lesson Fourteen　Getting a Haircut

B：请您拿着^{G3}毛巾到这边坐。您是要剪短还是改变发型？
　　Qǐng nín názhe[G3] máojīn dào zhèbian zuò. Nín shì yào jiǎnduǎn háishi gǎibiàn fàxíng?

A：剪短一点儿就可以了，不要改变发型。
　　Jiǎnduǎn yìdiǎnr jiù kěyǐ le, bú yào gǎibiàn fàxíng.

B：剪多少？
　　Jiǎn duōshao?

A：一寸左右[4]。两鬓剪短一些，后面不要剪太多。
　　Yí cùn zuǒyòu[4]. Liǎngbìn jiǎnduǎn yìxiē, hòumiàn bú yào jiǎn tài duō.

B：顶上要不要剪？
　　Dǐng shang yào bu yào jiǎn?

A：稍微去掉^{G4}一点儿。最好剪成^{G4}梯型的。
　　Shāowēi qùdiào[G4] yìdiǎnr. Zuìhǎo jiǎnchéng[G4] tīxíng de.

B：要刮胡子吗^{G5}？
　　Yào guā húzi ma[G5]?

A：不要。请把连鬓胡子修短一点儿。
　　Bú yào. Qǐng bǎ liánbìn húzi xiūduǎn yìdiǎnr.

……

B：您拿着镜子，看看这样可以吗？
　　Nín názhe jìngzi, kànkan zhèyàng kěyǐ ma?

A：能不能把脖子后面用推子推干净，再上点儿发油？
　　Néng bu néng bǎ bózi hòumiàn yòng tuīzi tuī gānjìng, zài shàng diǎnr fàyóu?

B：没问题。
　　Méi wèntí.

（三号理发师来了 Sān hào lǐfàshī lái le）

C：您好。我是三号美发师，为您服务。您要染发吗？要不要烫发？
　　Nín hǎo. Wǒ shì sān hào měifàshī, wèi nín fúwù. Nín yào rǎn fà ma? Yào bu yào tàng fà?

D：不用烫发。请您先把我的头发剪短一点儿，不要改变发型，再染发。
　　Búyòng tàng fà. Qǐng nín xiān bǎ wǒ de tóufa jiǎnduǎn yìdiǎnr, bú yào gǎibiàn fàxíng, zài rǎn fà.

---

4. "左右 zuǒyòu" (literally "left-right") may appear after a numeral with the meaning "more or less": "一寸左右 yí cùn zuǒyòu" (an inch, more or less).

C：可以。您要染什么颜色？
　　Kěyǐ. Nín yào rǎn shénme yánsè?

D：您有没有跟我头发颜色一样[G6]的染发剂？
　　Nín yǒu méiyǒu gēn wǒ tóufa yánsè yíyàng[G6] de rǎnfàjì?

C：有。这个颜色看起来更自然。
　　Yǒu. Zhège yánsè kàn qilai gèng zìrán.

D：好。我试试。
　　Hǎo. Wǒ shìshi.

……

C：好了。您在镜子里看看怎么样？
　　Hǎo le. Nín zài jìngzi li kànkan zěnmeyàng?

D：非常好。谢谢你。
　　Fēicháng hǎo. Xièxie nǐ.

C：不用谢。请您到前台去付款。欢迎再来。
　　Búyòng xiè. Qǐng nín dào qiántái qù fù kuǎn. Huānyíng zài lái.

New Words

1	理发/理髮	lǐ fà	VO	to style hair, to cut hair
	发/髮	fà	BF	hair on human head
2	理发师/理髮師	lǐfàshī	N	barber, hairdresser
3	广州/廣州	Guǎngzhōu	PropN	Guangzhou, Canton (a city in Guangdong)
4	家	jiā	N / Meas	family, household, home; *for families, businesses*
5	瑞士	Ruìshì	PropN	Switzerland
6	工作	gōngzuò	V/N	to work; occupation, job, work
7	过/過	guo	Part	*a verb suffix that indicates that the action has happened at some time in the past*
8	理发店/理髮店	lǐfàdiàn	N	barber shop, hair salon
9	头发/頭髮	tóufa	N	hair
10	长/長	zhǎng	V	to grow
11	长/長	cháng	Adj	long, for a long time
12	染发/染髮	rǎn fà	Phrase	to dye hair, to color hair

第十四课 理发
Lesson Fourteen Getting a Haircut

	染	rǎn	V	to dye, to color
13	进去/進去	jìnqu	V	to go in, to enter
14	久	jiǔ	Adj	long, for a long time
15	不用	búyòng	Adv	need not
16	美发师/美髮師	měifàshī	N	hairdresser
17	为/為	wèi	Prep	for (the sake of), on behalf of
18	修面	xiū miàn	VO	to shave (the face)
19	专业/專業	zhuānyè	Attr	professional
20	太太	tàitai	N	wife, Mrs. (form of address for older women)
21	女士	nǚshì	N	lady, miss (polite form of address or reference)
22	优先/優先	yōuxiān	V	to take precedence, to have priority
23	没关系/沒關係	méi guānxi	Phrase	it doesn't matter, never mind
24	剪	jiǎn	V	to cut (with scissors), to clip
25	吹	chuī	V	to blow (of wind), to play (a wind instrument)
26	慢	màn	Adj	slow
27	洗头/洗頭	xǐ tóu	Phrase	to wash hair, to shampoo
28	剪发/剪髮	jiǎn fà	Phrase	to have one's hair cut, to cut hair
29	吹风/吹風	chuī fēng	VO	to blow dry (one's hair); to be in a draft
	风/風	fēng	N	wind
30	洗发剂/洗髮劑	xǐfàjì	N	shampoo
31	国产/國產	guóchǎn	Attr	domestic product (i.e. made in China)
32	韩国/韓國	Hánguó	PropN	South Korea
33	德国/德國	Déguó	PropN	Germany
34	进口/進口	jìnkǒu	VO	to import
35	收费/收費	shōu fèi	Phrase	to collect fees, to be not free
36	水洗	shuǐxǐ	V	wet wash (in contrast to "dry clean")
37	干洗/乾洗	gānxǐ	V	dry wash, dry clean
38	按	àn	Prep/V	according to, based on; to press, to push down, to massage

真实生活汉语
Chinese for Living in China 2

39	按摩	ànmó	V	to massage
40	头部/頭部	tóubù	N	head, front part (e.g.: "a nose cone")
41	后背/後背	hòubèi	N	the back (of the body, etc.), at the back, in the rear
42	肩膀	jiānbǎng	N	the shoulder
43	着/著	zhe	Part	durative verb suffix
44	短	duǎn	Adj	short, brief
45	改变/改變	gǎibiàn	V	to change, to transform
46	发型/髮型	fàxíng	N	hair style
	型	xíng	BF	form, style
47	寸	cùn	Meas	Chinese inch (1/30 meter)
48	左右	zuǒyòu	PW	more or less, approximately (after an expression of quantity)
49	两鬓/兩鬢	liǎngbìn	N	hair on the temples
50	后面/後面	hòumiàn	PW	at the back, afterwards, later
51	顶上/頂上	dǐng shang	Phrase	the top, peak, highest point
52	稍微	shāowēi	Adv	a bit, slightly
53	去掉	qùdiào	V-RC	to get rid of
	掉	diào	V/RC	to fall, to drop; away, off, out, etc.
54	成	chéng	V/RC	to become, to turn into, to succeed; into
55	梯型	tīxíng	N	ladder-shaped, terraced, layered (of hair)
	梯	tī	N	ladder
56	刮	guā	V	to scrape, to scratch, to shave
57	胡子/鬍子	húzi	N	beard, moustache, facial hair
58	连鬓胡子/連鬢鬍子	liánbìn húzi	Phrase	full beard, sideburns
59	镜子/鏡子	jìngzi	N	a mirror
60	这样/這樣	zhèyàng	Pron	so, like this, this way
61	脖子	bózi	N	the neck, the neck (of a vessel, a vase, etc.)
62	推子	tuīzi	N	clippers
63	推	tuī	V	to shove, to push, to promote

Lesson Fourteen   Getting a Haircut

64	干净/乾淨	gānjìng	Adj	clean, trim
65	发油/髮油	fàyóu	N	hair oil
66	烫发/燙髮	tàng fà	VO	to perm
67	颜色/顏色	yánsè	N	color
68	一样/一樣	yíyàng	Adj	identical, alike, the same ("跟 gēn……一样 yíyàng", the same as…)
69	看起来/看起來	kàn qilai	V-DirC	to look as if, to seem to be, to appear to be
70	自然	zìrán	Adj	natural
71	试/試	shì	V	to test, to try, to experiment
72	怎么样/怎麼樣	zěnmeyàng	IntPron	how, how are things
73	欢迎/歡迎	huānyíng	V	to welcome, to receive favorably

Re-enacting the Dialogue

A: George   B: Barber #1   C: Barber #3   D: Linda

Linda and George are working for a Swiss Company in Guangzhou. They've been living in Guangzhou for over a month, and haven't been to a barbershop yet. By now, their hair has grown too long, and Linda also needs to have her hair colored. They found a barbershop in the neighborhood, and seeing that there weren't many people there, they went in.

A: "Shifu", we need haircuts, how long's the wait?

B: No wait. We have lots of hairdressers here. I'm #1 hairdresser, at your service. Do you both want haircuts?

A: I'd like a haircut and a facial; she wants hair coloring.

B: I can do your hair and the facial first; when the hair coloring specialist arrives, we'll do your wife's coloring, is that OK?

A: Fine. We can't have "ladies first" today, Linda.

C: No problem, I'll wait.

B: Please sit over here. Do you want a "wash-cut-dry"?

A: Speak a bit slower, please. What's a "wash-cut-dry"?

B: A "wash-cut-dry" is a shampoo, a haircut and a blow dry. You want everything?

A: Yes. Can I take a look at the shampoo you use?

B: Sure. We have a domestic product, and Korean and German imports.

A: Is the one from Germany expensive?

B: The shampoo is free. A wet wash is 20 *yuan*. If you want a dry wash, then it's priced according to the cost of the shampoo.

A: I'd like a wet wash, and please use the imported shampoo from Germany.

B: Do you want a massage with your shampoo? It's free of charge.

A: Free? Then of course!

B: Do you want just your head massaged, or back and shoulders as well?

A: The whole thing.

……

B: Please take the towel with you and sit over here. Do you want just a cut, or styling as well?

A: Just cut it a bit shorter – that'll be fine; don't change the style.

B: How much do you want off?

A: About an inch. Cut the sides a bit shorter, don't cut the back too much.

B: Do you want the top cut?

A: Take a bit off. It would be best if you cut it in a tapered style.

B: Do you need a shave?

A: No. Please make the sideburns a little shorter.

……

B: Hold the mirror and take a look to see if this is all right.

A: Could you shave the back of my neck clean, and then put some hair oil on?

B: No problem.

(#3 Hairdresser comes)

C: Hello. I'm #3 hairdresser, at your service. Do you want to dye your hair? Would you like a perm too?

D: No perm. Please cut my hair a bit shorter first, don't change the style; then color it.

C: Fine. What color would you like?

D: Do you have a dye that's the same color as my hair?

C: We do. This color looks more natural.

D: OK, I'll try it.

……

C: OK, take a look in the mirror – what do you think?

D: Great. Thanks a lot.

C: You're welcome. Please pay up front. Come again.

Lesson Fourteen Getting a Haircut

第十四课 理发

Grammar

▶ **G1.** The verb suffix "过 guo" (usually with neutral tone)

In Lesson 6 of Volume I in the series, you saw examples of "过 guò" used as a full verb, with the meaning "to cross, to pass over": "您过了马路往南走 Nín guòle mǎlù wǎng nán zǒu" (Cross the road and head south). In this lesson, "过 guo" (usually with neutral tone) is used as a verb suffix with a specialized meaning of "have (ever) done something":

① 你去过中国的理发店吗？ Have you ever been to a Chinese hair salon?
　　Nǐ qùguo Zhōngguó de lǐfàdiàn ma?

In this example, the time in question extends back indefinitely, so the English translation allows "ever". However, it should be noted that the "过 guo" suffix can also co-occur with a restricting time phrase, in which case the meaning is "within the time indicated" (and "ever" cannot be used):

② 你这个学期去过理发店吗？ Have you been to a hair salon this semester? (*ever)
　　Nǐ zhège xuéqī qùguo lǐfàdiàn ma?

The main dialogue gives you a nice example of a negative sentence containing the "过 guo" suffix:

③ 他们在广州住了一个多月了，还没有去过理发店。
　　Tāmen zài Guǎngzhōu zhùle yí ge duō yuè le, hái méiyǒu qùguo lǐfàdiàn.
　　They've been living in Guangzhou for over a month, and haven't been to a barbershop yet.

The example contrasts the two verbal suffixes, "了 le" and "过 guo". They behave differently under negation. Both make use of the helping verb "没 (有) méi (yǒu)". But while "了 le" is not preserved in the negative (还没吃呢 hái méi chī ne), "过 guo" is: "还没去过 hái méi qùguo" (haven't been yet).

The question is formed with "过 guo" and "没 (有) méi (yǒu)", with "没 (有)" filling in for "没有去过 méiyǒu qùguo":

④ A: 你去过上海没有？ Have you ever been to Shanghai (or not)?
　　　Nǐ qùguo Shànghǎi méiyǒu?

　　B: 还没去过，可是很想去。 Not yet, but I'd really like to.
　　　Hái méi qùguo, kěshì hěn xiǎng qù.

As with "了 le", it is important to distinguish verb-plus-objects from compound verbs: "理发 lǐ fà" is a verb-plus-object, so if you meet a two-year old on the street, and you want to ask her dad if she's ever had a haircut, you would place "过 guo" after the first element, the verb "理 lǐ": "她理过发没有？ Tā lǐguo fà méiyǒu?" However, if the verb were "工作 gōngzuò", a true two-syllable verb, not a verb-plus-object, then you would place "过 guo" after the second element:

⑤ 你在中国工作过没有？ Have you ever worked in China?
　　Nǐ zài Zhōngguó gōngzuòguo méiyǒu?

Other examples:

89

⑥ 我学过法文。 I've studied French (in the past).
　　Wǒ xuéguo Fǎwén.

⑦ 你们用过这个洗发剂吗？ Have you ever used this kind of shampoo?
　　Nǐmen yòngguo zhège xǐfàjì ma?

⑧ 我没买过国产的。 I've never bought the domestic product before.
　　Wǒ méi mǎiguo guóchǎn de.

▶ **G2. "的 de" used as a nominalizer**

　　Earlier, in Lessons 6 (G5) and 7 (G3) of Volume I, you were introduced to two of the main functions of the ubiquitous particle, "的 de", that is, possession ("你的", "毛老师的") and modification:

① 我房间的空调坏了。 The air-conditioning in my room is broken.
　　Wǒ fángjiān de kōngtiáo huài le.

If your air-conditioning were also broken, you could respond to the previous example without mentioning the air-conditioner at all – provided you left "的 de" in place to indicate that "房间 fángjiān" modified something. This is often called the nominalizing function of "的 de"; it substitutes for the omitted noun, i.e. "the one that …":

② 我房间的也坏了。 The one (that is) in my room's also broken.
　　Wǒ fángjiān de yě huài le.

"房间的 fángjiān de" could be translated as "the room's (air-conditioning)" or "the one in the room" (with "one" standing for "air-conditioning"). Other examples:

③ 我们有国产的洗发剂，也有韩国和德国进口的。
　　Wǒmen yǒu guóchǎn de xǐfàjì, yě yǒu Hánguó hé Déguó jìnkǒu de.
　　We have a domestic product, and Korean and German imports.

　In this example, "的 de" indicates that there's a missing noun, which the reader (or listener) can recover as "shampoo".

④ 是免费的。 It's a freebee.
　　Shì miǎnfèi de.

⑤ 最好剪成梯型的。 It would be best if you cut it in a tapered style (of haircut).
　　Zuìhǎo jiǎnchéng tīxíng de.

▶ **G3. The verb suffix "着 zhe"**

　　The third verbal suffix (after "了 le" and "过 guo") is "着 zhe", which is often characterized as "durative": "坐着 zuòzhe" (sitting), "睡着 shuìzhe" (sleeping), "站着 zhànzhe" (standing), "放着 fàngzhe" (sitting on, resting on – as a result of being "put" there). The last example clarifies the meaning of durative. "放 fàng" (to put, to place) is an action; but "放着 fàngzhe" describes an enduring state – which in English requires a shift in verb, from "put" to "rest", or "sit". (The fact that in English, verbs like "sit" or "stand" can be applied to things as well as to people probably strikes Chinese as strange – but English does not have a handy suffix like "着 zhe" to do the job.)

Lesson Fourteen   Getting a Haircut

① 桌子上放着镜子和推子。   There were a mirror and some clippers sitting on the table.
　　Zhuōzi shang fàngzhe jìngzi hé tuīzi.

In this function, "V-着" can be regarded as a more specific alternative to the existential pattern with "有 yǒu" (there is, there are): "桌子上有镜子和推子 Zhuōzi shang yǒu jìngzi hé tuīzi".

The examples of "V-着" in this lesson illustrate a different construction, involving two verbs, the first one of which is suffixed with "着 zhe", e.g.: "拿着 názhe……到 dào……". In such cases, the first verb provides a setting for the second: "holding the towel, go and sit over there", etc.

② 请您拿着毛巾到这边坐。   Please take the towel with you and sit here.
　　Qǐng nín názhe máojīn dào zhèbian zuò.

③ 您拿着镜子，看看这样可以吗？   Hold the mirror and take a look to see if this is all right.
　　Nín názhe jìngzi, kànkan zhèyàng kěyǐ ma?

These two functions of "着 zhe" share the property of describing the setting – the background – of an action. (Note: "着 zhe" is often followed by "呢 ne", the particle associated with both continued states and ongoing actions.)

④ 他在门外等着呢。   He's waiting at the door.
　　Tā zài mén wài děngzhe ne.

⑤ 她坐着空调大巴去上课。
　　Tā zuòzhe kōngtiáo dàbā qù shàng kè.
　　She takes an airconditioned big-bus to class. (i.e. "riding a bus goes to her class")

▶ **G4.** The verbs "掉 diào" and "成 chéng" used as resultative complements

The verbs "掉 diào" and "成 chéng" can also appear, in conjunction with a range of preceding verbs, as resultative complements (cf. Lesson 11, G7). As a main verb, "掉 diào" translates as "to fall, to drop". As a resultative complement, however, it has a more abstract meaning of "away" or "off": "去掉 qùdiào" (to get rid of), "扔掉 rēngdiào" (to throw away), "忘掉 wàngdiào" (to forget), "卖掉 màidiào" (to sell) and "死掉 sǐdiào" (to die). While it is useful to be able to characterize the meaning of "掉 diào" in this position as conveying a sense of "removal", in practice, it is better to remember the compounds themselves.

"成 chéng" as a full verb means "to turn into, to become". In combination with appropriate first verbs, it indicates a transformation, in which case, it requires an object (the result of the transformation): "听成 tīngchéng" (to hear as); "换成 huànchéng" (to change into); "写成 xiěchéng" (to write as).

① 他把"四"这个字写成了"西"。   She wrote the character "四" as "西".
　　Tā bǎ "sì" zhège zì xiěchéngle "xī".

② 他把"多"那个字听成了"都"。   He heard "多" as "都".
　　Tā bǎ "duō" nàge zì tīngchéngle "dōu".

③ 最好剪成梯型的。   It would be best if you cut it in a tapered style (of haircut).
　　Zuìhǎo jiǎnchéng tīxíng de.

Though both form combinations with initial verbs, "掉 diào" and "成 chéng" have different properties. "掉 diào" is in the same class as "懂 dǒng" in "听懂 tīngdǒng" (to understand) and "上 shàng" in "关上 guānshang" (to close [a door, etc.]). "成 chéng" (at least in its "become" meaning), however, requires a following object phrase: "换成大的 huànchéng dà de" (change to a bigger one). In that respect, "成 chéng" resembles post-verbal "到 dào" and "在 zài" in phrases like "走到那儿 zǒudào nàr" (walk over there) and "放在这儿 fàng zài zhèr" (put here) (cf. Lesson 12, G6).

▶ **G5. Omitted subjects and objects**

By now, you will have seen plenty of examples where Chinese, rather than using a pronoun, simply omits the subject (cf. Lesson 5, G3) or object. In the following examples, either the subject is omitted, the object, or in the last case, both. The English, on the other hand, has "you", "I", "it" and "anything":

① A: 要刮胡子吗？　Do [you] need a shave?
　　　Yào guā húzi ma?

　B: 不要。　No, [I] don't.
　　　Bú yào.

② A: 累不累？　Are [you] tired?
　　　Lèi bu lèi?

　B: 很累。　Yes, [I] am.
　　　Hěn lèi.

③ 我叫人来修。　I'll have someone come and fix [it].
　　Wǒ jiào rén lái xiū.

④ A: 您还要什么？　What else do [you] want?
　　　Nín hái yào shénme?

　B: 不要了。　[I] don't want [anything] else.
　　　Bú yào le.

In each case, who and what are being talked about can be recovered from the context. If context is not enough, the Chinese also has the option of providing pronouns. But even pronouns need to be interpreted in terms of the context: "it" is "the air-conditioning", etc. So omitting a known noun phrase (subject or object, etc.) rather than representing it with a pronoun is sometimes called "zero-pronominalization".

▶ **G6. Same or different: "A 跟 gēn B (不 bù) 一样 yíyàng"**

"一样 yíyàng" (and the negative "不一样 bù yíyàng") functions as a compound adjective meaning "the same" (literally "one-type"). The two entities being judged the same or not, are presented as a coordinate subject, usually linked by conjunctions such as "跟 gēn" (and, with), "和 hé" (and) or "同 tóng" (and, with).

① 我跟你一样。　I'm the same as you – like you.
　　Wǒ gēn nǐ yíyàng.

第十四课 理发
Lesson Fourteen Getting a Haircut

② 他和十年前不一样。 He's quite different from ten year's ago.
Tā hé shí nián qián bù yíyàng.

③ 染发剂的颜色跟我头发的颜色一样。
Rǎnfàjì de yánsè gēn wǒ tóufa de yánsè yíyàng.
The hair color is the same tone as the color of my own hair.

The construction can be expanded by adding an adjective afterwards.

④ 她跟我一样高。 She's the same height as me (as I am).
Tā gēn wǒ yíyàng gāo.

⑤ 这间教室跟那间一样大。 This classroom is the same size as that one.
Zhè jiān jiàoshì gēn nà jiān yíyàng dà.

⑥ 银行跟邮局一样远。 The bank is the same distance away as the post office.
Yínháng gēn yóujú yíyàng yuǎn.

The pattern can also be expanded by adding a clause after "一样 yíyàng", either with a pause, or not.

⑦ 乔治跟你一样在北大教英文。
Qiáozhì gēn nǐ yíyàng zài Běi Dà jiāo Yīngwén.
George and you are alike in both teaching English at Peking University.

⑧ 我的朋友跟我一样,都吃素。
Wǒ de péngyou gēn wǒ yíyàng, dōu chīsù.
My friend and I are alike – we are both vegetarians.

真实生活汉语
Chinese for Living in China 2

Consolidation & Practice

1. Exercises on the verb suffix "过 guo"

    (1) Ask and answer questions using the material provided

    Example: ① A: 你吃过中药吗？ Have you ever taken Chinese medicine?
    Nǐ chīguo zhōngyào ma?

    B: 我吃过（中药）。Yes, I have.
    Wǒ chīguo (zhōngyào).

    ② A: 你做没做过法国菜？ Have you ever cooked French food?
    Nǐ zuò méi zuòguo Fǎguó cài?

    B: 没做过。 No, I haven't.
    Méi zuòguo.

去 qù	早市 zǎoshì
在中国银行 zài Zhōngguó Yínháng	换钱 huàn qián
选 xuǎn	中国文学课 Zhōngguó wénxuékè
吃 chī	小王做的鱼 Xiǎo Wáng zuò de yú
染 rǎn	头发 tóufa
看 kàn	中国电影 Zhōngguó diànyǐng
做 zuò	家教 jiājiào
坐 zuò	北京的地铁 Běijīng de dìtiě
在北京 zài Běijīng	开车 kāi chē
上 shàng	长城 Chángchéng
在北京用 zài Běijīng yòng	信用卡 xìnyòngkǎ
买 mǎi	火车票 huǒchēpiào

第十四课　理发
Lesson Fourteen　Getting a Haircut

(2) Tell each other three bold or interesting things that you've done since coming to China

Example: 我吃过马肉。 I've eaten horse meat.
Wǒ chīguo mǎròu.

A. ....
....

B. ....
....

C. ....
....

2. Following the example, make use of "的 de" to avoid repetition of the noun in each sentence

Example: 那家理发店太贵，旁边的理发店便宜一点儿。
Nà jiā lǐfàdiàn tài guì, pángbiān de lǐfàdiàn piányi yìdiǎnr.
That barbershop is too expensive; the barbershop next to it is cheaper.

→ 那家理发店太贵，旁边的便宜一点儿。
Nà jiā lǐfàdiàn tài guì, pángbiān de piányi yìdiǎnr.
That barbershop is too expensive; the one next door is cheaper.

(1) ① 前边的车是空调车，后边的车没有空调。→ _____
Qiánbian de chē shì kōngtiáochē, hòubian de chē méiyǒu kōngtiáo.

② 留学生的宿舍都是新宿舍。→ _____
Liúxuéshēng de sùshè dōu shì xīn sùshè.

③ 我们学校里边的超市卖的日用品比这个超市卖的日用品贵一点儿。→ _____
Wǒmen xuéxiào lǐbian de chāoshì mài de rìyòngpǐn bǐ zhège chāoshì mài de rìyòngpǐn guì yìdiǎnr.

④ 这不是我的手机，我的手机是新手机。→ _____
Zhè bú shì wǒ de shǒujī, wǒ de shǒujī shì xīn shǒujī.

⑤ 我的发型跟他的发型不一样。→ _____
Wǒ de fàxíng gēn tā de fàxíng bù yíyàng.

⑥ 这个染发剂的颜色跟那个染发剂的颜色差不多。→ _____
Zhège rǎnfàjì de yánsè gēn nàge rǎnfàjì de yánsè chàbuduō.

(2) How do you say the following in Chinese?

① My mom's car is Japanese, my dad's is German, and mine's American.

_____

95

② Our dorms all have AC, but the Chinese students' don't.

_____

③ Produce sold at the morning market is the cheapest; that sold at the supermarket is the most expensive.

_____

④ I'd like to use domestic hair color; the imported stuff is too expensive.

_____

3. Study the examples and then, following the English cues, combine the phrases together

Example: ① 沙发上 / 放书　　　　　→　　沙发上放着书。
　　　　　　shāfā shang / fàng shū　　　　Shāfā shang fàngzhe shū.

② 您 / 拿 / 毛巾 / 到这边坐　　→　　您拿着毛巾到这边坐。
　　nín / ná / máojīn / dào zhèbian zuò　　Nín názhe máojīn dào zhèbian zuò.

(1) ① 开电视 / 做作业 → _____
　　　kāi diànshì / zuò zuòyè
　　　(I like to do my homework with the TV on.)

② 拿镜子 / 理发 → _____
　　ná jìngzi / lǐ fà
　　(The hairdresser asked me to hold the mirror while I get my hair cut.)

③ 说话 / 按摩 → _____
　　shuō huà / ànmó
　　(He chatted with me as he was giving me a massage.)

④ 桌子上 / 放 / 一些水果 → _____
　　zhuōzi shang / fàng / yìxiē shuǐguǒ
　　(There's some fruit sitting on the table.)

⑤ 教室前边 / 放 / 投影仪 → _____
　　jiàoshì qiánbian / fàng / tóuyǐngyí
　　(A projector's been put at the front of the classroom.)

⑥ 开冷气 / 睡觉 → _____
　　kāi lěngqì / shuì jiào
　　(I like to sleep with the AC on.)

⑦ 窗户旁边 / 放 / 新电视 → _____
　　chuānghu pángbian / fàng / xīn diànshì
　　(A new TV's been placed next to the window.)

Lesson Fourteen   Getting a Haircut

(2) Provide each other with the desired information

① what's sitting on your desk. (放着 fàngzhe)

_____

② what's next to the window. (放着 fàngzhe)

_____

③ that you like to listen to music while you eat. (看着 kànzhe)

_____

④ that you often call your friends while riding on the bus. (坐着 zuòzhe)

_____

4. Complete the sentences below, choosing the correct resultative complement "成 chéng, 掉 diào"

Example: ① 你叫了五个菜，太多了，去掉一个吧！
Nǐ jiàole wǔ ge cài, tài duō le, qùdiào yí ge ba!
You've ordered five dishes – that's too many. Why don't you remove one?

② 请把中文菜单换成英文的。
Qǐng bǎ Zhōngwén càidān huànchéng Yīngwén de.
Please exchange the Chinese menu for an English one.

(1) 我们买的水果太多了，拿（   ）两个吧！
Wǒmen mǎi de shuǐguǒ tài duō le, ná (   ) liǎng ge ba!

(2) 我们要的肉菜太多了，换（   ）一个素菜吧。
Wǒmen yào de ròucài tài duō le, huàn (   ) yí ge sùcài ba.

(3) 我没有人民币了，得把这十美元换（   ）人民币。
Wǒ méiyǒu rénmínbì le, děi bǎ zhè shí měiyuán huàn (   ) rénmínbì.

(4) 这个学期我选课选得太多了，想退（   ）一门课。
Zhège xuéqī wǒ xuǎn kè xuǎn de tài duō le, xiǎng tuì (   ) yì mén kè.

(5) 这个毛巾旧了，把它扔（   ）吧！
Zhège máojīn jiù le, bǎ tā rēng (   ) ba!

5. Read through the following dialogues and omit whichever of the underlined noun phrases you feel is redundant

Example: A: 今天吃点儿什么？
Jīntiān chī diǎnr shénme?

B: 有清炒豆苗吗？
Yǒu qīngchǎo-dòumiáo ma?

A: 有。来一个吗?
Yǒu. Lái yí ge ma?

B: 来一个吧!
Lái yí ge ba!

A: 你今天去哪儿了? 我一上午都没看到你。
Nǐ jīntiān qù nǎr le? Wǒ yí shàngwǔ dōu méi kàndào nǐ.

B: 我去理发了。你看我的新发型怎么样?
Wǒ qù lǐ fà le. Nǐ kàn wǒ de xīn fàxíng zěnmeyàng?

A: 你的新发型挺不错的。你染发了吧?
Nǐ de xīn fàxíng tǐng bú cuò de. Nǐ rǎn fà le ba?

B: 我染了。你喜欢这个颜色吗? 这个颜色比以前的颜色红一点儿。
Wǒ rǎn le. Nǐ xǐhuan zhège yánsè ma? Zhège yánsè bǐ yǐqián de yánsè hóng yìdiǎnr.

A: 我喜欢这个颜色,这个颜色比以前的颜色好看。你用的是进口的染发剂吗?
Wǒ xǐhuan zhège yánsè, zhège yánsè bǐ yǐqián de yánsè hǎokàn. Nǐ yòng de shì jìnkǒu de rǎnfàjì ma?

B: 是进口的染发剂。
Shì jìnkǒu de rǎnfàjì.

A: 进口的染发剂贵吗?
Jìnkǒu de rǎnfàjì guì ma?

B: 进口的染发剂比国产的染发剂贵一点儿,可是进口的染发剂颜色自然。
Jìnkǒu de rǎnfàjì bǐ guóchǎn de rǎnfàjì guì yìdiǎnr, kěshì jìnkǒu de rǎnfàjì yánsè zìrán.

A: 你是在哪儿买的这个进口的染发剂?
Nǐ shì zài nǎr mǎi de zhège jìnkǒu de rǎnfàjì?

B: 我是从美国带来的这个进口的染发剂。你喜欢这个进口的染发剂吗?
Wǒ shì cóng Měiguó dàilái de zhège jìnkǒu de rǎnfàjì. Nǐ xǐhuan zhège jìnkǒu de rǎnfàjì ma?

我给你一个这个进口的染发剂。
Wǒ gěi nǐ yí ge zhège jìnkǒu de rǎnfàjì.

A: 真的吗? 你以后不用这个进口的染发剂了吗?
Zhēn de ma? Nǐ yǐhòu bú yòng zhège jìnkǒu de rǎnfàjì le ma?

B: 我还有这个进口的染发剂。
Wǒ hái yǒu zhège jìnkǒu de rǎnfàjì.

A: 那我太感谢你了!
Nà wǒ tài gǎnxiè nǐ le!

Lesson Fourteen Getting a Haircut

第十四课 理发

6. Following the example, express "same" or "different", incorporating the material given in each item

A 跟 gēn B+ (不 bù) 一样 yíyàng (+Adj).

Example: 这个房间跟那个（房间）一样大。 This room's the same size as that one.
Zhège fángjiān gēn nàge (fángjiān) yíyàng dà.

(1)
这家理发店 zhè jiā lǐfàdiàn	那家理发店 nà jiā lǐfàdiàn	贵 guì
菜市场的西红柿 càishìchǎng de xīhóngshì	超市的西红柿 chāoshì de xīhóngshì	新鲜 xīnxian
韩国的染发剂 Hánguó de rǎnfàjì	德国的染发剂 Déguó de rǎnfàjì	贵 guì
上次用的洗发剂 shàng cì yòng de xǐfàjì	这次用的洗发剂 zhè cì yòng de xǐfàjì	好 hǎo
上次吃饭要的菜 shàng cì chī fàn yào de cài	这次吃饭要的菜 zhè cì chī fàn yào de cài	多 duō
头部按摩 tóubù ànmó	后背、肩膀按摩 hòubèi, jiānbǎng ànmó	舒服 shūfu
铁板牛肉 tiěbǎn-niúròu	糖醋鱼 tángcùyú	好吃 hǎochī
中国大学生 Zhōngguó dàxuéshēng	美国大学生 Měiguó dàxuéshēng	喜欢上网 xǐhuan shàng wǎng

(2) Tell each other three things about Chinese university campuses that are just like American campuses

A. ....
....

B. ....
....

C. ....
....

真实生活汉语 2
Chinese for Living in China

Listening Comprehension

1. Listen to the dialogue and then answer the questions

   (1) Why did the man want to get a haircut?

   (2) Where is the barbershop located?

   (3) When does the barbershop open?

   (4) Why did the woman go to the barbershop as well?

   (5) Did the hairdresser change the man's hairstyle?

   (6) Did the man use shampoo at all?

   (7) How much did the man pay altogether?

   (8) How much did the woman pay altogether?

   (9) Did the woman have to pay for her facial massage?

New Words

这么 zhème Pron this way, so

摩丝 mósī N mousse

2. Listen to the dialogue and then answer the questions

   (1) What kind of services did the woman get?

   (2) When is the busiest time of the day according to the hairdresser?

   (3) How many inches did the woman originally want taken off her hair?

   (4) How much did the hairdresser actually cut off? How come?

   (5) How did the woman like her new haircut?

   (6) What color did the woman choose to dye her hair?

   (7) Why did the woman choose to use American haircolor?

   (8) How much did the hairdresser charge the woman?

   (9) How much money did the woman try to give to the hairdresser?

   (10) Why didn't the hairdresser accept it?

New Words

忙 máng Adj busy

通常 tōngcháng Adv usually

牌子 páizi N brand, trademark

Lesson Fourteen　Getting a Haircut

第十四课　理 发

Communication Activities

Pair Work

Scenario I: Have a conversation with your partner incorporating Chinese versions of the following expressions:

(1) a hair dryer
(2) head and back massage
(3) change the hair style
(4) blow dry (my hair) a little bit
(5) cut (my hair) a bit shorter
(6) shave (face)
(7) a roll of toilet paper
(8) a bottle of imported shampoo
(9) use the hair clippers to trim clean my neck
(10) a domestic hair dye

Scenario II: Ask the following questions in Chinese, and answer incorporating the items given in parenthesis:

(1) How often do you have a haircut?　(多长时间 duō cháng shíjiān, 一次 yí cì)
(2) Have you been to a hair salon since you came to China?　(V + 过 guo)
(3) What kind of hair-style did you get?　(什么样的发型 shénme yàng de fàxíng)
(4) Do you find Chinese hairdressers like American, or not?　(A 跟 gēn B (不 bù) 一样 yíyàng)
(5) What did you have in addition to a haircut?

　　(剪发 jiǎn fà, 理发 lǐ fà, 烫发 tàng fà, 染发 rǎn fà, 刮胡子 guā húzi, 修面 xiū miàn,
　　吹风 chuī fēng, 按摩 ànmó, 头部 tóubù, 背部 bèibù)

(6) How much did you pay for these services?
(7) What kind of products did your hairdresser use?

　　(进口的 jìnkǒu de, 国产的 guóchǎn de, 洗发剂 xǐfàjì, 染发剂 rǎnfàjì)

(8) Did you tip your hairdresser?
(9) How did you like your hairdresser?

Scenario III: Compare the services in Chinese hair salons with those of barbers and hairdressers in your home town. Use the following words:

预约 yùyuē	等很久 děng hěn jiǔ	慢 màn	免费 miǎnfèi	洗头 xǐ tóu
吹风 chuī fēng	发油 fàyóu	镜子 jìngzi	按摩 ànmó	修面 xiū miàn
刮胡子 guā húzi	进口的 jìnkǒu de	国产的 guóchǎn de	小费 xiǎofèi	

真实生活汉语 2
Chinese for Living in China

Role-Play

Scenario I: At the hair salon. One of you is a customer at the hair salon, the other is the barber or hairdresser. As customer, you want a haircut (with no change of style), a shampoo and blow dry. The hairdresser offers a free head and back massage.

剪短一点儿	发型	洗头	吹风
jiǎn duǎn yìdiǎnr	fàxíng	xǐ tóu	chuī fēng
按摩	背部	免费	
ànmó	bèibù	miǎnfèi	

Scenario II: Getting a haircut in China. You're both overseas students in Beijing, but one of you has been there for a year, the other has just arrived. The older student advises the recent arrival on the art of getting your haircut at a salon. Be guided by the following word list:

剪发	理发	烫发	染发	刮胡子
jiǎn fà	lǐ fà	tàng fà	rǎn fà	guā húzi
修面	吹风	按摩	头部	背部
xiū miàn	chuīfēng	ànmó	tóubù	bèibù
等很久	慢	免费	洗头	吹风
děng hěn jiǔ	màn	miǎnfèi	xǐ tóu	chuī fēng
发油	进口的	国产的	小费	（不）一样
fàyóu	jìnkǒu de	guóchǎn de	xiǎofèi	(bù) yíyàng

Group Activities

You're at a hair salon. Four of you are customers waiting for services – hair cut, shampoo, etc. A fifth is at the front desk with the job of finding out what each person wants and then directing them to a barber/hairdresser and a seat. Use the following vocabulary:

不用	很久	等	师傅	专业染发师
búyòng	hěn jiǔ	děng	shīfu	zhuānyè rǎnfàshī
这边坐	按摩	头部	背部	
zhèbian zuò	ànmó	tóubù	bèibù	
收费	进口的	国产的	（不）一样	
shōu fèi	jìnkǒu de	guóchǎn de	(bù) yíyàng	

第十四课　理 发
Lesson Fourteen　Getting a Haircut

Review Exercises

1. Fill in the blanks with "过 guo" or "着 zhe"

(1) 我去（　　　）北京大学一次，知道怎么走。
　　Wǒ qù (　　　) Běijīng Dàxué yí cì, zhīdào zěnme zǒu.

(2) 他今天没课，在家看（　　　）电视休息呢。
　　Tā jīntiān méi kè, zài jiā kàn (　　　) diànshì xiūxi ne.

(3) 那个外教学（　　　）中文，所以听得懂我们的话。
　　Nàge wàijiāo xué (　　　) Zhōngwén, suǒyǐ tīng de dǒng wǒmen de huà.

(4) 现在才八点，超市还开（　　　）门呢！
　　Xiànzài cái bā diǎn, chāoshì hái kāi (　　　) mén ne!

(5) 昨天因为天太热，所以他开（　　　）空调睡觉。
　　Zuótiān yīnwèi tiān tài rè, suǒyǐ tā kāi (　　　) kōngtiáo shuìjiào.

(6) A: 你去（　　　）校园西边那个理发店吗？
　　　Nǐ qù (　　　) xiàoyuán xībian nàge lǐfàdiàn ma?

　　B: 去（　　　），可是我没有理发。
　　　Qù (　　　), kěshì wǒ méiyǒu lǐ fà.

　　A: 为什么？
　　　Wèi shénme?

　　B: 因为我那天去的时候理发店快关门了，还有三个人在那儿等（　　　）呢。
　　　Yīnwèi wǒ nàtiān qù de shíhou lǐfàdiàn kuài guān mén le, hái yǒu sān ge rén zài nàr děng (　　　) ne.

(7) A: 你做（　　　）家教吗？
　　　Nǐ zuò (　　　) jiājiào ma?

　　B: 做（　　　），可是我现在不做了。
　　　Zuò (　　　), kěshì wǒ xiànzài bú zuò le.

　　A: 为什么？是因为钱少吗？
　　　Wèi shéme? Shì yīnwèi qián shǎo ma?

　　B: 钱挺多的，可是我太忙了，常常没有时间做作业。有时候，我等（　　　）汽车看课文。
　　　Qián tǐng duō de, kěshì wǒ tài máng le, chángcháng méiyǒu shíjiān zuò zuòyè. Yǒu shíhou, wǒ děng (　　　) qìchē kàn kèwén.

(8) A: 你来中国以后去看（　　　）电影吗？
　　　Nǐ lái Zhōngguó yǐhòu qù kàn (　　　) diànyǐng ma?

真实生活汉语 2
Chinese for Living in China

B: 看（　　　），可是我没看完就出来了。
　　Kàn (　　　), kěshì wǒ méi kànwán jiù chūlai le.

A: 为什么？是因为看不懂吗？
　　Wèi shénme? Shì yīnwèi kàn bu dǒng ma?

B: 一是因为看不懂，二是因为我前边的人看（　　　）电影聊天儿。
　　Yī shì yīnwèi kàn bu dǒng, èr shì yīnwèi wǒ qiánbian de rén kàn (　　　) diànyǐng liáo tiānr.

2. Comment on the differences, using "A 跟 gēn B (不 bù) 一样 yíyàng (Adj)"

   Example: 剪长发十五元，剪短发只要八元。→ 剪长发跟剪短发不一样。
   　　　　　Jiǎn chángfà shíwǔ yuán, jiǎn duǎnfà zhǐ yào bā yuán.

   (1) 进口的染发剂 128 块钱，国产的 88 块钱。→ _____
   　　Jìnkǒu de rǎnfàjì yìbǎi èrshíbā kuài qián, guóchǎn de bāshíbā kuài qián.

   (2) 去教室用十分钟，去学生宿舍也用十分钟。→ _____
   　　Qù jiàoshì yòng shí fēnzhōng, qù xuéshēng sùshè yě yòng shí fēnzhōng.

   (3) 坐空调大巴花五块钱，坐出租车花二十块钱。→ _____
   　　Zuò kōngtiáo dàbā huā wǔ kuài qián, zuò chūzūchē huā èrshí kuài qián.

   (4) 你的发型 / 你朋友的发型 → _____
   　　nǐ de fàxíng / nǐ péngyou de fàxíng

   (5) 中国理发店的服务 / 美国理发店的服务 → _____
   　　Zhōngguó lǐfàdiàn de fúwù / Měiguó lǐfàdiàn de fúwù

   (6) 中国大学的校历 (school calendar) / 美国大学的校历 → _____
   　　Zhōngguó dàxué de xiàolì / Měiguó dàxué de xiàolì

   (7) 中国大学生的宿舍 / 美国大学生的宿舍 → _____
   　　Zhōngguó dàxuéshēng de sùshè / Měiguó dàxuéshēng de sùshè

3. Fill the blanks with resultative complements "掉 diào" or "成 chéng"

   (1) 小王，请帮我把这封信翻译（　　　）英文。
   　　Xiǎo Wáng, qǐng bāng wǒ bǎ zhè fēng xìn fānyì (　　　) Yīngwén.

   (2) 你前边的头发太长了，剪（　　　）一点儿吧。
   　　Nǐ qiánbian de tóufa tài cháng le, jiǎn (　　　) yìdiǎnr ba.

   (3) 我觉得这学期的文学课有点儿难，打算换（　　　）口语课。
   　　Wǒ juéde zhè xuéqī de wénxuékè yǒudiǎnr nán, dǎsuàn huàn (　　　) kǒuyǔkè.

   (4) 我们两个人要了四个菜，太多了，去（　　　）一个吧！
   　　Wǒmen liǎng ge rén yàole sì ge cài, tài duō le, qù (　　　) yí ge ba!

   (5) 服务员，我的床单太脏 (dirty) 了，请换（　　　）吧，谢谢！
   　　Fúwùyuán, wǒ de chuángdān tài zāng le, qǐng huàn (　　　) ba, xièxie!

第十四课 理发
Lesson Fourteen   Getting a Haircut

(6) 你下学期要做家教，又选了四门课，太忙了。我建议你去（　　　）一门课。
Nǐ xià xuéqī yào zuò jiājiào, yòu xuǎnle sì mén kè, tài máng le. Wǒ jiànyì nǐ qù (　　　) yì mén kè.

4. In a hair salon, request the following services from your barber/hairdresser

   (1) You need your hair cut about an inch shorter, plus a shampoo followed by a blow-dry.

   ....

   (2) You need your beard shaved off. Or you need your hair dyed – same color.

   ....

   (3) Find out what kinds of shampoo are used – and which one the stylist thinks is best for you; say you'll try the local one this time.

   ....

   (4) Ask if a head and back massage is free.

   ....

   (5) Ask your barber if he can use the hair clippers to trim the back of your neck. Or ask to take a look in the mirror.

   ....

   (6) You'd like a little oil on your hair. Or you'd like the back trimmed just a little shorter.

   ....

5. You have been living in China for a couple of months now and you've just visited a hair salon for the first time. Write an entry in your Chinese diary about your experience, describing what you saw and what you felt about the place. Incorporate at least 12 of the items in the following list:

预约 yùyuē	等很久 děng hěn jiǔ	慢 màn	免费 miǎnfèi	洗头 xǐ tóu
吹风 chuī fēng	发油 fàyóu	镜子 jìngzi	按摩 ànmó	刮脸 guā liǎn
头部 tóubù	刮胡子 guā húzi	进口的 jìnkǒu de	国产的 guóchǎn de	小费 xiǎofèi
剪发 jiǎn fà	理发 lǐ fà	烫发 tàng fà	染发 rǎn fà	修面 xiū miàn
背部 bèibù	A 跟 B (不)一样 (Adj) A gēn B bù yíyàng (Adj)	V 着 V zhe	V 成 V chéng	V 掉 V diào

Culture Notes

1. Shampooing

Shampooing is standard in Chinese hairdressers and barbershops, for both women and men. Those who don't want the regular shampoo can ask for a gentler one.

2. Massage

Chinese hairdressers, in addition to washing, cutting and styling hair, usually also provide massage of the head, upper back, and shoulders. Sometimes it is free and sometimes there is an additional charge.

Lesson Fifteen   Shopping for Clothes

第十五课   买衣服
Dì-shíwǔ Kè   Mǎi Yīfu

In this lesson you will learn how to do the following
- Find out what sort of clothes are appropriate for particular occasions
- Find out where to buy clothes
- Talk about size and color
- Compare items
- Request slightly different sizes or colors
- Bargain

Grammar
- The position of question words
- More examples of the adverb "就 jiù"
- Coordinate verb phrases
- Questions with "多 duō"
- Comparison: "比 bǐ" and "没有 méiyǒu" patterns
- "还可以 hái kěyǐ" as an expression of acceptance

Culture Notes
- Weights and measures: Length and distance
- Height
- Converting metric to non-metric
- International shoe sizes
- Receipts: "小票 xiǎopiào"

真实生活汉语
Chinese for Living in China 2

Dialogue

A：简妮，外教
　　Jiǎnnī, wàijiào

B：查理，外教
　　Chálǐ, wàijiào

C：黄老师，联络老师
　　Huáng lǎoshī, liánluò lǎoshī

D：商场服务员
　　shāngchǎng fúwùyuán

　　简妮和查理一起到上海一所九年制的学校教英语。简妮教小学，查理教初中。今天联络老师通知他们[1]：9月10号是教师节；市教育局的领导请全市的外教聚餐；那天他们应该穿得正式些。他们没想到会在中国遇上这样的场合，没有从美国带正式的服装来，所以决定今天赶快去买。他们先向[2]黄老师打听该买些什么衣服。

　　Jiǎnnī hé Chálǐ yìqǐ dào Shànghǎi yì suǒ jiǔniánzhì de xuéxiào jiāo Yīngyǔ. Jiǎnnī jiāo xiǎoxué, Chálǐ jiāo chūzhōng. Jīntiān liánluò lǎoshī tōngzhī tāmen[1]: Jiǔyuè shí hào shì Jiàoshī Jié; Shì Jiàoyùjú de lǐngdǎo qǐng quánshì de wàijiào jù cān; Nà tiān tāmen yīnggāi chuān de zhèngshì xiē. Tāmen méi xiǎngdào huì zài Zhōngguó yùshang zhèyàng de chǎnghé, méiyǒu cóng Měiguó dài zhèngshì de fúzhuāng lái, suǒyǐ juédìng jīntiān gǎnkuài qù mǎi. Tāmen xiān xiàng[2] Huáng lǎoshī dǎting gāi mǎi xiē shénme yīfu.

A：黄老师，女士穿什么[G1]算是比较正式的？
　　Huáng lǎoshī, nǚshì chuān shénme[G1] suàn shì bǐjiào zhèngshì de?

B：还有男士应该怎么穿才算正式？我看[3]校长平时都穿翻领的T恤衫，那是不是正装？
　　Háiyǒu nánshì yīnggāi zěnme chuān cái suàn zhèngshì? Wǒ kàn[3] xiàozhǎng píngshí dōu chuān fānlǐng de T xù shān, nà shì bu shì zhèngzhuāng?

Notes

1. "他们 tāmen": It was only relatively recently that a gender distinction was created in the written forms of the third person pronouns, "tā" and "tāmen". In Giles' Chinese-English Dictionary, for example, first published in 1892, "他" is glossed as "he, she, it". It was only later, on the model of English and other European languages, that modified characters were created for male and female and "it": "他", "她" and "它" (all pronounced "tā" still). The plural forms "他们" and "她们", refer to groups of males or mixed groups, and to all female groups, respectively. The fact that even Chinese who otherwise speak English with great fluency often fail to distinguish "he" and "she" in speech (where there is less time to monitor) reflects the relative primacy of the spoken language.

2. "向 xiàng" can be a verb with the meaning of "to face (a direction)": "向南 xiàng nán" (it faces south). More commonly, it is used as a preposition forming a phrase before an associated verb: "向前看 xiàng qián kàn" (to look ahead). As a preposition, it is also associated with verbs such as "打听 dǎting" (to inquire of) to mark the person to whom the action is directed (i.e. an extension of the "towards" meaning): "向她打听 xiàng tā dǎting" (to ask her, to inquire of her).

3. "我看 wǒ kàn", literally "I see", but in this context, the sense is "as I see it, in my opinion".

第十五课　买衣服
Lesson Fifteen　Shopping for Clothes

C：不是。老师和校领导们平时上班穿得干净整洁就[G2]可以了，不用穿正装。但出席宴会，男士最好穿西服，打领带，穿皮鞋[G3]。女士最好穿裙子或套装，不要穿短袜。
Bú shì. Lǎoshī hé xiàolǐngdǎomen píngshí shàng bān chuān de gānjìng zhěngjié jiù[G2] kěyi le, búyòng chuān zhèngzhuāng. Dàn chūxí yànhuì, nánshì zuìhǎo chuān xīfú, dǎ lǐngdài, chuān píxié[G3]. Nǔshì zuìhǎo chuān qúnzi huò tàozhuāng, bú yào chuān duǎnwà.

A：谢谢您。我们应该去哪儿买这样的衣服？
Xièxie nín. Wǒmen yīnggāi qù nǎr mǎi zhèyàng de yīfu?

C：大商场和购物中心都可以。如果你们要买名牌，还有很多名牌服装专卖店。
Dà shāngchǎng hé gòuwù zhōngxīn dōu kěyǐ. Rúguǒ nǐmen yào mǎi míngpái, hái yǒu hěn duō míngpái fúzhuāng zhuānmàidiàn.

B：谢谢。那我们先去附近的大商场看看。
Xièxie. Nà wǒmen xiān qù fùjìn de dà shāngchǎng kànkan.

（在商场 Zài shāngchǎng）

D：您好，您要买什么？
Nín hǎo, nín yào mǎi shénme?

B：我要买一套[4]西服和一件衬衫。
Wǒ yào mǎi yí tào[4] xīfú hé yí jiàn chènshān.

D：您穿多[G4]大号的？
Nín chuān duō[G4] dà hào de?

B：中号的。
Zhōnghào de.

D：这套西服怎么样？
Zhè tào xīfú zěnmeyàng?

B：我想要深灰色的，你们有没有？
Wǒ xiǎng yào shēnhuīsè de, nǐmen yǒu méiyǒu?

---

4. Four measure words are introduced in this lesson. "套 tào" is used for sets or collections of things: "一套房间 yí tào fángjiān" (a suite of rooms); "两套西服 liǎng tào xīfú" (two suits). "件 jiàn" is a measure for a disparate group of things, including suitcases, items of business and items of clothing: "一件衬衫 yí jiàn chènshān" (a shirt). "条 tiáo" is a measure for rivers, roads, and various other long, narrow, non-rigid things, including trousers: "两条裤子 liǎng tiáo kùzi" (two pairs of trousers). Pairs of things are measured with "双 shuāng": "一双鞋(子) yì shuāng xié(zi)" (a pair of shoes); "一双筷子 yì shuāng kuàizi" (a pair of chopsticks). "双 shuāng" also functions as a modifier meaning "double", as in expressions such as "双人间 shuāngrénjiān" (double room).

D： 有。您试试这套怎么样？
Yǒu. Nín shìshi zhè tào zěnmeyàng?

B： 西装外套很合适，就是裤子太长了，也有点儿肥。有没有瘦点儿的？
Xīzhuāng wàitào hěn héshì, jiùshì kùzi tài cháng le, yě yǒu diǎnr féi. Yǒu méiyǒu shòu diǎnr de?

D： 您试试这条长裤。这条比^{G5}那条瘦，也没有那条长^{G5}。
Nín shìshi zhè tiáo chángkù. Zhè tiáo bǐ^{G5} nà tiáo shòu, yě méiyǒu nà tiáo cháng^{G5}.

B： 好，很合适。我就^{G2}买这套吧。
Hǎo, hěn héshì. Wǒ jiù^{G2} mǎi zhè tào ba.

D： 这件衬衫怎么样？
Zhè jiàn chènshān zěnmeyàng?

B： 衬衫大小还可以^{G6}，可是这颜色跟西服不配。我觉得浅蓝色的更配。
Chènshān dàxiǎo hái kěyǐ^{G6}, kěshì zhè yánsè gēn xīfú bú pèi. Wǒ juéde qiǎnlánsè de gèng pèi.

D： 蓝色的在这边，您挑一下儿。
Lánsè de zài zhèbian, nín tiāo yíxiàr.

B： 好，我就要这件。简妮，你挑好了吗？
Hǎo, wǒ jiù yào zhè jiàn. Jiǎnnī, nǐ tiāohǎo le ma?

A： 我有裙子，买双鞋就可以了。服务员，我可以试试这双鞋吗？
Wǒ yǒu qúnzi, mǎi shuāng xié jiù kěyǐ le. Fúwùyuán, wǒ kěyǐ shìshi zhè shuāng xié ma?

D： 可以。
Kěyǐ.

A： 这双太紧了。有没有大点儿的？
Zhè shuāng tài jǐn le. Yǒu méiyǒu dà diǎnr de?

D： 您穿几号的鞋？
Nín chuān jǐ hào de xié?

A： 我穿三十九号半的。可是这双我穿不下。
Wǒ chuān sānshíjiǔ hào bàn de. Kěshì zhè shuāng wǒ chuān bu xià.

D： 这双是四十号的，您试试。
Zhè shuāng shì sìshí hào de, nín shìshi.

A： 很合适，能便宜点儿吗？
Hěn héshì, néng piányi diǎnr ma?

D： 原价六百八，今天打七折，四百七十六。
Yuánjià liùbǎi bā, jīntiān dǎ qīzhé, sìbǎi qīshí liù.

第十五课 买衣服
Lesson Fifteen Shopping for Clothes

A：好，在哪儿付钱？
　　Hǎo, zài nǎr fù qián?

D：收款台在那边。
　　Shōukuǎntái zài nàbian.

A：谢谢。查理，你不买双皮鞋吗？
　　Xièxie. Chálǐ, nǐ bù mǎi shuāng píxié ma?

B：我有皮鞋，不买了。我们去付款吧。
　　Wǒ yǒu píxié, bù mǎi le. Wǒmen qù fù kuǎn ba.

New Words

1	联络/聯絡	liánluò	V/N	to make contact with, to contact; liaison ("联络老师 liánluò lǎoshī", contact teacher)
2	售货员/售貨員	shòuhuòyuán	N	sales clerk, shop assistant, salesperson
3	九年制	jiǔniánzhì	N	grades 1-9
4	小学/小學	xiǎoxué	N	elementary school, primary school, elementary education
5	初中	chūzhōng	N	junior secondary school, junior middle school
6	通知	tōngzhī	V/N	to notify, to inform; a note, notice, circular
7	他们/他們	tāmen	Pron	they, them
8	教师节/教師節	Jiàoshī Jié	PropN	Teachers' Day (10 September)
9	市	shì	N	city, municipality, market, marketplace
10	教育局	jiàoyùjú	N	education bureau
11	领导/領導	lǐngdǎo	N/V	leader, boss; to lead
12	全市	quán shì	Phrase	the entire city, city-wide
13	聚餐	jù cān	VO	to get together for a meal, to dine together (e.g. a work unit or school on a festive occasion)
14	穿	chuān	V	to wear, to put on (clothing), to pass through
15	正式	zhèngshì	Adj	formal, official
16	没想到	méi xiǎngdào	Phrase	not to have expected, not have thought
17	遇上	yùshang	V-DirC	to encounter, to meet with, to happen upon
	遇	yù	V	to meet, to encounter
18	场合/場合	chǎnghé	N	occasion, situation

真实生活汉语
Chinese for Living in China 2

19	带/帶	dài	V	to carry, to bring or take
20	服装/服裝	fúzhuāng	N	clothing, costume, dress, apparel
21	决定	juédìng	V/N	to decide, to make up one's mind; decision
22	赶快/趕快	gǎnkuài	Adv	quickly
23	向	xiàng	V/Prep	to face towards; towards, to
24	打听/打聽	dǎting	V	to make inquiries, to ask about
25	男士	nánshì	N	man, gentleman (often facetious)
26	校长/校長	xiàozhǎng	N	principal, headmaster of a K-12 school president or chancellor of a college
27	翻领/翻領	fānlǐng	N	turndown collar
28	T恤衫	T xù shān	N	T-shirt, (Guangzhou) shirt
29	正装/正裝	zhèngzhuāng	N	formal attire
30	校领导/校領導	xiàolǐngdǎo	N	leader(s) of a school
	校	xiào	N	school
31	整洁/整潔	zhěngjié	Adj	tidy, neat and clean
32	出席	chūxí	V	to attend, to be present (at a meeting, etc.)
33	宴会/宴會	yànhuì	N	banquet, dinner party
34	西服	xīfú	N	suit, Western-style clothing
35	打领带/打領帶	dǎ lǐngdài	V	to hit, to strike, to make, to tie (a tie), to take (a taxi), etc.
36	领带/領帶	lǐngdài	N	tie, necktie
37	皮鞋	píxié	N	leather shoes
38	裙子	qúnzi	N	skirt, dress
39	套装/套裝	tàozhuāng	N	suit (for woman), coverall (garment for upper and lower body)
40	短袜/短襪	duǎnwà	N	(short) socks (in contrast to stockings)
41	商场/商場	shāngchǎng	N	department store, the business world
42	购物中心/購物中心	gòuwù zhōngxīn	Phrase	shopping mall, shopping center
	购物/購物	gòu wù	Phrase	to buy goods, things
	中心	zhōngxīn	N	center

第十五课 买衣服
Lesson Fifteen　Shopping for Clothes

43	名牌	míngpái	N	name brand
44	专卖店/專賣店	zhuānmàidiàn	N	specialty store
45	套	tào	Meas	*for sets of things or collections, e.g. an apartment suite or a suit of clothes*
46	件	jiàn	Meas	*for clothing, luggage, items of furniture, documents*
47	衬衫/襯衫	chènshān	N	shirt
48	多大号/多大號	duō dà hào	Phrase	what size (of clothing, etc.)
	多大	duō dà	Phrase	how old, how big (question or exclamation)
	号/號	hào	N	number (of house), size (of clothing)
49	中号/中號	zhōnghào	N	medium-size (cf. "大号 dàhào", large size; "小号 xiǎohào", small size)
50	深灰色	shēnhuīsè	N	dark gray color
	深灰	shēnhuī	Adj	dark gray
	色	sè	BF	color
51	西装/西裝	xīzhuāng	N	suit, Western-style clothing
52	外套	wàitào	N	overcoat, outer garment
53	合适/合適	héshì	Adj	suitable, fitting
54	裤子/褲子	kùzi	N	pants, trousers
55	肥	féi	Adj	loose (of clothing); fat, greasy
56	长裤/長褲	chángkù	N	long pants, trousers
57	比	bǐ	V/Prep	to compare; than
58	大小	dàxiǎo	N	size
59	还可以/還可以	hái kěyǐ	Phrase	(colloquial) to be OK, not bad, so-so
60	不配	búpèi	Adj	ill-matched, not fit
	配	pèi	Adj	well-matched, fit
61	觉得/覺得	juéde	V	to feel (tired, etc.), to think, to believe
62	浅蓝色/淺藍色	qiǎnlánsè	N	light blue (color)
63	双/雙	shuāng	Meas/Attr	*for pairs*; double, even (number)
64	鞋	xié	N	shoes
65	紧/緊	jǐn	Adj	tight, urgent, pressing, in short supply

真实生活汉语
Chinese for Living in China 2

66	原价/原價	yuánjià	N	original price, original value
67	打折	dǎ zhé	VO	to give a discount
68	付钱/付錢	fù qián	Phrase	to pay, to make a payment
69	收款台/收款臺	shōukuǎntái	N	cashier's booth, counter
	收款	shōu kuǎn	Phrase	to make collections
	台/臺	tái	N	platform, counter, (broadcasting) station

Re-enacting the Dialogue

A: Jennie, a foreign teacher **B: Charlie, a foreign teacher**
C: Huang laoshi, a school contact teacher **D: a salesclerk**

Jenny and Charley teach English at a "Grade 1-9 school" in Shenzhen. Jenny is teaching at the elementary school, Charley is at the middle school. Today, the contact teacher notified them that the 10th of September is Teacher's Day. The head of the municipal Education Bureau would be inviting all the foreign teachers in town for a dinner gathering. They should dress up a bit on the day. Now they hadn't expected to run into such an event in China and hadn't brought any formal clothes with them from the US. So today, they have decided to go and buy some right away. First, they asked Huang laoshi what sort of clothes they should buy.

A: Huang laoshi, what sort of clothes count as formal for females?

B: And what sort of clothes count as formal for males? I see the principal generally wears "golf shirts" – is that formal wear?

C: No, the teachers and the principal generally wear something clean and neat when they are at work and that's fine, they don't have to wear formal clothes. But at a banquet, it's best for men to wear suits, ties and leather shoes. Women should wear skirts or suits, and shouldn't wear socks.

A: Thanks. Where should we go to buy clothes like that?

B: Malls or shopping centers are fine. If you want to buy brand names, there are also lots of specialty stores that sell brand name clothing.

C: Thanks. In that case, first we'll go and take a look at the local mall.

(In the mall)

D: How do you do? What would you like to buy?

B: I'd like to buy a suit and a dress shirt.

D: What's your size?

B: I'm medium.

D: How's this suit?

B: I'd like one in a dark grey color – do you have one?

Lesson Fifteen   Shopping for Clothes

D: We do. Why don't you try this one on?

B: The suit jacket fits fine; but the trousers are long, and they're a bit loose. Do you have a smaller one?

D: Try these trousers on. These are narrower than those, and not as long.

B: Good, they fit well. I'll take this suit.

D: How do you like this shirt?

B: The size of the shirt's fine, but the color doesn't match the suit. I think a light blue would match better.

D: The blue ones are here – your choice.

B: OK, I'll have this one. Jennie, have you made a selection?

A: I have a dress, now all I need is a pair of shoes. Clerk, can I try on this pair?

D: Sure.

A: They're too tight. Do you have some that are a bit bigger?

D: What size shoe do you wear?

A: I wear a 39 1/2. But I can't get this pair on.

D: These are size 40 – please try them.

A: They fit fine; can you lower the price?

D: The original price was ￥680. They are 30% off today, ￥476.

A: OK. Where do we pay?

D: The cashier's booth is over there.

A: Thanks. Charlie, aren't you going to buy a pair of dress shoes?

B: No, I'm not – I have dress shoes. Let's go and pay.

Grammar

▶ G1. The position of question words

The major types of questions have by now almost all been introduced: yes-no questions, with "吗 ma"; content questions, with "什么 shénme", "多少 duōshao", "几 jǐ", "多 duō" (see also G4 below), "怎么 zěnme", "哪儿 nǎr" or "哪里 nǎli", "谁 shéi/shuí", "多久 duō jiǔ", etc., and "or" questions with "还是 háishi" (Lesson 12, G3).

It is worth reiterating that for the first two types, Chinese word order differs radically from that of English. In English, such questions involve adding material (such as "do"), and reordering: "She knows" > "Does she know?"; "She speaks Chinese" > "What does she speak?" Most notably, in normal content questions, question words come at the head of the sentence. Chinese has none of this. In Chinese, the form of the question is parallel to the form of the answer. Question words occupy the same position as the answer to be supplied. Compare the English translations with the Chinese in the following questions and answers:

① 女士穿什么算是比较正式的？（女士穿裙子算是比较正式的。）
Nǚshì chuān shénme suàn shì bǐjiào zhèngshì de?
(Nǚshēng chuān qúnzi suàn shì bǐjiào zhèngshì de.)
What sort of clothes count as formal for females?

② 我们应该去哪儿买这样的衣服？（我们应该去商场买这样的衣服。）
Wǒmen yīnggāi qù nǎr mǎi zhèyàng de yīfu?
(Wǒmen yīnggāi qù shāngchǎng mǎi zhèyàng de yīfu.)
Where should we go to buy clothes like that?

③ 这套西服怎么样？（这套西服很合适。）
Zhè tào xīfú zěnmeyàng? (Zhè tào xīfú hěn héshì.)
How's this suit?

▶ G2. More examples of the adverb "就 jiù"

This lesson also contains additional usages of the common adverb, "就 jiù" (cf. Lesson 12, G5). In one usage, "就 jiù" introduces a new state of affairs that comes into effect (hence "了 le") when prior conditions are met: "就好了 jiù hǎo le" (then it'll be fine, it's fine, etc.); "就可以了 jiù kěyǐ le" (then it'll be OK); "就好吃了 jiù hǎochī le" (then it'll taste good); "就不累了 jiù bú lèi le" (then I won't be tired anymore).

① 老师和校领导们平时上班穿得干净整洁就可以了。
Lǎoshī hé xiào lǐngdǎomen píngshí shàngbān chuān de gānjìng zhěngjié jiù kěyǐ le.
The teachers and the principal generally wear something that is clean and neat when they are at work and that's fine.

② 我有裙子，买双鞋就可以了。 I have a skirt; now all I need is a pair of shoes.
Wǒ yǒu qúnzi, mǎi shuāng xié jiù kěyǐ le.

In a slight variation on the same theme, "就 jiù" underscores a final decision (cf. English "so" in the first translation).

Lesson Fifteen Shopping for Clothes

第十五课　买衣服

③ 我就要这件。　So I'll take this one.
　　Wǒ jiù yào zhèi jiàn.

④ 很合适，我就买这条吧。　It fits fine, I'll take this pair, then.
　　Hěn héshì, wǒ jiù mǎi zhè tiáo ba.

▶ G3. Coordinate verb phrases

In Lesson 4 (G2), you were introduced to verbs in series: "我去商店买东西 Wǒ qù shāngdiàn mǎi dōngxi" (I'm going to the store to do some shopping). The two verb phrases ("去商店 qù shāngdiàn" and "买东西 mǎi dōngxi") appear in an order that corresponds to the sequence of events. Reversing the order of the phrases would signify a reverse order, buying then going – not very likely. This lesson has another type of example of multiple verb phrases forming a predicate:

出席宴会，男士最好穿西服，打领带，穿皮鞋。
Chūxí yànhuì, nánshì zuìhǎo chuān xīfú, dǎ lǐngdài, chuān píxié.
At a banquet, it's best for men to wear suits, ties, and leather shoes.

But this is not a case of verbs in series. The events are not in sequence. They are simply coordinate. They could be reordered without significant change in meaning. Notice that just as Chinese forgoes words like "to" and "for" in verbs in series, it also does without explicit conjunctions (such as "and") to conjoin verbs.

▶ G4. Questions with "多 duō"

"多 duō", in addition to its adjectival sense of "many" and "much", can occur as a question word, meaning "to what degree" (cf. the phrase "多远 duō yuǎn"—"how far" in Lesson 6). This is its function in the question phrase for duration: "多长时间 duō cháng shíjiān" (how much time, how long). As a question word, it usually only appears before a monosyllabic adjective (多长 duō cháng).

① 您穿多大号的衬衫？　What size shirt do you wear?
　　Nín chuān duō dà hào de chènshān?

② 您穿多大的鞋？　What size shoes do you wear?
　　Nín chuān duō dà de xié?

③ 理发要等多长时间？　How long is the wait for a haircut?
　　Lǐfà yào děng duō cháng shíjiān?

④ 这条裤子多长？　How long are these pants?
　　Zhè tiáo kùzi duō cháng?

▶ G5. Comparison: "比 bǐ" and "没有 méiyǒu" patterns

The preposition "比 bǐ" (than) introduces a comparison. Like other prepositions in Chinese such as "在 zài", "给 gěi" and "跟 gēn", "比 bǐ" appears with an object (e.g., "比我 bǐ wǒ") before the associated verb: "比昨天热 bǐ zuótiān rè" (warmer than yesterday). By contrast, "than phrases" in English appear after the adjective: "warmer than". Here are some examples:

① 她比我高一点儿。 She's a little taller than I am.
　　Tā bǐ wǒ gāo yìdiǎnr.

② 今天比昨天热。 It's hotter today than it was yesterday.
　　Jīntiān bǐ zuótiān rè.

③ 这条裤子比那条瘦。 This pair of trousers is tighter than that pair.
　　Zhè tiáo kùzi bǐ nà tiáo shòu.

"比 bǐ" can be negated: "她不比我高 Tā bù bǐ wǒ gāo" (It's not the case that she's taller than I am). But in ordinary discourse, it is more usual to say "not as", which in Chinese is expressed with "没有 méiyǒu":

④ 她没有我高。 She's not as tall as I am.
　　Tā méiyǒu wǒ gāo.

⑤ 昨天没有今天热。 Yesterday wasn't as hot as today.
　　Zuótiān méiyǒu jīntiān rè.

⑥ 那条没有这条瘦。 That pair isn't as tight as this pair.
　　Nà tiáo méiyǒu zhè tiáo shòu.

⑦ 拔牙没有补牙贵。 Having a tooth pulled isn't as expensive as having it filled.
　　Bá yá méiyǒu bǔ yá guì.

In formulaic terms, the two comparative patterns are:

A 比 bǐ B + Adj (+ 一点儿 yìdiǎnr, etc.).

⑧ 深蓝色的比浅蓝色的贵一点儿。
　　Shēnlánsè de bǐ qiǎnlánsè de guì yìdiǎnr.
　　The dark blue one is a bit more expensive than the light blue one.

A 没有 méiyǒu B + Adj

⑨ 这条裤子没有那条长。 This pair (of trousers) isn't as long as that pair.
　　Zhè tiáo kùzi méiyǒu nà tiáo cháng.

In some cases, comparison in Chinese is implicit: The question "谁高? Shéi gāo?" is comparative: "Who's taller?" The answer might be: "他高 Tā gāo." (He's taller). But adding "很 hěn" disallows the comparative reading: "他很高 Tā hěn gāo" (He's quite tall). Both comparatives and non-comparatives can be modified by "一点儿 yìdiǎnr" (a little, a bit). However, with comparatives, "一点儿 yìdiǎnr" follows the adjective: "高一点儿 gāo yìdiǎnr" (a bit taller). With non-comparatives, it precedes and requires the presence of "有 yǒu": "有(一)点高儿 yǒu (yì)diǎnr gāo" (be a rather tall).

⑩ 她高一点儿。 She's a bit taller.
　　Tā gāo yìdiǎnr.

⑪ 她有一点儿高。 She's rather (too) tall.
　　Tā yǒu yìdiǎnr gāo.

Lesson Fifteen　Shopping for Clothes

第十五课　买衣服

⑫ 有一点儿长。　It's a bit too long.
　　Yǒu yìdiǎnr cháng.

The presence of "too" in the English translation indicates that the second pattern, "有一点儿 yǒu yìdiǎnr + Adj", implies an unfavorable or slightly disparaging judgement.

▶ **G6.** "还可以 hái kěyǐ" as an expression of acceptance

The phrase, "还可以 hái kěyǐ", has acquired a conventional sense, rather like English "not bad" or "pretty good":

① A: 他的汉语说得怎么样？　How's his Chinese?
　　　Tā de Hànyǔ shuō de zěnmeyàng?

　　B: 还可以。　Not bad.
　　　Hái kěyǐ.

It is also common at the end of statements, expressing a not-too-enthusiastic acceptance:

② 衬衫大小还可以。　The shirt's about the right size.
　　Chènshān dàxiǎo hái kěyǐ.

Consolidation & Practice

I. Choose the appropriate position for question words such as "什么 shénme", "怎么 zěnme", "哪儿 nǎr", and "怎么样 zěnmeyàng" by filling in one of the blanks in the following sentences

(1) 周末外教聚会 _____ 我们穿 _____ 比较合适？　(什么 shénme)
　　Zhōumò wàijiào jùhuì _____ wǒmen chuān _____ bǐjiào héshì?

(2) 你说 _____ 我理 _____ 发型才好看 _____ ？　(什么 shénme)
　　Nǐ shuō _____ wǒ lǐ _____ fàxíng cái hǎokàn _____ ?

(3) _____ 我们应该去 _____ 买正式的服装 _____ ？　(哪儿 nǎr)
　　_____ wǒmen yīnggāi qù _____ mǎi zhèngshì de fúzhuāng _____ ?

(4) _____ 我们应该去 _____ 付款 _____ ？　(哪儿 nǎr)
　　_____ wǒmen yīnggāi qù _____ fù kuǎn _____ ?

(5) _____ 我们 _____ 要一个肉菜，两个素菜，_____ ？　(怎么样 zěnmeyàng)
　　_____ wǒmen _____ yào yí ge ròucài, liǎng ge sùcài, _____ ?

(6) _____ 你 _____ 没去上个星期的聚会 _____ ？　(怎么 zěnme)
　　_____ nǐ _____ méi qù shàng ge xīngqī de jùhuì _____ ?

(7) _____ 你觉得 _____ 我穿这条裙子 _____ ？　(怎么样 zěnmeyàng)
　　_____ nǐ juéde _____ wǒ chuān zhè tiáo qúnzi _____ ?

119

真实生活汉语
Chinese for Living in China 2

(8) _____ 你知道 _____ 打领带 _____ 吗？ (怎么 zěnme)
_____ nǐ zhīdào _____ dǎ lǐngdài _____ ma?

(9) 你染发想 _____ 染 _____ 颜色 _____ ？ (什么 shénme)
Nǐ rǎn fà xiǎng _____ rǎn _____ yánsè _____ ?

(10) _____ 你知道 _____ 卖西装外套 _____ 吗？ (哪儿 nǎr)
_____ nǐ zhīdào _____ mài xīzhuāng wàitào _____ ma?

2. Fill in the blanks, using the pattern "就可以了 jiù kěyǐ le", based on the English cues

   Example: 我有裙子，_____。
   Wǒ yǒu qúnzi, (I) just need to buy a pair of shoes

   → 我有裙子，买一双鞋就可以了。
   Wǒ yǒu qúnzi, mǎi yì shuāng xié jiù kěyǐ le.

(1) 我们明天晚上请客，_____。
   Wǒmen míngtiān wǎnshang qǐng kè, (we can go shopping tomorrow afternoon)

(2) 今天晚上的聚会不太正式，_____。
   Jīntiān wǎnshang de jùhuì bú tài zhèngshì, (if you wear a shirt that'll be fine)

(3) 我们两个人吃得都不多，_____。
   Wǒmen liǎng ge rén chī de dōu bù duō, (two dishes will be fine)

(4) 打的太贵了，我们_____。
   Dǎdī tài guì le, wǒmen (it'll be fine to take the subway)

(5) 师傅，我不要改变发型，稍微_____。
   Shīfu, wǒ bú yào gǎibiàn fàxíng, shāowēi (just shorten it a bit)

(6) 今天天气不太热，不用开空调，你_____。
   Jīntiān tiānqi bú tài rè, búyòng kāi kōngtiáo, nǐ (it'll do to open the window)

(7) 我也不知道退课的日期是几号，你_____。
   Wǒ yě bù zhīdào tuì kè de rìqī shì jǐ hào, nǐ (take a look at the school calendar, that should help)

(8) 你穿这条8号的裤子有点儿肥，_____。
   Nǐ chuān zhè tiáo bā hào de kùzi yǒudiǎnr féi, (size 7 would work for you)

3. In Chinese, ask the question, then answer with juxtaposed verb phrases

   Example: 男士最好穿西服，打领带，穿皮鞋。
   Nánshì zuìhǎo chuān xīfú, dǎ lǐngdài, chuān píxié.

(1) What do you need to do if you have a Chinese test tomorrow?
   我今天晚上得_____，_____，_____。
   Wǒ jīntiān wǎnshang děi _____, _____, _____.

第十五课　买衣服
Lesson Fifteen   Shopping for Clothes

(2) What do you need to do if you are inviting a couple of guests over for dinner tonight?

　　我今天得_____，_____，_____。
　　Wǒ jīntiān děi _____ , _____ , _____ .

(3) What do you need before going to bed at night?

　　我睡觉以前得_____，_____，_____。
　　Wǒ shuìjiào yǐqián děi _____ , _____ , _____ .

(4) What do you plan on doing this coming weekend?

　　我这个周末要_____，_____，_____。
　　Wǒ zhège zhōumò yào _____ , _____ , _____ .

(5) What do you have to do in order to be an English tutor?

　　我要_____，_____，_____。
　　Wǒ yào _____ , _____ , _____ .

4. Conduct interviews among yourselves to find out the information shown below, using the questions phrases "多大 duō dà", "多大号 duō dà hào", "多少 duōshao", "多远 duō yuǎn", "多长时间 duō cháng shíjiān", etc., and then report your findings to the class

　(1) The ages of brothers and sisters (if any), or of close friends.

　　…………………………………………………………………………………………………

　(2) Shoe sizes for each member of the family.

　　…………………………………………………………………………………………………

　(3) How much they paid for their computer, suitcase, suit and for last night's dinner.

　　…………………………………………………………………………………………………

　(4) How far away the supermarket/ morning market/ bank/ bus stop is from the dorm.

　　…………………………………………………………………………………………………

　(5) How long it takes to fly to Beijing from home.

　　…………………………………………………………………………………………………

　(6) How long it takes them to do their Chinese homework everyday.

　　…………………………………………………………………………………………………

　(7) How long it takes them to walk from the dorm to the classroom.

　　…………………………………………………………………………………………………

　(8) How long it takes for the mail from Beijing to their parents' house.

　　…………………………………………………………………………………………………

5. Make comparisons with "比 bǐ" or "没有 méiyǒu"

A 比 bǐ B + Adj

Example: 这件衬衫比那件大。 This shirt is bigger than that one.
Zhè jiàn chènshān bǐ nà jiàn dà.

(1) 灰颜色 / 蓝颜色 / 好看 → _____
    huī yánsè / lán yánsè / hǎokàn

(2) 摄像机 / 照相机 / 贵 → _____
    shèxiàngjī / zhàoxiàngjī / guì

(3) 电视 / 电脑 / 便宜 → _____
    diànshì / diànnǎo / piányi

(4) 教室 / 食堂 / 远 → _____
    jiàoshì / shítáng / yuǎn

(5) 这双鞋 / 那双鞋 / 紧 → _____
    zhè shuāng xié / nà shuāng xié / jǐn

(6) 这条裤子 / 那条裤子 / 短 → _____
    zhè tiáo kùzi / nà tiáo kùzi / duǎn

(7) 这个理发店 / 那个理发店 / 好 → _____
    zhège lǐfàdiàn / nàge lǐfàdiàn / hǎo

A 没有 méiyǒu B + Adj

Example: 国产的电脑没有进口的贵。
Guóchǎn de diànnǎo méiyǒu jìnkǒu de guì.
Domestically produced computers aren't as expensive as imported ones.

(1) 这双鞋 / 那双鞋 / 合适 → _____
    zhè shuāng xié / nà shuāng xié / héshì

(2) 衬衫 / T恤衫 / 舒服 → _____
    chènshān / T xù shān / shūfu

(3) 坐公共汽车 / 坐地铁 / 快 → _____
    zuò gōnggòng qìchē / zuò dìtiě / kuài

(4) 饭店的菜 / 早市的菜 / 便宜 → _____
    fàndiàn de cài / zǎoshì de cài / piányi

(5) 我的头发 / 你的头发 / 长 → _____
    wǒ de tóufa / nǐ de tóufa / cháng

(6) 穿裙子 / 穿裤子 / 正式 → _____
    chuān qúnzi / chuān kùzi / zhèngshì

(7) 历史课的作业 / 中文课的作业 / 多 → _____
    lìshǐkè de zuòyè / Zhōngwénkè de zuòyè / duō

第十五课 买衣服
Lesson Fifteen Shopping for Clothes

Listening Comprehension

1. Listen to the dialogue and then answer the questions

   (1) Where did the second man go last weekend?

   (2) Where was the shop?

   (3) What was the price?

   (4) What size?

   (5) What color?

   (6) What colors were available?

   (7) When is the first man going to look?

2. Listen to the dialogue and then answer the questions

   (1) What did the customer want to look at?

   (2) What size shoe?

   (3) What color did the customer eventually purchase?

   (4) For how much?

   (5) What was the original price?

   (6) Why were the shoes on sale?

   (7) Did the customer buy the shoes because they were cheaper than another pair?

New Words

肥瘦　féishòu　N
width, degree of tightness

打五折　dǎ wǔ zhé　Phrase
50% off

真实生活汉语
Chinese for Living in China 2

Communication Activities

Pair Work

Scenario I: Compare and contrast the clothes and shoes that you and your partner are wearing now. Mention the size, color, and how well they fit. Use "A 比 bǐ B + Adj", "A 跟 gēn B 一样 yíyàng + Adj", "A 没有 méiyǒu B + Adj", and try to incorporate the items below.

颜色	大小	肥瘦	长短	浅	深
yánsè	dàxiǎo	féishòu	chángduǎn	qiǎn	shēn
价钱	便宜	贵	正式	舒服	
jiàqián	piányi	guì	zhèngshì	shūfu	

Scenario II: Make a comparison between the banquet given by the municipal Education Bureau and the party at your Chinese friend's house, in terms of food, clothes, atmosphere, etc. Use the comparative or the "same" constructions, and try to incorporate the items below.

好吃	正式	有意思	多	贵
hǎochī	zhèngshì	yǒu yìsi	duō	guì
便宜	随便	舒服	时间长	时间短
piányi	suíbiàn	shūfu	shíjiān cháng	shíjiān duǎn

Scenario III: Make a comparison between two restaurants you have visited, in terms of the taste of the food, drink, variety of food, quantity, quality, price, service, etc. Use the comparative or the "same" constructions, and try to incorporate the items below.

好吃	甜	咸	油多	贵
hǎochī	tián	xián	yóu duō	guì
便宜	等的时间	服务态度	（服务员）漂亮	
piányi	děng de shíjiān	fúwù tàidu	(fúwùyuán) piàoliang	

Role-Play

Scenario I: A is shopping for a shirt and a pair of pants. B is the store clerk, who comes over to assist. A talks about color and size; the clerk makes suggestions. Use the following items.

喜欢	穿	多大号	怎么样	试试
xǐhuan	chuān	duō dà hào	zěnmeyàng	shìshi
打折	合适	原价	A 比 B + Adj	
dǎ zhé	héshì	yuánjià	A bǐ B + Adj	

Lesson Fifteen   Shopping for Clothes

第十五课   买衣服

除了……以外, 还……
chúle…… yǐwài, hái……

Scenario II: In pairs, take the roles of a salesperson and a customer. As a customer you have bought a pair of shoes that are too small and want to exchange them for a larger pair. Use the following items.

不舒服	太小了	有一点儿紧	大一号
bù shūfu	tài xiǎo le	yǒu yìdiǎnr jǐn	dà yí hào
不合适	换	A 没有 B + Adj	颜色
bù héshì	huàn	A méiyǒu B + Adj	yánsè
大小	不打折	还可以	
dàxiǎo	bù dǎ zhé	hái kěyǐ	

Scenario III: You've bought a pair of light blue trousers or pants for your boy/girlfriend, who feels the color's too light. Ask the salesperson if you can exchange them for a darker pair. It turns out the darker pair are more expensive. Try bargaining. Eventually, the salesperson offers a better price – on condition that you buy two pairs. Try to incorporate as many items below as possible.

喜欢	太浅了	颜色深一点儿的	大小	合适
xǐhuan	tài qiǎn le	yánsè shēn yìdiǎnr de	dàxiǎo	héshì
就便宜了	不打折	价钱	两条	换
jiù piányi le	bù dǎ zhé	jiàqián	liǎng tiáo	huàn
比	没有	一样		
bǐ	méiyǒu	yíyàng		

Group Activities

Three of you are shopping for clothes and shoes for a formal banquet. All do your best to find what you need, with assistance from the salesperson. Try to incorporate as many items below as possible.

喜欢	穿	多大号	怎么样	试试
xǐhuan	chuān	duō dà hào	zěnmeyàng	shìshi
（不）打折	合适	白色	灰色	蓝色
(bù) dǎ zhé	héshì	báisè	huīsè	lánsè
浅颜色	原价	太肥了	太瘦了	有一点儿紧
qiǎn yánsè	yuánjià	tài féi le	tài shòu le	yǒu yìdiǎnr jǐn
大一号	不合适	颜色	大小	还可以
dà yí hào	bù héshì	yánsè	dàxiǎo	hái kěyǐ
除了……以外	比	没有	一样	
chúle…… yǐwài	bǐ	méiyǒu	yíyàng	

Review Exercises

1. Select a measure word from the list to fill in the blanks

个 gè   件 jiàn   条 tiáo   双 shuāng   节 jié   套 tào   间 jiān   段 duàn

   (1) 一（　）时间　　　　　　(6) 两（　）书
   　　yī（　）shíjiān　　　　　　liǎng（　）shū

   (2) 两（　）裙子　　　　　　(7) 三（　）课
   　　liǎng（　）qúnzi　　　　　sān（　）kè

   (3) 三（　）衬衫　　　　　　(8) 一（　）卧室
   　　sān（　）chènshān　　　　yī（　）wòshì

   (4) 四（　）裤子　　　　　　(9) 一（　）收银台
   　　sì（　）kùzi　　　　　　　yī（　）shōuyíntái

   (5) 九（　）鞋　　　　　　　(10) 两（　）沙发
   　　jiǔ（　）xié　　　　　　　liǎng（　）shāfā

2. Use the material provided to describe a situation where, if the conditions are met (e.g. "吃药 chī yào"), things will work out (e.g. "就好了 jiù hǎo le")

   Example: 吃药 / 好 → 你吃了药就好了。
   　　　　　chī yào / hǎo → Nǐ chīle yào jiù hǎo le.

   (1) 不喝茶 / 能睡觉 → _____
   　　bù hē chá / néng shuì jiào

   (2) 洗澡 / 舒服 → _____
   　　xǐzǎo / shūfu

   (3) 穿一双皮鞋 / 正式 → _____
   　　chuān yì shuāng píxié / zhèngshì

   (4) 等一会儿 / 他来 → _____
   　　děng yíhuìr / tā lái

   (5) 喝一点儿水 / 舒服 → _____
   　　hē yìdiǎnr shuǐ / shūfu

   (6) 问一下儿老师 / 知道考试的时间 → _____
   　　wèn yíxiàr lǎoshī / zhīdào kǎoshì de shíjiān

   (7) 上网看一看 / 知道明天的天气 → _____
   　　shàng wǎng kàn yi kàn / zhīdào míngtiān de tiānqì

   (8) 坐332路汽车 / 到北京大学 → _____
   　　zuò sān-sān-èr lù qìchē / dào Běijīng Dàxué

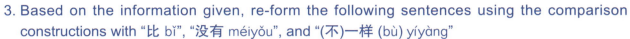

3. Based on the information given, re-form the following sentences using the comparison constructions with "比 bǐ", "没有 méiyǒu", and "(不)一样 (bù) yíyàng"

(1) 39号的鞋是白色的，38号半的鞋是红色的，都很好看。
Sānshíjiǔ hào de xié shì báisè de, sānshíbā hào bàn de xié shì hóngsè de, dōu hěn hǎokàn.
_____

(2) 这条黑裤子是30号，那条黑裤子是32号，都很便宜。
Zhè tiáo hēi kùzi shì sānshí hào, nà tiáo hēi kùzi shì sānshí'èr hào, dōu hěn piányi.
_____

(3) 这件红色的T恤衫有点儿肥，那件蓝色的T恤衫很合适，可是都很贵。
Zhè jiàn hóngsè de T xù shān yǒudiǎnr féi, nà jiàn lánsè de T xù shān hěn héshì, kěshì dōu hěn guì.
_____

(4) 这件白衬衫太肥了，那件灰衬衫太瘦了。
Zhè jiàn bái chènshān tài féi le, nà jiàn huī chènshān tài shòu le.
_____

(5) 剪长发十五元，剪短发只要八元。
Jiǎn chángfà shíwǔ yuán, jiǎn duǎnfà zhǐ yào bā yuán.
_____

(6) 这条十元的小号短裤有点儿紧，那条十元的中号短裤很合适。
Zhè tiáo shí yuán de xiǎohào duǎnkù yǒudiǎnr jǐn, nà tiáo shí yuán de zhōnghào duǎnkù hěn héshì.
_____

(7) 去大教室用十分钟，去学生宿舍也用十分钟。
Qù dà jiàoshì yòng shí fēnzhōng, qù xuésheng sùshè yě yòng shí fēnzhōng.
_____

(8) 坐空调大巴花五块钱，打的花十五块钱。
Zuò kōngtiáo dàbā huā wǔ kuài qián, dǎdī huā shíwǔ kuài qián.
_____

(9) 中国学生的宿舍住六个人，留学生宿舍住两个人。
Zhōngguó xuésheng de sùshè zhù liù ge rén, liúxuéshēng sùshè zhù liǎng ge rén.
_____

(10) 中国学生的教室没有空调，留学生的有空调。
Zhōngguó xuésheng de jiàoshì méiyǒu kōngtiáo, liúxuéshēng de yǒu kōngtiáo.
_____

4. What would you say?

(1) You're in an electrical appliance store. You brought your laptop from overseas, but its plug doesn't fit the socket in your room:

   a. Tell the clerk you want to buy an all-purpose socket for connecting your laptop.

   ....

   b. Ask the clerk if they have a surge protector and a voltage stabilizer.

   ....

   c. Tell the clerk that in addition to a mobile phone, you need 4 AA batteries.

   ....

(2) You are in a department store intending to buy some new clothes and shoes:

   a. Tell the clerk that you need to buy a pair of large-size black trousers.

   ....

   b. Tell the clerk that you like the white shirt, but it's too tight so you need a larger one.

   ....

   c. Ask the clerk if they have a special deal on the pants and/or the shirt.

   ....

   d. Ask the clerk if you can try the shoes on.

   ....

   e. Tell the clerk that size 9.5 shoes are a little too big; ask if they have a smaller size.

   ....

   f. Ask the clerk if it would be cheaper to buy two pairs of shoes (instead of one).

   ....

第十五课 买衣服

Lesson Fifteen　Shopping for Clothes

Culture Notes

1. Weights and measures: Length and distance

As noted earlier (in Lesson 12), China, officially, makes use of the metric system, but the traditional market system (市制 shìzhì) is still widely used. The following chart indicates how the three systems matchup:

	Market System	Metric System	American System
Length	1 寸 cùn	3.3 厘米 lí mǐ (centimeters)	1.3 英寸 yīngcùn (inches)
	1 尺 chǐ	0.33 米 mǐ (meters)	1.1 英尺 yīngchǐ (feet)
	1 丈 zhàng	3.3 米 mǐ (meters)	3.6 码 mǎ (yards)
Area	1 亩 mǔ	0.07 公顷 gōngqǐng (hectares)	0.16 英亩 yīngmǔ (acres)
	1 顷 qǐng	6.7 公顷 gōngqǐng (hectares)	16 英亩 yīngmǔ (acres)

2. Height

Height is measured in feet (the Chinese market system) or in meters (metric system):

Feet	Meters
5.0	1.52
5.1	1.55
5.2	1.58
5.3	1.62
5.4	1.66
5.5	1.68
5.6	1.71
5.7	1.74
5.8	1.77
5.9	1.80
6.0	1.82

3. Converting metric to non-metric

To convert centimeters to inches, multiply by 0.39.
To convert inches to centimeters, multiply by 2.54.
To convert length measurement:

　　　1 meter = 39.4 inches = 3.3 feet = 1.1 yards

　　　1 yard = 0.91 meters

　　　1 foot = 0.3 meters = 30 centimeters

4. International shoe size

Womens Shoe Size												
Europe	35.5	36	37	37.5	38	38.5	39	40	40.5	41	41.5	42
Britain (UK)	3.5	4	4.5	5	5.5	6	6.5	7	7.5	8	8.5	9
United States	5.5	6	6.5	7	7.5	8	8.5	9	9.5	10	10.5	11
Foot length (cm)	21.5	22	22.5	23	23.5	24	24.5	25	25.5	26	26.5	27

Mens Shoe Size												
Europe	39	40	41	42	43	43.5	44	44.5	45	45.5	46	47
Britain (UK)	6.5	7	7.5	8	8.5	9	9.5	10	10.5	11	11.5	12.5
United States	7	7.5	8	8.5	9	9.5	10	10.5	11	11.5	12	13
Foot length (cm)	25	25.5	26	26.5	27	27.5	28	28.5	29	29.5	30	31

5. Reciepts: "小票 xiǎopiào"

When you pay the cashier in a store, you receive a receipt on white, yellow, blue, or pink paper. It is called a "小票 xiǎopiào" (small receipt). You keep it as proof of purchase in case you find you need to exchange, return, or have repairs made to the merchandise within a few days. To get a receipt, one takes the "小票 xiǎopiào" to the cashier and asks for a store receipt.

Lesson Sixteen   At the Hospital

第十六课   在医院
Dì-shíliù Kè   Zài Yīyuàn

In this lesson you will learn how to do the following

- Explain your symptoms to a doctor
- Explain how you hurt yourself or got injured
- List any medicines you are taking
- Get instructions for your prescription

Grammar

- Resultative complements
- Events in succession: "先 xiān……然后 ránhòu……" (first... then...)
- Expressing uncertainty with "不知道 bù zhīdào" ([I] don't know if/whether)
- Directional complements ("下来 xiàlai", down here; "上去 shàngqu", up there, etc.)
- Ongoing action: the adverbs "正 zhèng", "在 zài" and "正在 zhèngzài"
- The intensifying suffix "得很 de hěn"

Culture Notes

- Registering at the hospital
- The medical examination room
- Payments
- The pharmacy

真实生活汉语 2
Chinese for Living in China

Dialogue

A：医生　　　　B：马克，外教　　　C：内科大夫　　　D：安妮，外教
　　yīshēng　　　　Mǎkè, wàijiào　　　nèikē dàifu　　　　Ānnī, wàijiào

　　马克在北京一所中学教英语。他喜欢放学后和学生们一起打篮球，锻炼身体。没想到^G1今天下午打球的时候，他摔了一跤，受伤了。学生们叫来了他的联络老师吴帮国。吴老师说学校的另一个外教安妮今天刚好也得¹去医院，他就带他们俩一起去医院看病²。到了医院，吴老师去给他们挂了号。他先把安妮带到内科，让她坐在候诊区等着，然后^G2带马克去看骨科急诊。

　　Mǎkè zài Běijīng yì suǒ zhōngxué jiāo Yīngyǔ. Tā xǐhuan fàng xué hòu hé xuéshēngmen yìqǐ dǎ lánqiú, duànliàn shēntǐ. Méi xiǎngdào^G1 jīntiān xiàwǔ dǎ qiú de shíhou, tā shuāile yì jiāo, shòu shāng le. Xuéshēngmen jiàoláile tā de liánluò lǎoshī Wú Bāngguó. Wú lǎoshī shuō xuéxiào de lìng yí ge wàijiào Ānní jīntiān zhènghǎo yě děi¹ qù yīyuàn, Tā jiù dài tāmen liǎ yìqǐ qù yīyuàn kàn bìng². Dàole yīyuàn, Wú lǎoshī qù gěi tāmen guàle hào. Tā xiān bǎ Ānní dài dào nèikē, ràng tā zuò zai hòuzhěnqū děngzhe, ránhòu^G2 dài Mǎkè qù kàn gǔkē jízhěn.

A：你是怎么受伤的？
　　Nǐ shì zěnme shòu shāng de?

B：我打篮球的时候摔了一跤，左脚扭伤了，左手臂也摔破了，疼极了^G3，不知道是不是骨折了^G4？
　　Wǒ dǎ lánqiú de shíhou shuāile yì jiāo, zuǒ jiǎo niǔshāng le, zuǒ shǒubì yě shuāipò le, Téngjí le^G3, bù zhīdào shì bu shì gǔzhé le^G4?

A：你流了很多血吗？
　　Nǐ liúle hěn duō xiě ma?

B：胳膊的皮破了，流了不少血。
　　Gēbo de pí pò le, liúle bù shǎo xiě.

Notes

1. "得 děi" is a modal verb (a verb that takes a verb phrase object) corresponding to English "have to", "must". The same character also writes the verb "dé" (to get, to obtain) ("得过高血压 déguo gāoxuèyā" - have had high blood pressure) and the particle "de" ("说得很好 shuō de hěn hǎo" - speak very well).
2. "看病 kàn bìng" (literally, "see illness"), said by a doctor, means "see a patient"; said by a patient, it can mean "see or consult a doctor". "看大夫 kàn dàifu", with "大夫 dàifu" (doctor), is unambiguous.

第十六课 在医院
Lesson Sixteen   At the Hospital

A：请你把左手臂往前伸，收起来^{G5}，再往上伸。好，放下。把左手指伸开，合起来。……看来你的手臂没有骨折。不过，伤口很大，我现在给你缝合。然后你去透视室给左脚照个片子，看看有没有骨折。
Qǐng nǐ bǎ zuǒ shǒubì wǎng qián shēn, shōu qǐlai^{G5}, zài wǎng shàng shēn. Hǎo, fàng xia. Bǎ zuǒ shǒuzhǐ shēnkāi, hé qǐlai. …… kànlái nǐ de shǒubì méiyǒu gǔzhé. Búguò, shāngkǒu hěn dà, wǒ xiànzài gěi nǐ fénghé. Ránhòu nǐ qù tòushìshì gěi zuǒ jiǎo zhào ge piānzi, kànkan yǒu méiyǒu gǔzhé.

B：好。谢谢。
Hǎo. Xièxie.

（马克照透视后发现，他的左脚没有骨折。他们就一起去内科找安妮。她已经进去了，正在^{G6}看大夫。Mǎkè zhào tòushì hòu fāxiàn, tā de zuǒ jiǎo méiyǒu gǔzhé. Tāmen jiù yìqǐ qù nèikē zhǎo Ānnī. Tā yǐjing jìnqu le, zhèngzài^{G6} kàn dàifu.）

C：你有什么不舒服³？
Nǐ yǒu shénme bù shūfu³?

D：大夫，我吐了，胃疼，不想吃东西。
Dàifu, wǒ tù le, wèi téng, bù xiǎng chī dōngxi.

C：你发烧吗？还有什么症状？
Nǐ fā shāo ma? Hái yǒu shénme zhèngzhuàng?

D：我不知道发不发烧。不过，我头很痛，肚子也疼得很^{G6}，还咳嗽，嗓子也疼。
Wǒ bù zhīdào fā bu fā shāo. Búguò, wǒ tóu hěn tòng, dùzi yě téng de hěn^{G6}, hái késou, sǎngzi yě téng.

C：你腹泻吗？
Nǐ fùxiè ma?

D：昨天晚上拉了好几次。
Zuótiān wǎnshang lāle hǎo jǐ cì.

C：我先量一下你的体温和血压，听听心脏。请脱掉你的外套。……张开嘴，把舌头伸出来……你的体温和血压都正常。
Wǒ xiān liáng yíxià nǐ de tǐwēn hé xuèyā, tīngting xīnzàng. Qǐng tuōdiào nǐ de wàitào. ……Zhāngkāi zuǐ, bǎ shétou shēn chulai. ……Nǐ de tǐwēn hé xuèyā dōu zhèngcháng.

---

3. "你有什么不舒服？Nǐ yǒu shénme bù shūfu?" Literally, "what do you have that's uncomfortable?" i.e.: "Where's the problem?" The question could also be formed as: "你哪儿不舒服？Nǐ nǎr bù shūfu?" "你怎么了？Nǐ zěnme le?" is also possible, but is more general, and could be translated as "What's up?" or "What's wrong?"

D：可是我觉得身上很难受。今天早上我去看过校医，她说现在正在流行肠胃感冒，我可能感染了，应该到医院来打点滴。
Kěshì wǒ juéde shēnshang hěn nánshòu. Jīntiān zǎoshang wǒ qù kànguo xiàoyī, tā shuō xiànzài zhèngzài liúxíng chángwèi gǎnmào, wǒ kěnéng gǎnrǎn le, yīnggāi dào yīyuàn lái dǎ diǎndī.

C：我开张化验单，你去化验室化验一下大便。如果不是细菌感染，最好不要输液或吃抗生素。
Wǒ kāi zhāng huàyàndān, nǐ qù huàyànshì huàyàn yíxià dàbiàn. Rúguǒ bú shì xìjūn gǎnrǎn, zuìhǎo bú yào shū yè huò chī kàngshēngsù.

（化验后，安妮又回来看大夫。 Huàyàn hòu, Ānnī yòu huílai kàn dàifu.）

C：你的化验结果正常，没有细菌感染。你可能吃了不干净的东西，消化不良。你的咳嗽跟腹泻没关系，可能是水土不服，对[4]空气污染过敏。我给你开[5]个药方，开止泻药和过敏药，多喝开水。
Nǐ de huàyàn jiéguǒ zhèngcháng, méiyǒu xìjūn gǎnrǎn. Nǐ kěnéng chīle bù gānjìng de dōngxi, xiāohuà bùliáng. Nǐ de késou gēn fùxiè méi guānxi, kěnéng shì shuǐtǔ bùfú, Duì[4] kōngqì wūrǎn guòmǐn. Wǒ gěi nǐ kāi[5] ge yàofāng, kāi zhǐxièyào hé guòmǐnyào, duō hē kāishuǐ.

D：好。这药怎么吃？
Hǎo. Zhè yào zěnme chī?

C：一天两次，一次一片[6]，饭后[7]吃。
Yì tiān liǎng cì, yí cì yí piàn[6], fàn hòu[7] chī.

D：谢谢您。
Xièxie nín.

---

4. "过敏 guòmǐn" is a verb meaning "to be sensitive to, to be allergic to"; the thing that causes the allergy is introduced with the preposition "对 duì", equivalent to English "to": "他对虾过敏 Tā duì xiā guòmǐn" (He's allergic to shrimp). "过敏 guòmǐn" can also be used in its literal meaning of "over-sensitive", in which case, it is an adjective: "你不要太过敏 Nǐ bú yào tài guòmǐn" (Don't be so sensitive).

5. "开 kāi" is a verb with a wide range of senses build around a core meaning of "to open" or "to start". With the object "药方（儿）yàofāng (r)" (prescription), it means "to write" or "to issue".

6. "片 piàn" is a measure word for slices and slice-like things: slices (of bread), blankets (of snow), expanses (of water), sheets (of flame) and for tablets (slices of cylinders) or pills.

7. "饭后 fàn hòu" is a succinct version of "吃饭以后 chī fàn yǐhòu".

第十六课 在医院
Lesson Sixteen　At the Hospital

New Words

#	汉字	Pinyin	词类	English
1	医院/醫院	yīyuàn	N	hospital, clinic
2	医生/醫生	yīshēng	N	doctor, physician
3	内科	nèikē	N	internal medicine, department of internal medicine
4	大夫	dàifu	N	doctor
5	北京	Běijīng	PropN	Beijing (Peking in some compounds)
6	放学/放學	fàng xué	VO	to finish classes for the day, to get out of school
7	篮球/籃球	lánqiú	N	basketball
8	锻炼/鍛煉	duànliàn	V	to engage in physical exercise
9	身体/身體	shēntǐ	N	the body
10	打球	dǎ qiú	Phrase	to play ball games
11	摔跤	shuāi jiāo	VO	to trip and fall, to fall down
	摔	shuāi	V	to fall, to tumble (after losing one's balance)
	跤	jiāo	BF	fall
12	受伤/受傷	shòu shāng	VO	to be wounded, to get injured
	受	shòu	V	to receive, to accept, to get, to suffer, to bear
	伤/傷	shāng	N	wound, injury
13	另	lìng	Pron	another, other
14	刚好/剛好	gānghǎo	Adv	just (in time), exactly, happen to
15	俩/倆	liǎ	Q	colloquial version of "两个 liǎng ge", the two of them
16	看病	kàn bìng	VO	to see a patient, to see a doctor
	病	bìng	V/N	to fall ill; illness
17	挂号/掛號	guà hào	VO	to register, to sign in (at a hospital, etc.)
18	候诊/候診	hòuzhěn	V	to wait to see a doctor (as in a hospital)
19	区/區	qū	BF	area, region
20	骨科	gǔkē	N	orthopedics
21	急诊/急診	jízhěn	N	emergency treatment, emergency call

135

真实生活汉语
Chinese for Living in China 2

22	脚/腳	jiǎo	N	foot, base (of a wall, hill, etc.)
23	扭伤/扭傷	niǔshāng	V-RC	to sprain
24	手臂	shǒubì	N	the arm
	臂	bì	BF	upper arm
25	破	pò	Adj / V	broken, damaged; to break, to cut
26	疼	téng	Adj / V	hurt, ache; to dote on, to love dearly
27	骨折	gǔzhé	N	bone fracture
28	流血	liú xiě	Phrase	to bleed, shed blood
	流	liú	V	to flow (of liquid), to wander
	血	xiě	N	blood
29	胳膊	gēbo	N	the arm
30	皮	pí	N	skin, peel, leather
31	伸	shēn	V	to stretch out, to extend, to spread
32	起来/起來	qǐlai	DirC	up, out
33	往上	wǎng shàng	Phrase	upwards
34	放下	fàngxia	V-DirC	to put down, to let go of
35	手指	shǒuzhǐ	N	finger
	指	zhǐ	V	to indicate, to point at
36	伸开/伸開	shēnkāi	V-RC	to stretch out, to extend, to spread open
37	合	hé	V	to close, to shut, to join, to combine
38	看来	kànlái	V	to look as if, to seem that
39	伤口/傷口	shāngkǒu	N	a wound
40	缝合/縫合	fénghé	V	to stitch up a wound
41	透视/透視	tòushì	N / V	X-ray; to see through
42	照	zhào	V	to shine, to illuminate, to take a photo
43	片子	piānzi	N	X-ray slide
	片	piàn	Meas	*for slice-like things, e.g. tablets*
44	正在	zhèngzài	Adv	be right in the process of
45	看大夫	kàn dàifu	Phrase	to go to a doctor

第十六课　在医院
Lesson Sixteen　At the Hospital

46	吐	tù	V	to vomit, to throw up, to cough up
47	胃	wèi	N	stomach
48	发烧/發燒	fā shāo	VO	to have a fever, to run a temperature
49	症状/症狀	zhèngzhuàng	N	symptom (of a disease)
50	痛	tòng	Adj	painful
51	肚子	dùzi	N	belly, abdomen ("拉肚子 lā dùzi", diarrhea)
52	咳嗽	késou	V/N	to cough; cough
53	嗓子	sǎngzi	N	throat
54	腹泻/腹瀉	fùxiè	N	diarrhea
	腹	fù	BF	belly, abdomen
55	拉	lā	V	to pull, to tug, to draw, to play (stringed instruments), to have a bowel movement
56	量	liáng	V	to measure sth. (with a measuring tape, yardstick, ruler, etc.), to estimate
57	体温/體溫	tǐwēn	N	body temperature
58	血压/血壓	xuèyā	N	blood pressure
59	听/聽	tīng	V	to hear, to listen, to obey
60	心脏/心臟	xīnzàng	N	heart
61	脱掉	tuōdiào	V-RC	to take off (clothes)
	脱	tuō	V	to take off (clothes), remove
62	张开/張開	zhāngkāi	V-RC	to open up, to spread open
	张/張	zhāng	V	to open, spread, stretch
63	嘴	zuǐ	N	mouth
64	舌头/舌頭	shétou	N	tongue
65	正常	zhèngcháng	Adj	normal, regular
66	身上	shēnshang	N	on one's body, on one's person (e.g. money, documents)
67	难受/難受	nánshòu	Adj	feel unwell, feel sad about
68	校医/校醫	xiàoyī	N	school doctor
69	流行	liúxíng	V/Adj	to spread, to rage (of disease); prevalent, in vogue
70	感冒	gǎnmào	V/N	to catch cold; a cold, the flu

真实生活汉语
Chinese for Living in China 2

71	感染	gǎnrǎn	V	to infect (literally or figuratively)
72	打点滴/打點滴	dǎ diǎndī	Phrase	to have an intravenous drip, receive an IV injection (also called "打吊针 dǎ diàozhēn")
73	化验单/化驗單	huàyàndān	N	laboratory test sheet
74	化验室/化驗室	huàyànshì	N	laboratory (for chemical testing)
75	化验/化驗	huàyàn	V	to do a chemical examination, to test
76	大便	dàbiàn	V/N	to defecate; feces, night soil
77	细菌	xìjūn	N	bacteria, germs
78	输液/輸液	shū yè	VO	to have an IV drip
79	抗生素	kàngshēngsù	N	antibiotic
80	结果/結果	jiéguǒ	N	outcome, result
81	消化不良	xiāohuà bùliáng	Phrase	to have indigestion
	消化	xiāohuà	N/V	digestion; to digest
	不良	bùliáng	Adj	not good, indisposed
82	水土不服	shuǐtǔ bùfú	Phrase	not used to the food, not acclimatized
	水土	shuǐtǔ	N	water and soil, natural environment
	不服	bùfú	V	not used to
83	对……过敏/對……過敏	duì……guòmǐn	Construction	to be allergic to…
	过敏/過敏	guòmǐn	V/N	to be over-sensitive to, to be allergic to; allergy
84	空气/空氣	kōngqì	N	air
85	污染	wūrǎn	N	pollution
86	止泻药/止瀉藥	zhǐxièyào	N	diarrhea medicine
87	药方/藥方	yàofāng	N	prescription
	药/藥	yào	N	medicine, drugs
88	开水/開水	kāishuǐ	N	boiled water, boiling water

第十六课　在医院
Lesson Sixteen　At the Hospital

Re-enacting the Dialogue

A: a doctor
B: Mark, a foreign teacher
C: internal medicine doctor
D: Annie, a foreign teacher

Mark is teaching English at a middle school in Beijing. After school, he likes playing basketball with students to get some exercise. This afternoon he accidentally fell down and hurt himself while playing basketball. The students called his contact teacher – Wu Bangguo over. Wu laoshi said it just so happened that another foreign teacher, Annie, also had to go to the hospital; he'd take the two of them to the hospital to see doctors. When they got to the hospital, Wu laoshi went and signed them in. First he took Annie to the Department of Internal Medicine and let her wait in the waiting room, then he took Mark to the orthopedics emergency room.

A: How did you hurt yourself?

B: I fell while playing basketball; I twisted my left foot and fell on my left arm. It's quite painful – I don't know if the bone's broken.

A: Did you lose a lot of blood?

B: I cut my arm and it bled quite a lot.

A: Move your left arm forwards and back, then up. OK, now put it down. Extend the fingers of your left hand, then close them … Doesn't look like you've broken the bone. But you've got quite a bad cut. I'm going to stitch it up for you right now. After that, go to the X-ray room and have your left foot X-rayed – to see if you've broken the bone.

B: OK, thanks.

(After having the X-ray, Mark finds out that his left foot isn't broken. Then they go to the Department of Internal Medicine together to look for Annie. She's already gone in and is seeing the doctor.)

C: What's bothering you?

D: Doctor, I threw up, my stomach hurts, and I don't feel like eating anything.

C: Do you have a fever? Any other symptoms?

D: I don't know if I have a fever or not, but I have a bad headache, my stomach hurts a lot, and I have a cough.

C: Do you have diarrhea?

D: Last night I had several bouts of diarrhea.

C: First, let me take your temperature and blood pressure, and listen to your heart. Take off your outer garments please … Open your mouth and stick out your tongue…. Your temperature and blood pressure are normal.

D: But I feel terrible. I went to see the school doctor this morning and she said that there was a lot of stomach flu going around, and that I may have got infected and should go to the hospital and get an IV.

C: I'll order a lab test; you go to the lab and get a stool test. If it's not a bacterial infection, it's best you not get an IV or take any antibiotics.

(Annie returns to the doctor after the test.)

C: Your lab test was normal, there's no viral infection. You probably ate something bad and couldn't digest it. The cough is not related to the diarrhea – it's probably just a problem of acclimatization, an allergic response to the polluted air. I'll give you a prescription for your diarrhea and for the allergies – drink a lot of boiled water.

D: OK. How do I take the medicine?

C: Take one pill twice a day after meals.

D: Thank you.

Grammar

▶ G1. Resultative complements

Resultative complements have been discussed in a number of prior grammar points. This lesson contains several examples. One is the verb "到 dào" which appears with verb "想 xiǎng" (think) in the set phrase "没想到 méi xiǎngdào" (to have not expected, unexpectedly, much to one's surprise).

① 没想到，今天下午打球的时候，他摔了一跤，受伤了。
Méi xiǎngdào, jīntiān xiàwǔ dǎ qiú de shíhou, tā shuāile yì jiāo, shòu shāng le.
Unexpectedly, when he was playing ball this afternoon, he fell and hurt himself.

As noted in Lesson 11 (G7), rather than its literal meaning of "to reach", "到 dào" used as a resultative complement has the meaning of "to succeed in, to manage to". Other examples include "找到 zhǎodào" (I've found it) and "买到 mǎidào" (I've managed to buy one).

Another resultative complement in this lesson is the verb "开 kāi", whose literal meaning is "to open". As a resultative complement, its sense ranges from "to open" to "out": "打开 dǎkāi" (to open [a window, etc.]); "伸开 shēnkāi" (to extend-open = to stretch out [one's hand, etc.]), "张开 zhāngkāi" (to expand-open = to open wide [one's mouth, etc.]).

② 把左手的手指伸开。 Open your left hand – unclench your fingers.
Bǎ zuǒshǒu de shǒuzhǐ shēnkāi.

③ 张开嘴。 Open wide your mouth.
Zhāngkāi zuǐ.

▶ G2. Events in succession: "先 xiān……然后 ránhòu……" (first... then...)

In Lesson 8 (G1), a succession of events was signaled with "先 xiān" (first) and another adverb, "再 zài" (then, later):

① 先买电话卡，再打电话。 First buy a phone card, then make your phone calls.
Xiān mǎi diànhuàkǎ, zài dǎ diànhuà.

"再 zài" often implies postponement or delay: "明天再说吧 Míngtiān zài shuō ba" (Let's talk about it tomorrow). "然后 ránhòu", whose literal meaning is close to "after that", is usually classified as a conjunction.

Unlike "再 zài" which as an adverb appears after a subject (if present), "然后 ránhòu" usually appears before the subject, though occasionally it can also be found after it.

② 我先量一下儿你的体温，然后你/你然后去化验一下儿大便。
Wǒ xiān liáng yíxiàr nǐ de tǐwēn, ránhòu nǐ/nǐ ránhòu qù huàyàn yíxiàr dàbiàn.
I'll take your temperature first; then afterwards, go and have your stool tested.

It is also possible to use all three, "先 xiān", "再 zài" and "然后 ránhòu", to indicate a more complicated sequence:

③ 他先挂号，再把安妮带到内科，然后带马克去看骨科急诊。
Tā xiān guà hào, zài bǎ Ānnī dàidào nèikē, ránhòu dài Mǎkè qù kàn gǔkē jízhěn.
He registers them first, then takes Annie to the Department of Internal Medicine; afterwards, he takes Mark to the orthopedic emergency room.

▶ **G3.** Expressing uncertainty with "不知道 bù zhīdào" ([I] don't know if/whether)

In English "I don't know" is followed by "if" or "whether", which indicate that there are in fact several options being considered. "I don't know if I can." Optionally, "or not" can be added to make the doubt more explicit: "I don't know if I can, or not."

In Chinese, the "or not" option – making the uncertainty explicit – is required. If what is in doubt is expressed, then it is expressed as a verb-not-verb question after "不知道 bù zhīdào": "我不知道他会不会说汉语 Wǒ bù zhīdào tā huì bu huì shuō Hànyǔ" (I don't know if he speaks Chinese, [or not]).

① 我不知道发不发烧。 I'm not sure if I have a fever (or not).
Wǒ bù zhīdào fā bu fāshāo.

② 他不知道能不能在那个站换车。
Tā bù zhīdào néng bu néng zài nàge zhàn huàn chē.
He's not sure whether you can change buses at that station.

③ 我不知道是不是骨折了。 I'm not sure if I've broken a bone or not.
Wǒ bù zhīdào shì bu shì gǔzhé le.

▶ **G4.** Directional complements ("下来 xiàlai", down here; "上去 shàngqu", up there, etc.)

Directional complements combine with verbs to indicate direction. They may be simple (one syllable) or compound (two syllables). "来 lái" and "去 qù", for example, combine with a preceding action verb to show direction towards the speaker, or away from the speaker, respectively. (As directional complements, "来 lái" and "去 qù" are usually untoned – i.e. in neutral tone.) In some cases, this allows Chinese to use a single verb where English has two: "拿来 nálai" (to bring), "拿去 náqu" (to take). Here are some examples:

① 请把东西拿来。 Please bring the things here.
Qǐng bǎ dōngxi nálai.

② 车票已经买来了。 I've already bought the tickets.
Chēpiào yǐjīng mǎilai le.

③ 我明天给你送去。 I'll deliver them to you tomorrow.
　　Wǒ míngtiān gěi nǐ sòngqu.

④ 我们带来的东西应该放在哪儿?
　　Wǒmen dàilái de dōngxi yīnggāi fàng zài nǎr?
　　Where shall we put the things we brought here?

Compound directional complements combine "来 lái" and "去 qù" with one of a number of verbs of movement in a direction ("上 shàng", "下 xià", "进 jìn", etc.) The 15 possible combinations are listed in the table below. (A 16th possible combination, "起去 qǐqu" – rise-away from speaker – is semantically anomalous and does not occur.)

	上	下	进	出	回	过	起
来	上来	下来	进来	出来	回来	过来	起来
去	上去	下去	进去	出去	回去	过去	/

Meanings are mostly additive: "拿上来 ná shanglai" (bring it up here), "拿下去 ná xiaqu" (take it down there); "放进来 fàng jinlai" (put it in here), "放进去 fàng jinqu" (put it in there); "走过来 zǒu guolai" (walk over here), "走过去 zǒu guoqu" (walk over there); "站起来 zhàn qilai" (stand up). Here is an example from the main dialogue:

① 把舌头伸出来。 Stick out your tongue.
　　Bǎ shétou shēn chulai.

Combinations with "起来 qǐlai", in particular, tend to extend the literal meaning of "rise up" in idiomatic ways, as the two examples from the dialogue in this lesson show:

② 请把左手臂往前伸……收起来。 Move your left left arm forwards… bring it back.
　　Qǐng bǎ zuǒ shǒubì wǎng qián shēn……shōu qilai.

③ 把左手的手指伸开,合起来。 Extend the fingers of your left hand, then close them.
　　Bǎ zuǒshǒu de shǒuzhǐ shēnkāi, hé qilai.

Like resultative complements, directional complements can be turned into potential compounds (cf. Lesson 11 G2) by the insertion of "得 de" or "不 bu":

④ A: 拿得上来拿不上来? Can you carry it up here [or not]?
　　　Ná de shànglai ná bu shànglái?

　　B: 拿得上来　Yes, I can.
　　　Ná de shànglái.

In such cases, both syllables of the directional complements tend to be fully toned, as shown.

▶ **G5. Ongoing action: the adverbs "正 zhèng", "在 zài", and "正在 zhèngzài"**

In some cases, a final "呢 ne" is sufficient to indicate ongoing action: "你做什么呢? Nǐ zuò shénme ne?" (What are you doing?) Ongoing action can be made more explicit by placing "在 zài" before the verb, as if functioning as an adverb: "我在吃饭呢 Wǒ zài chī fàn ne" (I'm having my meal).

If the emphasis is on a point in time, the adverb "正 zhèng" (precisely, just) can be used: "我正吃午饭呢 Wǒ zhèng chī wǔfàn ne" (I'm just eating my lunch); "她正在医院看大夫 Tā zhèngzài yīyuàn kàn dàifu" (She's seeing a doctor at the hospital). "正 zhèng" is particularly common with interruptions:

① 我正要出门，电话铃就响了。 I was just about to go out when the phone rang.
Wǒ zhèng yào chū mén, diànhuàlíng jiù xiǎng le.

Finally, to put even more emphasis on the ongoing nature of the action, "正 zhèng" and "在 zài" can be combined as "正在 zhèngzài" to give the sense of "right in the middle of":

② 她已经进去了，正在看大夫。 She's already gone in and is seeing the doctor.
Tā yǐjīng jìnqu le, zhèngzài kàn dàifu.

Ongoing action can be contrasted with the persistent states associated with V- "着 zhe". (Note that both are associated with, but not always translated as, the ing-form of the verb in English.)

③ 她们在沙发上坐着呢。 They're sitting on the sofa.
Tāmen zài shāfā shang zuòzhe ne.

④ 她们正在工作呢。 They are at work right now.
Tāmen zhèngzài gōngzuò ne.

▶ G6. The intensifying suffix "得很 de hěn"

The intensifying suffix "极了 jí le" was discussed in Lesson 13 (G2). It follows adjectives (but not usually derogatory ones) to indicate a superlative degree:

① 我的左手臂摔破了，疼极了。 My left arm's broken – it's extremely painful.
Wǒ de zuǒ shǒubì shuāipò le, téngjí le.

Another way of intensifying adjectives is to add "得很 de hěn", literally "to the extent of 'very'". "很 hěn", used as an ordinary adverb, is not very intensifying. In fact, at times it does little more than provide support for the adjective: "她很高" (She's tall; she's quite tall). To get a real sense of "very", the "得很 de hěn" suffix can be used:

② 我的肚子也疼得很。 My stomach hurts a lot, too.
Wǒ de dùzi yě téng de hěn.

③ 她那个发型好看得很。 That's a beautiful hairdo she has.
Tā nàge fàxíng hǎokàn de hěn.

Consolidation & Practice

I. Fill in the blanks with items from the list of V-Resultative Complements and V-Directional Complements provided that fit the English meanings

看懂 kàndǒng	想到 xiǎngdào	看见 kànjiàn	看清楚 kàn qīngchu	找到 zhǎodào
看完 kànwán	拿走 názǒu	记住 jìzhù	做完 zuòwán	伸开 shēnkāi
张开 zhāngkāi	买回来 mǎi huilai			

(1) A: 你为什么_____作业？(not finish doing)
Nǐ wèishéme _____ zuòyè?

B: 因为我_____你的问题。(not understand)
Yīnwèi wǒ _____ nǐ de wèntí.

(2) A: 你发烧三天了，怎么没有去医院看病？
Nǐ fā shāo sān tiān le, zěnme méiyǒu qù yīyuàn kàn bìng?

B: 因为我_____这次感冒这么严重。(not expect)
Yīnwèi wǒ _____ zhè cì gǎnmào zhème yánzhòng.

(3) A: 你_____大夫刚给我的药方了吗？(see)
Nǐ _____ dàifu gāng gěi wǒ de yàofāng le ma?

B: (I didn't see) 我想是吴老师_____了。(take away)
Wǒ xiǎng shì Wú lǎoshī _____ le.

(4) A: _____嘴，让我看一下儿你的嗓子。(open wide)
_____ zuǐ, ràng wǒ kàn yíxiàr nǐ de sǎngzi.

B: 您刚才看过了。
Nín gāngcái kànguo le.

A: 对，可是_____。(not see clearly)
Duì, kěshì _____.

(5) A: 大夫，这药怎么吃？
Dàifu, zhè yào zěnme chī?

B: 我已经告诉你了。
Wǒ yǐjīng gàosu nǐ le.

A: 对不起，我_____。(not remember)
Duìbuqǐ, wǒ _____.

第十六课　在医院
Lesson Sixteen　At the Hospital

(6) A: 你＿＿＿＿＿＿昨天我放在桌子上的三个西红柿了吗？(see)
　　　Nǐ ＿＿＿＿＿＿ zuótiān wǒ fàng zài zhuōzi shang de sān ge xīhóngshì le ma?

　　B: 我送给小王了。
　　　Wǒ sòng gěi xiǎo Wáng le.

　　A: 那是我刚从超市＿＿＿＿＿＿的。(buy and bring back here)
　　　Nà shì wǒ gāng cóng chāoshì ＿＿＿＿＿＿ de.

(7) A: 你的手怎么了？
　　　Nǐ de shǒu zěnme le?

　　B: 打篮球的时候受伤了。
　　　Dǎ lánqiú de shíhou shòu shāng le.

　　A: 骨折了吗？
　　　Gǔzhé le ma?

　　B: 我的手还能＿＿＿＿＿＿，应该没有问题。(stretch out)
　　　Wǒ de shǒu hái néng ＿＿＿＿＿＿, yīnggāi méiyǒu wèntí.

(8) A: 马克去医院怎么还没回来？
　　　Mǎkè qù yīyuàn zěnme hái méi huílai?

　　B: 我也不知道，可能还没＿＿＿＿＿＿病吧。(finish seeing the doctor)
　　　Wǒ yě bù zhīdào, kěnéng hái méi ＿＿＿＿＿＿ bìng ba.

　　A: 你有他的电话号码吗？我给他打一个电话。
　　　Nǐ yǒu tā de diànhuà hàomǎ ma? Wǒ gěi tā dǎ yí ge diànhuà.

　　B: 他那天告诉我了，可是我＿＿＿＿＿＿。你去问丽莎吧。(not remember)
　　　Tā nà tiān gàosu wǒ le, kěshì wǒ ＿＿＿＿＿＿. Nǐ qù wèn Lìshā ba.

　　A: 我去她的宿舍找过她，可是＿＿＿＿＿＿。(not find)
　　　Wǒ qù tā de sùshè zhǎoguo tā, kěshì ＿＿＿＿＿＿.

2. Describe actions in succession

(1) Answer the questions, using the phrases provided and "先 xiān" (first), "然后 ránhòu" (then, after that)

　　Example: 我回家以后先吃饭，然后吃药。
　　　　　　 Wǒ huí jiā yǐhòu xiān chī fàn, ránhòu chī yào.
　　　　　　 After I get home, I'll have my meal and then take my medicine.

　　① What will happen if you go to see a doctor?

量血压	听心脏
liáng xuèyā	tīng xīnzàng

② What are you going to do tomorrow?

> 看病　　买药
> kàn bìng　　mǎi yào

③ You caught a cold, and went to the campus clinic. What do you expect there?

> 量体温　　化验
> liáng tǐwēn　　huàyàn

④ What are you going to do when you get home?

> 吃药　　睡觉
> chī yào　　shuì jiào

⑤ You're invited by the school dean to a banquet. How do you prepare for it?

> 洗澡　　换正式的衣服
> xǐ zǎo　　huàn zhèngshì de yīfu

⑥ You are having a Chinese test tomorrow. How do you prepare for it?

> 复习生词　　做语法练习
> fùxí shēngcí　　zuò yǔfǎ liànxí

(2) Answer the questions, using the phrases provided and "先 xiān" (first), "再 zài" (then) and "然后 ránhòu" (after that)

Example: 我今天有很多事要做。我得先去商店买东西，再去邮局，然后去学校学习。
Wǒ jīntiān yǒu hěn duō shì yào zuò. Wǒ děi xiān qù shāngdiàn mǎi dōngxi, zài qù yóujú, ránhòu qù xuéxiào xuéxí.

① This is your first weekend in China; today you have to do the following:

> 换钱　　去超市买日用品　　去菜市场买水果
> huàn qián　　qù chāoshì mǎi rìyòngpǐn　　qù càishìchǎng mǎi shuǐguǒ

② You felt sick yesterday and went to the clinic. Describe what happened – "the nurse came in and….":

> 量体温　　量血压　　听心脏
> liáng tǐwēn　　liáng xuèyā　　tīng xīnzàng

③ You're invited to a Chinese friend's wedding. What do you have to do?

> 买礼物　　买正式的服装　　去理发
> mǎi lǐwù　　mǎi zhèngshì de fúzhuāng　　qù lǐ fà

第十六课 在医院
Lesson Sixteen   At the Hospital

④ You will have an interview for an English-teaching position next week. What do you have to do to prepare for it?

⑤ Your parents are coming to China to visit you in two weeks. Where do you plan to take them?

⑥ You just had your first haircut in China. Describe the occasion:

3. **Express the following, using suffixes** "极了 jí le" or "得很 de hěn"

   Example: ① 我的头疼极了。 I am suffering from a terrible headache.
   　　　　　　Wǒ de tóu téng jí le.

   　　　　　② 那个理发店贵得很。 That hairsalon is extremely expensive.
   　　　　　　Nàge lǐfàdiàn guì de hěn.

   (1) Tell your friend that your Chinese professor is REALLY nice.

   ....

   (2) Tell your doctor that your stomach hurts SO much.

   ....

   (3) Tell your Chinese host that the dishes she cooked are REALLY delicious.

   ....

   (4) Tell your roommate that the Chinese students you tutor now are SO smart.

   ....

   (5) Tell your friend that the produce and fruit at the morning market are EXTREMELY fresh and cheap.

   ....

   (6) Tell your Chinese friend that you have found that China has A LOT of rich people. ("中国的富人 Zhōngguó de fùrén", rich Chinese)

   ....

4. Answer the questions along the lines of the English cues, making your doubts clear (and using the phrases in parentheses)

Example: 我不知道我对这种药过敏不过敏。 I don't know if I'm allergic to this medicine or not.
Wǒ bù zhīdào wǒ duì zhè zhǒng yào guòmǐn bu guòmǐn.

(1) A: 你还来得及吃早饭吗？
Nǐ hái láidejí chī zǎofàn ma?

B: 我不知道_____。(if there's time to eat breakfast)

(2) A: 你的胳膊有没有骨折？
Nǐ de gēbo yǒu méiyǒu gǔzhé?

B: 我不知道_____。(if I broke my arm or not)

(3) A: 你现在发烧吗？
Nǐ xiànzài fā shāo ma?

B: 我不知道_____。(if I'm running a fever or not)

(4) A: 今天晚上的宴会教育局的领导来不来？
Jīntiān wǎnshang de yànhuì Jiàoyùjú de lǐngdǎo lái bu lái?

B: 我不知道_____。(if he will show up or not)

(5) A: 你下个学期还做不做家教？
Nǐ xià ge xuéqī hái zuò bu zuò jiājiào?

B: 我不知道_____。(if I have time to do it)

(6) A: 你放假的时候想去哪儿旅游？
Nǐ fàng jià de shíhou xiǎng qù nǎr lǚyóu?

B: 我不知道_____。(if I have the money to travel around)

(7) A: 你明年打算做什么？
Nǐ míngnián dǎsuàn zuò shénme?

B: 我不知道_____。(if I should return to the States)

5. Fill in the blanks with requests, using appropriate directional compounds

Example: 请过来。   请上来。
Qǐng guòlai.   Qǐng shànglai.

上来	下来	进来	出来	回来	过来	起来
上去	下去	进去	出去	回去	过去	/

(1) Ask your friend to come down stairs. _____

第十六课　在医院
Lesson Sixteen　At the Hospital

(2) Ask your friend to get in (the car). _____

(3) Ask your friend to come over. _____

(4) Ask your friend to get up. _____

(5) Your friend asks you to come upstairs. _____

(6) Your friend asks you to come out. _____

(7) Tell your friend that you are going back. _____

(8) Tell your friend to get out of the car. _____

(9) Tell your friend to go over there. _____

(10) Tell your friend to go into the doctor's office. _____

(11) Tell your friend to run back. _____ (跑 pǎo)

(12) Tell your friend to put the book back. _____ (放 fàng)

(13) Tell your friend to take out the textbook. _____ (拿 ná)

(14) Tell your friend to bring over some fruit (for the party). _____ (拿 ná)

(15) Tell your friend to put the thermometer in his mouth. _____ (放 fàng)

(16) Tell your friend to put the prescription over there. _____ (放 fàng)

6. Talk to people in your class and find out if they were doing the activities listed at the times that you designate with "正 zhèng", "在 zài", or "正在 zhèngzài"

   Example: A: 你今天早上九点钟在做作业吗？
   Nǐ jīntiān zǎoshang jiǔ diǎnzhōng zài zuò zuòyè ma?
   At 9 o'clock this morning, were you doing your homework?

   B: 没有，我在做早饭呢。 No, I was making breakfast.
   Méiyǒu, wǒ zài zuò zǎofàn ne.

(1) 洗衣服 xǐ yīfu	(7) 在理发店理发 zài lǐfàdiàn lǐ fà
(2) 上课 shàng kè	(8) 跟朋友吃饭 gēn péngyou chī fàn
(3) 看病 kàn bìng	(9) 睡觉 shuì jiào
(4) 买菜 mǎi cài	(10) 做中文作业 zuò Zhōngwén zuòyè
(5) 上网 shàng wǎng	(11) 在宿舍看电视 zài sùshè kàn diànshì

(6) 给妈妈/朋友打电话	(12) 在图书馆看书
gěi māma / péngyou dǎ diànhuà	zài túshūguǎn kàn shū

7. Match the diagnoses in column A with the symptoms in column B

Example: A: 水土不服的时候会有什么症状？
　　　　　Shuǐtǔ bùfú de shíhou huì yǒu shénme zhèngzhuàng?

　　　　B: 水土不服的时候会嗓子不舒服。
　　　　　Shuǐtǔ bùfú de shíhou huì sǎngzi bù shūfu.

A
诊断 zhěnduàn	diagnosis
水土不服 shuǐtǔ bùfú	not acclimatized
消化不良 xiāohuà bùliáng	indigestion
血压高 xuèyā gāo	high blood pressure
感冒 gǎnmào	cold, flu
骨折 gǔzhé	a broken bone
过敏 guòmǐn	allergy
扭伤 niǔshāng	to sprain

B
发烧 fā shāo	to have a fever
发炎 fā yán	to have inflammation
嗓子疼 sǎngzi téng	sore throat
咳嗽 késou	to cough or to have a cough
头疼 tóu téng	to have a headache
背疼 bèi téng	to have back pain, to have a backache
腹泻 fùxiè/拉肚子 lā dùzi	diarrhea
胃痛 wèi tòng	stomach ache
感染 gǎnrǎn	to infect
流血 liú xiě	to bleed, to shed blood
嗓子不舒服 sǎngzi bù shūfu	discomfort in the throat
胳膊疼 gēbo téng	sore arm
脚疼 jiǎo téng	sore foot

第十六课 在医院
Lesson Sixteen   At the Hospital

Listening Comprehension

1. Listen to the dialogue and then answer the questions

(1) What's wrong with the patient?

(2) How long has the patient had the problem?

(3) Is the patient running a fever?

(4) Does the patient have a headache?

(5) How about the patient's blood pressure?

(6) Did the patient get any tests?

(7) What was the doctor's diagnosis?

(8) What did the patient have for dinner the previous evening?

(9) What did the patient have for lunch that day? (Mention 4 things.)

(10) What did the doctor recommend besides taking some medicine? (Mention 2 things.)

New Words

正常 zhèngcháng Adj normal

宫保鸡丁 gōngbǎo-jīdīng Phrase spicy diced chicken with peanuts

葱爆牛肉 cōngbào-niúròu Phrase quick fried beef with scallions

猪肉 zhūròu N pork

饿 è Adj hungry

但是 dànshì Conj but

2. Listen to the dialogue and then answer the questions

(1) What brought the patient to the doctor's office? (Mention at least 2 things.)

(2) Does the patient have a fever?

(3) What were the test results?

(4) What was the doctor's diagnosis?

(5) Did the patient take any medicine before coming to see the doctor?

(6) What did the doctor prescribe?

(7) What were the instructions regarding the medicine?

(8) What did the doctor tell the patient particularly not to do?

New Words

呼吸 hūxī V to breathe

困难 kùnnan Adj difficult

胸口 xiōngkǒu N chest

阿司匹林 āsīpǐlín N aspirin

Communication Activities

Pair Work

Scenario I: Tell your partner about your experiences visiting a doctor. Use the following items:

挂号	预约	大夫	得过	量
guà hào	yùyuē	dàifu	déguo	liáng
听	化验	症状	先……然后……	
tīng	huàyàn	zhèngzhuàng	xiān……ránhòu……	
药方	一天……次	一次……片		
yàofāng	yì tiān……cì	yí cì……piàn		

Scenario II: Work together with your partner to determine a diagnosis for the given symptoms, then suggest a treatment:

(1)
发烧	发冷	咳嗽	头疼	感冒
fā shāo	fā lěng	késou	tóu téng	gǎnmào
输液	吃抗生素	一天……次	一次……片	
shū yè	chī kàngshēngsù	yì tiān……cì	yí cì……piàn	

(2)
血压有点儿高	心脏不正常	头疼	睡不好觉
xuèyā yǒudiǎnr gāo	xīnzàng bú zhèngcháng	tóu téng	shuì bu hǎo jiào
太紧张了	休息	早睡觉	多运动
tài jǐnzhāng le	xiūxi	zǎo shuì jiào	duō yùndòng

(3)
拉肚子	不想吃东西	吐	大便不正常
lā dùzi	bù xiǎng chī dōngxi	tù	dàbiàn bú zhèngcháng
水土不服	不干净的东西	开水	
shuǐtǔ bùfú	bù gānjìng de dōngxi	kāishuǐ	

Role-Play

Scenario I: Stomach problems. Roles: patient and doctor. You, the patient, ate some leftovers last night and a couple of hours later, you got a stomach ache and had to get up to go to the bathroom a lot in the night. Eventually you go to the doctor. The doctor examines you, asks questions, and makes a diagnosis. He/She prescribes some medicine and gives some advice. Make use of the following items:

拉肚子	疼极了	不想吃东西	吐	腹泄
lā dùzi	téngjí le	bù xiǎng chī dōngxi	tù	fùxiè
厕所	不干净的东西	化验	一天……次	
cèsuǒ	bù gānjìng de dōngxi	huàyàn	yì tiān……cì	

第十六课　在医院
Lesson Sixteen　At the Hospital

Scenario II: Sick leave. Roles: teacher and student. You, the student, tell your teacher that you don't know whether you'll be able to make it to class the next day: you have a cold and cough, and you feel feverish. Teacher suggests you go and see a doctor and get the problem taken care of; you don't want to infect your classmates.

感冒	头疼	嗓子	发烧	不知道
gǎnmào	tóu téng	sǎngzi	fā shāo	bù zhīdào
能不能	挂号	化验	开药方	
néng bu néng	guà hào	huàyàn	kāi yàofāng	

Group Activities

Roles: a nurse and three patients. The nurse has to find out the patients' symptoms, then assign each patient to a doctor. Use the following items:

Nurse:
哪儿不舒服　nǎr bù shūfu
量体温　liáng tǐwēn
血压　xuèyā
预约　yùyuē
先……再……　xiān……zài……
正常　zhèngcháng
化验血/大便/小便　huàyàn xiě/dàbiàn/xiǎobiàn

Patient A:	发烧 fā shāo	发冷 fā lěng	咳嗽 késou
	有一点儿 yǒu yìdiǎnr	头疼 tóu téng	

Patient B:	得过高血压 déguo gāoxuèyā	心脏不舒服 xīnzàng bù shūfu	头疼 tóu téng
	睡不好觉 shuì bu hǎo jiào	呼吸困难 hūxī kùnnan	

Patient C:	拉肚子 lā dùzi	不想吃东西 bù xiǎng chī dōngxi	吐 tù
	大便不正常 dàbiàn bú zhèngcháng	消化不良 xiāohuà bùliáng	

Review Exercises

1. Tell each other at least three things that have impressed you or shocked you since you have been in China

   Example: 中国菜好吃极了！
   Zhōngguócài hǎochī jí le!

真实生活汉语 2
Chinese for Living in China

北京的马路上德国车多得很!
Běijīng de mǎlù shang Déguóchē duō de hěn!

(1) _____

(2) _____

(3) _____

(4) _____

(5) _____

(6) _____

2. What would you do in the following situations? Answer with "先 xiān……然后 ránhòu……"

(1) 你的朋友吐了，还拉肚子。
Nǐ de péngyou tù le, hái lā dùzi.

_____

(2) 你看不懂老师给的作业。
Nǐ kàn bu dǒng lǎoshī gěi de zuòyè.

_____

(3) 你的老师请你去参加市教育局的宴会。
Nǐ de lǎoshī qǐng nǐ qù cānjiā Shì Jiàoyùjú de yànhuì.

_____

(4) 你觉得很不舒服，头疼，发冷，嗓子也疼。
Nǐ juéde hěn bù shūfu, tóu téng, fā lěng, sǎngzi yě téng.

_____

(5) 明天你要去面试一个家教的工作。
Míngtiān nǐ yào qù miànshì yí ge jiājiào de gōngzuò.

_____

(6) 在理发店，美发师问你需要什么服务。
Zài lǐfàdiàn, měifàshī wèn nǐ xūyào shénme fúwù.

_____

(7) 坐公共汽车的时候，售票员告诉你坐错方向了。
Zuò gōnggòng qìchē de shíhou, shòupiàoyuán gàosu nǐ zuòcuò fāngxiàng le.

_____

第十六课 在医院
Lesson Sixteen   At the Hospital

(8) 你要请中国朋友来家里吃饭。
Nǐ yào qǐng Zhōngguó péngyou lái jiāli chī fàn.

_____

(9) 你星期五有一个很重要的中文考试。
Nǐ xīngqīwǔ yǒu yí ge hěn zhòngyào de Zhōngwén kǎoshì.

_____

3. **One of you asks the question, the other answers using "正 zhèng", "在 zài" or "正在 zhèngzài"**

(1) A: 今天早上九点钟你在做什么？
　　　Jīntiān zǎoshang jiǔ diǎnzhōng nǐ zài zuò shénme?

　　B: _____。(做作业 zuò zuòyè)

(2) A: 昨天晚上九点钟你在做什么？
　　　Zuótiān wǎnshang jiǔ diǎnzhōng nǐ zài zuò shénme?

　　B: _____。(洗衣服 xǐ yīfu)

(3) A: 明天下午两点你会在做什么？
　　　Míngtiān xiàwǔ liǎng diǎn nǐ huì zài zuò shénme?

　　B: _____。(上英文课 shàng Yīngwénkè)

(4) A: 我给你打电话的时候你在做什么？
　　　Wǒ gěi nǐ dǎ diànhuà de shíhou nǐ zài zuò shénme?

　　B: _____。(看病 kàn bìng)

(5) A: 你的同屋洗衣服的时候你在做什么？
　　　Nǐ de tóngwū xǐ yīfu de shíhou nǐ zài zuò shénme?

　　B: _____。(做饭 zuò fàn)

(6) A: 为什么你得喝很多水？
　　　Wèi shénme nǐ děi hē hěn duō shuǐ?

　　B: _____。(发烧 fā shāo)

(7) A: 安妮怎么没来上课？
　　　Ānnī zěnme méi lái shàng kè?

　　B: _____。(看病 kàn bìng)

(8) A: 马克为什么没来吃饭？
　　　Mǎkè wèi shénme méi lái chī fàn?

　　B: _____。(打篮球 dǎ lánqiú)

155

4. Ask your partner if he/she knows the following (using "知道 zhīdào") and see how your partner responds

   (1) Where the restaurant with the best food is.

   ....

   (2) If you can find (找到 zhǎodào) a position teaching English.

   ....

   (3) Where you can watch a movie in English.

   ....

   (4) Where you can buy Tylenol.

   ....

   (5) If there's a subway station near the school.

   ....

5. Explain your symptoms to the doctor, following the English statements

   (1) You have indigestion and you vomited twice this morning.

   ....

   (2) You have a bad headache but you're not sure if you have a fever.

   ....

   (3) Your stomach aches, but you don't have diarrhea.

   ....

   (4) You have discomfort in your throat and your eyes itch. Find out if you have an allergy and explain that, back in the States, you have allergies in the spring. But since it's summer in Beijing, you think it might be the air pollution.

   ....

Lesson Sixteen   At the Hospital

第十六课   在医院

Culture Notes

1. Registering at the hospital

When you want to see a doctor in a hospital, your first step is to go to a window marked "挂号 guà hào" (registration). Registration costs about five *yuan* for a foreign patient. You get a registration number and a medical record book, which looks like this:

In China, patients keep their own medical record books, not doctors.

2. The medical examination room

Unlike in the West, patients at most Chinese hospitals are not seen first by nurses. The doctor sits in an examination room with the door open and patients enter and leave on their own. Often two doctors share an examination room, each seeing patients. Doctors will examine you and, if needed, give you a prescription. It is not standard procedure in China to take temperature or blood pressure before seeing a doctor.

3. Payments

All fees, including the examination fee and fees for prescriptions, are paid at the cashier's window. After payment, medicine can be picked up at the pharmacy window.

4. The pharmacy

In China, pharmacies are usually in the hospital. Once you have paid your fees, you take your prescription with the payment receipt to the pharmacy window and give them to the pharmacist to fill while you wait. The pharmacist will explain how to take the medicine and give written instructions.

Lesson Seventeen   Mary's Apartment

第十七课   玛丽的公寓
Dì-shíqī Kè   Mǎlì de Gōngyù

In this lesson you will learn how to do the following
- Talk about your co-worker(s) or classmates
- Describe your place of work
- Describe where you live in terms of rooms, furniture, utility bills, etc.
- Talk about preparing a meal and the kitchen implements you use

Grammar
- The preposition "被 bèi" (by)
- The three "de's": "的", "地", and "得"
- Purpose with "为了 wèile" (in order to)
- Concession, with "虽然 suīrán……但是 dànshì……" (although…[but]…)
- Coordination, with "不但 búdàn……而且 érqiě……" (not only…but also…)
- Simultaneous actions, with "一边 yìbiān……一边 yìbiān……" (while…, as well as…)

Culture Notes
- How to address people
- Visitors who come by unannounced
- What to bring as a gift
- Work units and the provision of daily-use items

第十七课　玛丽的公寓
Lesson Seventeen　Mary's Apartment

Dialogue

A：小兰，玛丽的同事　　　　B：玛丽　　　　C：小红，玛丽的同事
Xiǎolán, Mǎlì de tóngshì　　　Mǎlì　　　　Xiǎohóng, Mǎlì de tóngshì

　　玛丽在上海一家外贸公司工作。在公司写字楼工作的人被[G1]称为[1]"白领阶层"。白领们一般都很年轻，受过良好教育，收入稳定。他们穿名牌服装，拿名牌提包，老百姓都认为他们很有钱。白领一起出去吃饭都是AA制[2]，各付各的[3]钱。刚开始到公司工作的时候，同事们都对玛丽非常好，大家一起出去吃饭，他们常常请她，不要她付钱。渐渐地[G2]，玛丽发现这些白领同事不像人们想的那么富有。她不再要同事请客了。为了[G3]表示回报，这个周末玛丽想请她的同事到自己在上海的公寓吃饭。可是同事们大多数愿意自己过周末，只有两个女同事答应来。

　　Mǎlì zài Shànghǎi yì jiā wàimào gōngsī gōngzuò. Zài gōngsī xiězìlóu gōngzuò de rén bèi[G1] chēngwéi[1] "báilǐng jiēcéng". Báilǐngmen yìbān dōu hěn niánqīng, shòuguo liánghǎo jiàoyù, shōurù wěndìng. Tāmen chuān míngpái fúzhuāng, ná míngpái tíbāo, lǎobǎixìng dōu rènwéi tāmen hěn yǒuqián. Báilǐng yìqǐ chūqu chī fàn dōu shì AA zhì[2], gè fù gè de[3] qián. Gāng kāishǐ dào gōngsī gōngzuò de shíhou, tóngshìmen dōu duì Mǎlì fēicháng hǎo, dàjiā yìqǐ chūqu chī fàn, tāmen chángcháng qǐng tā, bú yào tā fù qián. Jiànjiàn de[G2], Mǎlì fāxiàn zhèxiē báilǐng tóngshì bú xiàng rénmen xiǎng de nàme fùyǒu. Tā bú zài yào tóngshì qǐng kè le. Wèile[G3] biǎoshì huíbào, zhège zhōumò Mǎlì xiǎng qǐng tā de tóngshì dào zìjǐ zài Shànghǎi de gōngyù chī fàn. Kěshì tóngshìmen dàduōshù yuànyì zìjǐ guò zhōumò, zhǐ yǒu liǎng ge nǚ tóngshì dāying lái.

A：玛丽在吗？
　　Mǎlì zài ma?

B：在。请进。不用脱鞋了。你们先坐在这边的沙发上。我去给你们沏茶。
　　Zài. Qǐng jìn. Búyòng tuō xié le. Nǐmen xiān zuò zài zhèbian de shāfā shang. Wǒ qù gěi nǐmen qī chá.

C：你的公寓好大，真漂亮。
　　Nǐ de gōngyù hǎo dà, zhēn piàoliang.

Notes

1. "称为 chēngwéi" means "to address as, to call". "为 wéi" (rising tone) originally meant "to be, to become, to serve as". Cf. "以为 yǐwéi" (to regard as). "称 chēng" and "为 wéi" can also be separated by an object: "有人称他们为白领阶层 Yǒu rén chēng tāmen wéi báilǐng jiēcéng" (Some people call them the "white-collar class").
2. "AA制 AA zhì" is, literally "the AA system", slang for "splitting the bill" or "going Dutch". It is assumed that the term originated as an abbreviation, but hypothetical sources like "algebraic average" or "all apart" are not very convincing.
3. "各付各的钱 gè fù gè de qián", literally "each pays each's expenses", i.e. "to pay separately". This is slightly different from "AA制 AA zhì", in which the total is split (usually).

真实生活汉语 2
Chinese for Living in China

A：这里虽然在市中心，附近很热闹，但是[G4]你的公寓真安静。你有几间房间？
Zhèli suīrán zài shì zhōngxīn, fùjìn hěn rènao, dànshì[G4] nǐ de gōngyù zhēn ānjìng. Nǐ yǒu jǐ jiān fángjiān?

B：一间卧室，一个客厅，一个卫生间和一个厨房。
Yì jiān wòshì, yí ge kètīng, yí ge wèishēngjiān hé yí ge chúfáng.

A：房租一定很贵吧？
Fángzū yídìng hěn guì ba?

B：这是公司给我租的房子，这些家具也是公司的。
Zhè shì gōngsī gěi wǒ zū de fángzi, zhèxiē jiājù yě shì gōngsī de.

C：客厅里的书柜和电视也是公司的吗？
Kètīng li de shūguì hé diànshì yě shì gōngsī de ma?

B：是。我没有书房，所以客厅就是我的书房。我什么家具都没买。卧室里的双人床、床头柜和衣柜也是公司的。这些家具都不是新的，可能是以前住在这儿的外国员工留下来的。
Shì. Wǒ méiyǒu shūfáng, suǒyǐ kètīng jiù shì wǒ de shūfáng. Wǒ shénme jiājù dōu méi mǎi. Wòshì li de shuāngrénchuáng, chuángtóuguì hé yīguì yě shì gōngsī de. Zhèxiē jiājù dōu bú shì xīn de, kěnéng shì yǐqián zhù zài zhèr de wàiguó yuángōng liú xialai de.

A：公司不但给你付房租，而且给你付水电费吗[G5]？
Gōngsī búdàn gěi nǐ fù fángzū, érqiě gěi nǐ fù shuǐdiànfèi ma[G5]?

B：是的。房租、水电费公司全包了。
Shì de. Fángzū, shuǐdiànfèi gōngsī quán bāo le.

C：你在上海市中心有这样一套公寓，所有的白领都会羡慕你。
Nǐ zài Shànghǎi shì zhōngxīn yǒu zhèyàng yí tào gōngyù, suǒyǒu de báilǐng dōu huì xiànmù nǐ.

B：我知道我是很幸运的。你们先坐着喝茶，我去厨房做饭。
Wǒ zhīdào wǒ shì hěn xìngyùn de. Nǐmen xiān zuòzhe hē chá, wǒ qù chúfáng zuò fàn.

A&C：我们也去厨房和你一起做饭吧。大家还可以一边做饭一边聊天儿[G6]。
Wǒmen yě qù chúfáng hé nǐ yìqǐ zuò fàn ba. Dàjiā hái kěyǐ yìbiān zuò fàn yìbiān liáo tiānr[G6].

B：好。我正在学做中国菜，还做得不好。我已经烤好了一只鸡，放在冰箱里了，过一会儿在微波炉里加热就好了。我再做一个炒洋白菜，一个青椒肉丝，我们就能开饭了。
Hǎo. Wǒ zhèngzài xué zuò zhōngguócài, hái zuò de bù hǎo. Wǒ yǐjīng kǎohǎole yì zhī jī, fàng zài bīngxiāng li le, guò yíhuìr zài wēibōlú li jiārè jiù hǎo le. Wǒ zài zuò yí ge chǎo yángbáicài, yí ge qīngjiāo ròusī, wǒmen jiù néng kāi fàn le.

第十七课　玛丽的公寓
Lesson Seventeen　Mary's Apartment

C：我帮你切肉丝吧。菜刀在哪儿？
　　Wǒ bāng nǐ qiē ròusī ba. Càidāo zài nǎr?

B：在抽屉里。
　　Zài chōuti li.

A：我来煮饭。
　　Wǒ lái zhǔ fàn.

B：那我就摆盘子、碗、叉子、勺子，还有纸巾。你们用筷子吗？
　　Nà wǒ jiù bǎi pánzi、wǎn、chāzi、sháozi, háiyǒu zhǐjīn. Nǐmen yòng kuàizi ma?

A&C：用。
　　Yòng.

B：哦，还要拿杯子。我们先喝一点儿红酒。来，干杯！
　　Ò, hái yào ná bēizi. Wǒmen xiān hē yìdiǎnr hóngjiǔ. Lái, gān bēi!

A&C：干杯！
　　Gān bēi!

New Words

1	外贸/外貿	wàimào	N	foreign trade
2	写字楼/寫字樓	xiězìlóu	N	office building
3	称为/稱為	chēngwéi	V	to address as, to be called, to be known as
4	白领/白領	báilǐng	N	white collar
5	阶层/階層	jiēcéng	N	social class, social stratum
6	一般	yìbān	Adj	commonplace, ordinary, average
7	年轻/年輕	niánqīng	Adj	young
8	良好	liánghǎo	Adj	good, desirable
9	教育	jiàoyù	N/V	education; to teach, to educate
10	收入	shōurù	N/V	income; to include
11	稳定/穩定	wěndìng	Adj	stable
12	提包	tíbāo	N	shopping bag, handbag
13	老百姓	lǎobǎixìng	N	the common folk, civilians
14	认为/認為	rènwéi	V	to believe that, to think that, to regard to be

真实生活汉语 2

15	有钱/有錢	yǒuqián	Adj	wealthy
16	出去	chūqu	V	to go out, to exit
17	AA制	AA zhì	Exp	"AA" = split the bill, go Dutch
	制	zhì	BF	system
18	各……各……	gè……gè……	Construction	each…each…
	各	gè	Pron	each, every
19	开始/開始	kāishǐ	V	to begin, to start
20	大家	dàjiā	N	everyone, all of us
21	份（儿）/份（兒）	fèn (r)	Meas	*for newspapers, shares or portions*
22	渐渐/漸漸	jiànjiàn	Adv	gradually, by degrees
23	地	de	Part	*follows adjectives to mark them as adverbials*
24	这些/這些	zhèxiē	Pron	these
25	像	xiàng	V	to resemble, to look as if
26	人们/人們	rénmen	N	people, humanity
27	那么/那麼	nàme	Pron/Conj	in that way, so; well, in that case
28	富有	fùyǒu	Adj	wealthy, rich
29	不再	bú zài	Phrase	no more, no longer
30	请客/請客	qǐng kè	VO	to entertain guests, to treat (someone to a meal)
31	为了/為了	wèile	Prep	for, in order to, for the sake of
32	表示	biǎoshì	V	to show, to express, to indicate
33	回报/回報	huíbào	V	to report back, to repay, to get one's own back
34	大多数/大多數	dàduōshù	N	great majority
35	愿意/願意	yuànyì	Aux	to be willing, to want
36	只有	zhǐ yǒu	Phrase	only, there are only
37	答应/答應	dāying	V	to answer, to reply, to agree, to promise
38	脱鞋	tuō xié	Phrase	to take off shoes (cf. "拖鞋 tuōxié", sandals)
39	沙发/沙發	shāfā	N	a sofa
40	沏茶	qī chá	Phrase	to brew tea

第十七课 玛丽的公寓
Lesson Seventeen Mary's Apartment

41	好大	hǎo dà	Phrase	so big, really big
	好	hǎo	Adv	(*used before adjectives with exclamatory force*) very, quite, so
42	漂亮	piàoliang	Adj	beautiful, splendid
43	虽然/雖然	suīrán	Conj	though, although
44	市中心	shì zhōngxīn	Phrase	in the center of town
45	热闹/熱鬧	rènao	Adj/V/N	lively, buzzing with excitement; to have a good time; excitement, fun
46	卧室	wòshì	N	bedroom
47	安静/安靜	ānjìng	Adj	quiet, peaceful
48	但是	dànshì	Conj	but
49	客厅	kètīng	N	living room
50	厨房/廚房	chúfáng	N	kitchen
51	房租	fángzū	N	rent (money)
52	租	zū	V	to rent, to lease, to hire
53	房子	fángzi	N	house, building, room or apartment
54	家具	jiājù	N	furniture
55	书柜/書櫃	shūguì	N	bookcase
56	书房/書房	shūfáng	N	study
57	双人床/雙人床	shuāngrén-chuáng	N	double bed
58	床头柜/床頭櫃	chuángtóuguì	N	bedside cupboard
	柜/櫃	guì	BF	cabinet
59	衣柜/衣櫃	yīguì	N	wardrobe, closet, cupboard
60	新	xīn	Adj	new
61	可能	kěnéng	Adj/Aux/N	possible, probable; to be possible, may; possibility
62	以前	yǐqián	TW	before in the past
63	外国/外國	wàiguó	N	foreign country
64	员工/員工	yuángōng	N	staff, personnel
65	留	liú	V	to remain, to stay
66	不但	búdàn	Conj	not only

真实生活汉语 2
Chinese for Living in China

67	而且	érqiě	Conj	moreover, in addition
68	水电费/水電費	shuǐdiànfèi	N	charges for water and electricity, utility bills
	水	shuǐ	N	water
	电/電	diàn	N	electricity
69	全	quán	Adv/Adj	totally, entirely; complete, whole
70	包	bāo	V/N/Meas	to undertake the whole thing, to wrap, to guarantee; bundle, bag; *for objects in packets, etc.*
71	所有	suǒyǒu	Attr	all, every
72	羡慕	xiànmù	V	to envy, to admire
73	幸运/幸運	xìngyùn	Adj/N	fortunate; good fortune, luck
74	做饭/做飯	zuò fàn	Phrase	to cook
75	一边(儿)……一边(儿)……/一邊(兒)……一邊(兒)……	yìbiān (r)……yìbiān (r)……	Construction	while…, one the one hand…on the other
76	聊天儿/聊天兒	liáo tiānr	VO	(col) to chat, to gossip
	聊	liáo	V	to chat
77	烤	kǎo	V	to bake, to roast, to toast, to warm (hands)
78	冰箱	bīngxiāng	N	refrigerator, icebox
79	微波炉/微波爐	wēibōlú	N	microwave oven
80	加热/加熱	jiārè	V	to heat, to warm up
81	洋白菜	yángbáicài	N	cabbage
82	肉丝/肉絲	ròusī	N	shredded pork
83	开饭/開飯	kāi fàn	VO	to serve a meal
84	切	qiē	V	to cut, to slice
85	菜刀	càidāo	N	kitchen knife
86	抽屉/抽屜	chōuti	N	drawer
87	煮饭/煮飯	zhǔ fàn	Phrase	(col) to cook rice
88	盘子/盤子	pánzi	N	tray, dish
89	碗	wǎn	N	bowl

第十七课 玛丽的公寓
Lesson Seventeen Mary's Apartment

90	叉子	chāzi	N	fork
91	勺子	sháozi	N	spoon, ladle, scoop
92	纸巾/紙巾	zhǐjīn	N	paper napkin
93	筷子	kuàizi	N	chopsticks
94	哦	ò	Int	*expressing realization, understanding, etc.*
95	红酒/紅酒	hóngjiǔ	N	red wine
96	干杯/乾杯	gān bēi	VO/Exp	to drink a toast; cheers

Re-enacting the Dialogue

A: Xiaolan, Mary's colleague   B: Mary, a foreigner   C: Xiaohong, Mary's colleague

Mary works at a foreign trading company in Shanghai. People who work at the company office building are referred to as the "white collar class". White collar people are generally quite young, well-educated and have a stable income. They wear brand-name clothes and carry brand-name handbags; ordinary people believe they're rich. When they go out to eat together, they go "AA system" (i.e. "Dutch"), each paying their own way. When she started working at the company, her colleagues were very nice to her, when they all went out to eat together. They often treated her, not allowing her to pay for her portion. Gradually, she realized that those white collar people weren't as well off as people thought. She doesn't want her colleagues to treat her anymore. In order to reciprocate, this weekend Mary is planning to invite her colleagues over to her Shanghai apartment for a meal. However, most of her colleagues have their own plans for the weekend; only two of them agree to come.

A: Is Mary in?

B: Yes, please come in. No need to take your shoes off. Have a seat on this sofa first; I'll go and brew some tea for you both.

C: Your apartment's big – it's really attractive.

A: Even though it's in the center of the city and in a lively district, the apartment's really quiet. How many rooms do you have?

B: Four altogether: a bedroom, a living room, a bathroom and a kitchen.

A: It must be expensive.

B: The company rented it for me – the furniture is the company's too.

C: Are the bookcase and TV in the living room also the company's?

B: Yes. I don't have a study, so the living room is my study. I haven't bought any furniture. The double-bed, the night stands and the bureau in the bedroom are also the company's. The furniture's not new; it was probably left by the foreign employee who lived here before.

A: The company not only pays your utility bills, it pays your rent as well?

B: It does. Everything's covered by the company – rent and utilities.

C: Having an apartment like this in the center of Shanghai! All the white collar workers will be envious of you!

B: Yes, I realize I'm very lucky. Sit down and have some tea while I go to the kitchen and prepare the meal.

A&C: Why don't we come to the kitchen and cook with you? We can chat while we're preparing the meal.

B: OK. I'm just learning how to cook Chinese food – I'm still not very good at it. I've already baked a chicken and put it in the fridge. It'll be ready shortly, after I heat it up in the microwave. We can eat after I stir-fry a cabbage and do a green pepper with shredded beef.

C: I'll help you cut the meat into shreds. Where's your kitchen knife?

B: In the drawer.

A: I'll cook the rice.

B: OK, so I'll put out the plates, bowls, forks and spoons – and the napkins. Will you use chopsticks?

A&C: Yes.

B: Oh. Take a glass. Let's start with some red wine. Here – cheers!

A&C: Cheers!

第十七课　玛丽的公寓
Lesson Seventeen　Mary's Apartment

Grammar

▶ G1. The preposition "被 bèi" (by)

Faced with an event involving an action, it is possible to take the perspective of the initiating agent – the "do-er" – or the perspective of the patient – the person or thing "done to". Say, for example, you left your shoes at the door and without telling you, someone removes them and puts them outside. You report as follows:

① 我的鞋被拿走了。　My shoes have been removed.
　Wǒ de xié bèi názǒu le.

You start with the object of interest – your shoes, and express the fact that someone took them by using "被 bèi" before the verb-resultative compound, "拿走 názǒu" (take-away) — "被拿走了 bèi názǒu le" (got taken away). If someone knows who took them, he could add the agent as the object of the preposition, "被 bèi":

② 你的鞋被小红拿走了。　Your shoes were removed by Xiaohong.
　Nǐ de xié bèi Xiǎohóng názǒu le.

Finally, if Xiaohong herself appears and confesses, she can make herself the subject and report the event using "把 bǎ" to focus on what she did do to the shoes:

③ 对不起，我把你的鞋拿走了。　Sorry, I removed your shoes.
　Duìbuqǐ, wǒ bǎ nǐ de xié názǒu le.

To some degree, "被 bèi"-sentences correspond to English passive sentences, which also serve to shift the perspective around – from the agent to the patient: (Active) "Xiaohong took the shoes" → (Passive) "The shoes were taken (or got taken) by Xiaohong." The order of words changes; the form of the verb also changes. The correspondence to Chinese is suggestive, but not exact. For one thing, the form of the verb in Chinese doesn't change. For another, a "被 bèi"-sentence often does not translate very easily into an English passive. English can achieve the same effects by other means – intonation, for example, or use of an indefinite subject, as the following examples show:

④ 鞋被我找到了。　I've found my shoes!
　Xié bèi wǒ zhǎodào le.

⑤ 窗户被人打破了。　Someone's broken the window.
　Chuānghu bèi rén dǎpò le.

⑥ 那本书被我扔掉了。　I threw that book out.
　Nà běn shū bèi wǒ rēngdiào le.

And conversely, Chinese sentences without "被 bèi" can often require the English passive in the translation:

⑦ 可能是以前住在这儿的外国员工留下来的。
　Kěnéng shì yǐqián zhù zài zhèr de wàiguó yuángōng liú xialai de.
　It was probably left by the foreign employee who lived here before.

For now, it is enough to know that if Chinese needs to indicate unambiguously the agent of an action, it can do so with the preposition "被 bèi". Try it: How would you say: "The food (cài) has been eaten up (chīdiào le)"? "菜

167

被吃掉了 Cài bèi chīdiào le". Now state who the culprit is – Mǎkè: "菜被马克吃掉了 Cài bèi Mǎkè chīdiào le". Now state simply that "Mark ate the food up": "马克把菜吃掉了 Mǎkè bǎ cài chīdiào le". Those are the relevant options.

As these examples – and the earlier ones – show, "被 bèi" sentences usually involve adverse or unfortunate events – something breaking, something lost, etc. Such cases typically also involve verbs with following resultative or directional complements, e.g., "拿走 názǒu", "吃掉 chīdiào", "打破 dǎpò". Here is the example from the dialogue in this lesson:

⑧ 在公司写字楼工作的人被称为"白领阶层"。
　Zài gōngsī xiězìlóu gōngzuò de rén bèi chēngwéi "báilǐng jiēcéng".
　People who work at the company office building are referred to as the "white collar class".

"被 bèi"-sentences are rare in the negative; but if they do occur, they are formed with "没(有) méi (yǒu)":

⑨ 她没被细菌感染。　She was not infected by the bacteria.
　Tā méi bèi xìjūn gǎnrǎn.

▸ **G2. The three "de's": "的", "地", and "得"**

As you have seen, particles pronounced "de" are ubiquitous in Chinese: "nǐ de" (yours), "yàodiàn de pángbiān" (next to the drugstore), "shì yuángōng liú xialai de" (it was left by the staff), "shuō de hěn hǎo" (you speak it well), "tīng de dǒng" (I understand it), "rè de hěn" (it's hot as heck), and a new function in this lesson, "jiànjiàn de" (gradually). Not so very long ago, all these "de's" were written one way, regardless of function, much as the two "le's" (verb suffix "le" and sentence "le") are both written "了". In fact, that is the case in one of the most famous books on Chinese grammar, Chao Yuen Ren's *A Grammar of Spoken Chinese* (Berkeley, 1968). However, over the years, conventions for writing the various "de's" differently have arisen, and now they are strictly adhered to. Here they are:

A. 的: This is the modification particle. It generally implies a following noun phrase, which may be omitted if it is understood, e.g.:"白色的 báisè de" [the white one(s)]. It also represents the "de" of the "是 shì……的 de" pattern (Lesson 7, G2), which in most cases, ends the sentence.

① 你的　yours
　nǐ de

② 药店的旁边　next to the drugstore
　yàodiàn de pángbiān

③ 是员工留下来的　It was left by the staff
　shì yuángōng liú xialai de

B. 得: By origin, a verb meaning "get" or "obtain", it was extended to function as a particle that introduces either adjectival phrases, or verbs in potential compounds. It also occurs in the intensifying suffix, "得很 de hěn".

④ 说得很好　you speak it well
　shuō de hěn hǎo

⑤ 听得懂　I understand it
　　tīng de dǒng

⑥ 热得很　It's hot as heck
　　rè de hěn

C. 地: Marks the preceding word as an adverb. The use of a character that is otherwise pronounced "dì" (e.g. in "地方 dìfang") stems from the fact that the adverbial particle is pronounced "di" rather than "de" in certain regions: jiànjiàn di.

⑦ 渐渐地　gradually
　　jiànjiàn de

⑧ 慢慢地　slowly [= "mànmān (r) de" in northern Mandarin]
　　mànmàn de

⑨ 她渐渐地发现白领不像人们想的那么富有。
　　Tā jiànjiàn de fāxiàn báilǐng bú xiàng rénmen xiǎng de nàme fùyǒu.
　　She gradually realized that those white collar people were not as well off as people thought.

▶ **G3.** Purpose with "为了 wèile" (in order to)

"为 wèi" (without the "了 le") serves as a preposition, with the meaning of "for, for the sake of, on behalf of". In that function, it introduces a noun phrase, e.g.: "为人民服务 wèi rénmín fúwù" (to serve the people). "为了 wèile" (with the "了 le", a part of the word) is also a preposition that introduces a full clause (often separated by a comma) that constitutes a reason or purpose:

① 我为了在中国找工作学习汉语。
　　Wǒ wèile zài Zhōngguó zhǎo gōngzuò xuéxí Hànyǔ.
　　I'm studying Chinese in order to find work in China.

② 为了表示回报，这个周末玛丽想请她的同事吃饭。
　　Wèile biǎoshì huíbào, zhège zhōumò Mǎlì xiǎng qǐng tā de tóngshì chī fàn.
　　In order to reciprocate, this weekend Mary is planning to invite her colleagues for a meal.

The purpose clause (with "为了 wèile") does not have to appear at the head of the sentence. In the previous example, "Mary" can be given more prominence by appearing first:

③ 玛丽为了感谢她的同事，这个周末请他们来家里吃晚饭。
　　Mǎlì wèile gǎnxiè tā de tóngshì, zhège zhōumò qǐng tāmen lái jiāli chī wǎnfàn.

▶ **G4.** Concession, with "虽然 suīrán……但是 dànshì……" (although … [but]…)

Concession ("although, granted") can be expressed by the pairing of "虽然 suīrán" with "但(是) dàn (shì)" – or, instead of "但是 dànshì", some other adversative, such as "可是 kěshì", "不过 búguò" or "却 què":

① 虽然是五月，但是天气还是很冷。　Although it's May, the weather's still quite cold.
　　Suīrán shì wǔyuè, dànshì tiānqì háishi hěn lěng.

② 她虽然汉语说得很好，但是还没去过中国。
Tā suīrán Hànyǔ shuō de hěn hǎo, dànshì hái méi qùguo Zhōngguó.
Although she speaks Chinese quite well, she's never been to China.

③ 这里虽然在市中心，附近很热闹，但是你的公寓真安静！
Zhèli suīrán zài shì zhōngxīn, fùjìn hěn rènao, dànshì nǐ de gōngyù zhēn ānjìng!
Although it's in the center of the city and quite bustling, the apartment's really quiet.

④ 那个教室虽然有空调，可是还是很热。
Nàge jiàoshì suīrán yǒu kōngtiáo, kěshì háishi hěn rè.
Although there is air-conditioning in that classroom, it is still very hot.

⑤ 虽然小张喜欢那个发型，不过我不喜欢。
Suīrán xiǎo Zhāng xǐhuan nàge fàxíng, búguò wǒ bù xǐhuan.
Granted, young Zhang likes that hair style, but I don't.

Notice that while Chinese generally requires both members of the construction to be present, "虽然 suīrán" and "但(是) dàn (shì)", English favors only the first ("although", etc.)

▶ **G5. Coordination, with "不但 búdàn……而且 érqiě……" (not only...but also…)**

Clauses can also be linked with "不但 búdàn" (not only) and "而且 érqiě" (but also). When both clauses apply to a single subject – as is usually the case, the subject is generally exposed at the head of the sentence with "不但 búdàn" placed after it.

① 她不但聪明而且漂亮。 She's smart as well as good looking.
Tā búdàn cōngming érqiě piàoliang.

② 这种手机不但太贵, 而且太大。
Zhè zhǒng shǒujī búdàn tài guì, érqiě tài dà.
This kind of cellphone is not just expensive, it's too big as well.

③ 公司不但给你付房租，而且给你付水电费吗？
Gōngsī búdàn gěi nǐ fù fángzū, érqiě gěi nǐ fù shuǐdiànfèi ma?
Does the company pay your rent as well as your utilities?

Various other words may stand instead of "而且 érqiě", including adverbs "还 hái", and "也 yě":

④ 我不但要理发，还要染发。 I want to color my hair as well as have it cut.
Wǒ búdàn yào lǐ fà, hái yào rǎn fà.

⑤ 她不但是我的老师，也是我的朋友。 She's my teacher, as well as my friend.
Tā búdàn shì wǒ de lǎoshī, yě shì wǒ de péngyou.

▶ **G6. Simultaneous actions, with "一边 yìbiān……一边 yìbiān……" (while …, as well as …)**

Recall that one of the functions of Verb- "着 zhe" was to mark the first of two verbal events as background to the second (Lesson 14, G3):

第十七课　玛丽的公寓
Lesson Seventeen　Mary's Apartment

① 看着电视做作业　watch television while doing your homework
　　kànzhe diànshì zuò zuòyè

A similar effect can be achieved with the construction "一边 yìbiān……一边 yìbiān……", with "一边 yìbiān" (one side) treated as an adverb and placed before both verbs.

② 他一边看电视，一边做作业。　He does his homework while watching television.
　　Tā yìbiān kàn diànshì, yìbiān zuò zuòyè.

③ 大家还可以一边做饭一边聊天儿。We can chat while we're preparing the meal.
　　Dàjiā hái kěyǐ yìbiān zuò fàn yìbiān liáo tiānr.

With single syllable verbs, the "一 yī" of "一边 yìbiān" is often elided:

④ 他们边走边谈。　They walked along chatting.
　　Tāmen biān zǒu biān tán.

真实生活汉语
Chinese for Living in China 2

Consolidation & Practice

1. Compose sentences that incorporate the Chinese material and express the agent (the "doer"), along the lines suggested by the English

   Item + 被 bèi + Agent + Complex Verb.

   Example: 昨天的啤酒 / 她 / 喝完 → 昨天的啤酒被她喝完了。
   zuótiān de píjiǔ / tā / hēwán (Yesterday's beer – it all got drunk by her.)

   (1) 我的书 / 朋友 / 拿走 → _____
   wǒ de shū / péngyou / názǒu (My book, it got taken away by (my) friend.)

   (2) 他的头发 / 美发师 / 剪短 → _____
   tā de tóufa / měifàshī / jiǎnduǎn (It was the hairdresser who cut his hair short.)

   (3) 我的作业 / 同学 / 拿走 → _____
   wǒ de zuòyè / tóngxué / názǒu (My homework got taken by (my) classmate.)

   (4) 昨天的饺子 / 小王 / 吃完 → _____
   zuótiān de jiǎozi / xiǎo Wáng / chīwán (Yesterday's dumplings all got eaten by young Wang.)

   (5) 妈妈买的新提包 / 玛丽 / 丢 → _____
   māma mǎi de xīn tíbāo / Mǎlì / diū
   (Mom's new handbag that she'd just bought – it was Mary that lost it.)

   (6) 我今天买的红酒 / 朋友 / 喝完 → _____
   wǒ jīntiān mǎi de hóngjiǔ / péngyou / hēwán
   [The wine that I bought today, it was finished up by (my) friends.]

   (7) 烤鸡 / 我 / 放在微波炉里 → _____
   kǎojī / wǒ / fàng zài wēibōlú li (The roast chicken – it was put in the microwave by me.)

   (8) 菜刀 / 他 / 放在抽屉里 → _____
   càidāo / tā / fàng zài chōuti li (The kitchen knife – it was put in the drawer by him.)

2. Provide the correct character ("的", "地", or "得") for the missing "de's"

   (1) 他今天下午高兴（　　　）告诉我，他找到了一个教英文（　　　）工作。
   Tā jīntiān xiàwǔ gāoxìng (　　) gàosu wǒ, tā zhǎodàole yí ge jiāo Yīngwén (　　) gōngzuò.

   (2) 他今天好像病了，走路走（　　　）很慢，吃饭吃（　　　）也很少。
   Tā jīntiān hǎoxiàng bìng le, zǒu lù zǒu (　　) hěn màn, chī fàn chī (　　) yě hěn shǎo.

   (3) 那是公司给她租（　　　）房子，水电费都包了。
   Nà shì gōngsī gěi tā zū (　　) fángzi, shuǐdiànfèi dōu bāo le.

   (4) 她跟男朋友出去吃饭都是AA制，各付各（　　　）钱。
   Tā gēn nánpéngyou chūqu chī fàn dōu shì AA zhì, gè fù gè (　　) qián.

172

第十七课 玛丽的公寓
Lesson Seventeen Mary's Apartment

(5) 你是在哪家理发店染（　　　）头发？染（　　　）很自然。
　　Nǐ shì zài nǎ jiā lǐfàdiàn rǎn (　　) tóufa? Rǎn (　　) hěn zìrán.

(6) 你昨天怎么没有去市教育局（　　　）宴会？宴会（　　　）饭菜可好吃了！
　　Nǐ zuótiān zěnme méiyǒu qù Shì Jiàoyùjú (　　) yànhuì? Yànhuì (　　) fàncài kě hǎochī le!

(7) 昨天路上堵车堵（　　　）厉害，所以我回来（　　　）很晚。
　　Zuótiān lùshang dǔ chē dǔ (　　) lìhai, suǒyǐ wǒ huílai (　　) hěn wǎn.

(8) 你慢慢（　　　）吃，吃（　　　）太快会消化不良。
　　Nǐ mànmàn (　　) chī, chī (　　) tài kuài huì xiāohuà bùliáng.

(9) 他在上海市一家外贸公司工作，工资很高。所有（　　　）朋友都很羡慕他。
　　Tā zài Shànghǎi shì yì jiā wàimào gōngsī gōngzuò, gōngzī hěn gāo. Suǒyǒu (　　) péngyou dōu hěn xiànmù tā.

(10) A: 你今天烤（　　　）鸡真好吃，教教我，好吗？
　　　　Nǐ jīntiān kǎo (　　) jī zhēn hǎochī, jiāojiao wǒ, hǎo ma?

　　 B: 我做饭做（　　　）好，可是不一定教做饭教（　　　）好。
　　　　Wǒ zuò fàn zuò (　　) hǎo, kěshì bù yídìng jiāo zuò fàn jiāo (　　) hǎo.

　　 A: 没关系，我是个聪明（　　　）学生，学什么都学（　　　）好。
　　　　Méi guānxi, wǒ shì ge cōngming (　　) xuésheng, xué shénme dōu xué (　　) hǎo.

3. Choose the correct slot for the preposition "为了 wèile"

(1) _____ 玛丽 _____ 毕业以后在中国工作 _____ 学中文。
　　_____ Mǎlì _____ bìyè yǐhòu zài Zhōngguó gōngzuò _____ xué Zhōngwén.

(2) _____ 明天的工作面试 _____ 马克特意去商场 _____ 买了一条新领带。
　　_____ míngtiān de gōngzuò miànshì _____ Mǎkè tèyì qù shāngchǎng _____ mǎile yì tiáo xīn lǐngdài.

(3) 我 _____ 准备今天的考试 _____ 昨天一夜没有 _____ 睡觉。
　　Wǒ _____ zhǔnbèi jīntiān de kǎoshì _____ zuótiān yí yè méiyǒu _____ shuì jiào.

(4) 他 _____ 给女朋友 _____ 买生日礼物 _____ 在服装店看了四个小时。
　　Tā _____ gěi nǚpéngyou _____ mǎi shēngri lǐwù _____ zài fúzhuāngdiàn kànle sì ge xiǎoshí.

(5) _____ 成绩我 _____ 得 _____ 退掉一门课。
　　_____ chéngjì wǒ _____ děi _____ tuìdiào yì mén kè.

(6) _____ 参加篮球比赛他 _____ 今天没有去 _____ 上课。
　　_____ cānjiā lánqiú bǐsài tā _____ jīntiān méiyǒu qù _____ shàng kè.

(7) 他 _____ 感谢朋友陪他 _____ 去医院看病 _____ 请朋友看了一场新电影。
　　Tā _____ gǎnxiè péngyou péi tā _____ qù yīyuàn kàn bìng _____ qǐng péngyou kànle yì chǎng xīn diànyǐng.

(8) _____最近玛丽_____健康_____不吃肉了。
_____ zuìjìn Mǎlì _____ jiànkāng _____ bù chī ròu le.

(9) 你为什么学中文？ (Find out from three of your classmates why they chose to study Chinese.)
Nǐ wèishénme xué Zhōngwén?
_____

4. Following the example, connect the following phrases with the "虽然 suīrán……但是 dànshì……" construction

   Example: 这个菜很贵 / 很好吃 → 这个菜虽然很贵，但是很好吃。
            zhège cài hěn guì / hěn hǎochī   Zhège cài suīrán hěn guì, dànshì hěn hǎochī.

   (1) 外边很热闹 / 公寓里边很安静 → _____
       wàibian hěn rènao / gōngyù lǐbian hěn ānjìng

   (2) 这件衣服的颜色很好 / 大小对你不合适 → _____
       zhè jiàn yīfu de yánsè hěn hǎo / dàxiǎo duì nǐ bù héshì

   (3) 没有骨折 / 胳膊很疼 → _____
       méiyǒu gǔzhé / gēbo hěn téng

   (4) 文学课很难 / 特别有意思 → _____
       wénxuékè hěn nán / tèbié yǒu yìsi

   (5) 地铁比公共汽车贵一点儿 / 比公共汽车快得多 → _____
       dìtiě bǐ gōnggòng qìchē guì yìdiǎnr / bǐ gōnggòng qìchē kuài de duō

   (6) 这家饭馆的菜便宜 / 没有那家饭馆的菜好吃 → _____
       zhè jiā fànguǎn de cài piányi / méiyǒu nà jiā fànguǎn de cài hǎochī

5. Connect the following phrases using the "不但 búdàn……而且 érqiě……" construction, along the lines of the example

   Example: 我们公司给我宿舍 / 还给我家具 →
            wǒmen gōngsī gěi wǒ sùshè / hái gěi wǒ jiājù

            我们公司不但给我宿舍，而且还给我家具。
            Wǒmen gōngsī búdàn gěi wǒ sùshè, érqiě hái gěi wǒ jiājù.

   (1) 买了电话卡 / 买了手机 → _____
       mǎile diànhuàkǎ / mǎile shǒujī

   (2) 教英语 / 学汉语 → _____
       jiāo Yīngyǔ / xué Hànyǔ

   (3) 理发 / 染发 → _____
       lǐ fà / rǎn fà

第十七课　玛丽的公寓
Lesson Seventeen　Mary's Apartment

  (4) 看孩子 / 做饭 → _____
    kān háizi / zuò fàn

  (5) 付房租 / 付水电费 → _____
    fù fángzū / fù shuǐdiànfèi

  (6) 发烧 / 拉肚子 → _____
    fā shāo / lā dùzi

  (7) 烤了一只鸡 / 炒了三个菜 → _____
    kǎole yì zhī jī / chǎole sān ge cài

  (8) 得穿西服 / 要打领带 → _____
    děi chuān xīfú / yào dǎ lǐngdài

6. You're good at multi-tasking, so using the "一边（儿）yìbiān(r)……一边（儿）yìbiān(r)……" pattern, explain how you often do the following pairs of tasks at the same time

  Example: 吃饭 / 看电视　→　我常常一边吃饭一边看电视。
      chī fàn / kàn diànshì　　Wǒ chángcháng yìbiān chī fàn yìbiān kàn diànshì.

  (1) 做作业 / 听音乐 → _____
    zuò zuòyè / tīng yīnyuè

  (2) 跑步 / 听音乐 → _____
    pǎo bù / tīng yīnyuè

  (3) 看书 / 上网 → _____
    kàn shū / shàng wǎng

  (4) 吃饭 / 给朋友打电话 → _____
    chī fàn / gěi péngyou dǎ diànhuà

  (5) 开车 / 听音乐 → _____
    kāi chē / tīng yīnyuè

  (6) 洗澡 / 唱歌 → _____
    xǐ zǎo / chàng gē

  (7) 学中文 / 教英文 → _____
    xué Zhōngwén / jiāo Yīngwén

  (8) 做饭 / 聊天儿 → _____
    zuò fàn / liáo tiānr

  (9) 烤鸡 / 炒菜 → _____
    kǎo jī / chǎo cài

  (10) 坐车 / 看书 → _____
    zuò chē / kàn shū

Listening Comprehension

1. Listen to the dialogue and then answer the questions

   (1) What is the first speaker looking for?

   (2) How much is the landlord asking for the place?

   (3) Is the apartment far from Peking University?

   (4) Mention at least four things in the apartment.

   (5) Which room is not furnished?

   (6) What are the surroundings like?

   (7) How much for the utilities?

   (8) What kind of deal did the landlord offer in order to try to convince the viewer?

   (9) What did the person looking for a room decide?

New Words

出租 chūzū V to rent

用具 yòngjù N utensil

2. Listen to the passage and then answer the questions

   (1) Who is young Ying?

   (2) What does she do?

   (3) Where does she live?

   (4) Does she have to commute far everyday?

   (5) How much is her rent?

   (6) Which of the items in her living room did she pay for?

   (7) Where does she eat usually?

   (8) Did she buy anything for the kitchen?

   (9) What is she learning to do?

   (10) Has she already invited Chinese friends over for dinner?

New Words

加拿大 Jiānádà PropN Canada

菜板 càibǎn N chopping board

Lesson Seventeen Mary's Apartment

第十七课 玛丽的公寓

Communication Activities

Pair Work

Scenario I: Biographical data. Tell your partner about your family and/or some of your friends. Cover subjects such as education, jobs, where they live, what kind of place they live in and how it's furnished, what they do on weekends, etc. Feel free to elaborate for the sake of using the material in the lesson, such as the following:

受过……教育 shòuguo……jiàoyù	在……公司工作 zài……gōngsī gōngzuò	收入不错 shōurù búcuò
X间卧室 X jiān wòshì	一个客厅 yí ge kètīng	卫生间 wèishēngjiān	厨房 chúfáng	书房 shūfáng
羡慕 xiànmù	出去吃饭 chūqu chī fàn	穿名牌服装 chuān míngpái fúzhuāng	幸运 xìngyùn

Scenario II: Your apartment. Tell your partner how many rooms you have in your apartment unit. Explain why you like the place, or not. Use the following items:

不但……而且…… búdàn……érqiě……	虽然……但是…… suīrán……dànshì……	比较 bǐjiào	非常 fēicháng
热闹 rènao	安静 ānjìng	冰箱 bīngxiāng	微波炉 wēibōlú

Scenario III: Furnishings. Tell your partner what furniture you have in your living room and bedroom. Use the following items:

不但……而且…… búdàn……érqiě……	另外 lìngwài	双人床 shuāngrénchuáng	衣柜 yīguì
床头柜 chuángtóuguì	电视 diànshì		

Scenario IV: The kitchen. Tell your partner which kitchen utensils and appliances the school has provided, and which you have bought yourself. Consider: a cutting board, a kitchen knife, chopsticks, spoons, and forks. Use the following:

不但……而且…… búdàn……érqiě……	另外 lìngwài	发给 fā gěi	厨房用具 chúfáng yòngjù
免费 miǎnfèi	虽然……但是…… suīrán……dànshì……	自己 zìjǐ	买 mǎi

真实生活汉语
Chinese for Living in China 2

Scenario V: Your dorm room. Compare and contrast your dorm room in China with one back home in terms of size, furniture, environment, convenience, and utility costs. Use the following items:

房子	卧室	住	家具	比
fángzi	wòshì	zhù	jiājù	bǐ
付	热闹	安静	房租	水电费
fù	rènao	ānjìng	fángzū	shuǐdiànfèi
电话费	免费	什么都……	漂亮	方便
diànhuàfèi	miǎnfèi	shénme dōu……	piàoliang	fāngbiàn
极了				
jí le				

Role-Play

Scenario I: One of you is looking for a place to live, the other is a landlord with apartments to rent out. Have a dialogue about the apartment being shown, using the following:

Landlord	Student
几室几厅 jǐ shì jǐ tīng	非常漂亮 / 安静 fēicháng piàoliang/ānjìng
离……远/近 lí……yuǎn/jìn	又大又方便 yòu dà yòu fāngbiàn
家具 jiājù	卧室 wòshì
房租 fángzū	厨房 chúfáng
包 bāo	有/没有卫生间 yǒu/méiyǒu wèishēngjiān
有/没有家具 yǒu/méiyǒu jiājù	不但……而且…… búdàn……érqiě……
水电费 shuǐdiànfèi	方便 fāngbiàn
卫生间 wèishēngjiān	虽然……可是…… suīrán……kěshì……
安静 ānjìng	免费 miǎnfèi
因为……所以…… yīnwèi……suǒyǐ……	

Lesson Seventeen Mary's Apartment

第十七课 玛丽的公寓

Scenario II: You have just moved into your dream apartment. A friend is visiting. After looking the place over, your friend is impressed and has all sorts of questions for you. You answer as best as you can. Use the following items:

房租 fángzū	一个月多少…… yí ge yuè duōshao……		水电费 shuǐdiànfèi	免费 miǎnfèi
邻居 línjū	附近 fùjìn	安静 ānjìng	买东西 mǎi dōngxi	方便 fāngbiàn
厨房用具 chúfáng yòngjù	微波炉 wēibōlú	冰箱 bīngxiāng	自己 zìjǐ	第一个月 dì-yī ge yuè
上网费 shàngwǎngfèi	付 fù			

Group Activities

Scenario I: One of you (A) is an architect, drawing a floor plan for a house for the three-generation Wang family. Two of you are the grandfather and grandmother (B and C), hoping the house will be comfortable, with easy access to conveniences. Two of you are the young couple with a nine-year old child, who want a house with a spacious living room, multiple bathrooms and a fully equipped kitchen. All four of the family need to work together with the architect to come up with a house plan that suits them all. Use the following items:

最 zuì	方便 fāngbiàn	楼上 lóu shàng	楼下 lóu xià	腿疼 tuǐ téng	心脏不好 xīnzàng bù hǎo
高血压 gāoxuèyā	舒服 shūfu	不但……而且…… búdàn……érqiě……		客厅 kètīng	卫生间 wèishēngjiān
卧室 wòshì	容易 róngyi	出去 chūqu	虽然……但是…… suīrán……dànshì……		
因为……所以…… yīnwèi……suǒyǐ……	另外 lìngwài		比较 bǐjiào	非常 fēicháng	漂亮 piàoliang

Scenario II: One of you is a Chinese talk-show host (A). You are interviewing three Chinese speaking Americans (B, C, D) about the problem of grown children living at home, which is becoming increasingly common. Talk about the advantages and disadvantages, and see if you can find common values that cross cultural boundaries. Use the following items:

退休 tuì xiū	生病 shēng bìng	照顾 zhàogù	看孩子 kān háizi	外地 wàidì	方便 fāngbiàn
贵极了 guìjí le	不再 bú zài	富有 fùyǒu	免费 miǎnfèi	房租 fángzū	水电费 shuǐdiànfèi

179

真实生活汉语 2
Chinese for Living in China

什么都没…… shénme dōu méi……	工作 gōngzuò	比较 bǐjiào	非常 fēicháng	合适 héshì
不但……而且…… búdàn……érqiě……	另外 lìngwài	因为……所以…… yīnwèi……suǒyǐ……		虽然……但是…… suīrán……dànshì……
便宜 piányi	愿意 yuànyì	不像人们想的那么…… bú xiàng rénmen xiǎng de nàme……		各付各的 gè fù gè de
自己 zìjǐ	住 zhù	A 跟 B 一样 A gēn B yíyàng		

Review Exercises

1. Write in Chinese characters

(1) List five defining characteristics of "white collar" workers in big cities such as Beijing or Shanghai.

----

(2) Write down the names of the rooms in your house or apartment back home.

----

(3) Write out all the furniture you have in your house or apartment back home.

----

(4) Write out the names of the appliances.

----

(5) Name your kitchen utensils.

----

2. Convert these "把 bǎ"-sentences into "被 bèi"-sentences

Example: 我把这盘菜吃完了。 → 这盘菜被我吃完了。
　　　　 Wǒ bǎ zhèi pán cài chīwán le.　 Zhè pán cài bèi wǒ chīwán le.

(1) 政府把这个网页关了。 → _____
　　 Zhèngfǔ bǎ zhège wǎngyè guān le.

(2) 学生把作业给老师了。 → _____
　　 Xuésheng bǎ zuòyè gěi lǎoshī le.

第十七课 玛丽的公寓
Lesson Seventeen Mary's Apartment

(3) 他把行李放到床上了。→ _____
    Tā bǎ xíngli fàngdào chuáng shang le.

(4) 我把烤好的鸡放在桌子上了。→ _____
    Wǒ bǎ kǎohǎo de jī fàng zài zhuōzi shang le.

(5) 玛丽把菜刀放在抽屉里了。→ _____
    Mǎlì bǎ càidāo fàng zài chōuti li le.

(6) 他把红酒放在冰箱里了。→ _____
    Tā bǎ hóngjiǔ fàng zài bīngxiāng li le.

(7) 吴老师把安妮带到内科去了。→ _____
    Wú lǎoshī bǎ Ānnī dàidào nèikē qù le.

(8) 大夫把马克的伤口缝好了。→ _____
    Dàifu bǎ Mǎkè de shāngkǒu fénghǎo le.

(9) 他把昨天的菜都吃完了。→ _____
    Tā bǎ zuótiān de cài dōu chīwán le.

(10) 他把化验单拿走了。→ _____
    Tā bǎ huàyàndān názǒu le.

3. Add "不但 búdàn……而且 érqiě……" to the following sentences so as to make the logical connections clearer

(1) 用电话卡打电话又方便又便宜。→ _____
    Yòng diànhuàkǎ dǎ diànhuà yòu fāngbiàn yòu piányi.

(2) 早市的蔬菜很新鲜也很便宜。→ _____
    Zǎoshì de shūcài hěn xīnxian yě hěn piányi.

(3) 他住在外教宿舍，又不用付房租，又不用付水电费。→ _____
    Tā zhù zài wàijiào sùshè, yòu búyòng fù fángzū, yòu búyòng fù shuǐdiànfèi.

(4) 大夫说他得打点滴，还要吃止泻药。→ _____
    Dàifu shuō tā děi dǎ diǎndī, hái yào chī zhǐxièyào.

(5) 他的厨房里又有冰箱又有微波炉。→ _____
    Tā de chúfáng li yòu yǒu bīngxiāng yòu yǒu wēibōlú.

(6) 那件衬衫太大了，颜色也不好看。→ _____
    Nèi jiàn chènshān tài dà le, yánsè yě bù hǎokàn.

(7) 他去理发店剪了头发，还作了按摩。→ _____
    Tā qù lǐfàdiàn jiǎnle tóufa, hái zuòle ànmó.

(8) 他都79岁了，没有心脏病，也没有高血压。→ _____
    Tā dōu qīshíjiǔ suì le, méiyǒu xīnzàngbìng, yě méiyǒu gāoxuèyā.

(9) 我朋友学中文，也教英文。→ _____
　　Wǒ péngyou xué Zhōngwén, yě jiāo Yīngwén.

(10) 800路公共汽车有空调，里边也很大。→ _____
　　Bā-líng-líng lù gōnggòng qìchē yǒu kōngtiáo, lǐbian yě hěn dà.

4. Use "虽然 suīrán……但是 dànshì……" to connect the phrases

   Example: 美国人 / 说中文　　→ 我虽然是美国人，但是会说中文。
   　　　　Měiguórén / shuō Zhōngwén　Wǒ suīrán shì Měiguórén, dànshì huì shuō Zhōngwén.

   (1) 带了人民币 / 忘了带身份证 → _____
   　　dàile rénmínbì / wàngle dài shēnfènzhèng

   (2) 吃了不干净的东西 / 没拉肚子 → _____
   　　chīle bù gānjìng de dōngxi / méi lā dùzi

   (3) 我自己从来没买过家具 / 我的公寓有不少家具 → _____
   　　wǒ zìjǐ cónglái méi mǎiguo jiājù / wǒ de gōngyù yǒu bù shǎo jiājù

   (4) 对学生很严格 / 我的学生都很喜欢我 → _____
   　　duì xuésheng hěn yángé / wǒ de xuésheng dōu hěn xǐhuan wǒ

   (5) 我是美国人 / 不喜欢吃美国饭 → _____
   　　wǒ shì Měiguórén / bù xǐhuan chī měiguófàn

   (6) 马克胳膊受伤了 / 还去打篮球 → _____
   　　Mǎkè gēbo shòu shāng le / hái qù dǎ lánqiú

   (7) 昨天她打了点滴 / 现在还发烧 → _____
   　　zuótiān tā dǎle diǎndī / xiànzài hái fā shāo

   (8) 她刚来中国一个月 / 已经交了很多朋友 → _____
   　　tā gāng lái Zhōngguó yí ge yuè / yǐjīng jiāole hěn duō péngyou

5. You paid a visit to your Chinese friend, young Zhang, at his home. Write down what you saw and learned, as follows

   (1) Young Zhang's house is located in the centre of the city. It's in a lively district, but the neighborhood is quite quiet.

   _____

   (2) The house has three bedrooms, a living room, a kitchen and two bathrooms.

   _____

(3) Young Zhang's father is a doctor; his mother was a Chinese language professor, who retired last year because she has heart disease and high blood pressure.

....

(4) Young Zhang's parents live in the master bedroom, which is furnished with a double bed and a bookcase, in addition to a sofa.

....

(5) Young Zhang and his wife live in the bedroom on the left. They have a computer, a bookcase, a wardrobe, and two chairs.

....

(6) Young Zhang's son lives in the next room, which is furnished with a small bed, a small wardrobe, and a bookshelf.

....

(7) The kitchen has a refrigerator, a microwave, dishes, and other cooking utensils. They were not bought. The school provided them because Zhang's mother used to work for the university.

....

(8) They don't need to pay rent and utilities – the school pays for those. However, they do have to pay 50 *yuan* a month for internet service (上网费 shàngwǎngfèi).

....

(9) Young Zhang has an older brother, who works for a company that deals with international trade. He also has a younger sister, who is an English teacher. They both live in another city. All the members of Zhang's family are well-educated, with stable jobs, and make pretty decent salaries.

....

(10) Compare Young Zhang's family with a typical middle-class family in your hometown, in terms of education, housing, standard of living, life-style, and health.

....

Culture Notes

1. How to address people

People who are older in age or higher in professional rank and social status than the speaker are usually addressed by surname and title: "王总 Wáng zǒng", for CEO Wang, "李经理 Lǐ jīnglǐ", for manager Li, "张老师 (教授) Zhāng lǎoshī (jiàoshòu) ", for Teacher (or Professor) Zhang.

A casual form of address for peers, colleagues or friends makes use of "小 xiǎo" (young) or "老 lǎo" (old) before surname: "小王 xiǎo Wáng", "老张 lǎo Zhāng".

2. Visitors who come by unannounced

In China, neighbors, friends or relatives often drop by unannounced. If a guest appears at the door, they would expect to be invited in. If you are truly busy and cannot attend to a guest, then you can apologize and say that the visitor is welcome to come back some other time.

3. What to bring as a gift

When you visit a Chinese friend's home, especially for the first time, it is polite to bring a small gift such as fruit, chocolate, liquor, or something from your hometown. Chinese people generally won't open the gift in front of you, but will wait until after you have left. Some gifts are to be avoided because their names have bad associations: "钟 zhōng" (clock), for example is a homonym of "终 zhōng" meaning "end" or "death". And "伞 sǎn" (umbrella) sounds like "散 sǎn" (to come loose, to fall apart).

4. Work units and the provision of daily-use items

Under the Communist system in China, each "work unit" (school, company, government agency, factory, etc.) provided working personnel with housing, furniture, food, and daily-use items. Since the economic reforms of the late 1980s, the system has been changing. But many schools and companies in China still provide some daily-use items for their employees – even foreign employees.

Lesson Eighteen   Traveling over Chinese New Year
第十八课   春 运
Dì-shíbā Kè   Chūnyùn

In this lesson you will learn how to do the following
- Talk about vacation plans
- Talk about the problems of traveling over the "Spring Rush" period
- Discuss train and other forms of transportation in China
- Buy train tickets, and choose types of seat or berth, etc.

Grammar
- The adverb "才 cái" (only then, not until)
- The paired adverbs "一 yī……就 jiù……" (once, as soon as, whenever)
- Complete action with "了 le" and "没(有) méi (yǒu)"
- Double negatives, expressing insistence: "不能不 bù néng bù", etc.
- "只要 zhǐyào……就 jiù……" (so long as… [then]…)
- "为什么不 wèi shénme bù……" (why don't…, how come [you] don't…)

Culture Notes
- How to buy a train or airplane ticket
- Types of trains in China
- Types of tickets
- Round-trip and one-way tickets
- Things to take when you travel by train
- Meals or snacks on the train

Dialogue

A：刘教授，艾德的同事
　　Liú jiàoshòu, Àidé de tóngshì

B：艾德，外教
　　Àidé, wàijiào

C：售票员
　　shòupiàoyuán

　　艾德在武汉大学外语系教美国文学和戏剧。武汉大学上个学期给外教们开了两次派对：一次是感恩节，一次是圣诞节。圣诞节在西方是家人团聚的节日，也是在中国的西方人最想家的时候。过了圣诞节，艾德才^{G1}觉得在中国的生活安定了下来。可是这时候学校里的中国老师和学生都开始准备放寒假了。中国学校放寒假的时间每年不一样：因为是在中国的春节前后¹放假，而²春节每年的时间不一样：有时³在阳历的一月，有时在二月。今年春节在一月，所以一^{G2}过圣诞节，寒假就快到了。寒假有差不多一个月的时间，学校里没有人了。艾德正在考虑去哪儿过寒假，这时系里的刘教授来找他。

　　Àidé zài Wǔhàn Dàxué wàiyǔxì jiāo Měiguó wénxué hé xìjù. Wǔhàn Dàxué shàng ge xuéqī gěi wàijiàomen kāile liǎng cì pàiduì: yí cì shì Gǎn'ēn Jié, yí cì shì Shèngdàn Jié. Shèngdàn Jié zài Xīfāng shì jiārén tuánjù de jiérì, yě shì zài Zhōngguó de Xīfāngrén zuì xiǎng jiā de shíhou. Guòle Shèngdàn Jié, Àidé cái^{G1} juéde zài Zhōngguó de shēnghuó āndìngle xiàlai. Kěshi zhè shíhou xuéxiào li de Zhōngguó lǎoshī hé xuésheng dōu kāishǐ zhǔnbèi fàng hánjià le. Zhōngguó xuéxiào fàng hánjià de shíjiān měi nián bù yíyàng: yīnwèi shì zài Zhōngguó de Chūn Jié qiánhòu¹ fàng jià, ér² Chūn Jié měi nián de shíjiān bù yíyàng—yǒushí zài yánglì de yīyuè, yǒushí zài èryuè. Jīnnián Chūn Jié zài yīyuè, suǒyǐ yí^{G2} guò Shèngdàn Jié, hánjià jiù kuài dào le. Hánjià yǒu chàbuduō yí ge yuè de shíjiān, xuéxiào li méiyǒu rén le. Àidé zhèngzài kǎolù qù nǎr guò hánjià, zhè shí xì li de Liú jiàoshòu lái zhǎo tā.

A：艾老师，您寒假去哪儿，计划了没有^{G3}？
　　Ài lǎoshī, nín hánjià qù nǎr, jìhuàle méiyou^{G3}?

B：还没有计划呢。
　　Hái méiyǒu jìhuà ne.

Notes

1. "前后 qiánhòu", a compound of "before" and "after", can function as a place word, suffixed to a noun, meaning "around (the time of)": "在春节前后回家 zài Chūn Jié qiánhòu huí jiā" (return home around the time of the Spring Festival). It also means "altogether": "我前后看了两三次 Wǒ qiánhòu kànle liǎng-sān cì" (I've seen it two or three times altogether).
2. "而 ér" (and, but) links verbs or adjectives, especially in concise expressions such as "摔倒而受伤 shuāidǎo ér shòushāng" (fall down and injure oneself), or "三思而行 sān sī ér xíng" (think thrice before acting), in which the first verb phrase conditions the second.
3. "有时 yǒushí" (sometimes, at times) is shortened from "有的时候 yǒu de shíhou".

第十八课 春运
Lesson Eighteen　Traveling over Chinese New Year

A：我老家在西安。西安有世界闻名的兵马俑。您要不要跟我一起回我老家过春节，同时也去看看兵马俑？
Wǒ lǎojiā zài Xī'ān. Xī'ān yǒu shìjiè wénmíng de Bīngmǎyǒng. Nín yào bu yào gēn wǒ yìqǐ huí wǒ lǎojiā guò Chūn Jié, tóngshí yě qù kànkan Bīngmǎyǒng?

B：那太好了。会不会太麻烦您？
Nà tài hǎo le. Huì bu huì tài máfan nín?

A：不会的。还没有外国人到过我家。我的家人一定会很高兴。不过，春运期间很难买到火车票，我们需要早一点儿走。
Bú huì de. Hái méiyǒu wàiguórén dàoguo wǒ jiā. Wǒ de jiārén yídìng huì hěn gāoxìng. Búguò, chūnyùn qījiān hěn nán mǎidào huǒchēpiào, wǒmen xūyào zǎo yìdiǎnr zǒu.

B：什么是"春运"？
Shénme shì "chūnyùn"?

A："春运"是中国人在春节前15天到春节后25天，这40天时间里大家都要旅行回家去过年。所有的交通运输：飞机、火车、长途汽车、轮船都非常拥挤，很难买到票。坐火车的人最多，很多人只能在火车上站十几个小时回家。据说2015年有3亿多[4]人在春运期间旅行。
"Chūnyùn" shì Zhōngguórén zài Chūn Jié qián shíwǔ tiān dào Chūn Jié hòu èrshíwǔ tiān, zhè sìshí tiān shíjiān li dàjiā dōu yào lǚxíng huí jiā qù guò nián. Suǒyǒu de jiāotōng yùnshū——fēijī, huǒchē, chángtú qìchē, lúnchuán dōu fēicháng yōngjǐ, hěn nán mǎidào piào. Zuò huǒchē de rén zuì duō, hěn duō rén zhǐ néng zài huǒchē shang zhàn shí jǐ ge xiǎoshí huí jiā. Jùshuō 2015 nián yǒu sānyì duō[4] rén zài chūnyùn qījiān lǚxíng.

B：所以我最近听到大家的话题都是买票啊，什么时候回家啊，等等[5]。大家过年的时候不能不[G4]回老家吗？
Suǒyǐ wǒ zuìjìn tīngdào dàjiā de huàtí dōu shì mǎi piào a, shénme shíhou huí jiā a, děngděng[5]. Dàjiā guò nián de shíhou bù néng bù[G4] huí lǎojiā ma?

A：中国的传统吧。过年时一家人只要[G5]能团聚在一起就是幸福。回家过年可以看到很多亲戚、朋友、同学，还有很多好吃的东西。
Zhōngguó de chuántǒng ba. Guò nián shí yìjiārén zhǐyào[G5] néng tuánjù zài yìqǐ jiù shì xìngfú. Huí jiā guò nián kěyǐ kàndào hěn duō qīnqi, péngyou, tóngxué, hái yǒu hěn duō hǎochī de dōngxi.

---

4. "3亿多 sānyì duō" (more than 300 million); for "多 duō" after units of ten, cf. Lesson 13, G3.
5. "等等 děngděng" appears at the end of enumerations, with much the same meaning as English "etc., and so on". The sense is probably "and such and such class of things", extended from "等 děng" (class, rank, grade) (cf. "二等 èr děng" - second class).

B: 这么多中国人喜欢做的事，我应该体验一下。好，我去你家过年。
Zhème duō Zhōngguórén xǐhuan zuò de shì, wǒ yīnggāi tǐyàn yíxià. Hǎo, wǒ qù nǐ jiā guò nián.

A: 那今天下午我就带你去买票。现在买票实行"实名制"[6]，别忘了带上你的护照。
Nà jīntiān xiàwǔ wǒ jiù dài nǐ qù mǎi piào. Xiànzài mǎi piào shíxíng "Shímíngzhì,"[6] Bié wàngle dàishang nǐ de hùzhào.

B: 好。
Hǎo.

（在售票处 Zài shòupiàochù）

B: 我要买一张从武汉去西安的车票。
Wǒ yào mǎi yì zhāng cóng Wǔhàn qù Xī'ān de chēpiào.

C: 从武汉到西安的火车有直达特快火车Z138。11个小时27分钟到。硬座135.5元，硬卧下247.5元，软卧下377.5元。
Cóng Wǔhàn dào Xī'ān zuì kuài de huǒchē shì zhídá tèkuài huǒchē Z yī-sān-bā. Shíyī ge xiǎoshí èrshíqī fēnzhōng dào. Yìngzuò yìbǎi sānshíwǔ diǎn wǔ yuán, yìngwò xià èrbǎi sìshíqī diǎn wǔ yuán, ruǎnwò xià sānbǎi qīshíqī diǎn wǔ yuán.

B: 什么是"硬卧下""软卧下"？
Shénme shì "yìngwò xià" "ruǎnwò xià"?

C: 硬卧有上铺、中铺、下铺，软卧有上铺和下铺。你要什么票？
Yìngwò yǒu shàngpù, zhōngpū, xiàpù, ruǎnwò yǒu shàngpù hé xiàpù. Nǐ yào shénme piào?

B: 请等一下儿。刘老师，坐火车要十几个小时，我们为什么不[G6]坐飞机？坐飞机比坐火车贵得多吗？
Qǐng děng yíxiàr. Liú lǎoshī, zuò huǒchē yào shíjǐ ge xiǎoshí, wǒmen wèi shénme bú[G6] zuò fēijī? Zuò fēijī bǐ zuò huǒchē guì de duō ma?

A: 坐飞机差不多贵好几倍[7]。我们坐软卧晚上八点上车，在车上睡一晚上，第二天早上就到了。
Zuò fēijī chàbuduō guì hǎo jǐ bèi[7]. Wǒmen zuò ruǎnwò wǎnshang bā diǎn shàng chē, zài chē shang shuì yí wǎnshang, dì-èr tiān zǎoshang jiù dào le.

---

6. "实名制 shímíngzhì", the "real-name-system" (cf. AA zhì in Lesson 17). The "实名制 shímíngzhì" requires people to show up in person to pick up tickets.

第十八课 春 运
Lesson Eighteen　Traveling over Chinese New Year

B：好。我买后天去西安的软卧下铺。
　　Hǎo. Wǒ mǎi hòutiān qù Xī'ān de ruǎnwò xiàpù.

C：对不起，现在已经没有春节前的票了。
　　Duìbuqǐ, xiànzài yǐjing méiyou Chūn Jié qián de piào le.

B：那我们怎么办呢？
　　Nà wǒmen zěnme bàn ne?

A：那我们买高铁票吧。
　　Nà wǒmen mǎi gāotiě piào ba.

C：春运的高铁票也没有了。
　　Chūnyùn de gāoètiě piào yě méiyǒu le.

A：都怪我，一直忙工作，忘了今年春运预购票提前到60天了。看来我们只能坐飞机了。
　　Dōu guài wǒ, yìzhí máng gōngzuò, wàngle jīnnián Chūnyùn yùgòu piào tíqián dào liùshí tiān le. Kàn lái wǒmen zhǐ néng zuò fēijī le

C：其实高铁票有时候比机票还贵。机票打折时比坐高铁便宜。
　　Qíshí gāotiě piào yǒu shíhou bǐ jīpiào hái guì. Jīpiào dǎ zhé shí bǐ zuò gāotiě piányi.

A：谢谢您。我们回去上网买机票吧。
　　Xièxiè nín. Wǒmen huíqù shàng wǎng mǎi jīpiào ba.

B：太好了，坐飞机从武汉到西安才一个半小时。
　　Tài hǎo le, zuò fēijī cóng Wǔhàn dào Xī'ān cái yí ge bàn xiǎoshí.

---

7. "倍 bèi", a measure for "multiples = by X times", e.g.: "多一倍 duō yí bèi" (twice as many).

真实生活汉语
Chinese for Living in China 2

New Words

#				
1	春运/春運	chūnyùn	N	spring rush (traveling over Chinese New Year)
2	教授	jiàoshòu	N	professor
3	武汉/武漢	Wǔhàn	PropN	Wuhan (a city in "湖北 Húběi" Province)
4	戏剧/戲劇	xìjù	N	theater, drama, a play
5	派对/派對	pàiduì	N	a transcription of the English word "party" ("开派对 kāi pàiduì", to have a party)
6	感恩节/感恩節	Gǎn'ēn Jié	PropN	Thanksgiving, Thanksgiving Day ("feel-kindness-festival")
7	圣诞节/聖誕節	Shèngdàn Jié	PropN	Christmas ("sacred-birth-festival")
8	西方	xīfāng/Xīfāng	N/PropN	the west; the West
9	家人	jiārén	N	family (members) (cf. "一家人 yìjiārén", whole family, members of a family)
10	团聚/團聚	tuánjù	V	to reunite, to have a reunion, to come together
11	节日/節日	jiérì	N	holiday, festival day
12	西方人	Xīfāngrén	PropN	Westerner
13	想家	xiǎng jiā	Phrase	to be homesick ("think of home")
14	生活	shēnghuó	N/V	life, livelihood; to live
15	安定	āndìng	Adj/V	stable, settled, quiet; to stabilize
16	这时候/這時候	zhè shíhou	Phrase	at this time
17	准备/準備	zhǔnbèi	V	to prepare, to make ready, to plan, to intend
18	寒假	hánjià	N	winter vacation
19	春节/春節	Chūn Jié	PropN	The Spring Festival, Chinese New Year, the Lunar New Year
20	前后/前後	qiánhòu	PW	around (the time of)
21	放假	fàng jià	VO	to have (or grant) a vacation or holiday
22	而	ér	Conj	and, and thus, but
23	阳历/陽曆	yánglì	N	solar calendar
24	差不多	chàbuduō	Adj/Adv	more or less the same; nearly, almost
25	考虑/考慮	kǎolǜ	V	to consider, to think over, to reconsider

第十八课 春运
Lesson Eighteen　Traveling over Chinese New Year

26	这时/這時	zhè shí	Phrase	at this time
27	计划/計劃	jìhuà	V/N	to plan; plan, program
28	老家	lǎojiā	N	native place, home town, home country
29	西安	Xī'ān	PropN	Xi'an (in "陕西 Shǎnxī" Province)
30	闻名/聞名	wénmíng	Adj	well known, famous, renowned
31	兵马俑/兵馬俑	bīngmǎyǒng	N	figures of warriors and horses buried with the dead
32	同时/同時	tóngshí	N/Conj	at the same time; besides, moreover
33	麻烦/麻煩	máfan	Adj/N	be a nuisance, bothersome; trouble, bother
34	高兴/高興	gāoxìng	Adj	happy, glad
35	期间/期間	qījiān	N	time, period, duration
36	难/難	nán	Adj	difficult
37	火车票/火車票	huǒchēpiào	N	train ticket
38	旅行	lǚxíng	V	to travel, to take a tour
39	运输/運輸	yùnshū	N/V	transport; to transport
40	回家	huí jiā	Phrase	to return home
41	过年/過年	guò nián	VO	to celebrate the Spring Festival or New Year
42	交通运输/交通運輸	jiāotōng yùnshū	Phrase	communications and transportation
	交通	jiāotōng	N	traffic, communications, transport, transportation
43	飞机/飛機	fēijī	N	airplane
44	火车/火車	huǒchē	N	train
45	轮船/輪船	lúnchuán	N	steamer, steamship
46	拥挤/擁擠	yōngjǐ	Adj/V	crowded, jammed; to crowd, to jam (of people, traffic, etc.)
47	只能	zhǐ néng	Phrase	can only
48	据说/據說	jùshuō	V	it's said that, supposedly
49	亿/億	yì	Num	100 million
50	话题/話題	huàtí	N	topic of conversation
	话/話	huà	N	speech, language

#	汉字	Pinyin	POS	Meaning
51	买票/買票	mǎi piào	Phrase	to buy tickets
52	啊	a	Part	*used after each item in an enumeration*
53	等等	děngděng	Part	etc., and so on, and so forth
54	传统/傳統	chuántǒng	N/Attr	tradition, convention; traditional
55	幸福	xìngfú	N/Adj	happiness; happy
56	亲戚/親戚	qīnqi	N	relatives
57	这么/這麼	zhème	Pron	this way, so
58	事	shì	N	thing, matter, event
59	体验/體驗	tǐyàn	V	to experience, to learn through practice
60	实行/實行	shíxíng	V	to implement, to put into practice, to carry out
61	实名制	shímíngzhì	N	"real-name-system"
62	别	bié	Adv/BF	don't; other
63	忘	wàng	V	to forget, to leave behind
64	售票处/售票處	shòupiàochù	N	ticket office
65	硬座	yìngzuò	N	hard seat (equivalent to a second-class seat)
66	硬卧	yìngwò	N	soft berth (equivalent to a second-class berth)
67	软卧/軟卧	ruǎnwò	N	soft berth (a first-class seat)
68	上铺/上鋪	shàngpù	N	upper berth
69	中铺/中鋪	zhōngpù	N	middle berth
70	下铺/下鋪	xiàpù	N	lower berth
71	倍	bèi	Meas	for multiples, times, -fold
72	对不起/對不起	duìbuqǐ	Exp	excuse me, I'm sorry, pardon me
73	预购/預購	yùgòu	V	to purchase in advance
74	高铁/高鐵	gāotiě	N	high-speed rail (short for "高速鐵路/高速铁路 gāosù tiělù")
75	怪	guài	V	to blame
76	其实	qíshí	Adv	in fact, actually

第十八课 春 运
Lesson Eighteen   Traveling over Chinese New Year

Re-enacting the Dialogue

A: Professor Liu, a colleague of Ed   B: Ed, a foreign professor in China   C: a ticket saleswoman

Ed teaches American literature and drama in the Department of Foreign Languages at Wuhan University. Last semester, Wuhan University hosted two parties for foreign teachers: one was at Thanksgiving and one was at Christmas. In the West, Christmas is a holiday when families get together; it's the time when Westerners in China feel most homesick. After Christmas, Ed finally felt that he was settling into life in China. But at that time, the Chinese teachers and students at the school were beginning to get ready for the winter break. The time of the winter break at Chinese universities varies year by year: sometimes it's in January (of the Western calendar); sometimes, it's in February. This year, Chinese New Year is in January, so as soon as Christmas in done with, it's almost winter break. The winter break is roughly a month long; there'll be no one on campus. Just as Ed is contemplating where to go for the winter break, in comes Professor Liu (from Ed's department), looking for him.

A: Professor Ed, have you planned where you're going to go for the winter break?

B: Not yet.

A: My home's in Xi'an. Xi'an has the world famous terra-cotta soldiers. Would you like to come home with me for the Spring Festival and go to see the terra-cotta soldiers at the same time?

B: That'd be great. Won't that be a lot of trouble for you?

A: Not at all. There haven't been any foreigners to visit my home yet. My family would definitely be excited. But it's really hard to get train tickets during the Spring Rush, so we'll need to go a little earlier.

B: What's the Spring Rush?

A: The Spring Rush is "traveling over Chinese New Year". During the 40 days around the Spring Festival – 15 days before and 25 days after – Chinese people all travel back home for Chinese New Year. All types of transportation – planes, trains, long-distance buses, or boats – are extremely crowded and it's really hard to get tickets. The largest number of people take trains, and a lot of people end up standing for more than ten hours on the way home. I've heard that in 2015, over 300 million people traveled in the Spring Rush period.

B: That's why I've heard so many people talking about buying tickets, what time they're going home, and so on. Does everyone have to return to their hometowns over New Year?

A: It's a Chinese tradition! At New Year, it's good luck for families to get together. Going home at New Year, you can see a lot of relative, friends and classmates – and eat lots of nice food.

B: I should get a feel for something that so many Chinese like to do! OK, I'll go home with you.

A: So this afternoon, then, I'll take you to get tickets. Because tickets are now sold on the "real-name-system", you have to show up in person before the ticket seller will sell a ticket to you. Don't forget to bring your passport.

B: OK.

(At the ticket office)

B: I'd like to buy a ticket from Wuhan to Xi'an.

C: The express from Wuhan to Xi'an is the Z138. It takes 11 hours and 27 minutes. Hard seats are 135.5 *yuan*, lower hard berths are 247.5 *yuan*, and lower soft berths are 377.5 *yuan*.

B: What are lower hard berths and soft berths?

C: Hard berths have upper, middle and lower levels; soft berths have upper and lower. Which kind would you like?

B: Hang on a minute, please. Prof. Liu, the train takes over ten hours. Why don't we fly there? Is the plane much more expensive than the train?

A: Flying is about several times as expensive as taking the train. If we take a soft berth and board the train at 8, we can sleep the night on the train and arrive the morning of the next day.

B: Okay, I'll buy a soft berth lower level to Xi'an for the day after tomorrow.

C: Sorry, Spring Rush tickets have been sole out, we don't have any anymore.

B: So what should we do?

A: Well, why don't we buy a ticket on the high-speed train?

C: During Spring Rush, high-speed train tickets also have been sold out.

A: It's all my fault. I've been so busy that I forgot that Spring Rush tickets have to be bought 60 days in advance. Looks like we'll have to go by plane.

C: Actually, high-speed train tickets are sometimes more expensive than air tickets. When they discount air tickets they're cheaper than high-speed trains.

A: Thanks. Let's go back and buy air tickets online.

B: That's great. It only takes an hour and a half to fly from Wuhan to Xi'an.

第十八课　春　运
Lesson Eighteen　Traveling over Chinese New Year

Grammar

▶ G1. The adverb "才 cái" (only then, not until)

When "才 cái" is used after a time phrase, it implies that the time is relatively later than expected; often the English translation is "not until". Here are some examples from this lesson:

① 过了圣诞节，艾德才觉得在中国的生活安定了下来。
　　Guòle Shèngdàn Jié, Àidé cái juéde zài Zhōngguó de shēnghuó āndìngle xiàlai.
　　Ed didn't feel that his life in China was settled until after Christmas.

② 你必须自己去那儿，售票员才会卖票给你。
　　Nǐ bìxū zìjǐ qù nàr, shòupiàoyuán cái huì mài piào gěi nǐ.
　　You have to go there in person; only then will the agent sell you a ticket.

Learners often use "才 cái" incorrectly for two reasons. One is that it often corresponds to a negative in English: "not until"; the other is that with the English expression, "not until", the time or quantity comes last – as both our examples show. With "才 cái", however, the quantity comes first: "八点才吃 bā diǎn cái chī" (not to eat until 8:00). The way to compensate for this interference from English is to use the English logical expression "then and only then" as a check. "Then and only then" not only captures the sense of "relatively late" presupposed by "才 cái"; but like "才 cái", it also follows the time or quantity expressions. "at 8 o'clock – then and only then – has dinner".

A quick check of your understanding of "才 cái": Announce that "you're not leaving until tomorrow morning". Remember to begin with the time or quantity – "tomorrow morning" (明天早上 míngtiān zǎoshang); and finish with the "then and only then" test: "I, tomorrow morning, then and only then, leave" (我明天早上才走 Wǒ míngtiān zǎoshang cái zǒu).

A few other notes about "才 cái": It can be associated with other elements, such as "只有 zhǐyǒu" (only), a conjunction that indicates that the time is the sole condition:

③ 她忙得很，只有吃饭的时候才可以休息一会儿。
　　Tā máng de hěn, zhǐyǒu chī fàn de shíhou cái kěyǐ xiūxi yíhuìr.
　　She's extremely busy; the only time she gets to rest for a bit is when she's eating.

"才 cái" is often contrasted with "就 jiù", another adverb that is frequently found in the same structural position in sentences (cf. Volume I, Lesson 9, G4 and Volume II, Lesson 15, G2). Whereas "才 cái" implies relatively later than expected, "就 jiù" is neutral or implies relatively earlier. The following example illustrates the contrast:

④ 我六点就吃晚饭，她八点才吃晚饭。
　　Wǒ liù diǎn jiù chī wǎnfàn, tā bā diǎn cái chī wǎnfàn.
　　I eat dinner (as early as) at 6:00 p.m., she doesn't eat until 8:00 p.m..

More generally, "就 jiù" and "才 cái" may follow expressions of quantity as well as time. In such cases, "就 jiù" implies conditions that are relatively neutral or minimal (normal, earlier, less), while "才 cái" indicates conditions that are relatively more severe (later, more, not until). The following example shows the contrast applied to quantity:

⑤ 我吃两碗就饱，他吃三四碗才饱。
　　Wǒ chī liǎng wǎn jiù bǎo, tā chī sān-sì wǎn cái bǎo.
　　I eat only two bowls and I'm full. He doesn't feel full until he's had three or four.

Finally, another contrast between the two adverbs: "就 jiù" often appear with sentence final "了 le"; but not "才 cái", which is incompatible with it.

⑥ 他们十一点就回家了。　They returned home at 11:00 p.m..
　　Tāmen shíyī diǎn jiù huí jiā le.

⑦ 他们十一点才回家（*了）。　They didn't get home until 11:00 p.m..
　　Tāmen shíyī diǎn cái huí jiā (*le).

▶ **G2.** The paired adverbs "一 yī……就 jiù……" (once, as soon as, whenever)

In earlier lessons, the numeral "一 yī" was always seen to precede measure words ("一个 yí ge", "一件 yí jiàn", etc.) But as examples in this lesson show, "一 yī" can also occur directly before verbs, in which case it functions as an adverb:

① 老师一进来，学生就站了起来。　Once the teacher entered, the students stood up.
　　Lǎoshī yí jìnlai, xuésheng jiù zhànle qilai.

As the example shows, "一 yī" before verbs is generally linked to a following "就 jiù", giving the sense of "once, as soon as… [then]" – in most cases, "then" will not appear in the English. Here are two examples – the first one from the dialogue:

② 今年春节在一月，所以一过圣诞节，寒假就快到了。
　　Jīnnián Chūn Jié zài yīyuè, suǒyǐ yí guò Shèngdàn Jié, hánjià jiù kuài dào le.
　　The Spring Festival's in January this year, so as soon as Christmas is done with, it's almost winter break.

③ 昨天我一吃完午饭就看电影去了。　Yesterday, right after eating lunch, I went to a movie.
　　Zuótiān wǒ yì chīwán wǔfàn jiù kàn diànyǐng qù le.

▶ **G3.** Completed action with "了 le" and "没(有) méi (yǒu)"

"了 le" was introduced in Lesson 5 (G5) as a signal of change of state, new situation, or current relevance. In that function, "了 le" appears at the foot of the sentence (after objects, duration phrases, etc.) and applies to the sentence as a whole: "上课了 shàngkè le" (it's time for class); "不早了 bù zǎo le" (it's getting late); "三年了 sān nián le" (three years so far).

"了 le" may also function as a verb suffix, appearing directly after verbs and modifying the verbal meaning rather than the sentence as a whole. It is associated with the onset or completion of actions (past, present or future). The text of an earlier lesson (Lesson 16) is a rich source of examples of the verb suffix "了 le":

① 他摔了一跤。　He fell down.
　　Tā shuāile yì jiāo.

第十八课 春 运
Lesson Eighteen Traveling over Chinese New Year

② 你可能吃了不干净的东西。 You probably ate something that wasn't clean.
Nǐ kěnéng chīle bù gānjìng de dōngxi.

The negative, indicating that an event has not taken place, is formed with "没 (有) méi (yǒu)" – with no "了 le".

③ 他们还没有下课。 They aren't out of class yet.
Tāmen hái méiyǒu xià kè.

Verb-not-verb questions combine positive "了 le" with negative "没 (有) méi (yǒu)":

④ 饭吃完了没有？/ 饭吃完了吗？ Have you finished eating yet (or not)?
Fàn chīwánle méiyǒu? / Fàn chīwánle ma?

⑤ 您寒假去哪儿，计划了没有？
Nín hánjià qù nǎr, jìhuàle méiyou?
Have you planned where you're going to go for the winter break?

The sense of completed action, associated with the "了 le" as a verb suffix is most obvious in those cases that involve one event being completed before another takes place, as in the following examples:

⑥ 到了医院吴老师去给他们挂号。
Dàole yīyuàn Wú lǎoshī qù gěi tāmen guà hào.
Once they reach the hospital, teacher Wu will go and register them.

⑦ A: 你今天几点回家？ When are you going home today?
Nǐ jīntiān jǐ diǎn huí jiā?

B: 我下了课就回家。 I'm going home after class.
Wǒ xiàle kè jiù huí jiā.

In both examples, "了 le" marks the first verb in a sequence of actions: they reach the hospital (到了医院 dàole yīyuàn) and then teacher Wu registers them; class gets out (下了课 xiàle kè) and then I go home.

English speakers are often tempted to identify "了 le" with tense. However, it should be noted first of all, that sentences containing "了 le" can be past, present or future, as the following examples show:

⑧ 昨天我在商店买了一双鞋。 (past)
Zuótiān wǒ zài shāngdiàn mǎile yì shuāng xié.
Yesterday, I bought a pair of shoes at the store.

⑨ 我每天都写了汉字才睡觉。 (present)
Wǒ měi tiān dōu xiěle Hànzì cái shuì jiào.
Everyday I go to bed only after I finish writing Chinese characters.

⑩ 明天我们看了电影就去吃饭。 (future)
Míngtiān wǒmen kànle diànyǐng qù chī fàn.
Tomorrow, we're going to see a movie and then going to eat.

It is also frequently the case that where English has past tense, Chinese has no "了 le" at all:

⑪ 昨天很热，我不想出去。 It was really hot yesterday, I didn't feel like going out.
Zuótiān hěn rè, wǒ bù xiǎng chūqu.

A final point: "了 le" may appear twice in a single sentence, once directly after the verb, and then again at the foot of the sentence (after a direct object, a duration phrase, etc.). For instance, you will often be asked in China how many years you have been studying Chinese. Your answer might be:

⑫ 我学了三年了。 I've been studying for three years.
　　Wǒ xuéle sān nián le.

The first "了 le" indicates the onset of study, the final "了 le" indicates that it continues – hence English "have been studying" rather than "have studied". It should be noted that the addition of a restricting adverb, such as "只 zhǐ" (only) or "才 cái" (in its meaning of "only"), cancels the "up to now" sense of the Chinese and disallows a final "了 le": 我只学了一年 Wǒ zhǐ xuéle yì nián (I've only been studying for one year) – the second, final "了 le" is no longer possible.]

▶ **G4.** Double negatives, expressing insistence: "不能不 bù néng bù", etc.

Certainty and necessity can be expressed by adverbs such as "一定 yídìng" and "得 děi": "我一定要去 Wǒ yídìng yào qù" (I'll be going for sure); "我得去 Wǒ děi qù" (I have to go). However, insistence is often expressed by a double negative, such as "不能不 bù néng bù" (simply have to), "不得不 bù dé bù" (have to) or "没有……不 méiyǒu……bù" (be obliged to).

① 大家过年的时候不能不回老家吗？
　　Dàjiā guò nián de shíhou bù néng bù huí lǎojiā ma?
　　Does everyone have to return to their hometowns over New Year?

② 我们不得不坐火车吗？ Do we have to take the train?
　　Wǒmen bù dé bú zuò huǒchē ma?

③ 领导的宴会没有人不穿西服吗？
　　Lǐngdǎo de yànhuì méiyǒu rén bù chuān xīfú ma?
　　Does absolutely everyone wear a suit to the banquet for the heads?

▶ **G5.** "只要 zhǐyào……就 jiù……" (so long as… [then]…)

The adverb "只 zhǐ" (only) and the auxiliary verb "要 yào" (need) often appear together to indicate minimal conditions: "as long as; so long as; all that's needed is". What follows from these conditions is often marked by "就 jiù" in the following clause:

① 只要公寓安静，我就去住。 As long as the apartment is quiet, I'll go and live there.
　　Zhǐyào gōngyù ānjìng, wǒ jiù qù zhù.

② 过年时，一家人只要能团聚在一起就是幸福。
　　Guònián shí, yìjiārén zhǐyào néng tuánjù zài yìqǐ jiù shì xìngfú.
　　At the New Year, so long as the whole family can get together, people are happy.

▶ **G6.** "为什么不 wèi shénme bù" (why don't…, how come [you] don't…)

In Chinese (as in English), posing a negative question is a common rhetorical device for bringing up other options:

Lesson Eighteen Traveling over Chinese New Year

第十八课 春运

① 我们为什么不坐飞机？坐飞机比坐火车贵得多吗？
Wǒmen wèi shénme bú zuò fēijī? Zuò fēijī bǐ zuò huǒchē guì de duō ma?
Why don't we take a plane? Is flying much more expensive than taking the train?

② 你为什么不跟你的中国朋友回老家呢？
Nǐ wèi shénme bù gēn nǐ de Zhōngguó péngyou huí lǎojiā ne?
How come you're not going back home with your Chinese friends?

Consolidation & Practice

1. Answer the questions along the lines of the English, using the adverb "才 cái" (not until, only then), and incorporating the material in parentheses

   Example: A: 他去网吧怎么还没有回来？
   Tā qù wǎngbā zěnme hái méiyǒu huílai?
   How come he hasn't come back from the internet café yet?

   B: 他晚上六点钟才去。He didn't go until 6:00 p.m..
   Tā wǎnshang liù diǎnzhōng cái qù.

(1) A: 你什么时候做饭？
   Nǐ shénme shíhou zuò fàn?

   B: _____
   (I won't start cooking until the guests are here.)

(2) A: 你什么时候去看电影？
   Nǐ shénme shíhou qù kàn diànyǐng?

   B: _____
   (I won't go see a movie until the weekend.)

(3) A: 你什么时候去买火车票？
   Nǐ shénme shíhou qù mǎi huǒchēpiào?

   B: _____
   (I won't go to buy the train tickets until I get out of class.)

(4) A: 我什么时候能上网？
   Wǒ shénme shíhou néng shàng wǎng?

   B: _____
   (You can't use the internet until you pay your deposit.)

(5) A: 我的房间怎么没有网络？
   Wǒ de fángjiān zěnme méiyǒu wǎngluò?

   B: _____

(You have to restart your computer to get connected.)

(6) A: 我什么时候才能见大夫?
Wǒ shénme shíhou cái néng jiàn dàifu?

B: _____
(You have to get the results of the test before seeing the doctor.)

(7) A: 你今天怎么八点才起床?
Nǐ jīntiān zěnme bā diǎn cái qǐ chuáng?

B: _____
(I didn't go to bed last night until midnight.)

(8) A: 你第一节课是几点?
Nǐ dì-yī jié kè shì jǐ diǎn?

B: _____
(My first class doesn't start until 10:10)

2. Connect the phrases below with "一 yī……就 jiù……"

Examples: ① 有钱 / 想买东西 → 他一有钱就想买东西。
yǒu qián / xiǎng mǎi dōngxi   Tā yì yǒu qián jiù xiǎng mǎi dōngxi.

② 买了电话卡 / 给父母打电话 → 他一买了电话卡就给父母打电话。
mǎile diànhuàkǎ / gěi fùmǔ dǎ diànhuà   Tā yì mǎile diànhuàkǎ jiù gěi fùmǔ dǎ diànhuà.

(1) 去理发店 / 想按摩 → _____
qù lǐfàdiàn / xiǎng ànmó

(2) 吃鱼 / 过敏 → _____
chī yú / guòmǐn

(3) 换了钱 / 去买飞机票 → _____
huànle qián / qù mǎi fēijīpiào

(4) 下了课 / 去看病 → _____
xiàle kè / qù kàn bìng

(5) 吃完晚饭 / 想睡觉 → _____
chīwán wǎnfàn / xiǎng shuì jiào

(6) 到周末 / 想看电影 → _____
dào zhōumò / xiǎng kàn diànyǐng

(7) 到圣诞节 / 想家 → _____
dào Shèngdàn Jié / xiǎng jiā

(8) 到中国 / 水土不服 → _____
dào Zhōngguó / shuǐtǔ bùfú

第十八课 春运
Lesson Eighteen Traveling over Chinese New Year

3. Following the English cues and incorporating the material in parentheses, ask the questions listed below, using [S V Resultative complement (了) 没有]

   Example: The express train tickets are sold out. Find out if tickets for the slow train are also sold out – or not. (卖完 màiwán)

   去西安的慢车票卖完了没有？
   Qù Xī'ān de mànchēpiào màiwánle méiyǒu?

   (1) Ask the ticket agent if there are any tickets for the express train to Shanghai.
   _____? (卖完 màiwán)

   (2) Ask your friend if her roasted chicken's cooked.
   _____? (烤好 kǎohǎo)

   (3) Ask your friend if she's found an English-teaching job?
   _____? (找到 zhǎodào)

   (4) Ask your friend who's just come from the hairdresser if he had a massage.
   _____? (按摩 ànmó)

   (5) Ask your friend if she's finished her homework.
   _____? (做完 zuòwán)

   (6) Ask your partner if he has finished shopping.
   _____? (买完 mǎiwán)

   (7) Ask your friend if she's taken her medicine.
   _____? (吃药 chī yào)

   (8) Ask your friend whether he has recovered from his bad cold.
   _____? (好 hǎo)

4. Rewrite the following questions or statements, using the "double negative" (不能不 bù néng bù) to indicate insistence

   Example: 你的血压很高，你一定得去看病。
   Nǐ de xuèyā hěn gāo, nǐ yídìng děi qù kàn bìng.

   → 你的血压很高，你不能不去看病。
   Nǐ de xuèyā hěn gāo, nǐ bù néng bú qù kàn bìng.

   (1) 明天的宴会很重要，你一定要参加。
   Míngtiān de yànhuì hěn zhòngyào, nǐ yídìng yào cānjiā.

   → _____

(2) 春节在中国是家人团聚的日子，我一定得回家。
　　Chūn Jié zài Zhōngguó shì jiārén tuánjù de rìzi, wǒ yídìng děi huí jiā.

　　→ _____

(3) 你的感冒还没有好，今天一定要去打篮球吗？
　　Nǐ de gǎnmào hái méiyǒu hǎo, jīntiān yídìng yào qù dǎ lánqiú ma?

　　→ _____

(4) 理发店快关门了，染发可能来不及了。你今天能不能不染发？
　　Lǐfàdiàn kuài guān mén le, rǎn fà kěnéng láibují le. Nǐ jīntiān néng bu néng bù rǎn fà?

　　→ _____

(5) 我们三个人吃饭，已经有四个菜了。我们一定要烤鸡吗？
　　Wǒmen sān ge rén chī fàn, yǐjīng yǒu sì ge cài le. Wǒmen yídìng yào kǎojī ma?

　　→ _____

(6) 你这个学期上四门课，还做家教。你一定要做家教吗？
　　Nǐ zhège xuéqī shàng sì mén kè, hái zuò jiājiào. Nǐ yídìng yào zuò jiājiào ma?

　　→ _____

5. Answer the questions, integrating the material in parentheses with the paired adverbs "只要 zhǐyào……就 jiù……"

　　Example: A: 过春节的时候，孩子要给父母买礼物吗？
　　　　　　　　 Guò Chūnjié de shíhou, háizi yào gěi fùmǔ mǎi lǐwù ma?

　　　　　　 B: 不用，只要孩子都回家过春节，父母就特别高兴。
　　　　　　　　 Búyòng, zhǐyào háizi dōu huí jiā guò Chūn Jié, fùmǔ jiù tèbié gāoxìng.

(1) A: 大夫，我什么时候可以不吃药了？
　　　Dàifu, wǒ shénme shíhou kěyǐ bù chī yào le?

　　B: _____（化验结果正常，可以不吃药）
　　　 _____(huàyàn jiéguǒ zhèngcháng, kěyǐ bù chī yào)

(2) A: 老师，我怎么提高口语水平？
　　　Lǎoshī, wǒ zěnme tígāo kǒuyǔ shuǐpíng?

　　B: _____（每天说中文，可以提高口语水平）
　　　 _____(měi tiān shuō Zhōngwén, kěyǐ tígāo kǒuyǔ shuǐpíng)

(3) A: 你要买名牌西服吗？
　　　Nǐ yào mǎi míngpái de xīfú ma?

　　B: 不一定要买名牌的，_____（穿着合适，买）
　　　 Bù yídìng yào mǎi míngpái de, _____(chuānzhe héshì, mǎi)

第十八课 春运
Lesson Eighteen Traveling over Chinese New Year

(4) A: 你想不想跟我去周末的派对?
　　　Nǐ xiǎng bu xiǎng gēn wǒ qù zhōumò de pàiduì?

　　B: _____（别回来太晚，去）
　　　　　　　　　　　　　　　　　　　　　　　　（bié huílai tài wǎn, qù）

(5) A: 我现在不吃肉了，因为我怕得心脏病。
　　　Wǒ xiànzài bù chī ròu le, yīnwèi wǒ pà dé xīnzàngbìng.

　　B: _____（别吃太多肉，没有关系）
　　　　　　　　　　　　　　　　　　　　　　　（bié chī tài duō ròu, méiyǒu guānxi）

(6) A: 你的腿受伤了，大夫说你还能打篮球吗?
　　　Nǐ de tuǐ shòu shāng le, dàifu shuō nǐ hái néng dǎ lánqiú ma?

　　B: 大夫告诉我，_____（注意一点儿，不会有问题）
　　　Dàifu gàosu wǒ,　　　　　　　　　　（zhùyì yìdiǎnr, bú huì yǒu wèntí）

(7) A: 你想要什么菜?
　　　Nǐ xiǎng yào shénme cài?

　　B: 我喜欢吃海鲜，_____（是海鲜，吃）
　　　Wǒ xǐhuan chī hǎixiān,　　　　　　　　　　　（shì hǎixiān, chī）

(8) A: 去西安的慢车票容易买到吗?
　　　Qù Xī'ān de mànchēpiào róngyì mǎidào ma?

　　B: _____（是去西安的票，都难买）
　　　　　　　　　　　　　　　　　　　　　（shì qù Xī'ān de piào, dōu nán mǎi）

6. Respond with a negative question "为什么不 wèi shénme bù" to emphasize other options, or options missed

(1) A: 糟糕，我忘记带护照了!
　　　Zāogāo, wǒ wàngjì dài hùzhào le!

　　B: _____?（早一点儿准备好 zǎo yìdiǎnr zhǔnbèi hǎo）

(2) A: 去西安的火车票都卖完了。
　　　Qù Xī'ān de huǒchēpiào dōu màiwán le.

　　B: _____?（坐飞机去西安 zuò fēijī qù Xī'ān）

(3) A: 我过敏一个星期了，还没有好。
　　　Wǒ guòmǐn yí ge xīngqī le, hái méiyǒu hǎo.

　　B: _____?（吃过敏药 chī guòmǐnyào）

(4) A: 我这个学期忙极了。
　　　Wǒ zhège xuéqī mángjí le.

　　B: _____?（辞掉家教的工作 cídiào jiājiào de gōngzuò）

(5) A: 我的同事对我都很好，我想请他们吃饭，可是我不会做中国饭。
　　　Wǒ de tóngshì duì wǒ dōu hěn hǎo, wǒ xiǎng qǐng tāmen chī fàn, kěshì wǒ bú huì zuò Zhōngguófàn.

　　B: _____？（给他们做美国饭吃 gěi tāmen zuò Měiguófàn chī）

(6) A: 名牌的包太贵了，真买不起。
　　　Míngpái de bāo tài guì le, zhēn mǎi bu qǐ.

　　B: _____？（买普通的包 mǎi pǔtōng de bāo）

Lesson Eighteen　Traveling over Chinese New Year

第十八课　春运

Listening Comprehension

1. Listen to the dialogue and then answer the questions

(1) When is the best time to visit Nanjing, according to the Nanjing native?

(2) How long would it take to fly to Nanjing from where they are?

(3) How much does it cost to take the express train to Nanjing?

(4) How long does it take to get to Nanjing by the express train?

(5) How long does it take to get to Nanjing by high-speed train?

(6) What is the advantage of taking the train rather than flying?

(7) What's the final decision about getting to Nanjing?

(8) Why did one of the speakers ask for the other's phone number?

New Words

累　lèi　Adj　tired

怕　pà　V　to fear, to be afraid

好玩儿　hǎowánr　Adj　to be fun, be enjoyable

2. Listen to the dialogue and then answer the questions

(1) What sort of ticket did the customer want?

(2) Why did the ticket agent suggest a different time?

(3) What sort of ticket did the agent ultimately come up with?

(4) How much was it?

(5) Why was it so expensive?

(6) Did the customer decide to purchase it?

(7) What prevented the purchase?

(8) Could the ticket agent do anything to help?

New Words

直达　zhídá　V　to be nonstop

涨　zhǎng　V　to rise

205

真实生活汉语
Chinese for Living in China 2

Communication Activities

Pair Work

Scenario I: Traveling by train. You're talking to a Chinese friend about train travel. You plan to travel around China by train during the break. Your friend's pretty knowledgeable about train travel, so it's a chance to ask questions. Be guided by the following list:

坐火车	交通运输	普快	特快	硬卧
zuò huǒchē	jiāotōng yùnshū	pǔkuài	tèkuài	yìngwò
软卧	硬座	软座	上铺	下铺
ruǎnwò	yìngzuò	ruǎnzuò	shàngpù	xiàpù
中铺	票价	非常拥挤	很难买到	贵一倍
zhōngpù	piàojià	fēicháng yōngjǐ	hěn nán mǎidào	guì yí bèi
坐飞机	卖完了	出发前二十天	带护照	体验
zuò fēijī	màiwán le	chūfā qián èrshí tiān	dài hùzhào	tǐyàn

Scenario II: Chinese New Year versus Thanksgiving. Compare and contrast the Chinese holiday and the American. Make use of the following phrases and expressions:

每年的时间不一样		差不多		只要……就……
měi nián de shíjiān bù yíyàng		chàbuduō		zhǐyào……jiù……
团聚	幸福	传统	亲戚	朋友
tuánjù	xìngfú	chuántǒng	qīnqi	péngyou
好吃的东西	非常拥挤	很难买到	贵几倍	坐火车
hǎochī de dōngxi	fēicháng yōngjǐ	hěn nán mǎidào	guì jǐ bèi	zuò huǒchē
开车	坐飞机	卖完了	交通运输	
kāi chē	zuò fēijī	màiwán le	jiāotōng yùnshū	
坐长途汽车	坐火车	特快	硬卧	软卧
zuò chángtú qìchē	zuò huǒchē	tèkuài	yìngwò	ruǎnwò
硬坐	软坐			
yìngzuò	ruǎnzuò			

Scenario III: Travel in China and the US. Talk about travel in the US versus China. Support your preferences and opinions. Consider benefits and drawbacks. Refer to the following list:

非常拥挤	贵得多	坐飞机	坐火车	开车
fēicháng yōngjǐ	guì de duō	zuò fēijī	zuò huǒchē	kāi chē

第十八课　春运
Lesson Eighteen　Traveling over Chinese New Year

特快	硬卧	软座	又快又方便
tèkuài	yìngwò	ruǎnzuò	yòu kuài yòu fāngbiàn
一边坐车一边聊天儿		交朋友	看风景
yìbiān zuò chē yìbiān liáotiānr		jiāo péngyou	kàn fēngjǐng
练习说中文		了解文化/社会	
liànxí shuō Zhōngwén		liǎojiě wénhuà/shèhuì	

Role-Play

Scenario I: Buying a train ticket. One of you is buying a train ticket from Shenzhen to Shanghai. The other is a ticket agent. The traveler needs to find out the following information that uses expressions like these:

票价	开车时间	到达时间	车次
piàojià	kāi chē shíjiān	dàodá shíjiān	chēcì
换不换车	餐车	第几站台	上车
huàn bu huàn chē	cānchē	dì jǐ zhàntái	shàng chē

The agent tries to help but sometimes needs clarification:

X比Y贵得多	特快/普快	软卧/硬卧	
X bǐ Y guì de duō	tèkuài/pǔkuài	ruǎnwò/yìngwò	
上铺/中铺/下铺	差不多	实名制	护照
shàngpù/zhōngpù/xiàpù	chàbuduō	shímíngzhì	hùzhào

Scenario II: The difficulty of returning home for the Spring Festival. An American student is talking to a friend from Anhui. The friend explains how difficult it is to return home at this time of year – hard to get tickets, having to stand for long periods, etc. Discuss these issues, being guided by the list of expressions:

春运期间旅行		非常拥挤	很难买到	太麻烦
chūnyùn qījiān lǚxíng		fēicháng yōngjǐ	hěn nán mǎidào	tài máfan
贵几倍	坐火车	卖完了	特快	硬卧
guì jǐ bèi	zuò huǒchē	màiwán le	tèkuài	yìngwò
软卧	软座	硬座	站十几个小时	
ruǎnwò	ruǎnzuò	yìngzuò	zhàn shíjǐ ge xiǎoshí	
坐高铁	一等软座	二等软座	坐飞机	
zuò gāotiě	yī děng ruǎnzuò	èr děng ruǎnzuò	zuò fēijī	
差不多	一……就……	为什么不……		
chàbuduō	yī……jiù……	wèi shénme bù……		

Group Activities

Scenario I: Best and worst travel experiences. Interview at least three of your classmates to find out the best or worst travel experience they have had in China. Then pick one and report it to the class. Be guided by the following:

旅行 lǚxíng	非常拥挤 fēicháng yōngjǐ	很难买到 hěn nán mǎidào	太麻烦 tài máfan	贵几倍 guì jǐ bèi
卖完了 màiwán le	特快 tèkuài	硬卧 yìngwò	软卧 ruǎnwò	软座 ruǎnzuò
硬座 yìngzuò	坐高铁 zuò gāotiě	一等软座 yī děng ruǎnzuò	二等软座 èr děng ruǎnzuò	差不多 chàbuduō
坐飞机 zuò fēijī	坐火车 zuò huǒchē	开车 kāi chē	一边坐车一边聊天儿 yìbiān zuò chē yìbiān liáo tiānr	
交朋友 jiāo péngyou	看风景 kàn fēngjǐng	练习说中文 liànxí shuō Zhōngwén	了解中国文化/社会 liǎojiě Zhōngguó wénhuà/shèhuì	
睡（不好）觉 shuì (bù hǎo) jiào	（不）舒服 (bù) shūfu	站十几个小时 zhàn shíjǐ ge xiǎoshí	厕所/洗手间/卫生间 cèsuǒ / xǐshǒujiān/wèishēngjiān	
西餐 xīcān	中餐 zhōngcān			

Scenario II: Going to Kunming. Four of you are planning to go to Kunming during the summer. You are discussing various ways of getting there – plane or train. Two of you prefer to fly, but two feel taking a hard-sleeper would be a more interesting experience. Here, for reference, is a list of words, most of which should by now be familiar:

非常拥挤 fēicháng yōngjǐ	贵得多 guì de duō	坐火车 zuò huǒchē	硬卧 yìngwò	软卧 ruǎnwò
差不多 chàbuduō	坐飞机 zuò fēijī	上铺 shàngpù	中铺 zhōngpù	下铺 xiàpù
不方便 bù fāngbiàn	一边坐车一边聊天儿 yìbiān zuò chē yìbiān liáo tiānr		交朋友 jiāo péngyou	看风景 kàn fēngjǐng
练习说中文 liànxí shuō Zhōngwén	了解中国文化/社会 liǎojiě Zhōngguó wénhuà/shèhuì		很难买票 hěn nán mǎi piào	
睡不好觉 shuì bu hǎo jiào	又……又…… yòu……yòu……			

第十八课 春 运
Lesson Eighteen Traveling over Chinese New Year

Review Exercises

1. Complete the sentences with "只有 zhǐyǒu……才 cái……" (only if, only when… [then]…)

    (1) _____ 能把中文学好。
    　　　　(Only when you come to China)　　　néng bǎ Zhōngwén xuéhǎo.

    (2) _____ 不会发烧。
    　　　　(Only if you take antibiotics)　　　bú huì fāshāo.

    (3) _____ 能买到快车票。
    　　　(Only if you arrive really early in the morning)　néng mǎidào kuàichēpiào.

    (4) _____ 能买到又便宜又新鲜的蔬菜。
    　　　　(Only if you go to the morning market)　néng mǎidào yòu piányi yòu xīnxian de shūcài.

    (5) _____ 出去吃饭。
    　　　(Only if we go to a Western restaurant)　chūqu chī fàn.

    (6) _____ 做很多菜。
    　　　(Only when I have guests over to my house)　zuò hěn duō cài.

2. Answer the questions using "一 yī……就 jiù……"

    (1) A: 你什么时候去买火车票?
    　　　Nǐ shénme shíhou qù mǎi huǒchēpiào?

    　　B: _____
    　　　(As soon as we finish the class.)

    (2) A: 你怎么又肚子疼了?
    　　　Nǐ zěnme yòu dùzi téng le?

    　　B: 我也不知道为什么。_____
    　　　Wǒ yě bù zhīdào wèi shénme.　(As soon as I drink something cold, I get a stomach-ache.)

    (3) A: 你打算什么时候去旅行?
    　　　Nǐ dǎsuan shénme shíhou qù lǚxíng?

    　　B: _____
    　　　(I'm going as soon as the semester's over.)

    (4) A: 你每天什么时候去打篮球?
    　　　Nǐ měi tiān shénme shíhou qù dǎ lánqiú?

    　　B: _____
    　　　(As soon as I get up in the morning.)

(5) A: 你是什么时候认识你的女/男朋友的？
Nǐ shì shénme shíhou rènshi nǐ de nǚ/nánpéngyou de?

B: _____
(I met him/her as soon as I arrived on campus.)

(6) A: 你什么时候回美国看父母？
Nǐ shénme shíhou huí Měiguó kàn fùmǔ?

B: _____
(I'm heading back as soon as I get a break.)

3. Ask questions about past events using the "了 le……没有 méiyǒu" question form

(1) Ask your partner if (s)he has eaten yet.

....

(2) Ask your partner if (s)he has done the homework.

....

(3) Ask your partner if (s)he's bought the train ticket for the upcoming holiday.

....

(4) Ask your partner if (s)he went to the hairdresser last week.

....

(5) Ask your partner if (s)he visited the new supermarket on the weekend.

....

(6) Ask your partner (who is coughing) if (s)he's had an X-ray.

....

4. Express the following, using the "不能不 bù néng bù" construction to emphasize your point

(1) Tell your friend to take some medicine for the cold.

....

(2) Tell your partner not to skip Friday's class.

....

(3) Tell the Chinese student (you are tutoring) that (s)he has to speak English to you.

....

(4) Tell your Chinese friend to be sure to come to your party.

....

第十八课 春 运
Lesson Eighteen   Traveling over Chinese New Year

(5) Tell your hairdresser that she has to take the tip. (小费 xiǎofèi)

....

(6) Tell your doctor that you have to have antibiotics for your fever.

....

5. Following the English, form Chinese sentences that incorporates "只要 zhǐyào……就 jiù……"

   (1) As long as you have money, you can travel to America or Europe.

   ....

   (2) With Chinese food, as long as you like to eat it, you can learn to cook it.

   ....

   (3) As long as you get up early and exercise, you can eat your favorite foods without worrying about your weight. (不用考虑体重 búyòng kǎolǜ tǐzhòng)

   ....

   (4) Provided you can speak Chinese, the Chinese will be happy to talk to you.

   ....

   (5) Provided you ask for them, your doctor will prescribe antibiotics for you.

   ....

   (6) As long as you have a fever, you'll get treated with intravenous fluid. (打点滴 dǎ diǎndī)

   ....

6. Ask questions appropriate to the situation

   (1) You need to go to Shenzhen for an important business meeting. At the high-speed train ticket window ask the clerk the following:

   ① Is there a train to Shenzhen today?

   ....

   ② Do I need to change trains?

   ....

   ③ How much is a round-trip ticket for a first-class soft seat?

   ....

   ④ How much for a second-class soft seat?

   ....

⑤ How many pieces of luggage am I allowed to bring with me?

....

(2) You are at the train station, buying a ticket to Shanghai. Ask the clerk the following information:

① If there's a soft-seat ticket to Shanghai today.

....

② If it's an express train, how many stops it makes, and whether you need to change.

....

③ If it's air-conditioned, and if there's a dining car.

....

④ When express train number 108 is leaving.

....

⑤ Where platform #3 is.

....

第十八课　春　运
Lesson Eighteen　Traveling over Chinese New Year

Culture Notes

1. How to buy a train or airplane ticket

In general, hotels with a three-star rating or higher will have a ticket office or counter that sells train and airplane tickets. You can also buy tickets at travel agencies or the ticket offices of airlines and train stations. You must bring some identification (such as your passport) with you when you make the booking.

One can also buy tickets online (e.g., at www.12306.cn, www.ctrip.com or www.tieyou.com), or make a telephone booking at the Ministry of Railways (Tel: 95105105).

2. Types of trains in China

Trains in China are labeled with letters according to their type and speed. The following chart shows the various types, ordered (roughly) by speed:

G (高铁 gāotiě): very high speed bullet trains; between large cities

D (动车 dòngchē): non-stop, inter-city, fast electric trains ("electric multiple units")

C (城际列车 chéngjì lièchē): short distance inter-city EMU trains

Z (直达特快 zhídá tèkuài): direct express with limited stops

T (特快 tèkuài): express trains stopping only at large stations

K (快车 kuàichē): regular inter-city trains stopping at medium to large stations (see N)

N (内 nèi): like K, except run by regional railway bureaus

L (临客 línkè): temporary passenger trains (peak season only)

Y (游车 yóuchē): special tourist trains (tourist routes only)

Numbers only (普快 pǔkuài, 普客 puke): local trains, frequent stops

3. Types of tickets

Airplanes are the same as in the United States, with first class, business class, and economy class seats. Trains have hard-seat (硬座 yìngzuò), soft-seat (软座 ruǎnzuò), soft-berth (软卧 ruǎnwò), and hard-berth (硬卧 yìngwò) tickets. The hard-berth (硬卧 yìngwò) carriage has tiers of three bunks (with mattress pads) and the carriage is divided into compartments without doors. The soft-berth carriage has tiers of two bunks in four-person closed compartments. The hard-berth tickets are divided into three categories: upper-level (上铺 shàngpù), mid-level (中铺 zhōngpù), and lower-level (下铺 xiàpù). The soft-berth tickets are divided into two categories: upper-level (上铺 shàngpù) and lower-level (下铺 xiàpù). The "高铁 gāotiě" (high-speed railway) has first-class seating (一等座 yīděngzuò), second-class seating (二等座 èrděngzuò), and luxury business class (豪华商务舱 háohuá shāngwùcāng).

4. Round-trip and one-way tickets

Chinese airlines do not usually sell round-trip ("来回 láihuí" or "往返 wǎngfǎn") tickets.

5. Things to take when you travel by train

When you travel by train in China, you need to bring a small towel for washing, and toilet paper. If you are traveling overnight, you will also need a toothbrush.

6. Meals or snacks on the train

Trains usually have a dining car, serving breakfast between 7:00 a.m. and 9:00 a.m., lunch from 11:00 a.m. to 1:30 p.m., and dinner at 6:00 p.m. to 7:30 p.m. You can also buy food from attendants, who push carts of packaged foods and snacks through the train.

Lesson Nineteen   How's the Weather?

第十九课   天气怎么样？
Dì-shíjiǔ Kè   Tiānqì Zěnmeyàng?

In this lesson you will learn how to do the following

- Talk about the weather and the seasons
- Become familiar with the language of weather reports
- Compare the weather in different areas

Grammar

- The scope of negation (e.g. "不都 bù dōu" versus "都不 dōu bù")
- Ambient sentences: describing the weather
- Vivid reduplication
- Comparison with "有 yǒu" and "没有 méiyǒu"
- The construction "以 yǐ……为 wéi……" (take…as…)
- Four-syllable expressions: a favorite type

Culture Notes

- "The 24 Solar Terms" of the traditional Chinese seasonal calendar
- Centigrade to Fahrenheit conversion table

Dialogue

A：艾德 Àidé　　**B**：刘教授 Liú jiàoshòu

　　艾德没想到这么快就买到了去西安的飞机票，他很兴奋：有机会去中国同事的老家过节，一路上还有中国同事做伴，学校的外国人不都[G1]是这么幸运。出发前他得赶快准备去西安旅行时穿的衣服和日用品，还要准备行李，给刘教授和他的家人买礼物等等。他不知道西安的天气怎么样，应该带什么衣服，所以去问刘教授。

　　Àidé méi xiǎngdào zhème kuài jiù mǎidàole qù Xī'ān de fēijīpiào, tā hěn xīngfèn: yǒu jīhui qù Zhōngguó tóngshì de lǎojiā guò jié, yílù shang hái yǒu Zhōngguó tóngshì zuò bàn, xuéxiào de wàiguórén bù dōu[G1] shì zhème xìngyùn. Chūfā qián tā děi gǎnkuài zhǔnbèi qù Xī'ān lǚxíng shí chuān de yīfu hé rìyòngpǐn, hái yào zhǔnbèi xíngli, gěi Liú jiàoshòu hé tā de jiārén mǎi lǐwù děngděng. Tā bù zhīdào Xī'ān de tiānqì zěnmeyàng, yīnggāi dài shénme yīfu, suǒyǐ qù wèn Liú jiàoshòu.

A：刘老师，您看，刮风了[G2]，天也阴了，会不会下雪？
　　Liú lǎoshī, nín kàn, guā fēng le[G2], tiān yě yīn le, huì bu huì xià xuě?

B：我看了天气预报，今天不会下雪，但是气温会下降。
　　Wǒ kànle tiānqì yùbào, jīntiān bú huì xià xuě, dànshì qìwēn huì xiàjiàng.

A：今天多少度？
　　Jīntiān duōshao dù?

B：天气预报说，武汉今天的气温只有零下一度，可是我感觉更冷一些。因为刮大风，而且武汉冬天屋子里没有暖气，冰冷冰冷[G3]的。
　　Tiānqì yùbào shuō, Wǔhàn jīntiān de qìwēn zhǐ yǒu líng xià yí dù, kěshì wǒ gǎnjué gèng lěng yìxiē. Yīnwèi guā dàfēng, érqiě Wǔhàn dōngtiān wūzi li méiyǒu nuǎnqì, bīnglěng bīnglěng[G3] de.

A：西安春节期间的天气怎么样？会不会有[G4]武汉这么冷？
　　Xī'ān Chūn Jié qījiān de tiānqì zěnmeyàng? Huì bu huì yǒu[G4] Wǔhàn zhème lěng?

B：虽然西安在武汉北边，但是没有武汉冷。
　　Suīrán Xī'ān zài Wǔhàn běibian, dànshì méiyǒu Wǔhàn lěng.

A：武汉冬天常常下大雪，西安也会下大雪吗？
　　Wǔhàn dōngtiān chángcháng xià dà xuě, Xī'ān yě huì xià dà xuě ma?

第十九课　天气怎么样？
Lesson Nineteen　How's the Weather?

B：西安春节期间常会下雪，如果刮大风就更冷了。我们上网查一下儿西安春节期间的天气吧。

Xī'ān Chūn Jié qījiān cháng huì xià xuě, rúguǒ guā dà fēng jiù gèng lěng le. Wǒmen shàngwǎng chá yíxiàr Xī'ān Chūn Jié qījiān de tiānqì ba.

……

B：网上天气预报说：春节长假[1]期间，西安市天气以晴为主[G5]，空气干燥。除夕那天气温会突然下降，在零下九度左右。可能有小雪。初一气温开始回升，多云转晴[G6]。

Wǎng shang tiānqì yùbào shuō: Chūn Jié chángjià[1] qījiān, Xī'ān shì tiānqì yǐ qíng wéi zhǔ[G5], kōngqì gānzào. Chúxī nà tiān qìwēn huì tūrán xiàjiàng, zài líng xià jiǔ dù zuǒyòu. Kěnéng yǒu xiǎo xuě. Chūyī qìwēn kāishǐ huíshēng, duōyún zhuǎn qíng[G6].

A：我需要带羽绒服吗？

Wǒ xūyào dài yǔróngfú ma?

B：你一定要带有帽子的羽绒服和毛衣，还有围巾和口罩。你老家的冬天也下大雪吗？

Nǐ yídìng yào dài yǒu màozi de yǔróngfú hé máoyī, hái yǒu wéijīn hé kǒuzhào. Nǐ lǎojiā de dōngtiān yě xià dà xuě ma?

A：我的老家在美国南方，从来不[2]下雪，跟云南昆明一样，四季如春。但是冬天常下雨，雨后还起大雾。

Wǒ de lǎojiā zài Měiguó nánfāng, cónglái bú[2] xià xuě, gēn Yúnnán Kūnmíng yíyàng, sìjì rú chūn. Dànshì dōngtiān cháng xià yǔ, yǔ hòu hái qǐ dà wù.

B：我老家西安四季分明：冬天很冷，春天暖和，夏天没有武汉热，秋天很凉快。

Wǒ lǎojiā Xī'ān sìjì fēnmíng: dōngtiān hěn lěng, chūntiān nuǎnhuo, xiàtiān méiyǒu Wǔhàn rè, qiūtiān hěn liángkuai.

A：武汉夏天很热吗？

Wǔhàn xiàtiān hěn rè ma?

Notes

1. "长假 chángjià" (long vacation). There are two official long vacations in China: "春节长假 Chūn Jié chángjià" (Spring Festival holiday); and "国庆节长假 Guóqìng Jié chángjià" (National Day holiday).
2. "从来 cónglái" is an adverb, commonly used in the negative, meaning "never". "从来不 cónglái bù" indicates that something never happens or never will: "从来不下雪 cónglái bú xià xuě" (it never snows [there]). "从来没 cónglái méi" (often with verb- "过 guo") indicates it has never happened: "从来没吃过海参 Wǒ cónglái méi chīguo hǎishēn" (I've never eaten sea-cucumber).

B：是。武汉的夏天又长又热，从五月到十月³都是夏季。七八月的时候最热，有时候达到四十多度。中国有"三大火炉"，指的就是武汉、重庆和南京。这三个城市都在长江边上。
Shì. Wǔhàn de xiàtiān yòu cháng yòu rè, cóng wǔyuè dào shíyuè³ dōu shì xiàjì. Qī-bāyuè de shíhou zuì rè, yǒushíhou dádào sìshí duō dù. Zhōngguó yǒu "sān dà huǒlú", zhǐ de jiù shì Wǔhàn、Chóngqìng hé Nánjīng. Zhè sān ge chéngshì dōu zài Cháng Jiāng biān shang.

A：我很怕热。夏天的时候我应该去哪儿避暑？
Wǒ hěn pà rè. Xiàtiān de shíhou wǒ yīnggāi qù nǎr bì shǔ?

B：你应该去东北避暑。东三省⁴是中国夏天最凉快的地方。你也可以到附近的庐山或黄山避暑。高山上都很凉快。
Nǐ yīnggāi qù Dōngběi bì shǔ. Dōng Sān Shěng⁴ shì Zhōngguó xiàtiān zuì liángkuai de dìfang. Nǐ yě kěyǐ dào fùjìn de Lú Shān huò Huáng Shān bì shǔ. Gāoshān shang dōu hěn liángkuai.

A：好。我先准备好去西安的事，以后再想夏天做什么吧。
Hǎo. Wǒ xiān zhǔnbèi hǎo qù Xī'ān de shì, yǐhòu zài xiǎng xiàtiān zuò shénme ba.

B：你去西安就住我家，不用带很多东西。
Nǐ qù Xī'ān jiù zhù wǒ jiā, búyòng dài hěn duō dōngxi.

A：好。谢谢。
Hǎo. Xièxie.

New Words

1	天气/天氣	tiānqì	N	weather
2	兴奋/興奮	xīngfèn	Adj	excited
3	机会/機會	jīhui	N	opportunity, chance
4	过节/過節	guò jié	VO	to celebrate a holiday
5	一路上	yílù shang	Phrase	throughout the whole journey

---

3. "从 cóng……到 dào……"(from… to…) can apply to time as well as to space (cf. Lesson 13, G5): "从四五月到十月 cóng sì-wǔyuè dào shíyuè" (from April or May to October).

4. "东三省 Dōng Sān Shěng" refers to the three provinces of "辽宁 Liáoníng", "吉林 Jílín", and "黑龙江 Hēilóngjiāng" plus the eastern part of the "内蒙古自治区 Nèiměnggǔ Zìzhìqū" (the Inner Mongolia Autonomous Region). The "东三省 Dōng Sān Shěng" was formerly known as Manchuria in English.

第十九课 天气怎么样?
Lesson Nineteen How's the Weather?

6	做伴	zuò bàn	VO	to keep sb. company, to be a companion
7	行李	xíngli	N	luggage, bags
8	礼物/禮物	lǐwù	N	present, gift
9	刮风/颳風	guā fēng	Phrase	for the wind to blow
	刮/颳	guā	V	to blow
10	阴/陰	yīn	Adj	overcast, cloudy
11	下雪	xià xuě	Phrase	for snow to fall, for it to snow
	雪	xuě	N	snow
12	天气预报/天氣預報	tiānqì yùbào	Phrase	weather report, weather forecast
	预报/預報	yùbào	V/N	to forecast; forecast
13	气温/氣溫	qìwēn	N	air temperature
14	下降	xiàjiàng	V	to drop, to fall, to descend, to decline
15	度	dù	Meas/V	degree; to spend, to pass (time)
16	零下	líng xià	Phrase	below zero
17	感觉/感覺	gǎnjué	V/N	to feel, to sense; feeling, sensation
18	冷	lěng	Adj	cold
19	大风/大風	dàfēng	N	strong wind
20	冬天	dōngtiān	N	winter
21	屋子	wūzi	N	room, house
22	暖气/暖氣	nuǎnqì	N	heating, central heating
23	冰冷	bīnglěng	Adj	ice cold, frosty (of expressions, etc.)
24	大雪	dàxuě	N	heavy snow
25	网上/網上	wǎng shang	Phrase	on the internet, online
26	长假/長假	chángjià	N	long vacation ("假期 jiàqī", period of leave, vacation)
27	以……为主/以……為主	yǐ……wéi zhǔ	Construction	to be basically…, to regard…as essential
28	晴	qíng	Adj	clear, fine (of weather) ("转晴 zhuǎn qíng", to chang to clear)
29	干燥/乾燥	gānzào	Adj	dry, arid (of weather), dry

30	除夕	chúxī	N	the eve of the Lunar New Year
31	突然	tūrán	Adv	suddenly, abruptly, unexpectedly
32	小雪	xiǎo xuě	N	light snow
33	初一	chūyī	N	New Year's Day, i.e. the first day of the New Year
34	回升	huíshēng	V	to rise again, to pick up (after a fall, etc.)
	升	shēng	V	to rise
35	多云/多雲	duōyún	N	lots of clouds, cloudy
	云/雲	yún	N	cloud
36	转/轉	zhuǎn	V	to turn, to shift to
37	羽绒服/羽絨服	yǔróngfú	N	down coat
38	帽子	màozi	N	hat, cap
39	毛衣	máoyī	N	woolen sweater
40	围巾/圍巾	wéijīn	N	scarf, muffler
41	口罩	kǒuzhào	N	gauze mask, surgical mask, flu mask
42	南方	nánfāng	PW	south, southern region, The South, the area to the south of the "长江 Cháng Jiāng"
43	从来/從來	cónglái	Adv	always, at all times, all along
44	云南/雲南	Yúnnán	PropN	Yunnan (province in the Southwest)
45	昆明	Kūnmíng	PropN	Kunming (a city in "云南 Yúnnán")
46	四季如春	sìjì rú chūn	Phrase	like spring all year round
	四季	sìjì	N	the four seasons
47	下雨	xià yǔ	Phrase	for it to rain
	雨	yǔ	N	rain
48	雨后/雨後	yǔ hòu	Phrase	after the rain
49	雾/霧	wù	N	fog, mist
50	分明	fēnmíng	Adj	clearly demarcated, distinct
51	春天	chūntiān	N	springtime, spring
52	暖和	nuǎnhuo	Adj	nice and warm, cozy
53	夏天	xiàtiān	N	summer

第十九课　天气怎么样?
Lesson Nineteen How's the Weather?

54	秋天	qiūtiān	N	autumn, fall
55	凉快	liángkuai	Adj/V	pleasantly cool; to cool oneself
56	夏季	xiàjì	N	summer season
57	达到/達到	dádào	V	to reach, to accomplish, to achieve
58	火炉/火爐	huǒlú	N	stove (for heating)
	炉/爐	lú	BF	stove, oven, furnace
59	重庆/重慶	Chóngqìng	PropN	Chongqing (a directly governed city)
60	城市	chéngshì	N	city, town
61	长江/長江	Cháng Jiāng	PropN	the Yangtze River
62	边上/邊上	biān shang	Phrase	on the banks of, beside
63	怕热/怕熱	pà rè	Phrase	to be sensitive to heat
	怕	pà	V	to fear, to be afraid
64	避暑	bì shǔ	VO	to avoid the heat, to go away for the summer holidays
65	东北/東北	dōngběi/ Dōngběi	PW/PropN	northeast; the Northeast China
66	东三省/東三省	Dōng Sān Shěng	PropN	the Three (North) Eastern Provinces, cf. the previous entry
67	庐山/廬山	Lú Shān	PropN	Mount Lu (in "江西 Jiāngxī" Province)
68	黄山	Huáng Shān	PropN	Mount Huang (in "安徽 Ānhuī" Province)

Re-enacting the Dialogue

A: Ed   B: Professor Liu

Ed didn't expect to be able to buy a plane ticket to Xi'an so quickly. He's quite excited about it: not all the foreigners at the school are so lucky as to have the chance to go to the hometown of a Chinese colleague on vacation, and to travel there with him as well. Before they start on their journey, Ed needs to get ready the clothes and everyday necessities that he's going to need on the journey to Xi'an, pack his bags, buy some gifts for Prof. Liu and his family, and so on. He's not sure what the weather's like in Xi'an and what clothes he should bring; so he's gone to ask Prof. Liu.

A: Look, Prof. Liu, it's windy and clouding over, do you think it's going to snow?
B: I saw today's weather report that it's not going to snow. But the temperature is dropping.

A: What's the temperature today?

B: The weather report says that the temperature in Wuhan will be only one degree below zero, but it feels colder to me – because it's quite windy, and in Wuhan, houses don't have heat; it's freezing.

A: How's the weather in Xi'an at Spring Festival time? Is it as cold as in Wuhan?

B: Although Xi'an is to the north of Wuhan, it's not as cold as in Wuhan.

A: It often snows a lot in the winter in Wuhan. Does Xi'an also get a lot of snow?

B: At the time of the Spring Festival, it often snows in Xi'an, and if the wind's blowing a lot, it's even colder. We'll go online and check out the weather at the time of the Spring Festival.

……

B: The weather report online says that during the long holiday for the Spring Festival, Xi'an is mainly dry. On the eve of the New Year, the temperature will drop precipitously to about 9 degrees below zero. There might be a little snow. On New Year's Day, the temperature will start to rise; it'll be overcast, then turning clear.

A: Should I bring a down jacket?

B: You should definitely bring a down jacket with a hood, and sweaters, and also a scarf and masks. Do you get lots of snow in the winter in your hometown too?

A: My home's in the southern part of the US; it never snows – it's like Kunming in Yunnan, every season's like spring. But it often rains in the winter, and after it rains, it gets foggy.

B: Xi'an, my hometown, has four clearly demarked seasons: winter's cold; spring is warm; the summer isn't as hot as Wuhan; and the fall is pleasantly cool.

A: Is it hot in the summer in Wuhan?

B: It is. Wuhan's summers are long and hot; they last from May till October. It's hottest in July and August, sometimes reaching more than 40 degrees. In the summer, China has "the three furnaces", which refer to Wuhan, Chongqing and Nanjing. All three are on the banks of the Yangtze River.

A: I'm quite fearful of hot weather. Where should I go in the summer to avoid the heat?

B: To avoid the heat, you should go to the Northeast; the Three Eastern Provinces are the three most comfortably cool places in the summer. Closer by, you can also go to Mount Lu or Mount Huang to escape the heat. It's always cool up in the mountains.

A: Good. First I'll get ready to go to Xi'an; later, I'll think about what to do in the summer.

B: When you go to Xi'an, you'll be staying at my home, so no need to bring a lot of things.

A: OK, thanks.

第十九课　天气怎么样?
Lesson Nineteen　How's the Weather?

Grammar

▶ G1. The scope of negation (e.g. "不都 bù dōu" versus "都不 dōu bù")

① 他们不都是留学生。　They're not all overseas students.
　　Tāmen bù dōu shì liúxuéshēng.

② 他们都不是留学生。　None of them is an overseas student.
　　Tāmen dōu bú shì liúxuéshēng.

Not surprisingly, the position of "不 bù" vis-à-vis other adverbs has semantic consequences. In Chinese, the scope relations are quite consistent, with adverbs on the right within the scope of those on the left: "不 bù (都是 dōu shì)" —not (all are); "都 dōu (不是 bú shì)"— all (are not). Unfortunately, English finds "all of them are not" awkward, and recasts it as "none of them is". But no such complications arise in the Chinese.

③ 学校的外国人不都是这么幸运。　Not all the foreigners at the school are so lucky.
　　Xuéxiào de wàiguórén bù dōu shì zhème xìngyùn.

④ 我们都不坐高铁。　None of us is taking the high-speed train.
　　Wǒmen dōu bú zuò gāotiě.

The same principle applies to other adverbs such as "太 tài" (too):

⑤ 今天天气太不好了。　The weather's awful today.
　　Jīntiān tiānqì tài bù hǎo le.

⑥ 今天天气不太好。　The weather's not very good today.
　　Jīntiān tiānqì bú tài hǎo.

▶ G2. Ambient sentences: describing the weather

Ambient sentences in Chinese, that is, sentences that describe many meteorological conditions, also often occur without subjects [cf. Lesson 5 (G3) and Lesson 14 (G5) on the omission of subjects]. Meteorological events are not initiated by any obvious entity, so the subject slot is simply left empty. (Note: in the examples, "了 le" provides context, suggesting that the event has just begun, or just been noticed.) In English, the subject slot is filled with the empty token "it". Here is a list of meteorological events. (It includes material not in this lesson, but of interest.)

① 下雨了。　　Xià yǔ le.　　(drops rain)　　It's raining.
　　刮风了。　　Guā fēng le.　　(blows wind)　　It's windy.
　　下雪了。　　Xià xuě le.　　(drops snow)　　It's snowing.
　　下雾了。　　Xià wù le.　　(drops fog)　　It's foggy.
　　打雷了。　　Dǎ léi le.　　(beats thunder)　　There's thunder.
　　打闪了。　　Dǎ shǎn le.　　(strikes lightning)　　There's lightning.

Place or time adjuncts can be placed in initial position:

② 外面在下冰雹。 It's hailing outside.
   Wàimiàn zài xià bīngbáo.

If you are simply making an observation that "There's rain falling", the order is: "下雨 xià yǔ", as above. But if you have something to say about the rain, then it becomes definite and can be placed in the subject position: "雨下得很大 Yǔ xià de hěn dà" (The rain is falling heavily), or more colloquially, "It's raining heavily." This holds true for the other meteorological expressions as well.

Note that not all meteorological events are formed on the model of "下雨 xià yǔ". "Cloudy" is "天阴了 Tiān yīn le", literally, "The sky is overcast."

▶ G3. Vivid reduplication

Adjectives can be elaborated by repetition to give them a vividness or liveliness: "高 gāo" (tall) → "高高 gāogāo" (good and tall); "客气 kèqi" (polite) → "客客气气 kèkeqiqi" (courteous and cordial).

Single syllable adjectives like "高 gāo" repeat, as shown. However, in northern Mandarin, they are usually repeated with a final -r and (often) a shift to level tone (if not already level tone, like "高 gāo"). So: "慢 màn" (slow) → "慢慢儿 mànmānr" (nice and slow).

Reduplication of two-syllable adjectives almost always has the form: AB → AABB: "清楚 qīngchu" → "清清楚楚 qīngqīngchǔchǔ". If, like "qīngchu", the final syllable is neutral tone, a full tone reappears in the reduplicated form: "qīngqīngchǔchǔ".

In a few cases, which should probably be regarded as exceptional, a two-syllable adjective reduplicates in the ABAB pattern. The example in the dialogue is one of these: "冰冷 bīnglěng" (ice-cold, frigid) → "冰冷冰冷 bīnglěngbīnglěng". This is not a common pattern, and most other cases that come to mind are specialized color terms: "雪白 xuěbái" (snowy white) → "雪白雪白 xuěbáixuěbái"; and "金黄 jīnhuáng" → "金黄金黄 jīnhuángjīnhuáng". The ABAB pattern is not productive. So faced with a new adjective, such as, say "轻松 qīngsōng" (relaxed, easy going), you can be sure that the reduplicated form is "轻轻松松 qīngqīngsōngsōng".

The reduplicated forms behave more or less like simple adjectives, though they cannot usually be intensified with adverbs such as "很 hěn". Here are some examples:

① 玛丽的公寓安安静静的。 Mary's apartment is nice and quiet.
   Mǎlì de gōngyù ānānjìngjìng de.

② 她把书放得整整齐齐的。 She put the books in neat order.
   Tā bǎ shū fàng de zhěngzhěngqíqí de.

When occurring at the foot of a sentence, reduplicated adjectives are followed by the "de" of modification, regardless of whether their function is adjectival or adverbial. However, they are also common in the adverbial position before a verb, in which case they are marked by "de", written "地" – the adverbial marker (cf. Lesson 17, G2).

③ 他客客气气地问我…… He asked me very politely...
   Tā kèkèqìqì de wèn wǒ……

G4. Comparison with "有 yǒu" and "没有 méiyǒu"

In Lesson 15 (G5), two types of comparative construction were discussed, one using "比 bǐ" and one with "没有 méiyǒu":

① 冬天，北京比上海冷。 In winter, Beijing's colder than Shanghai.
Dōngtiān, Běijīng bǐ Shànghǎi lěng.

② 冬天，上海没有北京（那么）冷。 In winter, Shanghai's not as cold as Beijing.
Dōngtiān, Shànghǎi méiyǒu Běijīng (nàme) lěng.

While the first construction establishes dominance (Beijing's colder), the second indicates parity or lack of parity (Shanghai's not as cold).

The examples in Lesson 15 involved lack of parity, with "没有 méiyǒu". This lesson shows the positive version, with "有 yǒu": "有武汉这么冷 yǒu Wǔhàn zhème lěng". Both "这么 zhème" (so, like this) and "那么 nàme" (so, like that) are possible before the adjective.

③ 西安春节期间的天气有武汉这么冷吗？
Xī'ān Chūn Jié qījiān de tiānqì yǒu Wǔhàn zhème lěng ma?
Will the weather in Xi'an over the Spring Festival be as cold as in Wuhan?

④ 虽然西安在武汉北边，但是没有武汉冷。
Suīrán Xī'ān zài Wǔhàn běibian, dànshì méiyǒu Wǔhàn lěng.
Although Xi'an is to the north of Wuhan, it is not as cold as Wuhan.

G5. The construction "以 yǐ……为 wéi……" (take…as…)

In earlier times, reflected in classical Chinese, both "以 yǐ" and "为 wéi" (to be contrasted with falling toned "为 wèi"—for the sake of) were verbs, the first meaning "to use, to employ", the second meaning "to do, to make" (cf. note 1 in Lesson 14). In the modern language, one or the other of the forms appear in compounds such as "可以 kěyǐ", "以后 yǐhòu" and "称为 chēngwéi" where their original functions are obscured. But their verbal origins are still perceivable in a few special constructions, such as the one under consideration here, "以 yǐ……为 wéi……", literally "take… to be…":

"以人为本 yǐ rén wéi běn" ("本 běn", root, base): "take people as basic", i.e. "people oriented"
"以和为贵 yǐ hé wéi guì" ("贵 guì", valuable): "regard harmony very highly"
"以避暑为主 yǐ bì shǔ wéi zhǔ" ("主 zhǔ", master, main thing): "to focus on avoiding the heat"

The construction appears in the dialogue for this lesson in the following form: "以晴为主 yǐ qíng wéi zhǔ", literally "to take clear (weather) as the main thing", or more idiomatically "be basically about clear skies" or "clear sky is the predominant factor".

春节长假期间，西安市天气以晴为主。
Chūn Jié chángjià qījiān, Xī'ān Shì tiānqì yǐ qíng wéi zhǔ.
During the long holiday for the Spring Festival, the weather in Xi'an is basically clear.

G6. Four-syllable expressions: a favorite type

A glance at almost any page of a comprehensive Chinese dictionary will reveal dozens of expressions made up of four syllables – or four characters. They may function as nouns, adjectives, onomatopoeic adverbs, or verbs. Here are six examples – the first four you will recognize from this and previous lessons:

四季如春	sìjì rú chūn	like spring all year round
四季分明	sìjì fēnmíng	having distinct seasons
三大火炉	sān dà huǒlú	the three furnaces
消化不良	xiāohuà bùliáng	indigestion
糊里糊涂	húlihútu	muddled
成千上万	chéngqiān-shàngwàn	thousands upon thousands

With the possible exception of "四季分明 sìjì fēnmíng", whose two parts can be used separately, the form of these expressions is fixed and it is best to learn them as units. However, even where fixed expressions are not used, there is a tendency for writing or formal styles to conform to the four-character pattern, as you can see from your brief exposure to weather reports:

多云转晴	duōyún zhuǎn qíng	cloudy, turning clear
不冷不热	bù lěng bú rè	neither hot nor cold
阴有中雨	yīn yǒu zhōngyǔ	clouds and moderate rain

第十九课　天气怎么样?
Lesson Nineteen　How's the Weather?

Consolidation & Practice

1. Fill in the blanks with the appropriate combinations of the adverbs "不都 bù dōu" or "都不 dōu bù"

   (1) 我们学校的留学生_____是美国人。
   　　Wǒmen xuéxiào de liúxuéshēng _____ shì Měiguórén.
   　　(Not all the foreign students on campus are American.)

   (2) 早市的蔬菜_____新鲜。(Not all the vegetables sold at the morning market are fresh.)
   　　Zǎoshì de shūcài _____ xīnxian.

   (3) 天气预报说北京这一个星期_____下雪。
   　　Tiānqì yùbào shuō Běijīng zhè yí ge xīngqī _____ xià xuě.
   　　(The weather forecast said that there will be no snow for this coming week in Beijing.)

   (4) A: 听说冬天在武汉，家里_____用暖气，是真的吗?
   　　　Tīngshuō dōngtiān zài Wǔhàn, jiāli _____ yòng nuǎnqì, shì zhēn de ma?
   　　　(I hear that none of the houses in Wuhan have heat in the winter – is that right?)

   　　B: _____是这样。有的人家用暖气。
   　　　_____ shì zhèyàng. Yǒu de rénjia yòng nuǎnqì.
   　　　(That's not true for everyone. Some people make use of heaters.)

   (5) A: 云南昆明从来_____下雪吗? (Does it ever snow in Kunming in Yunnan?)
   　　　Yúnnán Kūnmíng cónglái _____ xià xuě ma?

   　　B: 很少下雪。所以我听说那里的人_____会滑雪。
   　　　Hěn shǎo xià xuě. Suǒyǐ wǒ tīngshuō nàli de rén _____ huì huá xuě.
   　　　(Seldom. That's why none of the people there know how to ski, so I've heard.)

2. Describe the weather of your hometown, and a Chinese city with which you are familiar. Refer to the expressions provided below

   Example: 北京四季分明，天气以晴为主。春天常常刮大风，虽然气温不低，但是不暖和。夏天不常下雨，常常是多云天气。秋天天气比较好，晴天很多。冬天不常下雪，但是很冷，气温常常在零下。
   　　Běijīng sìjì fēnmíng, tiānqì yǐ qíng wéi zhǔ. Chūntiān chángcháng guā dà fēng, suīrán qìwēn bù dī, dànshì bù nuǎnhuo. Xiàtiān bù cháng xià yǔ, chángcháng shì duōyún tiānqì. Qiūtiān tiānqì bǐjiào hǎo, qíngtiān hěn duō. Dōngtiān bù cháng xià xuě, dànshì hěn lěng, qìwēn chángcháng zài líng xià.

下雨	刮风	下雪	下雾	凉快
xià yǔ	guā fēng	xià xuě	xià wù	liángkuai
暖和	热（极了）	（很）冷	多云	以晴为主
nuǎnhuo	rè (jí le)	(hěn) lěng	duōyún	yǐ qíng wéi zhǔ

真实生活汉语 2
Chinese for Living in China

春天	夏天	秋天	冬天	阴天
chūntiān	xiàtiān	qiūtiān	dōngtiān	yīntiān
晴天	气温	零下	降温	
qíngtiān	qìwēn	líng xià	jiàng wēn	

3. Choose from the list of reduplicated adjectives to describe the things designated below

高高兴兴的 (happy)
gāogāoxìngxìng de

甜甜的 (sweet)
tiántián de

冰冷冰冷的 (frosty, frigid)
bīnglěngbīnglěng de

安安静静的 (peaceful)
ānānjìngjìng de

舒舒服服的 (comfortable)
shūshufūfū de

暖暖和和的 (warm, cosy)
nuǎnnuanhuōhuō de

高高大大的 (tall, large, massive)
gāogāodàdà de

干干净净的 (clean)
gānganjīngjīng de

酸酸的 (sour)
suānsuān de

热热闹闹的 (lively)
rèrenāonāo de

(1) 玛丽的公寓_____
　　 Mǎlì de gōngyù _____

(2) 北京城里总是_____
　　 Běijīng chéngli zǒngshì _____

(3) 很多外国学生都是_____
　　 Hěn duō wàiguó xuésheng dōu shì _____

(4) 她做的菜汤_____
　　 Tā zuò de càitāng _____

(5) 冬天的时候，我的公寓_____
　　 Dōngtiān de shíhou, wǒ de gōngyù _____

(6) 我家旁边的早市每天都_____
　　 Wǒ jiā pángbiān de zǎoshì měi tiān dōu _____

(7) 马克的女朋友是日本人，不太爱说话，_____
　　 Mǎkè de nǚpéngyou shì Rìběnrén, bú tài ài shuō huà, _____

(8) 我很喜欢我的老师，每天上课时都_____
　　 Wǒ hěn xǐhuan wǒ de lǎoshī, měi tiān shàngkè shí dōu _____

(9) 我的宿舍虽然不大，可是_____
　　 Wǒ de sùshè suīrán bú dà, kěshì _____

第十九课　天气怎么样?
Lesson Nineteen　How's the Weather?

(10) 我的新羽绒服＿＿＿＿＿＿＿＿＿＿＿＿＿＿＿＿＿＿＿＿＿＿＿＿＿
　　　Wǒ de xīn yǔróngfú ＿＿＿＿＿＿＿＿＿＿＿＿＿＿＿＿＿＿＿＿＿

4. Following the examples, use the "有 yǒu" or "没有 méiyǒu" pattern with the adjectives to compare the items listed on the left

    Example: A: 冬天的时候，西安有武汉冷吗?
    　　　　　　Dōngtiān de shíhou, Xī'ān yǒu Wǔhàn lěng ma?

    　　　　 B: 在室内，西安没有武汉冷, 因为有暖气。
    　　　　　　Zài shì nèi, Xī'ān méiyǒu Wǔhàn lěng, yīnwèi yǒu nuǎnqì.

    (1) 日本饭 / 中国饭 / 好吃 → ＿＿＿＿＿＿＿＿＿＿＿＿＿＿＿＿＿＿
    　　Rìběnfàn / Zhōngguófàn / hǎochī

    (2) 武汉的夏天 / 上海的夏天 / 热 → ＿＿＿＿＿＿＿＿＿＿＿＿＿＿
    　　Wǔhàn de xiàtiān / Shànghǎi de xiàtiān / rè

    (3) 历史课 / 文学课 / 难 → ＿＿＿＿＿＿＿＿＿＿＿＿＿＿＿＿＿＿
    　　lìshǐkè / wénxué kè / nán

    (4) 你的宿舍 / 我的宿舍 / 大 → ＿＿＿＿＿＿＿＿＿＿＿＿＿＿＿＿
    　　nǐ de sùshè / wǒ de sùshè / dà

    (5) 坐高铁 / 坐飞机 / 贵 → ＿＿＿＿＿＿＿＿＿＿＿＿＿＿＿＿＿＿
    　　zuò gāotiě / zuò fēijī / guì

    (6) 庐山 / 黄山 / 远 → ＿＿＿＿＿＿＿＿＿＿＿＿＿＿＿＿＿＿＿＿
    　　Lú Shān / Huáng Shān / yuǎn

    (7) 重庆 / 上海 / 热闹 → ＿＿＿＿＿＿＿＿＿＿＿＿＿＿＿＿＿＿＿
    　　Chóngqìng / Shànghǎi / rènao

    (8) 国产染发剂的颜色 / 进口染发剂的颜色 / 自然 (natural) → ＿＿＿＿＿＿
    　　guóchǎn rǎnfàjì de yánsè / jìnkǒu rǎnfàjì de yánsè / zìrán

5. Complete the sentences with the construction "以 yǐ……为主 wéi zhǔ", making use of the material in parentheses

    (1) 北京的天气＿＿＿＿＿＿＿＿＿＿＿＿＿。（晴 qíng）
    　　Běijīng de tiānqì ＿＿＿＿＿＿＿＿＿＿＿.

    (2) 大学生可以打工，但是应该＿＿＿＿＿＿＿＿＿＿。（学习 xuéxí）
    　　Dàxuéshēng kěyǐ dǎ gōng, dànshì yīnggāi ＿＿＿＿＿＿＿＿＿.

    (3) 文学课跟口语课不一样，文学课＿＿＿＿，口语课＿＿＿＿。（讨论 tǎolùn, 说话 shuō huà）
    　　Wénxuékè gēn kǒuyǔkè bù yíyàng, wénxuékè ＿＿＿＿＿＿, kǒuyǔ kè ＿＿＿＿＿.

    (4) 他有高血压，大夫说他应该＿＿＿＿＿＿＿＿＿＿＿。（吃素 chī sù）
    　　Tā yǒu gāoxuèyā, dàifu shuō tā yīnggāi ＿＿＿＿＿＿＿＿＿＿.

(5) 这个医院是中医医院，治病_____。（中草药 zhōngcǎoyào）
　　 Zhège yīyuàn shì zhōngyī yīyuàn, zhì bìng _____.

6. Work with a partner to compose weather forecasts for two cities of your own choice; then present your reports to the class. Use at least 10 items from the list

会 huì	阴天 yīntiān	干燥 gānzào	以晴为主 yǐ qíng wéi zhǔ
下(小/大)雨 xià (xiǎo/dà) yǔ	刮（大）风 guā (dà) fēng	下雪 xià xuě	多云转晴 duōyún zhuǎn qíng
气温 qìwēn	下降 xiàjiàng	零下……度 líng xià……dù	回升 huíshēng
有雾 yǒu wù	暖和 nuǎnhuo	凉快 liángkuai	冷 lěng
更 gèng	A 有/没有 B + Adj A yǒu/méiyǒu B + Adj		

第十九课 天气怎么样?
Lesson Nineteen　How's the Weather?

Listening Comprehension

1. Listen to the dialogue and then answer the questions

   (1) Does Beijing have four seasons?

   (2) How about Shanghai?

   (3) In Beijing, does it ever snow?

   (4) Does it snow in Shanghai?

   (5) How cold does it get in Shanghai during the winter?

   (6) How is the weather in Shanghai in May? What do people have to carry with them all the time?

   (7) How is the weather in Beijing during the spring?

   (8) How hot does it get in Beijing during the summer?

   (9) What is the best season to visit Beijing?

   New Words
   雨伞　yǔsǎn　N　umbrella
   雨衣　yǔyī　N　raincoat
   季节　jìjié　N　season

2. Listen to the dialogue and then answer the questions

   (1) According to the woman, what's the ideal kind of weather? Why?

   (2) What does the woman like to do?

   (3) What makes the woman feel really happy?

   (4) What type of weather does the man like?

   (5) What's the argument against only liking one season?

   (6) What's the response in defense of "one season"?

   New Words
   景色　jǐngsè　N　view, scene, landscape
   跑步　pǎo bù　VO　to run

Communication Activities

Pair Work

Scenario I: **The seasons.** Work together to name the possible weather conditions that go along with each season:

春季： ....
chūnjì

夏季： ....
xiàjì

秋季： ....
qiūjì

冬季： ....
dōngjì

Scenario II: **Weather back home.** Describe the seasons in each of your hometowns, then compare and contrast. Try to use the following expressions:

你老家的天气怎么样？ Nǐ lǎojiā de tiānqì zěnmeyàng?		春天很暖和 chūntiān hěn nuǎnhuo	夏天很热 xiàtiān hěn rè
秋天很凉快 qiūtiān hěn liángkuai	冬天很冷 dōngtiān hěn lěng	夏天常常下雾 xiàtiān chángcháng xià wù	四季如春 sìjì rú chūn
不冷不热 bù lěng bú rè	从来不下雪 cónglái bú xià xuě	有时候刮台风 yǒushíhou guā táifēng	下雨 xià yǔ
冬天刮风 dōngtiān guā fēng	阴天 yīntiān	晴天 qíngtiān	比　　没有 bǐ　　méiyǒu

Scenario III: **Ideal weather.** With your partner, talk about the places that have the best weather. Refer to the list of expressions:

一般来说 yìbān lái shuō	经常 jīngcháng	从来不 cónglái bù	可以说 kěyǐ shuō
因为……所以…… yīnwèi……suǒyǐ……	从……到…… cóng……dào……	总是 zǒngshì	虽然……可是…… suīrán……kěshì……
春天 chūntiān	暖和 nuǎnhuo	不刮风 bù guā fēng	夏天 xiàtiān
不太热 bú tài rè	秋天 qiūtiān	很凉快 hěn liángkuai	冬天 dōngtiān

第十九课　天气怎么样?
Lesson Nineteen　How's the Weather?

很冷	四季如春	不冷不热	气温
hěn lěng	sìjì rú chūn	bù lěng bú rè	qìwēn
零上	干燥		
líng shàng	gānzào		

Role-Play

Scenario I: In pairs or groups, gather national weather reports off the internet about the day's weather. Report your findings to the class. Mention general weather conditions, temperature, changes through the day, regional differences (between north and south, for example) and trends in the five-day forecast.

Scenario II: Your friend's just returned wet and cold, from walking in the rain. You're worried about her or his health – catching a cold, and so on. Compose a dialogue using as many of the expressions provided as you can:

A	B
天气预报 tiānqì yùbào	怎么样 zěnmeyàng
晴转多云 qíng zhuǎn duōyún	会不会 huì bu huì
带 dài	发烧 fā shāo
雨伞 yǔsǎn	咳嗽 késou
太麻烦 tài máfan	感冒 gǎnmào
下大雨 xià dà yǔ	嗓子疼 sǎngzi téng
有点儿发冷 yǒudiǎnr fā lěng	虽然……但是…… suīrán……dànshì……
没什么 méi shénme	喝开水 hē kāishuǐ
从来不 cónglái bù	洗热水澡 xǐ rèshuǐ zǎo
	看大夫 kàn dàifu

真实生活汉语
Chinese for Living in China 2

Group Activities

Scenario I: Guessing game. Four of you are from different places in the US. Describe the weather for each place to a fifth person who has to guess where each person is from.

	Description	Where from
A		
B		
C		
D		

Scenario II: Anticipating the weather. Four of you are going on business trips to different places, each with different climates. The forecasts range from cold through warm, hot and extremely hot and humid. Each of you explains to all the others what sort of things you need to take. The fifth member of the group, having listened to the presentations, summarizes all four to the class.

	Weather	What to take
A		
B		
C		
D		

Review Exercises

1. Make comparisons between your hometown and the place you are currently living in. Consider the aspects listed – or add your own

   (1) 马路上的人 / 车 → _____
   mǎlù shang de rén / chē

   (2) 天气 / 气温 → _____
   tiānqì / qìwēn

   (3) 医院的医生 / 病人 → _____
   yīyuàn de yīshēng / bìngrén

   (4) 交通运输（火车 / 飞机）→ _____
   jiāotōng yùnshū (huǒchē / fēijī)

   (5) 饭馆的饭 / 菜 → _____
   fànguǎn de fàn / cài

   (6) 超市的东西 → _____
   chāoshì de dōngxi

第十九课　天气怎么样？
Lesson Nineteen　How's the Weather?

2. Use "能 néng" or "会 huì" to fill in the blanks according to the situation

   (1) 下雪的时候街上经常（　　　）堵车。
   　　Xià xuě de shíhou jiē shang jīngcháng (　　　) dǔ chē.

   (2) 我自己也没有伞，不（　　　）借给你。
   　　Wǒ zìjǐ yě méiyǒu sǎn, bù (　　　) jiè gěi nǐ.

   (3) 你的牙在发炎，今天不（　　　）补。
   　　Nǐ de yá zài fā yán, jīntiān bù (　　　) bǔ.

   (4) 天气预报说今天晚上（　　　）下雨。
   　　Tiānqì yùbào shuō jīntiān wǎnshang (　　　) xià yǔ.

   (5) 今年冬天我要去深圳，不（　　　）去北京。
   　　Jīnnián dōngtiān wǒ yào qù Shēnzhèn, bù (　　　) qù Běijīng.

   (6) 你的雨衣太瘦了，我不（　　　）穿。
   　　Nǐ de yǔyī tài shòu le, wǒ bù (　　　) chuān.

   (7) 现在有大雾，不（　　　）开车。
   　　Xiànzài yǒu dà wù, bù (　　　) kāi chē.

   (8) 如果你吃得太多，就（　　　）消化不良。
   　　Rúguǒ nǐ chī de tài duō, jiù (　　　) xiāohuà bùliáng

3. Following the model, each of you states three things that you'll never do, and three things that you've never done (Cf. note 2 in the dialogue)

   Example: ① 他从来不吃海鲜。　He never eats seafood.
   　　　　　　Tā cónglái bù chī hǎixiān.

   　　　　　② 他从来没吃过法国饭。　He has never had French food.
   　　　　　　Tā cónglái méi chīguo Fǎguófàn.

   (1) ....
   (2) ....
   (3) ....
   (4) ....
   (5) ....
   (6) ....

4. Read the following weather forecasts and then, guessing where needed, translate them into English

(1) 今天夜间，阴，有阵雨，偏南风2、3级，最低气温15度。
Jīntiān yèjiān, yīn yǒu zhènyǔ, piānnánfēng èr、sān jí, zuì dī qìwēn shíwǔ dù.

_____

(2) 明天白天，多云，偏北风1、2级，最高气温25度。
Míngtiān báitiān, duōyún, piānběifēng yī、èr jí, zuì gāo qìwēn èrshíwǔ dù.

_____

(3) 明天夜间，阴，有中雨，北部山区有大雨。偏西风2、3级，最低气温12度。
Míngtiān yèjiān, yīn yǒu zhōngyǔ, běibù shānqū yǒu dàyǔ. Piānxīfēng èr、sān jí, zuì dī qìwēn shí'èr dù.

_____

(4) 未来三天有小雨，气温偏低，不宜 (not suitable) 洗车。
Wèilái sān tiān yǒu xiǎo yǔ, qìwēn piān dī, bùyí xǐ chē.

_____

(5) 周末天气，阴转晴。北风2、3级，气温明显回升，最高气温可达30度。
Zhōumò tiānqì, yīn zhuǎn qíng. Běifēng èr、sān jí, qìwēn míngxiǎn huíshēng, zuì gāo qìwēn kě dá sānshí dù.

_____

5. What would you say? Relate the following in Chinese

(1) You're meeting with a group of new employees, in Shenzhen for the first time. You're telling them about the climate

① It can be said that there's no winter in Shenzhen, because it never gets colder than 5 or 6 degrees (Centigrade).

....

② It never snows here, but it rains a lot. So people carry umbrellas around all the time.

....

③ The summer is very long, from May to October, and the temperature can reach 40℃.

....

④ It is advisable to listen to or watch the weather report each day before going out.

....

第十九课　天气怎么样?
Lesson Nineteen　How's the Weather?

(2) You're going to Xi'an in July, so you're asking a friend who's from Xi'an about the weather

　① How is the weather in Xi'an in July? What's the hottest it gets?

　　..

　② Does it rain a lot? Is it windy?

　　..

　③ Is July in Xi'an as hot as in Beijing? Does it get cool in the evening?

　　..

　④ Do I need to bring a jacket (外衣 wàiyī) with me?

　　..

真实生活汉语
Chinese for Living in China

Culture Notes

1. "The 24 Solar Terms" of the traditional Chinese seasonal calendar

Since at least the Former Han dynasty, the Chinese have made use of an agricultural calendar that divides the year into seasons and each season into six segments of fifteen days, for a total of 24. These are referred to as the "二十四节气 èrshísì jiéqì", literally, "The 24 climatic periods", but usually translated in English as "The 24 Solar Terms", because they allude to the positions of the sun in its elliptic. Farmers and peasants would make reference to these periods in performing the tasks of the agricultural year.

The following is a list of the 24 solar terms, with their dates in the Western calendar:

1	立春 lìchūn	Start of Spring	February 3, 4 or 5
2	雨水 yǔshuǐ	Rain Water	February 18, 19 or 20
3	惊蛰 jīngzhé	Waking of Insects	March 5, 6 or 7
4	春分 chūnfēn	Spring Equinox	March 20, 21 or 22
5	清明 qīngmíng	Pure Brightness	April 4, 5 or 6
6	谷雨 gǔyǔ	Grain Rains	April 19, 20 or 21
7	立夏 lìxià	Start of Summer	May 5, 6 or 7
8	小满 xiǎomǎn	Grain Fills	May 20, 21 or 22
9	芒种 mángzhòng	Grain in Ear	June 5, 6 or 7
10	夏至 xiàzhì	Summer Solstice	June 21 or 22
11	小暑 xiǎoshǔ	Slight Heat	July 6, 7 or 8
12	大暑 dàshǔ	Great Heat	July 22, 23 or 24
13	立秋 lìqiū	Start of Fall	August 7, 8 or 9
14	处暑 chǔshǔ	Limit of Heat	August 22, 23 or 24
15	白露 báilù	White Dew	September 7, 8 or 9
16	秋分 qiūfēn	Autumnal Equinox	September 22, 23 or 24
17	寒露 hánlù	Cold Dew	October 8 or 9
18	霜降 shuāngjiàng	Frost Descends	October 23 or 24
19	立冬 lìdōng	Start of Winter	November 7 or 8
20	小雪 xiǎoxuě	Slight Snow	November 22 or 23
21	大雪 dàxuě	Great Snow	December 6, 7 or 8
22	冬至 dōngzhì	Winter Solstice	December 21, 22 or 23
23	小寒 xiǎohán	Slight Cold	January 5, 6 or 7
24	大寒 dàhán	Great Cold	January 20 or 21

第十九课　天气怎么样?

Lesson Nineteen　How's the Weather?

Each season is divided into six parts, with the first part announcing the season: "立春 lìchūn" (start of spring); "立夏 lìxià" (start of summer); and so on. Within the six parts of each season, the fourth is named for the important solar phenomena of the equinoxes and the solstices. The equinoxes, when day and night are equally divided, are expressed with "分 fēn" (to divide): "春分 chūnfēn", "秋分 qiūfēn". The solstices, when the day is at its longest or shortest, are expressed with "至 zhì" (to reach): "夏至 xiàzhì", "冬至 dōngzhì".

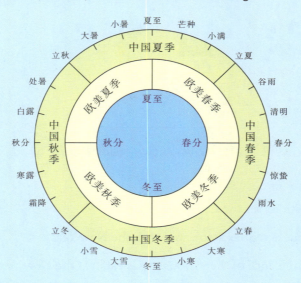

2. Centigrade to Fahrenheit conversion table

China uses the Centigrade (Celsius) system for temperature. The following table shows the Fahrenheit equivalents:

Centigrade (°C)	Fahrenheit (°F)
-20	-4
-15	5
-10	14
-5	23
0	32
5	41
10	50
15	59
20	68
25	77
30	86
35	95
40	104

239

Lesson Twenty   Celebrating the New Year

第二十课   过 年
Dì-èrshí Kè   Guò Nián

In this lesson you will learn how to do the following

- Talk about family
- Talk about preparations for the Chinese New Year
- Describe the various activities associated with the New Year
- Talk about the significance of the various foods eaten at the New Year

Grammar

- Topic-comment
- Providing reassurance with "没什么 (不) méi shénme (bù)"
- Comparison with "不如 bùrú" (not as [good as], be inferior to)
- Elliptical "的 de" phrases
- Rhetorical questions, with "不是 bú shì……吗 ma?"
- Coordinate clauses

Culture Notes

- "春节 Chūn Jié": The Spring Festival
- "压岁钱 yāsuìqián" (New Year's money)
- "拜年 bài nián" (Paying New Year's calls)

第二十课 过年
Lesson Twenty Celebrating the New Year

Dialogue

A：刘教授 Liú jiàoshòu　　B：艾德 Àidé

他头一次在中国坐飞机，坐在靠窗户的位子上，一直看着窗外，感觉不到时间在飞。他们是中午12:40离开武汉的,好像只在飞机上聊了一会儿天，就到西安了。出了机场，他们打的很快就到了刘教授家。

Tā tóu yí cì zài Zhōngguó zuò fēijī, zuò zài kào chuānghu de wèizi shang, yīzhí kàn zhe chuāngwài, gǎnjué bú dào shíjiān zài fēi. Tāmen shì zhōngwǔ shí'er diǎn sìshí líkāi Wǔhàn de, hǎoxiàng zhǐzài fēijī shang liáole yíhuìr tiānr, jiù dào Xī'ān le. Chūle jīchǎng, tāmen dǎ dī hěn kuài jiù dàole Liú jiàoshòu jiā.

A：艾老师，请进。这就是我的家。
　　Ài lǎoshī, qǐng jìn. Zhè jiù shì wǒ de jiā.

B：你家是四合院[1]啊？真漂亮。
　　Nǐ jiā shì sìhéyuàn[1] a?　Zhēn piàoliang.

A：这是我父母的房子。我的工资可买不起这样的房子[G1]。
　　Zhè shì wǒ fùmǔ de fángzi. Wǒ de gōngzī kě mǎi bu qǐ zhèyàng de fángzi[G1].

B：你和爸爸、妈妈住在一起吗？
　　Nǐ hé bàba、māma zhù zài yìqǐ ma?

A：对。我是独子。父母年纪大了，退休了，我有责任照顾他们。我在外地工作，我爱人和女儿跟我父母住在这儿，爸爸、妈妈也可以帮我们看看孩子。
　　Duì. Wǒ shì dúzǐ. Fùmǔ niánjì dà le, tuì xiū le, wǒ yǒu zérèn zhàogù tāmen. Wǒ zài wàidì gōngzuò, wǒ àiren hé nǚ'ér gēn wǒ fùmǔ zhù zài zhèr, bàba、māma yě kěyǐ bāng wǒmen kànkan háizi.

B：三代人一起住方便吗？
　　Sān dài rén yìqǐ zhù fāngbiàn ma?

Notes

1. "四合院（儿）sìhéyuàn(r)", a residence that consists of one-story buildings enclosing (合 hé) a courtyard (院 yuàn) on all four (四 sì) sides, is a traditional northern Chinese design, seen both in residences and in temples (houses for the spirits). "四合院 sìhéyuàn" can still be found on small alleys and lanes off the main roads in Beijing and other northern cities.

241

A: 我们住在一起很和谐，互相照顾，没什么不[G2]方便的。这边是你的房间。我帮你把行李拿进去。
Wǒmen zhù zài yìqǐ hěn héxié, hùxiāng zhàogù, méi shénme bù[G2] fāngbiàn de. Zhèbian shì nǐ de fángjiān. Wǒ bāng nǐ bǎ xíngli ná jinqu.

B: 谢谢。我什么时候可以见到你的家人？
Xièxie. Wǒ shénme shíhou kěyǐ jiàndào nǐ de jiārén?

A: 你先休息一下儿。吃晚饭的时候就见到我们全家了。
Nǐ xiān xiūxi yíxiàr. Chī wǎnfàn de shíhou jiù jiàndào wǒmen quánjiā le.

B: 刘老师，我在西安的时间怎么安排？
Liú lǎoshī, wǒ zài Xī'ān de shíjiān zěnme ānpái?

A: 我明天先带你去看兵马俑。过年时游人很多，非常拥挤，不如[G3]我们年前就去参观。
Wǒ míngtiān xiān dài nǐ qù kàn bīngmǎyǒng. Guònián shí yóurén hěn duō, fēicháng yōngjǐ, bùrú[G3] wǒmen nián qián jiù qù cānguān.

B: 好。中国人过年都有些什么活动？
Hǎo. Zhōngguórén guò nián dōu yǒu xiē shénme huódòng?

A: 中国人过年前一定要先"扫尘"。就是把房子打扫干净，把旧的[G4]、脏的、不好的东西都扫出去，迎接新的一年。
Zhōngguórén guònián qián yídìng yào xiān "sǎo chén". Jiù shì bǎ fángzi dǎsǎo gānjìng, bǎ jiù de[G4]、zāng de、bù hǎo de dōngxi dōu sǎo chuqu, yíngjiē xīn de yì nián.

B: 你不是说过我很会打扫办公室吗[G5]？我可以帮忙打扫。
Nǐ bú shì shuōguo wǒ hěn huì dǎsǎo bàngōngshì ma[G5]? Wǒ kěyǐ bāng máng dǎsǎo.

A: 你不用帮忙打扫房子，不过，你可以和我女儿一起贴春联，贴窗花，贴年画和"福"字[G6]。
Nǐ búyòng bāng máng dǎsǎo fángzi, búguò, nǐ kěyǐ hé wǒ nǚ'ér yìqǐ tiē chūnlián, tiē chuānghuā, tiē niánhuà hé "fú" zì[G6].

B: 好。
Hǎo.

A: 我爱人今天去买年货[2]，准备除夕晚上吃的东西。我爸爸、妈妈忙着包饺子。
Wǒ àiren jīntiān qù mǎi niánhuò[2], zhǔnbèi chúxī wǎnshang chī de dōngxi. Wǒ bàba、māma mángzhe bāo jiǎozi.

B: 除夕的晚饭很特别吗？
Chúxī de wǎnfàn hěn tèbié ma?

---

2. "年货 niánhuò" means "New Year's goods", i.e., purchases made for the New Year's celebration.

第二十课 过年
Lesson Twenty　Celebrating the New Year

A：对。除夕晚上全家人要团聚在一起吃年夜饭。吃的东西都是有寓意的。比如：鱼代表"有余"；饺子代表"和谐、有钱"；年糕代表"甜蜜"。想要孩子的人家还要吃花生、瓜子，意思是"儿子、女儿花着生"，"多子多孙"。

Duì. Chúxī wǎnshang quánjiārén yào tuánjù zài yìqǐ chī niányèfàn. Chī de dōngxi dōu shì yǒu yùyì de. Bǐrú: yú dàibiǎo "yǒuyú", jiǎozi dàibiǎo "héxié、yǒuqián", niángāo dàibiǎo "tiánmì". Xiǎng yào háizi de rénjiā hái yào chī huāshēng、guāzǐ, yìsi shì "érzi、nǚ'ér huāzhe shēng" "duō zǐ duō sūn".

B：真有意思！

Zhēn yǒu yìsi!

A：除夕我们全家还要在一起守岁。你可以先睡。不过，一过[3]十二点，新年到了，有很多人家放鞭炮，外面很吵。

Chúxī wǒmen quánjiā hái yào zài yìqǐ shǒu suì. Nǐ kěyǐ xiān shuì. Búguò, yí guò[3] shí'èr diǎn, xīnnián dào le, yǒu hěn duō rénjiā fàng biānpào, wàimiàn hěn chǎo.

B：那我跟你们一起守岁吧。我看到你把一个红包放到我枕头下边，这有什么寓意啊？

Nà wǒ gēn nǐmen yìqǐ shǒu suì ba. Wǒ kàn dào nǐ bǎ yí ge hóngbāo fàng dào wǒ zhěntou xiàbian, zhè yǒu shénme yùyì a?

A："那是"压岁钱"。通常，大人在除夕晚上把红包放在孩子枕头下，希望他一年都平平安安。因为你是外国客人，我也给你一个红包。

Nà shì "yāsuìqián". Tōngcháng, dàren zài chúxī wǎnshang bǎ hóngbāo fàng zài háizi zhěntou xià, xīwàng tā yì nián dōu píngpíng'ān'ān. Yīnwèi nǐ shì wàiguó kèren, wǒ yě gěi nǐ yí ge hóngbāo.

B：谢谢。

Xièxie.

A：初一那天我得和家人去给亲戚朋友拜年，你就不用跟我们去了。我可以先把你送到大雁塔去玩儿，我们拜完年后去接你，好吗？

Chūyī nà tiān wǒ děi hé jiārén qù gěi qīnqi、péngyou bài nián, nǐ jiù búyòng gēn wǒmen qù le. Wǒ kěyǐ xiān bǎ nǐ sòngdào Dàyàn Tǎ qù wánr, wǒmen bàiwán nián hòu qù jiē nǐ, hǎo ma?

B：不用了。除夕睡得晚，大年初一我正好在家睡觉，不出去玩儿了。

Búyòng le. Chúxī shuì de wǎn, dànián chūyī wǒ zhènghǎo zài jiā shuì jiào, bù chūqu wánr le.

---

3. "一过十二点 yí guò shí'èr diǎn" means "once past midnight", with "一 yī" used adverbially to mean "as soon as" (cf. Lesson 18, G2).

真实生活汉语 2
Chinese for Living in China

New Words

#	简体/繁體	Pinyin	Type	Meaning
1	离开/離開	líkāi	V	to leave
2	四合院	sìhéyuàn	N	residence made up of a courtyard enclosed by four single-story buildings
3	啊	a	Part	*a phrase particle associated with exclamation, surprise, heartiness*
4	父母	fùmǔ	N	father and mother, parents
	父	fù	BF	father
	母	mǔ	BF	mother, female (animal)
5	可	kě	Adv	really, in contrast, actually
6	买不起/買不起	mǎi bu qǐ	Pot	cannot afford
7	独子/獨子	dúzǐ	N	only son
8	年纪/年紀	niánjì	N	age, years old (of a person)
9	退休	tuì xiū	VO	to retire
10	责任/責任	zérèn	N	responsibility, duty, blame
11	照顾/照顧	zhàogù	V	to look after, to care for
12	外地	wàidì	N	place other than where one is
13	爱人/愛人	àiren	N	spouse, husband or wife, (girl/boy) friend
14	女儿/女兒	nǚ'ér	N	daughter
15	看孩子	kān háizi	Phrase	to babysit, to look after children
	看	kān	V	to look after
	孩子	háizi	N	child, children
16	代	dài	N	generation
17	方便	fāngbiàn	Adj	convenient
18	和谐/和諧	héxié	Adj	harmonious
19	互相	hùxiāng	Adv	each other
20	没什么/沒什麼	méi shénme	Phrase	for it not to matter, not to be anything (of consequence)
21	全家	quánjiā	N	the whole family
22	时间/時間	shíjiān	N	time, period of time

第二十课 过年
Lesson Twenty Celebrating the New Year

23	安排	ānpái	V/N	to arrange, to provide; plan
24	游人/遊人	yóurén	N	travelers, tourists
25	不如	bùrú	V	not as (good as), to be inferior to
26	年前	nián qián	Phrase	last year, before the New Year
27	参观/參觀	cānguān	V	to tour, to visit
28	活动/活動	huódòng	N/V	activity; to move about, to exercise
29	扫尘/掃塵	sǎo chén	VO	to sweep away dust, to clean house in the early New Year
	扫/掃	sǎo	V	to sweep
	尘/塵	chén	BF	dust
30	打扫/打掃	dǎsǎo	V	to sweep
31	旧/舊	jiù	Adj	worn, used, old, bygone
32	脏/髒	zāng	Adj	dirty
33	迎接	yíngjiē	V	to greet, to welcome, to take on (a challenge)
34	贴/貼	tiē	V	to paste, to stick, to subsidize
35	春联/春聯	chūnlián	N	New Year couplets (pasted on door frames)
36	窗花	chuānghuā	N	paper-cut window decoration
37	年画/年畫	niánhuà	N	paintings hung during the Lunar New Year, depicting themes of good luck and prosperity
38	福	fú	N	good fortune, blessing
39	年货/年貨	niánhuò	N	goods for the Lunar New Year
40	忙	máng	V/Adj	to busy oneself with; busy
41	特别	tèbié	Adj/Adv	special, particular; particularly
42	年夜饭/年夜飯	niányèfàn	N	family reunion dinner on the eve of the Lunar New Year
43	寓意	yùyì	N	implied or hidden meaning, moral message, implication
44	比如	bǐrú	V	for example, for instance
45	代表	dàibiǎo	V/N	to represent, to stand for; a delegate, proxy
46	有余/有餘	yǒuyú	V	to have enough with some to spare
47	年糕	niángāo	N	Lunar New Year cake (made with rice flour)
48	甜蜜	tiánmì	Adj	sweet, happy, affectionate

真实生活汉语
Chinese for Living in China 2

49	人家	rénjiā/rénjia	N/Pron	house-hold, family; other people, referring to a 3rd person (he/she/they)
50	花生	huāshēng	N	peanut
51	瓜子	guāzǐ	N	melon seeds, sunflower seeds
52	意思	yìsi	N	meaning, idea, opinion
53	儿子/兒子	érzi	N	son
54	花着生/花著生	huā zhe shēng	Phrase	to bear both sons and daughters
	花	huā	N/V	flower; to spend
	生	shēng	V	to give birth to, to bear
55	多子多孙/多子多孫	duō zǐ duō sūn	Phrase	to have many sons and grandsons
56	守岁/守歲	shǒu suì	VO	"to keep a watch on the year", i.e. welcome the New Year in by staying up all night
57	新年	xīnnián	N	new year
58	鞭炮	biānpào	N	firecrackers (collectively), a string of small firecrackers
59	吵	chǎo	Adj/V	noisy; to make a lot of noise, to quarrel
60	红包/紅包	hóngbāo	N	"red packets", i.e. envelopes containing money given as gifts, bonuses, bribes
61	枕头/枕頭	zhěntou	N	pillow
62	下边/下邊	xiàbian	PW	underneath, below, bottom
63	压岁钱/壓歲錢	yāsuìqián	N	a gift of money given to children on lunar New Year's Eve
64	通常	tōngcháng	Adv/Attr	usually, generally; normal
65	大人	dàren	N	adult (person)
66	希望	xīwàng	V/N	to hope (for/to/that), to wish (to/that), to want to; a wish, hope
67	平安	píng'ān	Adj	safe, well, peaceful
68	拜年	bài nián	VO	to pay a New Year's visit, to wish (sb.) a Happy New Year
	拜	bài	V	to pay respects, to visit, to call on
69	送	sòng	V	to give as a present, to deliver, to send, to take, to see (sb.) off, to accompany (sb. to his destination)
70	大雁塔	Dàyàn Tǎ	PropN	Wild Goose Pagoda (in Xi'an Prorince)
	大雁	dàyàn	N	wild goose

第二十课 过年
Lesson Twenty Celebrating the New Year

	塔	tǎ	N	pagoda (especially Buddhist), tower-like structure (e.g. a lighthouse)
71	玩儿/玩兒	wánr	V	to have fun, to amuse oneself, to play, to play (games)
72	接	jiē	V	to meet, to come in contact with, to connect, to receive
73	大年初一	dànián chūyī	Phrase	New Year's Day
74	正好	zhènghǎo	Adv	just right, just in time, happen to, chance to

Re-enacting the Dialogue

A: Professor Liu   B: Ed

Ed boarded the high-speed train with Prof. Liu. This is the first time he's taken a train that goes 350 kilometers an hour; he sat in a comfortable first-class seat and didn't feel the slightest vibration from the train. Their high-speed train left Wuhan at 12:40, and after chatting on the train for what seemed like a short time, they arrived in Xi'an at 4:35. They went out of the high-speed train station, got a taxi, and were soon at Porf. Liu's house.

A: Professor Ed, come on in. This is my home.
B: So your home is a courtyard house! It's lovely.
A: This is my parents' house. On my salary, I couldn't afford such a house.
B: Do you live with your mother and father?
A: Yes. I'm an only child. My parents are getting old, and they've retired, so it's my responsibility to look after them. I work away from home. My wife and daughter live here with my parents – Dad and Mom can also help us keep an eye on the children.
B: Is having three generations living together convenient?
A: We live together quite harmoniously; we look after each other, there's nothing to make it inconvenient. Your room is over here. I'll help you to bring in your luggage.
B: Thanks. When can I meet your family?
A: Rest up a bit first. At dinner, you'll meet the whole family.
B: Prof. Liu, how am I to organize my time while in Xi'an?
A: First of all, tomorrow I'll take you to see the Terra Cotta Soldiers. During the New Year time, there'll be a lot of visitors. It'll be extremely crowded. It'll be better if we visit there before the New Year.
B: Good. When Chinese celebrate the New Year, what sort of activities do they have?
A: Before the New Year, Chinese first of all have to "sweep the dust", that is, clean up their houses, and sweep out the old, the dirty, and the bad and welcome the new year.
B: Didn't you say that I was good at cleaning my office? I can help you clean.
A: No need for you to help me sweep the house, but you can help my daughter stick up the New Year couplets, the paper cutouts for the windows, and the New Year's pictures and good luck charms.
B: Good.

A: My wife is going to make some New Year's purchases today and she'll prepare things to eat for New Year's Eve. My mother and father are busy wrapping dumplings.

B: Is the New Year's Eve dinner special?

A: Yes, It is. On the Eve, the whole family gets together for the year-end dinner. Everything that's eaten has a special significance. For example, fish signifies abundance; dumplings signify harmony and wealth; New Year's sticky rice represents sweetness and affection. People who want a child also eat peanuts or sunflower seeds, which signify "having babies of both sexes" and "having lots of children and grandchildren".

B: That's fascinating.

A: On the Eve, the whole family gets together and welcomes in the New Year (by staying up the whole night). You can go to bed earlier. But, at midnight, when the New Year arrives, a lot of people set off firecrackers. It's very noisy outside.

B: In that case, I'll welcome the New Year in with everyone else. I see you've put a red envelope under my pillow. What the significance of that?

A: That's New Year's money. Normally, adults put a red packet under their children's pillows on the eve of the New Year in the hope that they will be safe and sound. Because you're a foreign guest, I gave you one too.

B: Thanks.

A: On the first day of the New Year, I have to go with my family and pay respects to friends and family; you don't need to come with us to pay respects. I'll take you to the Wild Goose Pagoda first so you can enjoy yourself; we'll pick you up after we finish doing our rounds, OK?

B: No need. If we go to bed late on the Eve of the New Year, it'll be just fine if I stay at home and sleep, and not go out for any fun.

第二十课 过年
Lesson Twenty Celebrating the New Year

Grammar

▶ G1. Topic-comment

Chinese is often characterized as a topic-prominent language, in contrast to languages like English, which are subject-prominent. In other words, in Chinese, sentences are composed of topic and comment rather than subject and predicate. Topic and comment are more loosely bound than subject and predicate, as the following sentence from the main dialogue illustrates:

① 我的工资可买不起这样的房子。 On my salary, I couldn't afford such a house.
   Wǒ de gōngzī kě mǎi bu qǐ zhèyàng de fángzi.

The Chinese makes the "salary" the topic (我的工资 wǒ de gōngzī) – it is what the sentence is about: "My salary just can't afford this kind of a house." But in English, people afford, not money. Subject-prominent languages prefer the person involved (if mentioned) to be subject: "I can't afford this kind of house on my salary". In the following two examples, notice the difference in the order of elements between Chinese and English:

② 除夕晚上吃饺子，是中国人的传统。
   Chúxī wǎnshang chī jiǎozi, shì Zhōngguórén de chuántǒng.
   Eating dumplings on New Year's Eve is Chinese tradition.

③ 我们的同学，两个是新加坡人。 Two of our classmates are from Singapore.
   Wǒmen de tóngxué, liǎng ge shì Xīnjiāpōrén.

As the last sentence illustrates, Chinese sentences often have a two-tiered structure, with an outer noun phrase (我们的同学 wǒmen de tóngxué) providing the general scope for an inner one (两个 liǎng ge): "of our classmates, two" = "two of our classmates".

▶ G2. Providing reassurance with "没什么 (不) méi shénme (bù)"

Politeness often requires you to reassure others. A common way to do this is to shrug off any possible problem, with a phrase like "没什么 méi shénme":

① 没什么不方便的。 There's nothing inconvenient about it.
   Méi shénme bù fāngbiàn de.

② 没什么困难。 There are no difficulties to speak of.
   Méi shénme kùnnan.

③ 没有什么不正常。 There's nothing abnormal about it.
   Méiyǒu shénme bú zhèngcháng.

Notice that "什么 shénme" in these examples is not used as a question word, but as an indefinite, not "what" but "whatever" or "anything". The remark made by "刘老师 Liú lǎoshī" in the dialogue is meant to reassure Ed that there is nothing problematical about three generations living together:

④ 三代人住在一起没有什么不方便。 Three generations live together quite harmoniously.
   Sān dài rén zhù zài yìqǐ méi shénme bù fāngbiàn.

G3. Comparison with "不如 bùrú" (not as [good as], be inferior to)

In Lesson 15 (G5), two comparative constructions were discussed, one with "比 bǐ", expressing dominance (e.g. bigger than), and one with "没有 méiyǒu", expressing parity (e.g. not as big as). The latter was expanded in Lesson 19 (G4) with examples with "有 yǒu" (as big as) as well as "没有 méiyǒu". The "不如 bùrú" construction discussed in this section is similar to the comparatives with "有 yǒu" and "没有 méiyǒu". However, since "不如 bùrú" is a verb, it can appear without a following adjective, meaning simply "not the equal of".

① 汉语呢，乔治不如琳达。
　　Hànyǔ ne, Qiáozhì bùrú Líndá.

② 汉语呢，乔治没有琳达（那么）好。
　　Hànyǔ ne, Qiáozhì méiyǒu Líndá (nàme) hǎo.

In terms of their Chinese, George isn't as good as Linda.

The example from this lesson is:

③ 过年时游人很多，非常拥挤，不如我们年前就去参观。
　　Guònián shí yóurén hěn duō, fēicháng yōngjǐ, bùrú wǒmen nián qián jiù qù cānguān.
　　During the New Year time there'll be a lot of visitors, and it will be extremely crowded. It will be better if we visit (there) before the New Year.

However, it is possible to specify how the comparison is unequal by adding an adjective after the comparison with "不如 bùrú". In the following example, the comparison is specified for speed (快 kuài):

④ 快车不如高铁快。　　Express trains aren't equal to high-speed trains in speed.
　　Kuàichē bùrú gāotiě kuài.　　(Express trains aren't as fast as high-speed trains.)

G4. Elliptical "的 de" phrases

Rather than repeating a noun phrase with a series of different modifiers, it is usual to omit it, leaving "的 de" to mark the ellipsis. Examples of this phenomenon were also illustrated in Lesson 14 (G2).

把旧的、脏的、不好的东西都扫出去，迎接新的一年。
Bǎ jiù de、zāng de、bù hǎo de dōngxi dōu sǎo chuqu, yíngjiē xīn de yì nián.
Sweep out the old, the dirty and the bad stuff and welcome the new year.

G5. Rhetorical questions, with "不是 bú shì……吗 ma?"

Politeness often demands that a statement be made in a round about way, either because it could be interpreted as critical, or because the speaker is not sure of the facts. One way avoid a possible affront is to ask a question:

① 这条裤子不是太长吗？　Aren't these pants a little long?
　　Zhè tiáo kùzi bú shì tài cháng ma?

② 你的生日不是在下个月吗？　Don't you have a birthday next month?
　　Nǐ de shēngri bú shì zài xià ge yuè ma?

③ 你不是刚买了一张去上海的机票吗？　Didn't you just buy a plane ticket to Shanghai?
　　Nǐ bú shì gāng mǎile yì zhāng qù Shànghǎi de jīpiào ma?

④ 您不是说过我很会打扫办公室吗?
   Nín bú shì shuōguo wǒ hěn huì dǎsǎo bàngōngshì ma?
   Didn't you say that I was good at cleaning my office?

▶ G6. Coordinate clauses

As noted in Lesson 15 (G3), clauses in Chinese can be strung together without any explicit conjunctions:

① 鱼代表"有余",饺子代表"和谐、有钱",年糕代表"甜蜜"。
   Yú dàibiǎo "yǒuyú", jiǎozi dàibiǎo "héxié、yǒuqián", niángāo dàibiǎo "tiánmì".
   Fish signifies abundance; dumplings signify harmony and wealth; New Year's sticky rice represents sweetness and affection.

But while English allows a string of objects to be listed with a single verb, Chinese generally repeats the verb with each object. Compare the Chinese with the English in the following example:

② 您可以和我女儿一起贴春联,贴窗花,贴年画和"福"字。
   Nín kěyǐ hé wǒ nǚ'ér yìqǐ tiē chūnlián, tiē chuānghuā, tiē niánhuà hé "fú" zì.
   You can help my daughter stick up the New Year couplets, the paper cutouts for the windows, and the New Year paintings and good luck Charms.

Consolidation & Practice

1. Following the model of the sample sentence, provide comments for each of the topics given below

                   TOPIC   COMMENT

   Example: 在美国上大学   越来越贵了。
   Zài Měiguó shàng dàxué yuè lái yuè guì le.

   (1) 在中国看病_____
   Zài Zhōngguó kàn bìng _____

   (2) 有了网络，交朋友_____
   Yǒule wǎngluò, jiāo péngyou _____

   (3) 来到中国，学做中国饭_____
   Láidào Zhōngguó, xué zuò Zhōngguófàn _____

   (4) 有了高铁，在中国旅行_____
   Yǒule gāotiě, zài Zhōngguó lǚxíng _____

   (5) 在北京买房子_____
   Zài Běijīng mǎi fángzi _____

   (6) 在北京开车_____
   Zài Běijīng kāi chē _____

2. Reassure the speaker by responding with "没什么 (不) méi shénme (bù)", along the lines of the English

   Example: A: 跟爸爸妈妈一起住会不方便吧？
   Gēn bàba māma yìqǐ zhù huì bù fāngbiàn ba?

            B: 我觉得没什么不方便的。
   Wǒ juéde méi shénme bù fāngbiàn de.

   (1) A: 实名制买票真麻烦！
   Shímíngzhì mǎi piào zhēn máfan!

     B: _____
   (It's not that troublesome!)

   (2) A: 你明天就要去面试了，现在紧张吗？
   Nǐ míngtiān jiù yào qù miànshì le, xiànzài jǐnzhāng ma?

     B: _____
   (There is nothing to be nervous about!)

第二十课 过年
Lesson Twenty　Celebrating the New Year

(3) A: 你今天看起来好像有点儿不高兴，怎么了？
　　　Nǐ jīntiān kàn qilai hǎoxiàng yǒudiǎnr bù gāoxìng, zěnme le?

　　B: _____
　　　(There is nothing to be unhappy about!)

(4) A: 你的化验结果都正常吗？
　　　Nǐ de huàyàn jiéguǒ dōu zhèngcháng ma?

　　B: _____
　　　(Everything seems to be normal!)

(5) A: 今年春天天气有点儿不正常，都四月了，还穿羽绒服！
　　　Jīnnián chūntiān tiānqì yǒudiǎnr bú zhèngcháng, dōu sìyuè le, hái chuān yǔróngfú!

　　B: 每年都是这样，_____
　　　Měi nián dōu shì zhèyàng,　(There's nothing strange about it!)

(6) A: 你真幸运，买到去西安的快车票了！
　　　Nǐ zhēn xìngyùn, mǎidào qù Xī'ān de kuàichēpiào le!

　　B: _____，只要你早去就能买到。
　　　(I'm not lucky)　　　　　　　　　　　zhǐyào nǐ zǎo qù jiù néng mǎidào.

3. **Make comparisons with "不如 bùrú", based on the material provided**

(1) 法国饭 / 美国饭 / 贵 → _____
　　Fǎguófàn / Měiguófàn / guì

(2) 美国的圣诞节 / 中国的春节 / 热闹 → _____
　　Měiguó de Shèngdàn Jié / Zhōngguó de Chūn Jié / rènao

(3) 历史课 / 文学课 / 有意思 → _____
　　lìshǐkè / wénxuékè / yǒu yìsi

(4) 我的公寓 / 玛丽的宿舍 / 大 → _____
　　wǒ de gōngyù / Mǎlì de sùshè / dà

(5) 坐高铁 / 坐飞机 / 快 → _____
　　zuò gāotiě / zuò fēijī / kuài

(6) 上海 / 广州 / 远 → _____
　　Shànghǎi / Guǎngzhōu / yuǎn

(7) 重庆 / 上海 / 热闹 → _____
　　Chóngqìng / Shànghǎi / rènao

(8) 进口洗发剂 / 国产洗发剂 / 便宜 → _____
　　jìnkǒu xǐfàjì / guóchǎn xǐfàjì / piányi

真实生活汉语
Chinese for Living in China 2

4. Reduce the redundancy by using elliptical "的 de" phrases in the following sentences

Example: 这张年画是旧年画。→ 这张年画是旧的。
Zhè zhāng niánhuà shì jiù niánhuà. → Zhè zhāng niánhuà shì jiù de.

(1) 这些年画都是新年画吗? → _____
Zhèxiē niánhuà dōu shì xīn niánhuà ma?

(2) 我的车是旧车，我太太的车是新车。→ _____
Wǒ de chē shì jiù chē, wǒ tàitai de chē shì xīn chē.

(3) 这是你的红包，她的红包放在枕头下边了。→ _____
Zhè shì nǐ de hóngbāo, tā de hóngbāo fàng zài zhěntou xiàbian le.

(4) 这是我父母的房子，我们的房子很小。→ _____
Zhè shì wǒ fùmǔ de fángzi, wǒmen de fángzi hěn xiǎo.

(5) 这是我的行李，你的行李呢? → _____
Zhè shì wǒ de xíngli, nǐ de xíngli ne?

(6) 你吃这盘肉饺子，那盘饺子是素饺子。→ _____
Nǐ chī zhè pán ròujiǎozi, nà pán jiǎozi shì sùjiǎozi.

(7) 你喜欢吃什么鱼? 清蒸鱼还是红烧鱼? → _____
Nǐ xǐhuan chī shénme yú? Qīngzhēngyú háishi hóngshāoyú?

(8) 我们有两种年糕，一种甜年糕，一种咸年糕。→ _____
Wǒmen yǒu liǎng zhǒng niángāo, yì zhǒng tián niángāo, yì zhǒng xián niángāo.

5. Recast the lead-in statement to form a rhetorical question with "不是 búshì……吗 ma", following the form of the example

Example: 你现在在北京，为什么还没去长城?
Nǐ xiànzài zài Běijīng, wèi shénme hái méi qù Chángchéng?

→ 你现在不是在北京吗? 为什么还没去长城?
Nǐ xiànzài bú shì zài Běijīng ma? Wèi shénme hái méi qù Chángchéng?

(1) 你要学汉语，为什么不去中国?
Nǐ yào xué Hànyǔ, wèi shénme bú qù Zhōngguó?

→ _____

(2) 你想早一点儿到武汉，怎么不坐飞机?
Nǐ xiǎng zǎo yìdiǎnr dào Wǔhàn, zěnme bú zuò fēijī?

→ _____

(3) 你说软卧很舒服，怎么不买软卧?
Nǐ shuō ruǎnwò hěn shūfu, zěnme bù mǎi ruǎnwò?

→ _____

Lesson Twenty   Celebrating the New Year

(4) 你要体验中国文化，为什么不跟你的中国朋友回老家过年？
Nǐ yào tǐyàn Zhōngguó wénhuà, wèi shénme bù gēn nǐ de Zhōngguó péngyou huí lǎojiā guò nián?

→ _____

(5) 你需要钱，为什么不找一个家教的工作？
Nǐ xūyào qián, wèi shénme bù zhǎo yí ge jiājiào de gōngzuo?

→ _____

(6) 你发烧了，为什么还去打篮球？
Nǐ fā shāo le, wèi shénme hái qù dǎ lánqiú?

→ _____

(7) 你想学包饺子，下星期跟我回家过除夕吧。
Nǐ xiǎng xué bāo jiǎozi, xià xīngqī gēn wǒ huí jiā guò chúxī ba.

→ _____

(8) 你想看兵马俑，我们俩放假一起去西安吧。
Nǐ xiǎng kàn bīngmǎyǒng, wǒmen liǎ fàng jià yìqǐ qù Xī'ān ba.

→ _____

6. **Answer the questions with coordinate clauses, along the lines of the example**

   Example: 你和我女儿一起贴春联，贴年画，贴窗花。
   Nǐ hé wǒ nǚ'ér yìqǐ tiē chūnlián, tiē niánhuà, tiē chuānghuā.

(1) What do Chinese eat on the eve of the Chinese New Year?
   ....

(2) When you visit a doctor, what does the nurse do first? (量 liáng)
   ....

(3) When you take a Chinese test, how do you prepare? (准备 zhǔnbèi)
   ....

(4) If you are inviting friends over to your apartment for dinner, what do you have to do?
   ....

(5) If you are going to a formal banquet, what do you need to buy first?
   ....

(6) You've been invited for a job interview. How are you going to answer the question of what courses are you going to teach?
   ....

7. Tell each other to do the following, using "把 bǎ······放在 fàng zài······"

 (1) Put your book under your chair.

 (2) Put your money on the desk.

 (3) Put your backpack under your chair.

 (4) Put your pen on your book.

 (5) Put your shoes under your desk.

 (6) Put your book under you (=sit on your book).

 (7) Put your pen under your money.

 (8) Put your money under my backpack.

 (9) Put your book under mine.

(10) Put your money into my backpack. (Thank you!)

第二十课 过年
Lesson Twenty Celebrating the New Year

Listening Comprehension

1. Listen to the narration and then answer the questions

    (1) What did the speaker do before Chinese New Year's Eve?

    (2) What did the speaker's dad and sister do?

    (3) What did the speaker and the speaker's mother buy?

    (4) What did the speaker's dad do when the speaker got home?

    (5) What did the speaker do afterwards?

    (6) What did they start cooking?

    (7) When did they start making dumplings?

    (8) When did people start setting off firecrackers?

    (9) When did they start eating dumplings?

    (10) What did everyone do at midnight?

New Words

团圆饭　tuányuánfàn　N　reunion meal

开心　kāixīn　Adj　happy

2. Listen to the passage and then answer the following questions

    (1) What happened on Chinese New Year's Eve?

    (2) How many people showed up?

    (3) What did males wear? And females?

    (4) What did the head of the school give everyone?

    (5) Who is Bai Daming? Is this his first Chinese New Year?

    (6) Why does he like red?

    (7) What was his plan for right after the Chinese New Year?

    (8) Who is Baoluo? When did he come to China?

    (9) What subjects is he interested in?

    (10) What is Baoluo's plan for the future? (Give details.)

New Words

男士　nánshì　N　men

女士　nǚshì　N　women

套装　tàozhuāng　N　suit

和平　hépíng　N　peace

购物卡　gòuwùkǎ　N　gift card

满街　mǎn jiē　Phrase　the whole street

将来　jiānglái　N　future

真实生活汉语
Chinese for Living in China 2

Communication Activities

Pair Work

Scenario I: Work together to list all the concepts, ideas and things that go along with the Chinese New Year celebrations.

Scenario II: Compare and contrast a holiday in your country that is comparable to Chinese New Year. Refer to the following list:

迎接	传统	春节	团聚	幸福
yíngjiē	chuántǒng	Chūn Jié	tuánjù	xìngfú
和谐	代表	吃年夜饭	年货	准备
héxié	dàibiǎo	chī niányèfàn	niánhuò	zhǔnbèi
全家	有意思	希望	饺子	鱼
quánjiā	yǒu yìsi	xīwàng	jiǎozi	yú
漂亮	热闹	礼物		
piàoliang	rènao	lǐwù		

Scenario III: Ask each other about your favorite holiday(s), and explain why you like them so much. Refer to the list:

迎接	文化	传统	圣诞节	感恩节
yíngjiē	wénhuà	chuántǒng	Shèngdàn Jié	Gǎn'ēn Jié
团聚	幸福	和谐	代表	吃年夜饭
tuánjù	xìngfú	héxié	dàibiǎo	chī niányèfàn
年货	准备	互相	送	礼物
niánhuò	zhǔnbèi	hùxiāng	sòng	lǐwù
全家	有意思	希望	漂亮	热闹
quánjiā	yǒu yìsi	xīwàng	piàoliang	rènao
安静	玩儿	看电视/电影		
ānjìng	wánr	kàn diànshì/diànyǐng		

第二十课 过年
Lesson Twenty　Celebrating the New Year

Role-Play

Scenario I: How different age groups celebrate Chinese New Year. With a partner, use the internet to find out how different age groups – the young, middle-aged working people and retirees – celebrate Chinese New Year. Report what you find out to the class.

Scenario II: A new way to pass the New Year? Two of you take the parts of a young Chinese couple. Each of you is an only child. So the question of whose family to spend Chinese New Year with is an issue. This year, you've come up with a new proposal: drop the traditional practice, and both families meet at a nice Chinese restaurant for a family banquet. You meet with one parent from each to thrash out the idea. The young couple try to convince their parents to adopt the idea, while the parents defend the traditional ways. Use as many of the items below as possible:

迎接 yíngjiē	文化 wénhuà	春节 Chūn Jié	团聚 tuánjù	幸福 xìngfú
和谐 héxié	代表 dàibiǎo	吃年夜饭 chī niányèfàn	独子 dúzǐ	责任 zérèn
照顾 zhàogù	互相 hùxiāng	全家 quánjiā	没什么……的 méi shénme……de	
年货 niánhuò	准备 zhǔnbèi	麻烦 máfan	有钱 yǒu qián	有意思 yǒu yìsi
希望 xīwàng	漂亮 piàoliang	热闹 rènao	计划 jìhuà	高兴 gāoxìng
体验 tǐyàn	应该 yīnggāi	兴奋 xīngfèn	机会 jīhuì	正好 zhènghǎo
休息 xiūxi				

Group Activities

Scenario I: Interview some Chinese friends, and ask them the following questions. Report your findings to the class and see whether the answers agree or not.

① 你过春节以前得做什么？你知道"扫尘"的意思吗？
　　Nǐ guò Chūn Jié yǐqián děi zuò shénme? Nǐ zhīdào "sǎochén" de yìsi ma?

② 你过春节的时候在家贴年画和"福"字吗？年画和"福"字代表什么？
　　Nǐ guò Chūn Jié de shíhou zài jiā tiē niánhuà hé "fú" zì ma? Niánhuà hé "fú" zì dàibiǎo shénme?

③ 为什么中国人过春节的时候常常吃鱼？鱼代表什么？
　　Wèi shénme Zhōngguórén guò Chūn Jié de shíhou chángcháng chī yú? Yú dàibiǎo shénme?

④ 为什么中国人过春节的时候常常吃年糕？年糕代表什么？
　　Wèi shénme Zhōngguórén guò Chūn Jié de shíhou chángcháng chī niángāo? Niángāo dàibiǎo shénme?

⑤ 你过春节的时候有压岁钱吗？"压岁钱"有什么意思？
　　Nǐ guò Chūn Jié de shíhou yǒu yāsuìqián ma? "Yāsuìqián" yǒu shénme yìsi?

Scenario II: Gather information from the internet about how many other countries celebrate a Lunar New Year and in what ways. Report what you find out to the class.

Country	How to celebrate

Review Exercises

1. Following the example, provide comments for the topics listed

　　　　　TOPIC　　　　　　　COMMENT
Example: 中国　　　　　　人多车多，饭好吃，东西便宜。
　　　　　Zhōngguó　　　　　rén duō chē duō, fàn hǎochī, dōngxi piányi.

(1) 美国＿＿＿＿＿＿＿＿＿＿＿＿＿＿＿＿＿＿＿＿＿
　　Měiguó ＿＿＿＿＿＿＿＿＿＿＿＿＿＿＿＿＿＿＿

(2) 意大利饭＿＿＿＿＿＿＿＿＿＿＿＿＿＿＿＿＿＿
　　Yìdàlìfàn ＿＿＿＿＿＿＿＿＿＿＿＿＿＿＿＿＿

(3) 在中国学中文＿＿＿＿＿＿＿＿＿＿＿＿＿＿＿＿
　　Zài Zhōngguó xué Zhōngwén ＿＿＿＿＿＿＿＿＿

(4) 在中国坐火车＿＿＿＿＿＿＿＿＿＿＿＿＿＿＿＿
　　Zài Zhōngguó zuò huǒchē ＿＿＿＿＿＿＿＿＿＿

(5) 在中国过春节＿＿＿＿＿＿＿＿＿＿＿＿＿＿＿＿
　　Zài Zhōngguó guò Chūn Jié ＿＿＿＿＿＿＿＿＿

(6) 西方的圣诞节＿＿＿＿＿＿＿＿＿＿＿＿＿＿＿＿
　　Xīfāng de Shèngdàn Jié ＿＿＿＿＿＿＿＿＿＿＿

第二十课 过年
Lesson Twenty Celebrating the New Year

2. Reassuring people by making use of the pattern "没什么 méi shénme……的 de"

   (1) What would you say to reassure a friend who's nervous about an upcoming interview?

   你准备得很好，_____。（紧张 jǐnzhāng）
   Nǐ zhǔnbèi de hěn hǎo, _____.

   (2) How would you reassure someone who's worried about X-ray results?

   你现在不发烧，也不咳嗽，_____。（担心 dānxīn）
   Nǐ xiànzài bù fāshāo, yě bù késou, _____.

   (3) How would you reassure someone who's upset because her boyfriend broke up with her?

   _____，你可以再找一个男朋友。（难过 nánguò）
   _____, nǐ kěyǐ zài zhǎo yí ge nánpéngyou.

   (4) What would you say if a new friend of yours kept apologizing for asking too many questions about life in Beijing?

   _____，我愿意帮助新来的学生。（麻烦 máfan）
   _____, wǒ yuànyì bāngzhù xīn lái de xuésheng.

   (5) What would you say to a friend who just failed a Chinese test?

   _____，下次考试以前，我们一起复习，你会考好的。（难过 nánguò）
   _____, xià cì kǎoshì yǐqián, wǒmen yìqǐ fùxí, nǐ huì kǎohǎo de.

3. While living in China, you've made some discoveries. List more discoveries, incorporating the "不如 bùrú" pattern, following the example

   Example: 美国的中国饭馆都不如中国的中国饭馆。
   Měiguó de Zhōngguó fànguǎn dōu bùrú Zhōngguó de Zhōngguó fànguǎn.

   (1) ....
   (2) ....
   (3) ....
   (4) ....
   (5) ....
   (6) ....

4. Make rhetorical questions to back up the question that is provided

   Example: 你不是想看中国电影吗？今天晚上咱们去看电影吧！
   Nǐ bú shì xiǎng kàn Zhōngguó diànyǐng ma? Jīntiān wǎnshang zánmen qù kàn diànyǐng ba!

真实生活汉语
Chinese for Living in China 2

(1) _____? 为什么不申请 (to apply for) 这个教英文的工作呢?
　　　　　　　　　　　 Wèi shénme bù shēnqǐng zhège jiāo Yīngwén de gōngzuò ne?

(2) _____? 为什么不跟你的中国朋友回家过春节呢?
　　　　　　　　　　　 Wèi shénme bù gēn nǐ de Zhōngguó péngyou huí jiā guò Chūn Jié ne?

(3) _____? 为什么不去医院检查呢?
　　　　　　　　　　　 Wèi shénme bú qù yīyuàn jiǎnchá ne?

(4) _____? 为什么不去商店买一件新的羽绒服呢?
　　　　　　　　　　　 Wèi shénme bú qù shāngdiàn mǎi yí jiàn xīn de yǔróngfú ne?

(5) _____? 为什么不去问问老师呢?
　　　　　　　　　　　 Wèi shénme bú qù wènwen lǎoshī ne?

(6) _____? 为什么不坐飞机呢?
　　　　　　　　　　　 Wèi shénme bú zuò fēijī ne?

5. Interview at least 6 of your classmates to find out about the make of her or his car, the color of the car, the brand of computer (s)he uses, and report your findings to the class, using "的 de" to save repetition

   Example: 我的车是日本的，是黑色的。我的电脑是戴尔（Dell）的。
   　　　　　Wǒ de chē shì Rìběn de, shì hēisè de. Wǒ de diànnǎo shì Dài'ěr de.

   (1) ....
   (2) ....
   (3) ....
   (4) ....
   (5) ....
   (6) ....

6. You are going on a trip to Shanghai, but unfortunately, you just broke your arm and you're having a hard time packing your carry-on bag. Your roommate has offered to help, though, so you can tell him what to do, using the following two constructions "把 bǎ + N + 放在 fàng zài……下 xià/上 shàng", tell your roommate where to put the following items

浅色/深色的 T 恤衫	西装	裤子	袜子
qiǎnsè/shēnsè de T xù shān	xīzhuāng	kùzi	wàzi
领带	皮鞋	中文书	英文报纸
lǐngdài	píxié	Zhōngwénshū	Yīngwén bàozhǐ

第二十课 过 年
Lesson Twenty Celebrating the New Year

(1) ....

(2) ....

(3) ....

(4) ....

(5) ....

(6) ....

Culture Notes

1. "春节 Chūn Jié": The Spring Festival

On September 27, 1949, the Gregorian calendar (the solar calendar that is used internationally) was officially adopted by the People's Republic of China. (It had been adopted much earlier by the Republic of China, but was not always used in the intervening period.) New Year's Day (called "元旦 Yuándàn" in Chinese) was made an official holiday. The Lunar Calendar was accepted for its traditional roles as well, particularly in designating the first day of the lunar year.

In Chinese tradition, the build-up to the New Year begins on the 8th day of the 12th lunar month (of the previous lunar year), with offerings of a specially prepared rice porridge (腊八粥 làbāzhōu) to the ancestors and household deities. It continues on the 28th day, with offerings to the Kitchen God (灶王爷 Zàowángye), who keeps track of family events. Around the same time, the household is swept to rid it of any baleful influences. New decorations replace the old: spring couplets are pasted on doorways, lucky characters on walls and doors, and paper-cuts on windows. Elders prepare lucky red paper envelopes containing money ("红包 hóngbāo", or more formally, "压岁钱 yāsuìqián" — see next entry) to give to children and young people.

On the Eve of the Spring Festival (除夕 chúxī), a reunion banquet is served, that includes foods that have symbolic value in addition to tasting good — foods like fish, whose name (鱼 yú) is homophonous with the word for plenty (余 yú). Late in the evening, modern audiences often watch the CCTV New Year's Gala (春节联欢晚会 Chūn Jié Liánhuān Wǎnhuì), which goes from 8:00 p.m. to after midnight. (It is, supposedly, the most watched TV program on earth.)

Once the New Year arrives, firecrackers (鞭炮 biānpào) are set of with wild abandon. In the north, people eat dumplings (饺子 jiǎozi), in the south, glutinous rice cakes (年糕 niángāo). Dumplings are shaped like traditional Chinese ingots of precious metal (元宝 yuánbǎo), so they are symbolic of wealth and prosperity. The name of the glutinous rice cakes that are eaten in the south (黏糕 niángāo) is a perfect pun on "New Year's cake" (年糕 niángāo). People generally stay up till dawn. On New Year's Day ("正月初一 zhēngyuè chūyī", the first day of the first month), people dress up and pay goodwill visits to friends (拜年 bài nián).

Traditionally, the New Year festivities extend to the 15th day of the first lunar month, the Yuanxiao (元宵 Yuánxiāo) or Shangyuan (上元 Shàngyuán) Festival, also known as the Lantern Festival.

2. "压岁钱 yāsuìqián" (New Year's money)

New Year's money (originally written with the homophonous "压祟钱 yāsuìqián" — suppress-mischief or harm-money") is believed to protect the recipient through the new year. It is placed in red packets (红包 hóngbāo) in certain lucky denominations, and either put under the pillow when the child is sleeping, or presented on New Year's Day when the younger generation pays respectful visits to the older.

3. "拜年 bài nián" (Paying New Year's calls)

On the first day of the first lunar month (正月初一 zhēngyuè chūyī), people get up early, put on their best clothes, and go out to make New Year's calls. They go from house to house, visiting family elders, relatives, friends and co-workers, conveying New Year's greetings to them and wishing them well for the coming year. Sometimes, colleagues congregate in a single place to give each other New Year's salutations (团拜 tuánbài).

Vocabulary 词汇表 Cíhuì Biǎo

A

Pinyin	Characters	Type	Meaning	Lesson
AA zhì	AA制	Exp	"AA" = split the bill, go Dutch	L17
a	啊	Part	used after each item in an enumeration	L18
a	啊	Part	a phrase particle associated with exclamation, surprise, heartiness	L20
àiren	爱人/愛人	N	spouse, husband or wife, (girl/boy) friend	L20
āndìng	安定	Adj/V	stable, settled, quiet; to stabilize	L18
ānjìng	安静	Adj	quiet, peaceful	L17
ānpái	安排	V/N	to arrange, to provide; plan	L20
àn	按	Prep/V	according to, based on; to press, to push down, to massage	L14
ànmó	按摩	V	to massage	L14

B

Pinyin	Characters	Type	Meaning	Lesson
bǎ	把	Prep	spotlights objects	L11
báibǎn	白板	N	whiteboard, white bulletin board	L11
báilǐng	白领/白領	N	white collar	L17
bǎi	摆/擺	V	to arrange, to lay out	L11
bài	拜	V	to pay respects, to visit, to call on	L20
bài nián	拜年	VO	to pay a New Year's visit, to wish (sb.) a Happy New Year	L20
bān	班	N	class	L11
bān	班	Meas	for scheduled buses, trains, airplanes	L13
bǎncār	板擦儿/板擦兒	N	(chalkboard or whiteboard) eraser	L11
bàngōngshì	办公室/辦公室	N	office	L11
bāng	帮/幫	V	to help, to lend a hand	L11
bāo	包	V/N/Meas	to undertake the whole thing, to wrap, to guarantee; bundle, bag; for objects in packets, etc.	L17
Běijīng	北京	PropN	Beijing (Peking in some compounds)	L16
bèi	倍	Meas	for multiples, times, -fold	L18
běnkē	本科	N	undergraduate, undergraduate course	L11
bǐ	比	V/Prep	to compare; than	L15
bǐjiào	比较/比較	Adv/V	comparatively, relatively; to compare, to contrast	L12
bǐrú	比如	V	for example, for instance	L20
bì shǔ	避暑	VO	to avoid the heat, to go away for the summer holidays	L19
bì	臂	BF	upper arm	L16

265

biān shang	边上/邊上	Phrase	on the banks of, beside	L19
biānpào	鞭炮	N	firecrackers (collectively), a string of small firecrackers	L20
biāoqiān	标签/標簽	N	label, tag (with the price, proof of inspection, etc.)	L12
biǎoshì	表示	V	to show, to express, to indicate	L17
biǎoxiàn	表现/表現	V/N	to show, to display, to do; performance, expression	L11
bié	别	Adv/BF	don't; other	L18
bīnglěng	冰冷	Adj	ice cold, frosty (of expressions, etc.)	L19
bīngxiāng	冰箱	N	refrigerator, icebox	L17
bīngmǎyǒng	兵马俑/兵馬俑	N	figures of warriors and horses buried with the dead	L18
bìng	病	V/N	to fall ill; illness	L16
bózi	脖子	N	the neck, the neck (of a vessel, a vase, etc.)	L14
búdàn	不但	Conj	not only	L17
búguò	不过/不過	Conj	but, however, nevertheless	L13
búpèi	不配	Adj	ill-matched, not fit	L15
búyòng	不用	Adv	need not	L14
bú zài	不再	Phrase	no more, no longer	L17
bùfú	不服	V	not used to	L16
bùliáng	不良	Adj	not good, indisposed	L16
bùrú	不如	V	not as (good as), to be inferior to	L20

C

cái	才	Adv	only then, just now, only (in reference to age or duration)	L13
cáiliào	材料	N	material, data, ingredients	L11
cài	菜	N	vegetables; dish (in a meal)	L12
càidāo	菜刀	N	kitchen knife	L17
càishìchǎng	菜市场/菜市場	N	food market, grocery store	L12
cānguān	参观/參觀	V	to tour, to visit	L20
chāzi	叉子	N	fork	L17
chá	查	V	to check, to examine, to inspect	L11
chàbuduō	差不多	Adj/Adv	more or less the same; nearly, almost	L18
cháng	长/長	Adj	long, for a long time	L14
chángjià	长假/長假	N	long vacation ("假期 jiàqī", period of leave, vacation)	L19
Cháng Jiāng	长江/長江	PropN	the Yangtze River	L19
chángkù	长裤/長褲	N	long pants, trousers	L15
chǎnghé	场合/場合	N	occasion, situation	L15
chǎo	吵	Adj/V	noisy; to make a lot of noise, to quarrel	L20

chē	车/車	N	bus, car, vehicle ("坐车 zuò chē", by bus, car, etc.)	L13
chēpiào	车票/車票	N	ticket (for bus, train)	L13
chén	尘/塵	BF	dust	L20
chènshān	衬衫/襯衫	N	shirt	L15
chēng	称/稱	V	to weigh	L12
chēngwéi	称为/稱為	V	to address as, to be called, to be known as	L17
chéng	成	V/RC	to become, to turn into, to succeed; into	L14
chéngshì	城市	N	city, town	L19
Chóngqìng	重庆/重慶	PropN	Chongqing (a directly governed city)	L19
chōu	抽	V	to take out, to draw forth, to obtain	L13
chōuchū	抽出	V-DirC	to draw out, to extract, to find (time)	L13
chōuti	抽屉/抽屜	N	drawer	L17
chūqínlǜ	出勤率	N	rate of attendance, amount of participation	L11
chūqu	出去	V	to go out, to exit	L17
chūxí	出席	V	to attend, to be present (at a meeting, etc.)	L15
chūyī	初一	N	New Year's Day, i.e. the first day of the New Year	L19
chūzhōng	初中	N	junior secondary school, junior middle school	L15
chúle	除了	Prep	except for, besides	L11
chúxī	除夕	N	the eve of the Lunar New Year	L19
chúfáng	厨房/廚房	N	kitchen	L17
chuān	穿	V	to wear, to put on (clothing), to pass through	L15
chuántǒng	传统/傳統	N/Attr	tradition, convention; traditional	L18
chuānghu	窗户	N	window	L11
chuānghuā	窗花	N	paper-cut window decoration	L20
chuángtóuguì	床头柜/床頭櫃	N	bedside cupboard	L17
chuī	吹	V	to blow (of wind), to play (a wind instrument)	L14
chuī fēng	吹风/吹風	VO	to blow dry (one's hair); to be in a draft	L14
Chūn Jié	春节/春節	PropN	The Spring Festival, Chinese New Year, the Lunar New Year	L18
chūnlián	春联/春聯	N	New Year couplets (pasted on door frames)	L20
chūntiān	春天	N	springtime, spring	L19
chūnyùn	春运/春運	N	spring rush (traveling over Chinese New Year)	L18
cì	次	Meas	occasion, time	L11
cónglái	从来/從來	Adv	always, at all times, all along	L19

cùn	寸	Meas	Chinese inch (1/30 meter)	L14

D

dāying	答应/答應	V	to answer, to reply, to agree, to promise	L17
dádào	达到/達到	V	to reach, to accomplish, to achieve	L19
dǎ lǐngdài	打领带/打領帶	Phrase	to hit, to strike, to make, to tie (a tie), to take (a taxi), etc.	L15
dǎ chē	打车/打車	VO	to go by taxi, to take a taxi	L13
dǎ diǎndī	打点滴/打點滴	Phrase	to have an intravenous drip, receive an IV injection (also "打吊针 dǎ diàozhēn")	L16
dǎ qiú	打球	Phrase	to play ball games	L16
dǎsǎo	打扫/打掃	V	to sweep	L20
dǎting	打听/打聽	V	to make inquiries, to ask about	L15
dǎ zhé	打折	VO	to give a discount	L15
dàbā	大巴	N	large bus, big bus ("空调大巴 kōngtiáo dàbā", *air-conditioned bus*)	L13
dàbiàn	大便	V/N	to defecate; feces, night soil	L16
dàduōshù	大多数/大多數	N	great majority	L17
dàfēng	大风/大風	N	strong wind	L19
dàjiā	大家	N	everyone, all of us	L17
dàkǎo	大考	N	final examination	L11
dànián chūyī	大年初一	Phrase	New Year's Day	L20
dàren	大人	N	adult (person)	L20
dàxiǎo	大小	N	size	L15
dàxué	大学/大學	N	university, college	L13
dàxuě	大雪	N	heavy snow	L19
dàyàn	大雁	N	wild goose	L20
Dàyàn Tǎ	大雁塔	PropN	Wild Goose Pagoda (in Xi'an city)	L20
dàifu	大夫	N	doctor	L16
dài	代	N	generation	L20
dàibiǎo	代表	V/N	to represent, to stand for; a delegate, proxy	L20
dài	带/帶	V	to carry, to bring or take	L15
dànshì	但是	Conj	but	L17
dào	到	V/Prep	to arrive, to succeed in; to, until	L11
Déguó	德国/德國	PropN	Germany	L14
de	地	Part	*follows adjectives to mark them as adverbials*	L17
děngděng	等等	Part	etc., and so on, and so forth	L18
dī	低	Adj/V	low; to lower (e.g. one's head)	L11
dì	第	Pref	*attached to cardinal numbers to form ordinals*, e.g.: "第三 dì-sān" (3rd)	L11

diàn	电/電	N	electricity	L17
diànnǎo	电脑/電腦	N	computer	L11
diào	掉	V/RC	to fall, to drop; away, off, out, etc.	L14
dǐng shang	顶上/頂上	Phrase	the top, peak, highest point	L14
dōngběi/Dōngběi	东北/東北	PW/PropN	northeast; the Northeast China	L19
Dōng Sān Shěng	东三省/東三省	PropN	the Three (North) Eastern Provinces, cf. the previous entry	L19
dōngtiān	冬天	N	winter	L19
dǒng	懂	V	to understand, to comprehend ("不懂 bù dǒng", *not to understand*)	L11
dúzǐ	独子/獨子	N	only son	L20
dú	读/讀	V	to read aloud, to read, to study (a subject in school)	L11
dǔ chē	堵车/堵車	VO	for there to be traffic jams, for traffic to be bad	L13
dùzi	肚子	N	belly, abdomen ("拉肚子 lā dùzi", *diarrhea*)	L16
dù	度	Meas/V	degree; to spend, to pass (time)	L19
duǎn	短	Adj	short, brief	L14
duǎnwà	短袜/短襪	N	(short) socks (in contrast to stockings)	L15
duànliàn	锻炼/鍛煉	V	to engage in physical exercise	L16
duì……guòmǐn	对……过敏/對……過敏	Construction	to be allergic to…	L16
duìbuqǐ	对不起/對不起	Exp	excuse me, I'm sorry, pardon me	L18
duō cháng	多长/多長	Phrase	how long (with "多 duō" here meaning "to what degree")	L13
duō cháng shíjiān	多长时间/多長時間	Phrase	how long	L13
duō dà	多大	Phrase	how old, how big (question or exclamation)	L15
duō dà hào	多大号/多大號	Phrase	what size (of clothing, etc.)	L15
duōméitǐ	多媒体/多媒體	N	multimedia	L11
duōyún	多云/多雲	N	lots of clouds, cloudy	L19
duō zǐ duō sūn	多子多孙/多子多孫	Phrase	to have many sons and grandsons	L20

E

érzi	儿子/兒子	N	son	L20
ér	而	Conj	and, and thus, but	L18
érqiě	而且	Conj	moreover, in addition	L17

F

fā	发/發	V	to send out, to issue, to launch, to produce	L11
fā shāo	发烧/發燒	VO	to have a fever, to run a temperature	L16
fà	发/髮	BF	hair on human head	L14

真实生活汉语

Chinese for Living in China 2

fàxíng	发型/髮型	N	hair style	L14
fàyóu	发油/髮油	N	hair oil	L14
fānqié	番茄	N	tomato ("番茄 fānqié" in Guangdong and Hong Kong, "西红柿 xīhóngshì" in North China)	L12
fānlǐng	翻领/翻領	N	turndown collar	L15
fāngbiàn	方便	Adj	convenient	L20
fāngxiàng	方向	N	direction, orientation, bearing	L13
fángzi	房子	N	house, building, room or apartment	L17
fángzū	房租	N	rent (money)	L17
fàng	放	V	to put down, to place ("放在 fàng zài", to put or place into or onto)	L12
fàng jià	放假	VO	to have (or grant) a vacation or holiday	L18
fàngxia	放下	V-DirC	to put down, to let go off	L16
fàng xué	放学/放學	VO	to finish classes for the day, to get out of school	L16
fēijī	飞机/飛機	N	airplane	L18
fēicháng	非常	Adv	very, extremely	L13
féi	肥	Adj	loose (of clothing); fat, greasy	L15
fēnmíng	分明	Adj	clearly demarcated, distinct	L19
fèn (r)	份（儿）/份（兒）	Meas	*for newspapers, shares or portions*	L17
fēng	风/風	N	wind	L14
fénghé	缝合/縫合	V	to stitch up a wound	L16
fúzhuāng	服装/服裝	N	clothing, costume, dress, apparel	L15
fú	福	N	good fortune, blessing	L20
fù	父	BF	father	L20
fùmǔ	父母	N	father and mother, parents	L20
fù	付	V	to pay	L12
fù kuǎn	付款	Phrase	to pay a sum of money	L12
fù qián	付钱/付錢	Phrase	to pay, to make a payment	L15
fùyǒu	富有	Adj	wealthy, rich	L17
fù	腹	BF	belly, abdomen	L16
fùxiè	腹泻/腹瀉	N	diarrhea	L16

G

gǎibiàn	改变/改變	V	to change, to transform	L14
gān	干/乾	Adj	dry, dried up, dried out	L11
gān bēi	干杯/乾杯	VO/Exp	to drink a toast; cheers	L17
gānjìng	干净/乾淨	Adj	clean, trim	L14
gānxǐ	干洗/乾洗	V	dry wash, dry clean	L14

gānzào	干燥/乾燥	Adj	dry, arid (of weather), dry	L19
gǎnkuài	赶快/趕快	Adv	quickly	L15
Gǎn'ēn Jié	感恩节/感恩節	PropN	Thanksgiving, Thanksgiving Day ("feelkindness-festival")	L18
gǎnjué	感觉/感覺	V/N	to feel, to sense; feeling, sensation	L19
gǎnmào	感冒	V/N	to catch cold; a cold, the flu	L16
gǎnrǎn	感染	V	to infect (literally or figuratively)	L16
gānghǎo	刚好/剛好	Adv	just (in time), exactly, happen to	L16
gāotiě	高铁/高鐵	N	high-speed rail (short for "高速铁路 gāosù tiělù")	L18
gāoxìng	高兴/高興	Adj	happy, glad	L18
gēbo	胳膊	N	the arm	L16
gè	各	Pron	each, every	L17
gè……gè……	各……各……	Construction	each…each…	L17
gōngzī	工资/工資	N	salary, wages, pay	L13
gōngzuò	工作	V/N	to work; occupation, job, work	L14
gōnggòng	公共	Attr	public, common, communal	L13
gōnggòng qìchē	公共汽车/公共汽車	Phrase	public bus	L13
gōngyù	公寓	N	apartment house, boarding house, rooming house ("教师公寓 jiàoshī gōngyù", teacher's dorm)	L12
gōngyuán	公园/公園	N	public park, town green	L13
gòu wù	购物/購物	Phrase	to buy goods, things	L15
gòuwù zhōngxīn	购物中心/購物中心	Phrase	shopping mall, shopping center	L15
gǔkē	骨科	N	orthopedics	L16
gǔzhé	骨折	N	bone fracture	L16
gùdìng	固定	Adj	fixed, regular, scheduled	L11
guāzǐ	瓜子	N	melon seeds, sunflower seeds	L20
guā	刮	V	to scrape, to scratch, to shave	L14
guā	刮/颳	V	to blow	L19
guā fēng	刮风/颳風	Phrase	for the wind to blow	L19
guà hào	挂号/掛號	VO	to register, to sign in (at a hospital, etc.)	L16
guài	怪	V	to blame	L18
guān	关/關	V	to close	L11
guān mén	关门/關門	VO	to close the door (literal or figurative)	L12
guānshang	关上/關上	V-RC	to close, to lock (a door, window, etc.)	L11
Guǎngzhōu	广州/廣州	PropN	Guangzhou, Canton (a city in Guangdong)	L14
guì	柜/櫃	BF	cabinet	L17
guóchǎn	国产/國產	Attr	domestic product (i.e. made in China)	L14
guò jié	过节/過節	VO	to celebrate a holiday	L19

pinyin	汉字/漢字	POS	English	Lesson
guòmǐn	过敏/過敏	V/N	to be over-sensitive to, to be allergic to; allergy	L16
guò nián	过年/過年	VO	to celebrate the Spring Festival or New Year	L18
guo	过/過	Part	a verb suffix that indicates that the action has happened at some time in the past	L14

H

pinyin	汉字/漢字	POS	English	Lesson
hái kěyǐ	还可以/還可以	Phrase	(colloquial) to be OK, not bad, so-so	L15
háizi	孩子	N	child, children	L20
hǎixiān	海鲜/海鮮	N	seafood	L12
Hánguó	韩国/韓國	PropN	South Korea	L14
hánjià	寒假	N	winter vacation	L18
Hànzì	汉字/漢字	PropN	Chinese character	L11
háng	行	Meas	line, row	L12
hǎo	好	Adv	(used before adjectives with exclamatory force) very, quite, so	L17
hǎo dà	好大	Phrase	so big, really big	L17
hào	号/號	N	number (of house), size (of clothing)	L15
hé	合	V	to close, to shut, to join, to combine	L16
héshì	合适/合適	Adj	suitable, fitting	L15
héxié	和谐/和諧	Adj	harmonious	L20
hóngbāo	红包/紅包	N	"red packets", i.e. envelopes containing money given as gifts, bonuses, bribes	L20
hóngjiǔ	红酒/紅酒	N	red wine	L17
hòubèi	后背/後背	N	the back (of the body, etc.), at the back, in the rear	L14
hòumiàn	后面/後面	PW	at the back, afterwards, later	L14
hòuzhěn	候诊/候診	V	to wait to see a doctor (as in a hospital)	L16
húzi	胡子/鬍子	N	beard, moustache, facial hair	L14
hùxiāng	互相	Adv	each other	L20
huā	花	N/V	flower; to spend	L20
huāshēng	花生	N	peanut	L20
huā zhe shēng	花着生/花著生	Phrase	to bear both sons and daughters	L20
huàyàn	化验/化驗	V	to do a chemical examination, to test	L16
huàyàndān	化验单/化驗單	N	laboratory test sheet	L16
huàyànshì	化验室/化驗室	N	laboratory (for chemical testing)	L16
huà	话/話	N	speech, language	L18
huàtí	话题/話題	N	topic of conversation	L18
huānyíng	欢迎/歡迎	V	to welcome, to receive favorably	L14
huàn chē	换车/換車	Phrase	to change vehicles (bus, train, etc.), to transfer, to switch	L13
huángguā	黄瓜	N	cucumber	L12

Huáng Shān	黄山	PropN	Mount Huang (in "安徽 Ānhuī")	L19
huíbào	回报/回報	V	to report back, to repay, to get one's own back	L17
huí jiā	回家	Phrase	to return home	L18
huíshēng	回升	V	to rise again, to pick up (after a fall, etc.)	L19
huódòng	活动/活動	N/V	activity; to move about, to exercise	L20
huǒchē	火车/火車	N	train	L18
huǒchēpiào	火车票/火車票	N	train ticket	L18
huǒlú	火炉/火爐	N	stove (for heating)	L19
huòzhě	或者	Conj	or, either	L11

J

jīhui	机会/機會	N	opportunity, chance	L19
jí	极/極	Adv	extremely	L13
jí le	极了/極了	Phrase	extremely, very (after adjectives)	L13
jízhěn	急诊/急診	N/V	emergency treatment, emergency call	L16
jǐ lù	几路/幾路	Phrase	bus number what, which bus	L13
jìhuà	计划/計劃	V/N	to plan; plan, program	L18
jìshù	技术/技術	N	technique, skill, technology	L11
jiā kè	加课/加課	Phrase	to add a class	L11
jiārè	加热/加熱	V	to heat, to warm up	L17
jiā	家	N/Meas	family, household, home; *for families, businesses*	L14
jiājù	家具	N	furniture	L17
jiārén	家人	N	family (members) (cf. "一家人 yìjiārén", whole family, members of a family)	L18
jiàgé	价格/價格	N	price, cost	L12
jiānbǎng	肩膀	N	the shoulder	L14
jiǎn	剪	V	to cut (with scissors), to clip	L14
jiǎn fà	剪发/剪髮	Phrase	to have one's haircut, to cut hair	L14
jiàn	件	Meas	*for clothing, luggage, items of furniture, documents*	L15
jiànjiàn	渐渐/漸漸	Adv	gradually, by degrees	L17
jiāotōng	交通	N	traffic, communications, transport, transportation	L18
jiāotōng yùnshū	交通运输/交通運輸	Phrase	communications and transportation	L18
jiāo shū	教书/教書	VO	to teach	L13
jiāo	跤	BF	fall	L16
jiǎo	脚/腳	N	foot, base (of a wall, hill, etc.)	L16
jiàocái	教材	N	teaching material	L11
jiàoshī	教师/教師	N	teacher	L11
Jiàoshī Jié	教师节/教師節	PropN	Teachers' Day (10 September)	L15

273

真实生活汉语 2
Chinese for Living in China

jiàoshì	教室	N	classroom	L11
jiàoshòu	教授	N	professor	L18
jiàowùchù	教务处/教務處	N	the dean's office, the administration office	L11
jiàoyánzǔ	教研组/教研組	N	teaching and research department or group	L12
jiàoyù	教育	N/V	education; to teach, to educate	L17
jiàoyùjú	教育局	N	education bureau	L15
jiēcéng	阶层/階層	N	social class, social stratum	L17
jiē	接	V	to meet, to come in contact with, to connect, to receive	L20
jiēshòu	接受	V	to accept, to receive (honors), to get ("接受采访 jiēshòu cǎifǎng", to be interviewed)	L13
jiérì	节日/節日	N	holiday, festival day	L18
jiéguǒ	结果/結果	N	outcome, result	L16
jǐn	紧/緊	Adj	tight, urgent, pressing, in short supply	L15
jìn kǒu	进口/進口	VO	to import	L14
jìnqu	进去/進去	V	to go in, to enter	L14
jìngzi	镜子/鏡子	N	a mirror	L14
jiǔniánzhì	九年制	N	grades 1-9	L15
jiǔ	久	Adj	long, for a long time	L14
jiù	旧/舊	Adj	worn, used, old, bygone	L20
jiù shì	就是	Phrase	to be right at, then it's, and that is	L13
jùshuō	据说/據說	V	it's said that, supposedly	L18
jù cān	聚餐	VO	to get together for a meal, to dine together (e.g. a work unit or school on a festive occasion)	L15
juédìng	决定	V/N	to decide, to make up one's mind; decision	L15
juéde	觉得/覺得	V	to feel (tired, etc.), to think, to believe	L15

K

kāi	开/開	V	to open, to start	L12
kāi fàn	开饭/開飯	VO	to serve a meal	L17
kāi mén	开门/開門	VO	to open the door (literal or figurative)	L12
kāishǐ	开始/開始	V	to begin, to start	L17
kāishuǐ	开水/開水	N	boiled water, boiling water	L16
kān	看	V	to look after	L20
kān háizi	看孩子	Phrase	to babysit, to look after children	L20
kǎn jià	砍价/砍價	VO	to bargain	L12
kàn bìng	看病	VO	to see a patient, to see a doctor	L16
kàn dàifu	看大夫	Phrase	to go to a doctor	L16

Pinyin	Characters	POS	Definition	Lesson
kànlái	看来/看來	V	to look as if, to seem that	L16
kàn qilai	看起来/看起來	V-DirC	to look as if, to seem to be, to appear to be	L14
kàngshēngsù	抗生素	N	antibiotic	L16
kǎolǜ	考虑/考慮	V	to consider, to think over, to reconsider	L18
kǎoshì	考试/考試	V/N	to take an exam or test; test, examination	L11
kǎo	烤	V	to bake, to roast, to toast, to warm (hands)	L17
kē	科	N	branch of learning, administrative section	L11
késou	咳嗽	V/N	to cough; cough	L16
kě	可	Adv	really, in contrast, actually	L20
kěnéng	可能	Adj/Aux/N	possible, probable; to be possible, may; possibility	L17
kèqi	客气/客氣	Adj	polite, courteous	L12
kètīng	客厅/客廳	N	living room	L17
kèbiǎo	课表/課表	N	schedule of classes, school timetable	L11
kètáng	课堂/課堂	N	classroom	L11
kōngqì	空气/空氣	N	air	L16
kǒuyǔ	口语/口語	N	spoken language	L11
kǒuzhào	口罩	N	gauze mask, surgical mask, flu mask	L19
kùzi	裤子/褲子	N	pants, trousers	L15
kuàizi	筷子	N	chopsticks	L17
Kūnmíng	昆明	PropN	Kunming (a city in "云南 Yúnnán")	L19

L

Pinyin	Characters	POS	Definition	Lesson
lā	拉	V	to pull, to tug, to draw, to play (stringed instruments), to have a bowel movement	L16
láidejí	来得及/來得及	Pot	can make it (in time) (the negative is "来不及 láibují")	L13
lánqiú	篮球/籃球	N	basketball	L16
láojià	劳驾/勞駕	Intj	excuse me (when asking sb. to move out of the way, etc.), would you mind…	L13
lǎobǎixìng	老百姓	N	the common folk, civilians	L17
lǎojiā	老家	N	native place, home town, home country	L18
lěng	冷	Adj	cold	L19
líkāi	离开/離開	V	to leave	L20
lǐwù	礼物/禮物	N	present, gift	L19
lǐ fà	理发/理髮	VO	to style hair, to cut hair	L14
lǐfàdiàn	理发店/理髮店	N	barbershop, hair salon	L14
lǐfàshī	理发师/理髮師	N	barber, hairdresser	L14
lìshǐ	历史/歷史	N	history	L11
liǎ	俩/俩	Q	colloquial version of "两个 liǎng ge", the two of them	L16

liánbìn húzi	连鬓胡子/連鬢鬍子	Phrase	full beard, sideburns	L14
liánluò	联络/聯絡	V/N	to make contact with, to contact; liaison ("联络老师 liánluò lǎoshī", contact teacher)	L15
liánghǎo	良好	Adj	good, desirable	L17
liángkuai	凉快	Adj/V	pleasantly cool; to cool oneself	L19
liáng	量	V	to measure sth. (with a measuring tape, yardstick, ruler, etc.), to estimate	L16
liǎngbìn	两鬓/兩鬢	N	hair on the temples	L14
liáo	聊	V	to chat	L17
liáo tiānr	聊天儿/聊天兒	VO	(col) to chat, to gossip	L17
liǎojiě	了解	V	to understand, to find out about, to look into, to learn about	L13
línjū	邻居/鄰居	N	neighbor	L12
líng xià	零下	Phrase	below zero	L19
lǐngdài	领带/領帶	N	tie, necktie	L15
lǐngdǎo	领导/領導	N/V	leader, boss; to lead	L15
lìng	另	Pron	another, other	L16
liú	留	V	to remain, to stay	L17
liú	流	V	to flow (of liquid), to wander	L16
liúxíng	流行	V/Adj	to spread, to rage (of disease); prevalent, in vogue	L16
liú xiě	流血	Phrase	to bleed, to shed blood	L16
Lú Shān	庐山/廬山	PropN	Mount Lu (in "江西 Jiāngxī" Province)	L19
lú	炉/爐	BF	stove, oven, furnace	L19
lù	路	N	road, path, (bus) route, line	L13
lùkǒu	路口	N	street intersection	L12
lúnchuán	轮船/輪船	N	steamer, steamship	L18
lǚxíng	旅行	V	to travel, to take a tour	L18

M

máfan	麻烦/麻煩	Adj/N	be a nuisance, bothersome; trouble, bother	L18
mǎi bu qǐ	买不起/買不起	Pot	cannot afford	L20
mǎi cài	买菜/買菜	Phrase	to buy vegetables, to buy groceries	L12
mǎi piào	买票/買票	Phrase	to buy tickets	L18
màn	慢	Adj	slow	L14
máng	忙	V/Adj	to busy oneself with; busy	L20
máoyī	毛衣	N	woolen sweater	L19
màozi	帽子	N	hat, cap	L19
méi guānxi	没关系/沒關係	Phrase	it doesn't matter, never mind	L14

méi shénme	没什么/沒什麼	Phrase	for it not to matter, not to be anything (of consequence)	L20
méi xiǎngdào	没想到	Phrase	not to have expected, not have thought	L15
měifàshī	美发师/美髮師	N	hairdresser	L14
mén	门/門	Meas/N	*for courses in school, skills*; door	L11
ménkǒu	门口/門口	N	doorway, entrance	L13
mìshū	秘书/秘書	N	secretary	L11
miànbāo	面包/麵包	N	bread	L12
miàn duì miàn	面对面/面對面	Phrase	face-to-face	L11
míngpái	名牌	N	name brand	L15
mǔ	母	BF	mother, female (animal)	L20

N

ná	拿	V	to hold, to grasp, to take	L12
nǎge	哪个/哪個	IntPron	which (of them), which one	L12
nàme	那么/那麼	Pron/Conj	in that way, so; well, in that case	L17
nánshēng	男生	N	male student, young man	L15
nánshì	男士	N	man, gentleman (often facetious)	L15
nánfāng	南方	PW	south, southern region, The South, the area to the south of the "长江 Cháng Jiāng"	L19
Nánjīng	南京	PropN	Nanjing (a city in "江苏 Jiāngsū") ("南京路 Nánjīng Lù", Nanjing Road)	L13
nán	难/難	Adj	difficult	L18
nánshòu	难受/難受	Adj	feel unwell, feel sad about	L16
nèikē	内科	N	internal medicine, department of internal medicine	L16
niángāo	年糕	N	Lunar New Year cake (made with rice flour)	L20
niánhuà	年画/年畫	N	paintings hung during the Lunar New Year, depicting themes of good luck and prosperity	L20
niánhuò	年货/年貨	N	goods for the Lunar New Year	L20
niánjì	年纪/年紀	N	age, years old (of a person)	L20
nián qián	年前	Phrase	last year, before the New Year	L20
niánqīng	年轻/年輕	Adj	young	L17
niányèfàn	年夜饭/年夜飯	N	family reunion dinner on the eve of the Lunar New Year	L20
niúnǎi	牛奶	N	milk	L12
niǔshāng	扭伤/扭傷	V-RC	to sprain	L16
nuǎnhuo	暖和	Adj	nice and warm, cozy	L19
nuǎnqì	暖气/暖氣	N	heating, central heating	L19

277

nǚ'ér	女儿/女兒	N	daughter, girl	L20
nǚshēng	女生	N	female student, (TW usage) girl, woman	L15
nǚshì	女士	N	lady, miss (polite form of address or reference)	L14

O

ò	哦	Int	expressing realization, understanding, etc.	L17

P

pà	怕	V	to fear, to be afraid	L19
pà rè	怕热/怕熱	Phrase	to be sensitive to heat	L19
pàiduì	派对/派對	N	a transcription of the English word "party" ("开派对 kāi pàiduì", to have a party)	L18
pánzi	盘子/盤子	N	tray, dish	L17
pèi	配	Adj	well-matched, fit	L15
pí	皮	N	skin, peel, leather	L16
píxié	皮鞋	N	leather shoes	L15
piānzi	片子	N	x-ray slide	L16
piàn	片	Meas	for slice-like things, e.g. tablets	L16
piàoliang	漂亮	Adj	beautiful, splendid	L17
píng'ān	平安	Adj	safe, well, peaceful	L20
píngshí	平时/平時	N	(in) ordinary times	L11
pò	破	Adj/V	broken, damaged; to break, to cut	L16

Q

qī chá	沏茶	Phrase	to brew tea	L17
qījiān	期间/期間	N	time, period, duration	L18
qīmò	期末	N	end of the school term	L11
qíshí	其实	Adv	in fact, actually	L18
qítā	其他	Pron	others, the rest, other	L12
qǐlai	起来/起來	DirC	up, out	L16
qìwēn	气温/氣溫	N	air temperature	L19
qìchē	汽车/汽車	N	motor vehicle, car, bus	L13
qiánbian	前边/前邊	PW	in front, ahead, preceding	L12
qiánhòu	前后/前後	PW	around (the time of)	L18
qiánmiàn	前面	PW	in front, ahead	L12
qiǎnlánsè	浅蓝色/淺藍色	N	light blue (color)	L15
qiē	切	V	to cut, to slice	L17
qīnqi	亲戚/親戚	N	relatives	L18
qīngjiāo	青椒	N	green peppers	L12

qīngchu	清楚	Adj	clear, distinct		L11
qíng	晴	Adj	clear, fine (of weather) ("转晴 zhuǎn qíng", to chang to clear)		L19
qǐng kè	请客/請客	VO	to entertain guests, to treat (someone to a meal)		L17
qiūtiān	秋天	N	autumn, fall		L19
qū	区/區	BF	area, region		L16
qùdiào	去掉	V-RC	to get rid of		L14
quán	全	Adv/Adj	totally, entirely; complete, whole		L17
quánjiā	全家	N	the whole family		L20
quán shì	全市	Phrase	the entire city, city-wide		L15
qúnzi	裙子	N	skirt, dress		L15

R

rǎn	染	V	to dye, to color		L14
rǎn fà	染发/染髮	Phrase	to dye hair, to color hair		L14
ràng	让/讓	V/Prep	to let, to allow, to have or make (sb. do sth.); by		L13
rènao	热闹/熱鬧	Adj/V/N	lively, buzzing with excitement; to have a good time; excitement, fun		L17
rénjiā/rénjia	人家	N/Pron	house-hold, family; other people, referring to a 3rd person (he/she/they)		L20
rénmen	人们/人們	N	people, humanity		L17
rénmín	人民	N	the people (of a country)		L13
rényuán	人员/人員	N	personnel, staff		L11
rèn	认/認	V	to recognize, to know		L11
rènwéi	认为/認為	V	to believe that, to think that, to regard to be		L17
Rìběn	日本	PropN	Japan		L11
rìqī	日期	N	date		L11
rìyòngpǐn	日用品	N	items of daily use, daily necessities		L12
ròu	肉	N	meat (default is "pork")		L12
ròusī	肉丝/肉絲	N	shredded pork		L17
ruǎnwò	软卧/軟卧	N	soft berth (a first-class seat)		L18
ruǎnzuò	软座/軟座	N	soft seat (on a train)		L18
Ruìshì	瑞士	PropN	Switzerland		L14

S

sǎngzi	嗓子	N	throat		L16
sǎo	扫/掃	V	to sweep		L20
sǎo chén	扫尘/掃塵	VO	to sweep away dust, to clean house in the early New Year		L20
sè	色	BF	color		L15

shāfā	沙发/沙發	N	a sofa	L17
shāng	伤/傷	N	wound, injury	L16
shāngkǒu	伤口/傷口	N	a wound	L16
shāngchǎng	商场/商場	N	department store, the business world	L15
shàngmiàn	上面	PW	above, on top of, on	L12
shàngpù	上铺/上鋪	N	upper berth	L18
shàng wǎng	上网/上網	VO	to go online, to get on the Internet	L11
shāowēi	稍微	Adv	a bit, slightly	L14
sháozi	勺子	N	spoon, ladle, scoop	L17
shétou	舌头/舌頭	N	tongue	L16
shēn	伸	V	to stretch out, to extend, to spread	L16
shēnkāi	伸开/伸開	V-RC	to stretch out, to extend, to spread open	L16
shēnshang	身上	N	on one's body, to have… with someone (e.g. money, documents)	L16
shēntǐ	身体/身體	N	the body	L16
shēnhuī	深灰	Adj	dark grey	L15
shēnhuīsè	深灰色	N	dark gray color	L15
Shēnzhèn	深圳	PropN	Shenzhen (a city in Guangdong Province)	L12
shēng	升	V	to rise	L19
shēng	生	V	to give birth to, to bear	L20
shēngcài	生菜	N	lettuce, romaine lettuce	L12
shēnghuó	生活	N/V	life, livelihood; to live	L18
Shèngdàn Jié	圣诞节/聖誕節	PropN	Christmas ("sacred-birth-festival")	L18
shīfàn	师范/師範	Attr	a "normal" or teacher's (college)	L13
shīfu	师傅/師傅	N	master (worker)	L11
shí	时/時	N	time, when, at (a certain time)	L13
shíjiān	时间/時間	N	time, period of time	L20
shímíngzhì	实名制	N	"real-name-system"	L18
shíxíng	实行/實行	V	to implement, to put into practice, to carry out	L18
shìjiè	世界	N	world	L11
shì	市	N	city, municipality, market, marketplace	L15
shì zhōngxīn	市中心	Phrase	in the center of town	L17
shì	事	N	thing, matter, event	L18
shì	试/試	V	to test, to try, to experiment	L14
shì	室	N	room, chamber	L11
shìyǒu	室友	N	roommate	L11
shōu fèi	收费/收費	Phrase	to collect fees, to be not free	L14

shōu kuǎn	收款	Phrase	to make collections	L15
shōukuǎntái	收款台/收款臺	N	cashier's booth, counter	L15
shōu qián	收钱/收錢	Phrase	to receive money, to collect debts	L12
shōurù	收入	N/V	income; to include	L17
shōuyíntái	收银台/收銀臺	N	cashier	L12
shǒubì	手臂	N	the arm	L16
shǒuzhǐ	手指	N	finger	L16
shǒu suì	守岁/守歲	VO	"to keep a watch on the year", i.e. welcome the New Year in by staying up all night	L20
shòu	受	V	to receive, to accept, to get, to suffer, to bear	L16
shòu shāng	受伤/受傷	VO	to be wounded, to get injured	L16
shòuhuòyuán	售货员/售貨員	N	sales clerk, shop assistant, salesperson	L15
shòupiàochù	售票处/售票處	N	ticket office	L18
shòupiàoyuán	售票员/售票員	N	ticket seller, bus conductor (female or male)	L13
shūfáng	书房/書房	N	study	L17
shūguì	书柜/書櫃	N	bookcase	L17
shūfu	舒服	Adj	comfortable, feel well	L13
shū yè	输液/輸液	VO	to have an IV drip	L16
shūcài	蔬菜	N	vegetables, greens	L12
shuāi	摔	V	to fall, to tumble (after losing one's balance)	L16
shuāi jiāo	摔跤	VO	to trip and fall, to fall down	L16
shuāng	双/雙	Meas/Attr	*for pairs*; double, even (number)	L15
shuāngrénchuáng	双人床/雙人床	N	double bed	L17
shuǐ	水	N	water	L17
shuǐbǐ	水笔/水筆	N	marker, water-color brush, fountain pen	L11
shuǐdiànfèi	水电费/水電費	N	charges for water and electricity, utility bills	L17
shuǐtǔ	水土	N	water and soil, natural environment	L16
shuǐtǔ bùfú	水土不服	Phrase	not used to the food, not acclimatized	L16
shuǐxǐ	水洗	V	wet wash (in contrast to "dry clean")	L14
sìhéyuàn	四合院	N	residence made up of a courtyard enclosed by four single-story buildings	L20
sìjì	四季	N	the four seasons	L19
sìjì rú chūn	四季如春	Phrase	like spring all year round	L19
sòng	送	V	to give as a present, to deliver, to send, to take, to see (sb.) off, to accompany (sb. to his destination)	L20
sùliào	塑料	N	plastic	L12

真实生活汉语
Chinese for Living in China 2

sùliàodài	塑料袋	N	plastic bag	L12
suàn	算	V	to count, to include, to consider as, to calculate	L11
suàn zhàng	算账/算賬	VO	to square or settle accounts (with sb.), to get even	L12
suīrán	虽然/雖然	Conj	though, although	L17
suíshí	随时/隨時	Adv	from time to time, as necessary, at all times	L11
suǒ	所	Meas	*for houses, schools, hospitals*	L12
suǒyǐ	所以	Conj	so, therefore, as a result	L11
suǒyǒu	所有	Attr	all, every	L17

T

T xù shān	T恤衫	N	T-shirt, (Guangzhou) shirt	L15
tāmen	他们/他們	Pron	they, them	L15
tǎ	塔	N	pagoda (especially Buddhist), tower-like structure (e.g. a lighthouse)	L20
tái	台/臺	N	platform, counter, (broadcasting) station	L15
tàitai	太太	N	wife, Mrs. (form of address for older women)	L14
tàng fà	烫发/燙髮	VO	to perm	L14
tào	套	Meas	*for sets of things or collections, e.g. an apartment suite or a suit of clothes*	L15
tàozhuāng	套装/套裝	N	suit (for woman), coverall (garment for upper and lower body)	L15
tèbié	特别	Adj/Adv	special, particular; particularly	L20
téng	疼	Adj/V	hurt, ache; to dote on, to love dearly	L16
tī	梯	N	ladder	L14
tīxíng	梯型	N	ladder-shaped, terraced, layered (of hair)	L14
tíbāo	提包	N	shopping bag, handbag	L17
tǐwēn	体温/體溫	N	body temperature	L16
tǐyàn	体验/體驗	V	to experience, to learn through practice	L18
tiānqì	天气/天氣	N	weather	L19
tiānqì yùbào	天气预报/天氣預報	Phrase	weather report, weather forecast	L19
tiánmì	甜蜜	Adj	sweet, happy, affectionate	L20
tiāo	挑	V	to select, to choose	L12
tiáo	调/調	V	to adjust, to mix, to blend	L11
tiáoliào	调料/調料	N	seasoning, flavoring	L12
tiē	贴/貼	V	to paste, to stick, to subsidize	L20
tīng	听/聽	V	to hear, to listen, to obey	L16
tōngcháng	通常	Adv/Attr	usually, generally; normal	L20
tōngzhī	通知	V/N	to notify, to inform; a note, notice, circular	L15

tóngshí	同时/同時	N/Conj	at the same time; besides, moreover	L18
tóngshì	同事	N	colleague, fellow worker ("同事们 tóngshìmen", *colleagues, fellow workers*)	L12
tòng	痛	Adj	painful	L16
tóu	头/頭	N	head, top, end of something	L12
tóubù	头部/頭部	N	head, front part (e.g.: "a nose cone")	L14
tóufa	头发/頭髮	N	hair	L14
tóuyǐngyí	投影仪/投影儀	N	projector	L11
tòushì	透视/透視	N/V	X-ray; to see through	L16
tūrán	突然	Adv	suddenly, abruptly, unexpectedly	L19
tù	吐	V	to vomit, to throw up, to cough up	L16
tuánjù	团聚/團聚	V	to reunite, to have a reunion, to come together	L18
tuī	推	V	to shove, to push, to promote	L14
tuīzi	推子	N	clippers	L14
tuì	退	V	to withdraw, to quit, to return (goods, money, etc.)	L11
tuì kè	退课/退課	Phrase	to drop a class	L11
tuì xiū	退休	VO	to retire	L20
tuō	脱	V	to take off, to remove, to cast off	L16
tuōdiào	脱掉	V-RC	to take off (clothes)	L16
tuō xié	脱鞋	Phrase	to take off shoes (cf. "拖鞋 tuōxié", *sandals*)	L17

W

wàibian	外边/外邊	PW	the outside, away from home, outside	L13
wàidì	外地	N	place other than where one is	L20
wàiguó	外国/外國	N	foreign country	L17
wàimào	外贸/外貿	N	foreign trade	L17
wàitào	外套	N	overcoat, outer garment	L15
wàiyǔ	外语/外語	N	foreign language	L13
wánr	玩儿/玩兒	V	to have fun, to amuse oneself, to play, to play (games)	L20
wǎn	碗	N	bowl	L17
wǎng	网/網	N	net, network	L11
wǎng shang	网上/網上	Phrase	on the internet, online	L19
wǎng shàng	往上	Phrase	upwards	L16
wàng	忘	V	to forget, to leave behind	L18
wēibōlú	微波炉/微波爐	N	microwave oven	L17
wéijīn	围巾/圍巾	N	scarf, muffler	L19
wèishēngzhǐ	卫生纸/衛生紙	N	toilet paper, sanitary paper	L12

283

真实生活汉语 2
Chinese for Living in China

wèi	为/為	Prep	for (the sake of), on behalf of	L14
wèile	为了/為了	Prep	for, in order to, for the sake of	L17
wèi	位	Meas	*for people* ("几位 jǐ wèi", *several people*)	L12
wèi	胃	N	stomach	L16
wēndù	温度	N	temperature	L11
wénxué	文学/文學	N	literature	L11
wénmíng	闻名/聞名	Adj	well known, famous, renowned	L18
wěndìng	稳定/穩定	Adj	stable	L17
wèntí	问题/問題	N	question, issue, problem	L11
wòshì	卧室	N	bedroom	L17
wūrǎn	污染	N	pollution	L16
wūzi	屋子	N	room, house	L19
Wǔhàn	武汉/武漢	PropN	Wuhan (a city in "湖北 Húběi" Province)	L18
wù	雾/霧	N	fog, mist	L19

X

Xī'ān	西安	PropN	Xi'an (in "陕西 Shǎnxī" Province)	L18
xīfāng/Xīfāng	西方	N/PropN	the west; the West	L18
Xīfāngrén	西方人	PropN	Westerner	L18
xīfú	西服	N	suit, Western-style clothing	L15
xīlánhuā	西蓝花/西藍花	N	broccoli	L12
xīzhuāng	西装/西裝	N	suit, Western-style clothing	L15
xīwàng	希望	V/N	to hope (for/to/that), to wish (to/that), to want to; a wish, hope	L20
xǐfàjì	洗发剂/洗髮劑	N	shampoo	L14
xǐ tóu	洗头/洗頭	Phrase	to wash hair, to shampoo	L14
xǐyīfěn	洗衣粉	N	washing powder, laundry powder	L12
xìjù	戏剧/戲劇	N	theater, drama, a play	L18
xìjūn	细菌/細菌	N	bacteria, germs	L16
xiàbian	下边/下邊	PW	underneath, below, bottom	L20
xià chē	下车/下車	Phrase	to get off of a vehicle (bus, train, etc.) (cf. "上车 shàngchē", *to get on a vehicle*)	L13
xiàjiàng	下降	V	to drop, to fall, to descend, to decline	L19
xiàpù	下铺/下鋪	N	lower berth	L18
xià xuě	下雪	Phrase	for snow to fall, for it to snow	L19
xià yǔ	下雨	Phrase	for it to rain	L19
xiàjì	夏季	N	summer season	L19
xiàtiān	夏天	N	summer	L19
xiànmù	羡慕	V	to envy, to admire	L17
xiǎng jiā	想家	Phrase	to be homesick ("think of home")	L18

xiàng	向	V/Prep	to face towards; towards, to	L15
xiàng	像	V	to resemble, to look as if	L17
xiāohuà	消化	N/V	digestion; to digest	L16
xiāohuà bùliáng	消化不良	Phrase	to have indigestion	L16
xiǎo	小	Adj/Pref	little, small; prefixed to a "姓 xìng", or when added to a last name, it indicates familiarity or endearment	L13
xiǎokǎo	小考	N	quiz	L11
xiǎoqū	小区/小區	N	area, a residential neighbourhood	L12
xiǎoxué	小学/小學	N	elementary school, primary school; elementary education	L15
xiǎoxuě	小雪	N	light snow	L19
xiào	校	N	school	L15
xiàolì	校历/校曆	N	school calendar	L11
xiàolǐngdǎo	校领导/校領導	N	leader(s) of a school	L15
xiàomén	校门/校門	N	school gate	L12
xiàoyī	校医/校醫	N	school doctor	L16
xiàozhǎng	校长/校長	N	principal, headmaster of a K-12 school president or chancellor of a college	L15
xiē	些	Meas	some, a few, several	L12
xié	鞋	N	shoes	L15
xiě	写/寫	V	to write, to compose, to draw	L11
xiě/xuè	血	N	blood	L16
xiězìlóu	写字楼/寫字樓	N	office building	L17
xīnzàng	心脏/心臟	N	heart	L16
xīn	新	Adj	new	L17
xīnnián	新年	N	new year	L20
xīnxian	新鲜/新鮮	Adj	fresh (of food, air, etc.), new	L12
xīngfèn	兴奋/興奮	Adj	excited	L19
xíngli	行李	N	luggage, bags	L19
xíng	型	BF	form, style	L14
xìngfú	幸福	N/Adj	happiness; happy	L18
xìngyùn	幸运/幸運	Adj/N	fortunate; good fortune, luck	L17
xiū miàn	修面	VO	to shave (the face)	L14
xuǎn	选/選	V	to choose, to select	L11
xuéqī	学期/學期	N	academic semester, school term	L11
xuéwèi	学位/學位	N	academic degree	L11
xuéxí	学习/學習	V	to study, to learn, to learn from	L13
xuě	雪	N	snow	L19
xuèyā	血压/血壓	N	blood pressure	L16

真实生活汉语
Chinese for Living in China 2

Y

pinyin	汉字	POS	English	Lesson
yāsuìqián	压岁钱/壓歲錢	N	a gift of money given to children on lunar New Year's Eve	L20
yánsè	颜色/顏色	N	color	L14
yànhuì	宴会/宴會	N	banquet, dinner party	L15
yánglì	阳历/陽曆	N	solar calendar	L18
yángbáicài	洋白菜	N	cabbage	L17
yángcōng	洋葱/洋蔥	N	onion	L12
yào	药/藥	N	medicine, drugs	L16
yàofāng	药方/藥方	N	prescription	L16
yīguì	衣柜/衣櫃	N	wardrobe, closet, cupboard	L17
yīshēng	医生/醫生	N	doctor, physician	L16
yīyuàn	医院/醫院	N	hospital, clinic	L16
yílù shang	一路上	Phrase	throughout the whole journey	L19
yíxiàr	一下儿/一下兒	Q	a bit, for a while (minimizing)	L11
yíyàng	一样/一樣	Adj	identical, alike, the same ("跟 gēn……一样 yíyàng", the same as…)	L14
yídòng	移动/移動	V	to move, to shift	L11
yǐ……wéi zhǔ	以……为主/以……為主	Construction	to be basically…, to regard…as essential	L19
yǐqián	以前	TW	before, in the past	L17
yǐzi	椅子	N	chair	L11
yìbān	一般	Adj	commonplace, ordinary, average	L17
yìbiān (r)……yìbiān (r)……	一边（儿）……一边（儿）……/一邊（兒）……一邊（兒）……	Construction	while…, one the one hand…on the other	L17
yìxiē	一些	Q	some, a few, several, a number of, a little	L12
yì	亿/億	Num	100 million	L18
yìsi	意思	N	meaning, idea, opinion	L20
yīnwèi	因为/因為	Conj	because, for, on account of	L11
yīn	阴/陰	Adj	overcast, cloudy	L19
Yīngyǔ	英语/英語	PropN	English, the English language (esp. spoken)	L11
yíngjiē	迎接	V	to greet, to welcome, to take on (a challenge)	L20
yìngwò	硬卧	N	hard berth (equivalent to a second-class berth)	L18
yìngzuò	硬座	N	hard seat (equivalent to a second-class seat)	L18
yōngjǐ	拥挤/擁擠	Adj/V	crowded, jammed; to crowd, to jam (of people, traffic, etc.)	L18

yōuxiān	优先/優先	V	to take precedence, to have priority	L14
yóurén	游人/遊人	N	travelers, tourists	L20
yǒuqián	有钱/有錢	Adj	wealthy	L17
yǒuyú	有余/有餘	V	to have enough with some to spare	L20
yòu	又	Adv	again, moreover, and	L12
yòu……yòu……	又……又……	Construction	(both)… and…	L12
yòu shì	又是	Phrase	also, again, moreover, besides	L13
yǔróngfú	羽绒服/羽絨服	N	down coat	L19
yǔ	雨	N	rain	L19
yǔ hòu	雨后/雨後	Phrase	after the rain	L19
yùbào	预报/預報	V/N	to forecast; forecast	L19
yùgòu	预购/預購		to purchase in advance	L18
yù	遇	V	to meet, to encounter	L15
yùshang	遇上	V-DirC	to encounter, to meet with, to happen upon	L15
yùyì	寓意	N	implied or hidden meaning, moral message, implication	L20
yuángōng	员工/員工	N	staff, personnel	L17
yuánjià	原价/原價	N	original price, original value	L15
yuànyì	愿意/願意	Aux	to be willing, to want	L17
yún	云/雲	N	cloud	L19
Yúnnán	云南/雲南	PropN	Yunnan (province in the Southwest)	L19
yùnxíng	运行/運行	V	to move, to be in motion	L18
yùnshū	运输/運輸	N/V	transport; to transport	L18

Z

zāng	脏/髒	Adj	dirty	L20
zǎoshì	早市	N	morning market	L12
zérèn	责任/責任	N	responsibility, duty, blame	L20
zěnmeyàng	怎么样/怎麼樣	IntPron	how, how are things	L14
zhàn	站	V/N	to stand, to stop; station	L13
zhànpái	站牌	N	sign identifying a bus stop (or train station, subway station, etc.)	L13
zhāng	张/張	V	to open, to spread, to stretch	L16
zhāngkāi	张开/張開	V-RC	to open up, to spread open	L16
zhǎng	长/長	V	to grow	L14
zhàng	账/賬	N	accounts, bill	L12
zhào	照	V	to shine, to illuminate, to take a photo	L16
zhàogù	照顾/照顧	V	to look after, to care for	L20
zhèli	这里/這裡	PW	here, this place	L12
zhème	这么/這麼	Pron	this way, so	L18

zhè shí	这时/這時	Phrase	at this time	L18
zhè shíhou	这时候/這時候	Phrase	at this time	L18
zhèxiē	这些/這些	Pron	these	L17
zhèyàng	这样/這樣	Pron	so, like this, this way	L14
zhe	着/著	Part	durative verb suffix	L14
zhěntou	枕头/枕頭	N	pillow	L20
zhěngjié	整洁/整潔	Adj	tidy, neat and clean	L15
zhèngcháng	正常	Adj	normal, regular	L16
zhènghǎo	正好	Adv	just right, just in time, happen to, chance to	L20
zhèngshì	正式	Adj	formal, official	L15
zhèngzài	正在	Adv	be right in the process of	L16
zhèngzhuāng	正装/正裝	N	formal attire	L15
zhèngzhuàng	症状/症狀	N	symptom (of a disease)	L16
zhī	支	Meas	*for long, thin, inflexible objects*	L11
zhǐxièyào	止泻药/止瀉藥	N	diarrhea medicine	L16
zhǐ néng	只能	Phrase	can only	L18
zhǐ yǒu	只有	Phrase	only, there are only	L17
zhǐjīn	纸巾/紙巾	N	paper napkin	L17
zhǐ	指	V	to indicate, to point at	L16
zhì	制	BF	system	L17
zhōnghào	中号/中號	N	medium-size (cf. "大号 dàhào", *large size*; "小号 xiǎohào", *small size*)	L15
zhōngjí	中级/中級	Attr	intermediate level, middle rank, secondary	L11
zhōngpù	中铺/中鋪	N	middle berth	L18
zhōngxīn	中心	N	center	L15
zhōngxué	中学/中學	N	middle school, high school, secondary education	L12
zhǔ fàn	煮饭/煮飯	Phrase	(col) to cook rice	L17
zhùcè	注册/註冊	V	to register	L11
zhuānmàidiàn	专卖店/專賣店	N	specialty store	L15
zhuānyè	专业/專業	Attr	professional	L14
zhuǎn	转/轉	V	to turn, to shift to	L19
zhǔnbèi	准备/準備	V	to prepare, to make ready, to plan, to intend	L18
zhuōzi	桌子	N	table, desk	L11
zìrán	自然	Adj	natural	L14
zì	字	N	character, word, letter	L11
zū	租	V	to rent, to lease, to hire	L17
zuǐ	嘴	N	mouth	L16

zuì jìn	最近	Phrase	nearest	L12
zuìjìn	最近	Adv	recently, of late, lately, in the near future	L13
zuǒyòu	左右	PW	more or less, approximately (after an expression of quantity)	L14
zuò bàn	做伴	VO	to keep sb. company, to be a companion	L19
zuò fàn	做饭/做飯	Phrase	to cook	L17

Listening Scripts 录音文本 Lùyīn Wénběn

第十一课 在中国学校

1. A：张老师，您好！
   B：大卫，你好！
   A：您现在有时间吗？我想问您一个问题。
   B：有时间。有什么问题？你说吧。
   A：我在美国的大学学了一年的汉语课。可是我们学得不多。今天我上了二年级的口语课，觉得很难。老师的话很多我都听不懂。现在我不知道自己应该上一年级的课还是二年级的课。
   B：学生常常有这个问题。没关系。你明天下午三点以后来我的办公室，我可以给你一个考试。要是考得不太好，你可以上一年级的口语课。
   A：好的。我明天三点半以后没事儿，三点三刻来您办公室可以吗？
   B：没问题。
   A：老师，我还有一个问题。要是我上一年级的口语课，那回美国大学算学分吗？
   B：这个问题我不太清楚。你应该问一下美国大学的教务处。
   B：好吧，我给他们发电子邮件。

2. 露西现在在北京大学英语系教英语，也学汉语。每天早上她都有四节课，八点上汉语课，下课以后上中国文学课。十点十分一直到十二点她教中国学生学英语。中午十二点吃午饭。一点到两点是中国人睡午觉的时间，露西也回宿舍休息一下儿。两点以后露西常常去办公室。她没有固定的办公室时间，可是每天都有学生去她的办公室跟她练习英语口语。露西发现中国学生跟美国学生很不一样。中国学生上课的时候不喜欢说话，可是在老师的办公室不但喜欢说，还说得很好。露西常常去北京大学外边的饭馆吃晚饭。晚饭以后她在房间做汉语作业。除了学习以外，她也上网跟她在美国的朋友聊天儿。露西平常十一点钟睡觉。

3. A：中国大学的教室很多都很大，是不是因为每个班的学生都很多？
   B：对，一个班常常有四五十人。教室前边有很大的白板，白板下边有水笔和板擦儿。老师写字要写得很大，学生才可以看清楚。
   A：有没有投影仪？
   B：有，在白板的前边。老师可以放PPT，也可以上网。
   A：这跟美国一样，美国的教室里都有投影仪，很有用。
   B：可是美国的教室只有空调，没有电扇。
   A：是，你说得很对！因为美国的教室空调的温度调得很低，所以我们觉得教室很冷。
   B：我听说在美国大学上课的时候学生可以吃饭，这是真的吗？

A：对，上课的时候学生可以吃饭。因为美国大学没有固定的午饭时间，所以学生常常把饭拿到教室来吃。

B：那中午休息吗？

A：更没有休息的时间了。

第十二课 在超市

1. 马丽莎来中国以后，每天都在学生食堂吃饭。今天是星期天，她想换一换，自己做饭吃。早上她起床以后，她就去学校附近的早市买菜。她买了两个青椒、半斤扁豆、五块钱的西红柿，还有别的蔬菜，都很新鲜，花了十八块钱。中午她用这些蔬菜做了素菜面条。晚上她想做一点儿肉菜，下午去了一家菜市场买肉。菜市场的肉不新鲜，可是水果很好，也很便宜。她香蕉、苹果、橘子每样买了两斤，一共花了三十五块钱。出了菜市场以后，她又去了旁边的超市买肉，那儿的肉太贵了，也不可以砍价，可是鱼不贵，也很新鲜。所以她买了三条，还买了六个鸡蛋和一些调料，花了五十二块六。她想今天晚上可以请她的中国学生来吃饭了。

2. 汤姆：钱明，学校附近哪儿可以买日用品？

   钱明：最近的小超市在教学楼对面，里面又有吃的，又有用的。我也要买两瓶饮料，我们一起去吧！

   汤姆：太好了！

   （在超市）

   钱明：到了，就这儿。你要买什么？

   汤姆：六卷卫生纸、一包洗衣粉、一块肥皂，还有一条毛巾。

   钱明：这些都在日用品那行。

   汤姆：这儿有食品吗？

   钱明：有，在右边那行，走到头就是。

   汤姆：你看，这两种面包很好，多少钱？

   钱明：水果面包一块八一个，黑面包两块一个。可是我觉得水果面包不太新鲜。

   汤姆：那我来三个黑面包。

   钱明：我也来一个，再来四个橘子罐头。你还要买别的吗？

   汤姆：我觉得他们的衣服很好看。

   钱明：可是不便宜，这儿你也不能砍价，最好不在这儿买。

   汤姆：好吧。

第十三课 坐 车

1. A：请问你知道去北京大学坐几路车吗？

B：332路、300路和802路都可以。
A：三路车的车票都一样吗？
B：332便宜一点儿，802路和300路贵一点儿，你上车以后问问司机吧。
A：好。车上有空调吗？
B：802路和300路都有。
A：要换车吗？
B：不用。
A：坐几站？
B：332路慢一点儿，坐10站；802和300空调车的站少一些，只要坐8站就到了。
A：下车以后往哪个方向走？
B：往前走一会儿就到北京大学门口了。
A：谢谢！

2. 北京地方很大，人多，车也很多。路不少，可是常常堵车。早上上班和下午下班的时候，你可以看到很多车都停在路口，不能走。坐公共汽车常常得花很长时间。如果你坐出租车，就只能坐在车上看打表。如果你有急事去远的地方，就最好先坐车到地铁站，再换地铁。地铁站常常在大路口，往西和往东方向的地铁都是三分钟来一次。

第十四课 理 发

1. A：今天上午我们要跟老师照相，可是我的头发太长了，想去理发馆剪一剪。
   B：东门外边就有一家理发馆，剪发只要二十块钱，又好又便宜。
   A：要不要等很久？我们十点照相，现在去来得及吗？
   B：九点一开门就去，来得及。我也想花二十块钱去按摩按摩我的头和背，休息一下儿。
   A：好，我们一起去吧！

   （在理发店）
   C：请问你们是理发还是按摩？
   B：他理发，我按摩。要等吗？
   C：不用，请这边来。剪发吗？
   A：对，头发太长了，剪短点儿。
   C：头发剪什么样的？
   A：后边剪两寸，旁边少剪点儿。
   C：要不要洗头？
   A：洗头另收费吗？
   C：如果您用进口的洗发剂，就再付二十块钱，国产的十块。
   A：那用进口的洗吧。

C：好。剪好了，您看看镜子，这么短可以吗？

A：可以。好像改变了发型。

C：没有给您改变发型，就是短了一点儿。您再付五块钱还可以给您做面部按摩。

A：按摩不要了。你就上点儿摩丝吹一吹。（指B）她要按摩。

C：可以。我给她吹了风，就给您按摩。

B：没问题。师傅，您按摩头的时候可以给我按摩一下脸吗？

C：对不起，我们不做脸部按摩。

2. A：请问您是理发还是染发？

B：我先剪发，再染发。要等吗？

A：不用，现在这会儿不忙了。中午吃饭的时候人多。请这边来！头发剪什么样的？

B：旁边剪短三寸，后边少剪点儿。

A：三寸太短了吧？我看最多剪一寸半。您的脸小，还是留长头发好看。

B：那就听你的吧。

A：剪好了，您看看镜子，喜欢吗？

B：喜欢，比我想的还要好。谢谢你！

A：头发染什么颜色？如果您用进口的洗发剂，就再付二十块钱，国产的十五块。

B：我想染成红一点儿的，你说好看吗？

A：我觉得可以。我们有进口的染发剂，德国的168，美国的128，国产的便宜一点儿，88块。您选哪一种？

B：用美国的吧。我在美国就是用这个牌子的染发剂。

（过了一会儿）

A：好了，看看怎么样。

B：真的很好！你比我在美国的美发师还好。可以给我按摩一下头部和面部吗？

A：可以。我给您稍微吹吹头发，就给您按摩。

B：真舒服。谢谢师傅！一共多少钱？

A：染发剂128，染发60，按摩15，一共203。

B：给您210块，别找钱了。

A：那可不行。这是中国，不是美国。您拿着这7块钱。

B：谢谢！我下次还会再来！

第十五课 买衣服

1. A：你的这件白衬衫很好看，是在哪儿买的？

B：学校旁边的那个服装店。

A：是刚买的吗？

B：对，上周末刚买的。
A：贵不贵？
B：很便宜，85块。
A：这件衬衫是多大号的？
B：中号的。你要不要试试？
A：我穿大号的。你的这件我穿不合适。
B：他们也有大号的。你可以去看看。
A：他们有浅蓝色的吗？
B：什么颜色的都有。
A：太好了，下课以后我就去看看。

2. A：售货员小姐，请给我看看那双鞋。
B：哪双？
A：那双带白边的黑鞋。
B：你穿多大号的？
A：38号的。
B：给你，四百块一双。你穿上试试。
A：有点儿紧。有没有大半号的？
B：对不起，黑色的没有。这双带黑边的白鞋是38号半的。
A：这双肥瘦很合适，白颜色也好看。这双多少钱？
B：原价四百二十，给你打五折，二百一，怎么样？
A：太好了！我要了。为什么这双鞋这么便宜？
B：因为只有这一双了。
A：在哪儿付钱？
B：前边的二号收款台。

第十六课 在医院

1. A：你哪儿不舒服？
B：我拉肚子。
A：几天了？
B：从昨天晚上到今天，上午还吐了一次。
A：发烧吗？
B：有一点儿热，头也疼得厉害。
A：来，我先给你量一下儿体温和血压，再听听心脏，然后你去化验大便。

（过了一会儿）

A：你的体温有点儿高，可是血压和心脏都正常。从大便看你是消化不良。你这些天都吃了什么东西？

B：昨天晚上在食堂吃了宫保鸡丁和葱爆牛肉，今天中午跟朋友去饭馆吃了糖醋鱼、猪肉扁豆、酸辣鱼，还有炒鸡蛋，喝了很多冷饮和啤酒，还有……

A：可能你吃得太多了，也可能吃了不新鲜的东西。还有，热的和冷的一起吃，肚子就吃坏了。我给你开一些中药，吃了就好。今天你最好一天都不吃饭，好好儿休息。

B：大夫，那我饿了怎么办？

A：你可以多喝水，但是要喝热水。

B：谢谢大夫！

2. A：你哪儿不舒服？

B：我咳嗽，呼吸有点儿困难，嗓子也不舒服。

A：发烧吗？

B：有一点儿，可是不太高。

A：请张开嘴，说"啊"。

B：啊……

A：你的嗓子有点儿发炎。我听听你的胸口……很正常。你有点儿感冒。先去楼下化验室做一个血的化验，然后回来我给你开一点儿药。

（过了一会儿）

A：血的化验不太正常，因为你现在有点儿发烧。吃点药吧。

B：我吃过两天感冒药，可是没有用。

A：你对阿司匹林过敏吗？

B：不过敏。

A：好的，吃这个药很快就好了。

B：怎么吃？

A：四个小时吃一次，一次两片，最好饭后吃。还有，多喝水，可是不要喝冷饮，多休息。

B：好的，谢谢！

第十七课 玛丽的公寓

1. A：我想找一个公寓，你有公寓出租吗？

B：几个人住？

A：我一个人。

B：有，一室一厅的公寓。

A：房租多少钱？

B：一个月 4500 块。

A：离北京大学远不远？

B：坐 320 公共汽车三站就到，非常近。

A：公寓里边有家具吗？

B：不但有家具，而且还是新家具。卧室里边有一张小床，客厅里边有一个双人沙发，一个书柜，另外厨房里还有一张桌子和两个椅子。

A：厨房和洗澡间大不大？

B：厨房不小，里边有不少厨房用具，你都可以用。卫生间比较小，里边也没有家具。

A：公寓附近安静吗？我是学生，常常要看书。

B：非常安静。公寓旁边很漂亮，买东西也很方便。另外，如果你住这里，水电费都是免费的。怎么样？要不要来住？

A：别的都很不错，就是房租贵了点儿。能便宜点儿吗？

B：因为你是学生，所以我给你第一个月免费，好吗？

A：真的吗？太好了。我现在就去看看，好吗？

B：好，我等你。

2. 小英是加拿大人，现在在北京大学教英文。她住在大学的外教宿舍里，宿舍离她的教室和办公室都不远，非常方便。小英的房租、水电都是免费的，宿舍里有一些常用的家具：单人床、沙发、桌子和椅子。小英自己还买了电视和电话，放在客厅里。宿舍的厨房里不但有冰箱，还有微波炉。另外，学校还给了她不少厨房用具：锅、碗、菜板和菜刀。小英常常在学校的食堂吃饭，但是有时候也换一换，自己在宿舍做点儿饭吃，所以她买了一些盘子、筷子、叉子和勺子。现在她正在学做中国饭，她想学好以后，请她的中国朋友来宿舍一起吃她自己做的中国饭。

第十八课 春 运

1. A：我从来没去过南京，今年秋天想去看看。你的老家在南京，对吗？

B：对。秋天的南京最漂亮！吃的地方、玩儿的地方、买东西的地方都很多。

A：太好了！你觉得我怎么去最合适？

B：坐飞机又快又方便，两个小时就到了。但是飞机票要 1500 块。坐火车便宜得多，特快 400 块就可以了，但是时间比较长，要十多个小时。我回家的时候，一般都坐火车。

A：坐十多个小时的火车太累了。

B：如果怕累，你就坐高铁。高铁，又快又舒服，5个小时就到了。

A：下次你回家的时候，我能和你一起去吗？

B：好啊！把你的手机号给我，我回去以前给你打电话，我们一起买票。

A：太好了！谢谢！

2. A：小姐，我要一张明天下午四点直达深圳的软卧下铺票。
   B：明天下午四点到深圳的软卧票都已经卖完了。后天早上的可以吗？
   A：我有急事，明天必须到深圳。你再帮我看看硬卧下铺有没有。
   B：稍等。
   A：多谢！
   B：对不起，硬卧下铺也都卖完了。有一张硬卧中铺，要不要？
   A：多少钱？
   B：700块。
   A：真贵啊！硬卧中铺还这么贵吗？
   B：现在票价涨了，所以就贵。只有这一张票了，你要不要啊？
   A：贵也不能不买呀！
   B：把你的身份证给我。
   A：啊呀，身份证怎么找不到了？应该是忘在宿舍了。小姐，我现在回去拿身份证，你能不能等我？
   B：那不行，要是有人要买这张票，我不能不卖啊！

第十九课 天气怎么样？

1. A：我是北京人，你的老家在哪里？
   B：在上海。
   A：上海也和北京一样，一年有四季吗？
   B：有，但是上海的秋天和冬天比较短，春天和夏天比较长。
   A：冬天也和北京一样经常下雪吗？
   B：一般不会，但是有时候会很冷，最冷的时候会到零下五六度。
   A：上海春、夏两季的天气怎么样？
   B：春天比较暖和，夏天很热。从五月到六月总下雨，人们每天都得带着雨伞，穿着雨衣。
   A：北京的春天就不一样了，春天不但雨不多，而且经常刮风。夏天非常热，最热的时候四十多度，但是下雨以后就凉快了。北京最好的季节是秋天，不冷也不热。

2. A：春夏秋冬，你最喜欢哪个季节？
   B：我只喜欢春天。因为我又怕热又怕冷。如果夏天凉快一点儿，冬天暖和一点儿，我就都喜欢了。
   A：那就没有四季了，而且也没有意思了。我喜欢不同的季节，不同的景色。
   B：四季如春最舒服了。而且，我喜欢在外边跑步。春天跑步最舒服，一边跑步，一边看景色，感觉好极了。

A：虽然你现在舒服，但是这跟吃饭一样，如果总吃一种东西，从来不换，过一段时间你就会不喜欢了。

B：我可以吃不同的东西，但是我会一直都喜欢春天。

第二十课 过 年

1. 我小的时候，最高兴的就是过春节的时候。春节时，每家都要准备很多吃的东西。大街上和商店里的人很多，非常热闹，大家都高高兴兴的。我十岁那年除夕的前一天，妈妈和我去买过年的东西，爸爸和姐姐在家打扫房子。我和妈妈买了春联和年画，还有很多好吃的东西。最让我高兴的是，我们还买了一些鞭炮。妈妈还给我买了新衣服。我们回家以后，爸爸和姐姐已经把家里打扫得干干净净的了。爸爸把我们买的春联和"福"字贴在门上，我把花生和瓜子都放在盘子里，再放到桌子上。

   除夕那天，穿上妈妈给我买的新衣服，我高兴极了！下午的时候爸爸、妈妈一起做了很多我爱吃的菜。晚上一起吃团圆饭的时候，全家人都很开心。吃完了团圆饭全家人坐在一起看电视上的春节晚会。电视节目很有意思。我们一家人一边看电视一边包饺子。快十二点了，很多人在外边放鞭炮。我和爸爸也拿着鞭炮跑到外边，我们放了很多鞭炮。我比爸爸放的鞭炮多。放完了鞭炮，我们开始吃饺子。夜里十二点，大家开始拜年，每个人都给我压岁钱。

2. 今年除夕，大学的领导请全校的外国留学生吃春节年饭。一共来了500多名留学生，坐满了50多张桌子。每张桌子上都放着各种各样的肉菜和素菜，还有很多很多饺子。大家都穿得很漂亮，男士们都穿着深色西服，打着红色领带；女士们都穿着红色的套装，或者红色的裙子。大学的领导给所有的外国留学生拜年，希望每个人都能开心、幸福，也希望世界和平、和谐。最后他们还给每个留学生一个红包，里面是一张购物卡。

   白大明来自美国。他说今年是第三年在中国过春节，他觉得很幸运。他非常喜欢中国的传统文化，更喜欢满街的红色，他说红色代表着爱和幸福。他打算春节以后和朋友们去上海玩儿一下儿，看看上海人怎么过春节。

   保罗是法国人，来中国才半年，但是已经能说很多中文了，因为他特别喜欢中国的历史和文化。最近他还交了一个中国女朋友。他计划将来和女朋友在中国买房子。他说："我希望学好中文，在中国买个房子，然后做老师，教法国历史和中国历史。"